高 等 学 校 教 材

仪器分析实验

主 编 陈家全
副主编 于清峰 陈 蓉

中国教育出版传媒集团
高等教育出版社 · 北京

内容提要

本书根据中国药科大学高质量发展、“双一流”建设和化学基础课程教学改革的需要编写而成，侧重药学研究领域仪器分析实验技能和科研思维的培养，同时关注了仪器分析实验新技术，力求培养学生的实验动手能力和分析问题、解决问题的能力。

本书分为6章，包括仪器分析实验基础知识、电化学分析、光谱分析、色谱分析、色谱-质谱联用法及设计类实验，共45个实验，以及6个设计实验选题。内容采用中英文对照，便于双语教学。

本书可作为高等学校药学类专业本科生仪器分析实验课程教材，也可供医学、食品及化学化工等相关学科实验教学和分析工作者的参考用书。

图书在版编目（C I P）数据

仪器分析实验 / 陈家全主编 ; 于清峰，陈蓉副主编
. -- 北京 : 高等教育出版社，2024.8
ISBN 978-7-04-061948-5

Ⅰ. ①仪… Ⅱ. ①陈… ②于… ③陈… Ⅲ. ①仪器分析-实验-高等学校-教材 Ⅳ. ①O657-33

中国国家版本馆CIP数据核字(2024)第052027号

YIQI FENXI SHIYAN

策划编辑 沈晚晴　　责任编辑 沈晚晴　　封面设计 张申申　　版式设计 杜微言
责任绘图 于　博　　责任校对 胡美萍　　责任印制 刘思涵

出版发行 高等教育出版社
社　　址 北京市西城区德外大街4号
邮政编码 100120
印　　刷 高教社（天津）印务有限公司
开　　本 787 mm × 1092 mm　1/16
印　　张 21.5
字　　数 530千字
购书热线 010-58581118
咨询电话 400-810-0598
网　　址 http://www.hep.edu.cn
　　　　 http://www.hep.com.cn
网上订购 http://www.hepmall.com.cn
　　　　 http://www.hepmall.com
　　　　 http://www.hepmall.cn
版　　次 2024年8月第1版
印　　次 2024年8月第1次印刷
定　　价 45.00元

物 料 号　61948-00

前　　言

党的二十大报告强调“教育、科技、人才是全面建设社会主义现代化国家的基础性、战略性支撑”。高校作为科技第一生产力、人才第一资源和创新第一动力的重要结合点，要打造世界重要人才中心和创新高地，切实发挥基础性、战略性支撑作用。构建新时代人才培养体系，要求高校不断提升实践创新人才培养能力，其中实验教学是培养理工类高质量创新创业人才的关键环节。另一方面，为切实贯彻中国药科大学高质量发展、“双一流”建设和化学基础课程教学改革相关要求，全面提升本科实验教学体系建设水平，全面提高教材建设质量，鉴此，我们编写了仪器分析实验课程教材。

仪器分析发展至今，形成了以光谱分析、电化学分析、色谱分析及色谱－质谱联用法为支柱的现代仪器分析，其内涵和外延非常丰富，与国民经济的各个领域密切相关，已成为研究各种化学理论及解决生命科学、环境科学、食品质量与安全和药学等领域中不可缺少的手段和工具。仪器分析是一门实践性和技术性很强的综合性课程，因此仪器分析实验在仪器分析的教学中占有重要的地位，是必不可少的环节。通过实验教学，学生能够加深对仪器分析的方法理论、仪器结构和基本原理的理解；掌握仪器分析研究中的基本实验技能和各类分析仪器的使用方法；学习正确处理实验数据和表达实验结果的方式；了解先进的仪器分析技术；培养实事求是的科学作风和解决问题的能力，具备基本的科学实验的思路和方法。

本书在中国药科大学理学院原分析化学教研室、仪器分析课程群多年的实验教学改革和双语实验教学的基础上，并参考了国内外仪器分析实验教材和相关文献，结合本校专业特色编写而成。本书包含了常用的仪器分析方法，侧重药物研究领域仪器分析方法的运用，彰显药学特色。在实验内容上，除基础类实验外，还增加了设计类实验的方案指导、案例和参考选题，学生可通过查阅文献资料，对所学的各类仪器分析方法加以灵活应用，自行设计实验方案，进一步提升分析问题和解决问题的能力。在教材的编排上，在每个实验中增加了实验指导部分，便于学生预习相应的理论知识、掌握影响实验关键因素和思考相关拓展性问题。

本书采用中英文对照编写，便于教师双语教学，利于学生尽早接触专业领域的英文，为进一步深造打下基础。

参与本书编写工作的有中国药科大学廖声华（第一章、第三章实验 3.14—3.18）、陈家全（第二章）、叶宝芬（第三章实验 3.1—3.13）、于清峰（第三章实验 3.19、第四章实验 4.1—4.7、第五章实验 5.3—5.4）、岳婉晴（第四章实验 4.8—4.13）、陈蓉（第五章实验 5.1—5.2、5.5—5.7、第六章）。全书由陈家全统稿。

感谢中国药科大学季一兵教授对编写工作的指导和关怀，感谢中国药科大学理学院领导、高等教育出版社沈晚晴编辑的大力支持。感谢中国药科大学教务处“十四五”校级规划教材（第二轮）立项资助。

由于编者水平有限，书中难免存在错误和不妥之处，恳请读者批评指正。

编　者

2023 年 3 月

Contents

Chapter 1 Basic Knowledge of Instrumental Analysis Experiment

Chapter 2 Electrochemical Analysis

Chapter 3 Spectral Analysis

目　录

第一章　仪器分析实验基础知识

第二章　电化学分析

第三章　光 谱 分 析

Chapter 4 Chromatographic Analysis

第四章　色 谱 分 析

第五章 色谱 – 质谱联用法

第六章 设计类实验

Chapter 1 Basic Knowledge of Instrumental Analysis Experiment

1.1 General Knowledge of Laboratory Safety

(1) Before entering the laboratory, you should be familiar with all kinds of emergency signs in the laboratory (such as exits, etc.), understand the storage location of all kinds of safety equipment in the laboratory (such as fire extinguisher, fume hood, shower and eye washer, etc.) and how to use safety equipment correctly.

(2) Do not try to prepare and store all kinds of food or drink in the chemical laboratory. Never drink all kinds of food in the chemical laboratory or use the experimental container as a water cup or tableware. Don't chew gum or smoke or apply all kinds of cosmetics and lip balm in the chemical laboratory, because cosmetics or food will absorb chemical vapor.

(3) When entering the laboratory at any time, you must wear goggles. It is not permitted to use glasses instead of goggles.

(4) Do not wear contact lenses in the laboratory. Because the gas produced during the experiment may stay between the contact lens and your eyeball, some gas may cause irrecoverable damage to your eyes.

(5) Wear the experimental clothes correctly. The experimental clothing should cover most of the body. It is not allowed to wear shorts, short skirts, suspenders, sleeveless T-shirts or other clothes made of mesh fabric in chemical laboratory. The backpack or clothes you bring should be placed in the designated areas by the teacher.

(6) It is not allowed to wear open toed shoes, slippers or other shoes that can't completely protect the feet to enter the laboratory, so as to prevent spills or broken glass instruments from damaging the feet.

(7) Before entering the laboratory, you should use a bandage or adhesive bandage to wrap any cut or open wound. Students with open wounds on their hands must wear disposable gloves.

(8) The working areas must be clean and neat which is good for reducing the probability of accidents, and is favored to observing experimental results.

(9) Don't leave the laboratory during the experiment. In case of an emergency, you can accurately tell the disposal personnel what chemicals exist.

(10) Do not inhale chemical gas directly. If it is necessary to determine the odor of certain chemicals, you should keep the container (such as beaker and test tube) away from your nasal cavity for a certain distance, and then wave your hand to make the odor of chemicals float into the nasal cavity.

第一章　仪器分析实验基础知识

1.1　实验室安全常识

（1）进入实验室前，应该熟悉实验室中的各种应急标志（如逃生通道等），了解实验室各种安全设备（如灭火器、通风橱、淋洗器和洗眼器等）存放的位置，以及如何正确使用这些安全设备。

（2）不要尝试在化学实验室制备和储存各种食物或饮料，也不能在化学实验室食用各种食物，更不能用实验容器作为水杯或餐具。不要在实验室嚼口香糖、吸烟或涂抹各种化妆品和润唇膏，因为化妆品及食物会吸附化学蒸气。

（3）在任何时候进入实验室，必须佩戴好护目镜，不能用眼镜代替护目镜。

（4）在实验室内不能佩戴隐形眼镜。因为实验过程中产生的气体可能会滞留在隐形眼镜和眼球之间，一些气体可能会对眼睛造成不可恢复的损伤。

（5）正确地穿戴好实验服。实验服要求能够覆盖身体的大部分，不允许穿短裤、短裙、吊带衫、无袖 T 恤衫或其他网状织物制成的衣服进入实验室。背包或衣服放在教师指定的位置。

（6）不允许穿露趾鞋、拖鞋或其他不能完全保护足部的鞋进入实验室，以防实验中产生的溢出物或破损的玻璃仪器对足部产生伤害。

（7）在进入实验室前，任何割伤或开放性伤口必须采用绷带或创可贴包裹，手部具有开放性伤口的学生必须佩戴一次性手套。

（8）工作区域必须干净、整齐。整洁有序的工作区域能够减少事故发生的概率，并能使学生更好地观察实验结果。

（9）实验过程中不要离开实验室。在紧急情况发生时，准确告知处置人员存在哪些化学药品。

（10）不要直接吸入化学气体。如果需要确定某些化学药品的气味，将存放该化学药品的容器（如烧杯、试管）远离鼻腔一段距离，然后挥动手使化学药品的气味飘入鼻腔。

（11）当可燃性物质存在时，不要使用明火加热。对于可燃性物质，可采用加热套或加热台加热。

（12）不要用嘴去吮吸移液管，应该采用洗耳球或吸液器。

（13）不要将多余的化学试剂放回原来的试剂瓶中。

(11) In the presence of flammable substances, it is not permitted to heat matters by open fire. Heating mantle or heatplate can be used for heating flammable chemical reagents.

(12) Never pipet by mouth. Always use pipet or suction bulb.

(13) Never return residue chemical reagent to the original container once they have been removed.

(14) Dispose of all laboratory waste properly. Solid waste produced in chemical laboratory should be put into solid waste container. Organic waste liquid or inorganic waste liquid should be put into waste liquid bucket separately. Broken glassware and used syringe needles should be put into designated container.

(15) Before leaving the laboratory, you should clean the working area, and turn off all instruments or equipment and cut off the power supply, and return all glass apparatus to their original positions, and wipe the experimental table. Always wash your hands and arms with soap and water before leaving the laboratory, even if you wore gloves.

（14）正确处置所有实验废弃物。固体废弃药品应该放入固体废弃物容器中，有机废液和无机废液应该分开放入废液桶中，破损的玻璃仪器和废弃尖锐物应该放入专用的容器内。

（15）离开实验室之前，清理工作区域，关闭所有仪器设备并切断电源，将所有的玻璃仪器放回原来的位置，并擦拭实验台面。即使在戴手套的情况下，也要用肥皂与水清洗手和手臂。

1.2 Experimental Report

To ensure the originality of experimental data and the integrity and repeatability of experimental procedures, it is very important to develop good experimental recording ability. Even if you participate in an experiment as a group member, you should complete your experimental report independently. Before entering the laboratory, you should have previewed the experiment you will carry out, understand the background knowledge and the purpose and the procedures of the experiment, and write a preview report. Once you enter into a laboratory, the data and conclusion produced in your experiment should be recorded in your experimental notebook. At the end of the experiment, a retrospective summary should be made to help you to reorganize and explain the phenomena found in the experiment. Specifically:

(1) The experimental report should be a bound notebook with page numbers. It is not allowed to tear any page or use a loose-leaf notebook as the experimental notebook.

(2) The experimental report will serve as an experimental dairy, so be sure to record truly the procedures, time and places, and the external conditions (such as temperature, humidity, etc.) of the experiment you carried out.

(3) The experimental report is complete and repeatable. Specifically, a complete experimental report should include the purpose, principles, instruments and reagents, detailed experimental procedures which can be represented by flow chart, results, notices, discussions, and the data analysis or the explanation for phenomena found during the experiment of experiment you have done.

(4) The experimental report should be written in permanent ink, such as a pen or a gel pen filled with black or blue-black ink. Never use a pencil to write the experimental report.

(5) The original data produced during the experiment should be accurately recorded in the experimental report at the same time of the experiment, and cannot be added after the end of the experiment, and cannot be recorded in the draft book, small pieces of paper or other places.

(6) If the original data was recorded wrongly in the experiment, you can draw a bar in the middle of the wrong data and record the correct data beside it. It is not permitted to modify or erase the wrong recording data with correction fluid or a rubber. It is not allowed to delete, or fabricate the experimental original data at will.

(7) The final experimental results should be expressed with appropriate significant figures, units, and standard deviation or error. If necessary, relevant charts should be attached.

(8) Discussion should include the comparison between the experimental data and the theoretical value or the value reported in the literature, and the analysis of the data error, the brief introduction and the explanation on the important experimental findings, the suggestions for the improvement of the experiment, etc.

(9) The experimental report should be neat and elaborately organized.

1.2　实验报告

为了保证实验数据的原始性及实验过程的完整性和可重复性，在实验中养成良好的实验记录习惯是非常重要的。即使以小组成员的身份参与实验时，也应该独立地完成实验报告。在进入实验室前，应该对即将进行的实验进行了预习并阅读了有关的背景知识，清楚实验目的及实验过程，并写好预习报告。进入实验室后，实验中的所有数据及结论均应完整地记录在实验报告中。实验结束后，应该进行回顾性总结，解释实验中所发现的现象，形成实验报告。

（1）实验报告本应该是装订好的记录本，并编好页码。不能撕毁任一页，更不能采用活页记录本作为实验报告本。

（2）实验报告是一份实验日志，应该真实地记录实验过程以及进行实验的时间、地点和外部环境因素（如温度、湿度等）。

（3）实验报告具有完整性及可重复性的特点。具体内容包括：实验目的、基本原理、仪器与试剂、详细的实验步骤（可采用流程图表示）、实验结果、注意事项，以及对相关实验结果或实验现象的讨论分析等。

（4）实验报告的书写应该采用永久性的墨水书写，如用黑色或蓝黑色的钢笔或中性笔书写，不能用铅笔进行书写。

（5）实验中的原始数据应该边实验边准确地记录在实验报告本上，不能等实验结束后再补记，更不能将原始数据记录在草稿本、小纸片或其他地方。

（6）对于实验中错误记录的原始数据，需在错误数据的中间画一杠，并在旁边记录上正确的数据。不能采用修正液进行修改或用橡皮擦除。任何随意删除、拼凑或杜撰实验数据的行为都是不允许的。

（7）最终的实验结果应该采用合适的有效数字、单位及标准偏差或误差表示，并应附上必要的图表。

（8）讨论部分应该包括实验数据与理论值或文献报道值的比较，并对数据误差进行分析；简述重要的实验发现并对其进行解释；对实验改进的建议等。

（9）实验报告应该是整洁的，其内容应该是经过精心组织的。

1.3 Disposal of Chemical Laboratory Waste

All kinds of wastes produced in the chemical laboratory include disposable laboratory vessels, filter papers, aqueous solution and dangerous chemicals. According to the physical and chemical properties of chemical laboratory wastes, different treatment methods should be adopted.

(1) Collect all kinds of chemical laboratory wastes in designated containers and store them in designated places for transportation to centralized collection places or recycling by special waste treatment companies.

(2) Never mix immiscible waste solvents. Solvents to be mixed must have good chemical compatibility to ensure that the other exothermic or effluent gas chemical reactions can't occur.

(3) Organic solvents containing halogen and halogen-free organic solvents should be collected in different containers because halogen-free organic solvents are more favorable to mix with the fuel.

(4) Different types of waste liquids should be collected in the appropriate container. Glass containers are not affected by most chemicals, but a risk of leakage exists in glass containers. Therefore, it is recommended to use plastic containers (such as polyethylene containers) or metal containers to collect liquid waste. However, it is not permitted that corrosive or containing amine waste liquid stored in metal containers.

(5) The container for collecting waste liquid must be sealed, and 10% space should be reserved above the solvent. The waste liquid cannot fill the whole container.

(6) Galvanized stainless-steel containers cannot be used to collect waste liquid containing halogen, which can corrode these containers.

(7) The soluble waste liquid in water should be collected separately from organic waste liquid. The harmless inorganic saline solution or the organic waste liquid miscible with water can be directly drained into the sewer in the laboratory equipped with wastewater treatment facilities, but the waste liquids containing flammable or harmful substances cannot be directly drained into the sewer, even if they can be miscible with water.

(8) Solid wastes, such as by-products formed after reaction, contaminated filter paper, or chromatographic media (such as silica gel, etc.), should be put into labeled containers for recycling. Expired chemical reagents can be put into the original reagent bottle for recycling, but the label of the original reagent bottle should be complete and clear.

(9) All containers containing chemical wastes should be labeled. The label should include the full name, hazard (such as flammability or corrosiveness), volume, date, and other relevant information of the waste chemicals.

1.3 化学实验室废弃物处理

化学实验室中产生各种废弃物,包括一次性使用的实验器皿、滤纸、水溶液和危险的化学物品。根据化学实验室废弃物的物理和化学性质的不同,应该采用不同的处理方法。

(1) 采用指定的容器收集各种化学实验室废弃物,并储存在指定地点,以便转运到集中收集点或由专门的废弃物处理公司回收。

(2) 不要将不相容的废弃物溶剂相互混合。能够相互混合的溶剂必须具有良好的化学相容性,以确保不会产生放热、逸出气体等化学反应。

(3) 含卤素的有机溶剂和不含卤素的有机溶剂应该采用不同的容器进行收集,因为不含卤素的有机溶剂更适合与燃料混合。

(4) 采用适当的容器收集废液。玻璃容器不受大多数化学物质的影响,但存在泄漏的危险。因此对于液体废液建议采用塑料容器(如聚乙烯容器)或金属容器,但不要在金属容器中储存含有胺类溶剂或具有腐蚀性的废液。

(5) 收集废液的容器必须密封,并且在溶剂上方应该预留 10% 的空间,废液不能装满整个容器。

(6) 不能采用镀锌的不锈钢容器收集含卤素的废液,因为含卤素的废液能够对这些容器产生腐蚀作用。

(7) 水溶性的废液应该与有机废液分开收集。安装有废水处理设施的实验室可将无害的无机盐水溶液或与水混溶的有机废液直接排放到下水道中,但含有可燃性物质或有害物质的废液不能直接排放到下水道中,即使它们能与水混溶。

(8) 对于固体废弃物,如反应的副产物、污染过的滤纸或色谱介质(如硅胶等)应该放入贴好标签的容器中等待回收。过期的化学试剂可放在原试剂瓶中等待回收,但原试剂瓶的标签应该是完整、清晰的。

(9) 所有装有化学实验室废弃物的容器应该贴好标签,标签应该包括废弃物的化学名称全称、危险性(如可燃性或腐蚀性)、体积及日期等相关信息。

1.4 Colored Cylinder Mark for Gases and the Precautions of Gas Cylinders for Use in Laboratory

1. Colored cylinder mark for gases

At present, the gas cylinders used in our country mainly include seamless steel cylinders, welded steel cylinders, dissolved acetylene cylinders, seamless aluminum-alloy cylinders, etc., but the gas cylinders used in the laboratory are mainly seamless steel cylinders. According to the Chinese national standards (*Colored Cylinder Mark for Gases*; GB/T 7144—2016) issued by the Standardization Administration of China, gas cylinders filled with different gases should be labelled with different colour marks for convenient identification. The colored cylinder marks of gas include body colour, text style, text colour and loop colour on the outer surface of gas cylinder according to relevant standards. The colored cylinder marks of commonly used gas in the chemical laboratory are listed in Table 1-1.

Table 1-1 The colored cylinder marks of commonly used gas in the chemical laboratory

Name of filled gas	Chemical formula	Body colour	Text style	Text colour	Loop colour
Air	Air	Black	空气	White	P=20, White, Single Loop P≥30, White, Double Loop
Argon	Ar	Silver Grey	氩	Dark Green	
Helium	He	Silver Grey	氦	Dark Green	
Nitrogen	N_2	Black	氮	White	
Oxygen	O_2	Light Blue	氧	Black	
Hydrogen	H_2	Light Green	氢	Red	P=20, Red, Single Loop P≥30, Red, Double Loop
Acetylene	C_2H_2	White	乙炔 (不可近火)	Red	—

Note:The "P" in the column of loop colour represents the nominal operating pressure with the unit of MPa of gas cylinders.

2. How to use gas cylinder

Before compressed gas stored in the gas cylinder is used and flows into the gas system, the pressure of gas must be reduced to the required range by adjusting the pressure reducing valve. The assembling schematic diagram of the pressure reducing valve and gas cylinder is shown in Figure 1-1.

The operation is as follows:

(1) At first, check whether the color mark of the gas cylinder is complete and in line with relevant regulations, whether there are grease pollutants in the cylinder and pressure reducing valve, and whether the connection between the cylinder and pressure reducing valve is in good airtightness.

(2) Check whether the gas outlet of the pressure reducing valve is closed. If the gas outlet of the pressure reducing valve is not closed, adjust the low-pressure adjusting screw anticlockwise to close it.

(3) Turn on the gas cylinder switch anticlockwise, and the pressure displayed in the high-pressure gauge is the pressure of the compressed gas stored in the gas cylinder.

(4) Adjust the low-pressure adjusting screw clockwise, and the pressure shown on the low-pressure gauge is the pressure of the output gas.

1.4　气体钢瓶的标识及其使用注意事项

1. 气体钢瓶的颜色标志

我国目前使用的气体钢瓶（简称气瓶）主要包括钢制无缝气瓶、钢制焊接气瓶、溶解乙炔气瓶、铝合金无缝气瓶等，但在实验室中使用的气瓶主要是钢制无缝气瓶。根据中华人民共和国国家标准《气瓶颜色标志》（GB/T 7144—2016）的相关规定，不同充装介质的气瓶应该采用不同的气瓶颜色标志作为识别气瓶气体的标志。其中气瓶颜色标志是根据相关标准对气瓶外表面涂敷的涂膜颜色、字样、字色、色环等内容进行规定的组合。表 1–1 列举了实验室常用的气瓶颜色标志。

表 1–1　实验室常用的气瓶颜色标志

<table>
<tr><th>充装气体名称</th><th>化学式（或符号）</th><th>体色</th><th>字样</th><th>字色</th><th>色环</th></tr>
<tr><td>空气</td><td>Air</td><td>黑</td><td>空气</td><td>白</td><td rowspan="5">P=20，白色单环
P≥30，白色双环</td></tr>
<tr><td>氩</td><td>Ar</td><td>银灰</td><td>氩</td><td>深绿</td></tr>
<tr><td>氦</td><td>He</td><td>银灰</td><td>氦</td><td>深绿</td></tr>
<tr><td>氮</td><td>N_2</td><td>黑</td><td>氮</td><td>白</td></tr>
<tr><td>氧</td><td>O_2</td><td>淡（酞）蓝</td><td>氧</td><td>黑</td></tr>
<tr><td>氢</td><td>H_2</td><td>淡绿</td><td>氢</td><td>大红</td><td>P=20，大红单环
P≥30，大红双环</td></tr>
<tr><td>乙炔</td><td>C_2H_2</td><td>白</td><td>乙炔
（不可近火）</td><td>大红</td><td>—</td></tr>
</table>

注：色环栏内的 P 是气瓶的公称工作压力，单位为兆帕（MPa）。

2. 气体钢瓶的使用方法

储存在气体钢瓶中的压缩气体使用时通过减压阀使气体压力降至所需范围后再输入气路系统中，气体钢瓶和减压阀组装示意图如图 1–1 所示。

具体的使用方法如下：

（1）使用前先检查气体钢瓶的颜色标志是否完整并符合相关规定，气体钢瓶和减压阀有无油脂污染物，气体钢瓶和减压阀的连接是否气密性良好。

（2）检查减压阀气体出口是否处于关闭状态。如减压阀气体出口未关闭，逆时针调节低压压力调节螺杆使其关闭。

（3）逆时针打开气体钢瓶开关，此时高压表中显示的压力为气体钢瓶中压缩气体的压力。

（4）顺时针调节低压压力调节螺杆，低压表中显示的压力为输出气体的压力。

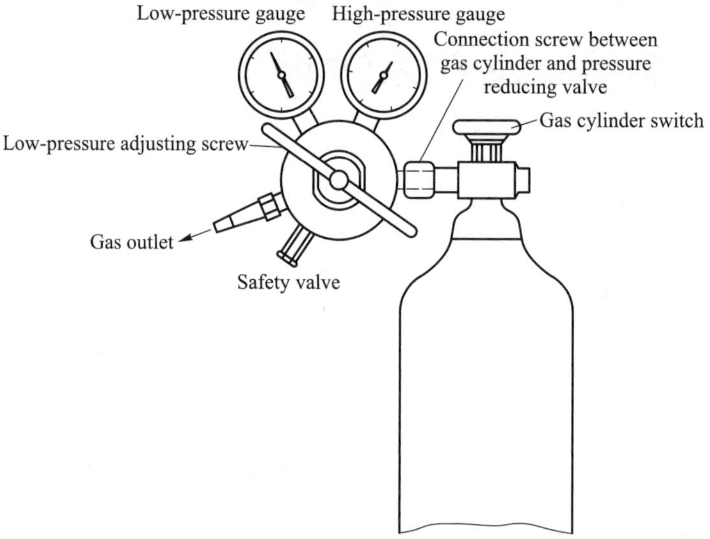

Figure 1-1 Assembling schematic diagram of the gas cylinder and pressure reducing valve

(5) After use, turn off the gas cylinder switch clockwise, and turn off the low pressure adjusting screw anticlockwise after the reading of the low-pressure gauge returns to zero.

3. Precautions for use of gas cylinder

(1) The storage of gas cylinders shall be managed by a specially assigned person. Empty, full, and unqualified gas cylinders should be stored in different areas.

(2) The gas cylinder should be stored in a cool, dry place, away from the sun, heating, furnace fire, and other heat sources, and the distance from the open fire should be more than 10 m. The room where gas cylinders are stored shall have the necessary ventilation.

(3) Gas cylinders should be placed vertically when they are used, and they should be fixed to prevent them from tipping.

(4) The cylinder can be moved by tilting and rolling with bare hands when it is moved in a short distance; when it is moved in a long distance, it can be transported by a portable cart, and the cylinder shall not be thrown, rolled, slid, or overturned.

(5) The cylinder body and valve of the cylinder storing oxygen or other strong oxidizing gas shall not be contaminated with grease or other combustibles. The working clothes, gloves, and handling tools of users shall not be stained with grease.

(6) When installing the pressure reducing valve, check whether the thread of the connecting nut is in good condition. The pressure reducing valve, connector, pipe, and pressure gauge used to connect the gas cylinder shall be marked and shall not be mixed.

(7) When turning on/off the gas cylinder switch, turn the gas cylinder switch slowly with hands or special wrench, and do not use a hammer, pipe wrench, long handle thread wrench, etc.

(8) The gas in the cylinder should not be used up, and there should be residual pressure. The gas in the cylinder shall not be transferred to other cylinders or the residual gas in the cylinder shall not be disposed of by oneself.

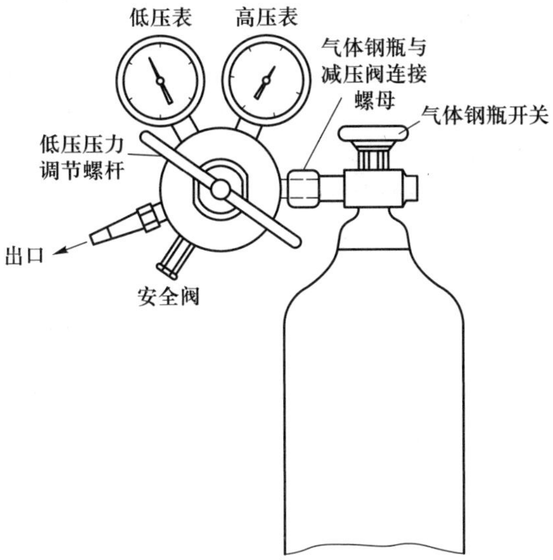

图 1-1 气体钢瓶和减压阀组装示意图

（5）使用完毕后，顺时针关闭气体钢瓶开关，并待低压表读数回到零后，逆时针关闭低压压力调节螺杆。

3. 气体钢瓶使用注意事项

（1）气体钢瓶的储存应有专人负责管理。空瓶、实瓶和不合格气体钢瓶应分别存放在不同的区域。

（2）气体钢瓶应存放在阴凉、干燥，远离阳光、暖气、炉火等热源的地方，与明火的距离要在 10 m 以上。储存气体钢瓶的房间应具有必要的通风设备。

（3）气体钢瓶使用时应立放，并将气体钢瓶加以固定，防止倾倒。

（4）近距离移动气体钢瓶，可采用徒手倾斜滚动的方式移动；远距离移动时，可用轻便小车运送，不应抛、滚、滑、翻气瓶。

（5）使用氧气或其他强氧化性气体的气体钢瓶，其瓶体、瓶阀不应沾染油脂或其他可燃物。使用人员的工作服、手套和装卸工具上不应沾有油脂。

（6）在安装减压阀时，应检查连接螺帽的螺纹是否完好。用于连接气体钢瓶的减压阀、接头、导管和压力表应涂以标记，不能混用。

（7）开启或关闭气体钢瓶开关时，用手或专用扳手缓慢转动气瓶开关，不应使用锤子、管钳、长柄螺纹扳手等。

（8）瓶内气体不应用尽，应留有余压。也不应将气体钢瓶内的气体向其他气体钢瓶倒装或自行处理瓶内的余气。

(9) If it is found that the cylinder valve is leaking, or there is no gas when it is turned on, or there are other defects, the switch of the cylinder shall be closed, marked, and returned to the filling unit for treatment. When the cylinder switch is frozen, the cylinder should be moved to a warmer place and thawed with warm water or heat source whose temperature is not more than 40 ℃ .

(10) The steel seal and colored marks of the gas cylinder shall not be changed without authorization.

(11) Seamless steel cylinders filled with active gas shall be inspected once every three years, seamless steel cylinders filled with inert gas shall be inspected once every five years, and seamless steel cylinders filled with corrosive gas shall be inspected once every two years. Unqualified cylinders shall be scrapped or degraded in time.

（9）发现瓶阀漏气，或打开无气体，或存在其他缺陷时，应将气体钢瓶开关关闭，并做好标记，返回气体钢瓶充装单位处理。气体钢瓶开关冻结时，应把气体钢瓶移到较温暖的地方，用温水或温度不超过 40 ℃的热源解冻。

（10）专瓶专用，不应擅自更改气体钢瓶的钢印和颜色标志。

（11）装有活性气体的无缝钢瓶每 3 年检验一次，装有惰性气体的无缝钢瓶每 5 年检验一次，装有腐蚀性气体的无缝钢瓶每 2 年检验一次，不合格的气体钢瓶要及时报废或降级使用。

1.5 Data Processing Software Commonly Used in Instrumental Analysis Experiments: Introduction to Origin 2018 Software

1. Briefly introduction to Origin 2018

Origin software is the data analysis and graphing software for scientists and engineers developed by OriginLab Company of the United States. Because of its simple and easy to learn, flexible operation, and powerful functions, it is deeply loved by the majority of scientific and technological workers. At present, more than 500 000 scientists and engineers are using Origin Software all over the world. Since 1992, origin has been serving the scientific and engineering communities for more than 30 years, and has become one of the standard graphing software recognized by the international science and technology publishing communities. This book introduces the application of Origin 2018 in instrumental analysis experiment course, mainly including linear curve fitting, two-dimensional graphing, peak analysis, etc. The working interface of origin 2018 software is shown in Figure 1–2, which mainly includes a menu bar, standard toolbar, project manager, file list, workspace, object manager, and Apps library.

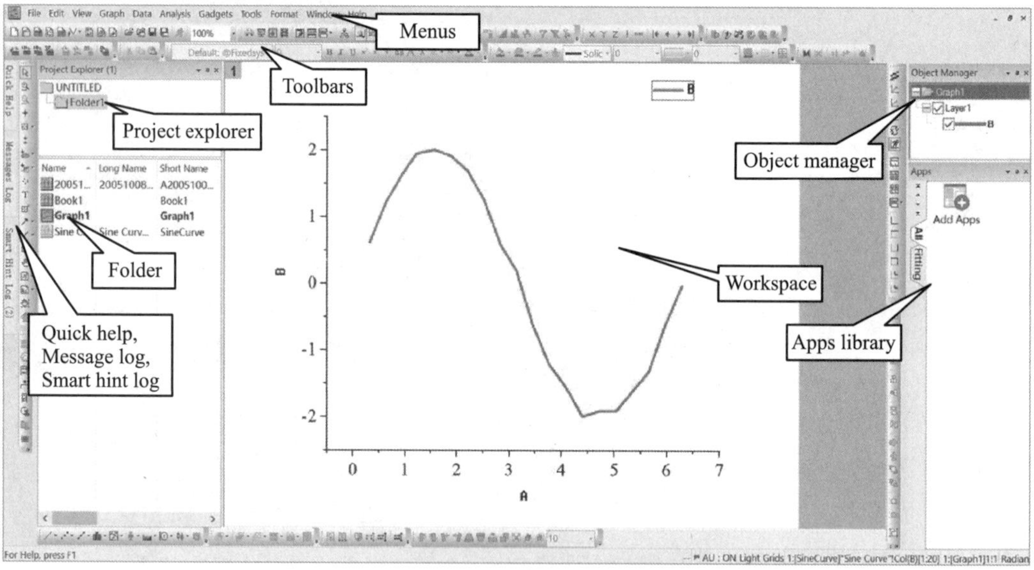

Figure 1–2 The working interface of Origin 2018

2. Linear curve fitting

Linear curve fitting is one of the most commonly used data processing methods in the standard curve method. In this part, the linear curve fitting method based on origin 2018 will be introduced by taking " Colorimetric Determination of Trace Iron in Water with 1,10-Phenanthroline" as an example. As shown in Figure 1-3 to Figure 1-6.

(1) Importing Data. After the Origin 2018 software is opened, a new workbook named "Book 1" will be created automatically in the Project Explorer, and Sheet1 of the workbook will be displayed in the workspace. In Sheet1, the concentration and absorbance of the standard curve solution are input in column A(X) and column B(Y), respectively. The first four rows with a light-yellow

1.5　仪器分析实验中常用数据处理软件——Origin 2018 简介

1. Origin 2018 简介

Origin 是由美国 OriginLab 公司开发的一款科技绘图及数据处理软件，具有简单易学、操作灵活、功能强大的特点，深受广大科技工作者的喜爱，目前全球已经有超过 50 万科学家和工程师正在使用 Origin 软件。从 1992 年开始，Origin 已经服务于科学和工程界超过 30 年，并成为国际科技出版界公认的标准作图软件之一。本书以 Origin 2018 软件为例，介绍其在仪器分析实验课程中的应用，主要包括线性拟合、二维图形的绘制和光谱峰分析等内容。Origin 2018 软件的工作界面如图 1-2 所示，主要包括菜单栏、标准工具栏、项目管理器、文件列表、工作区、对象管理器及 Apps 库。

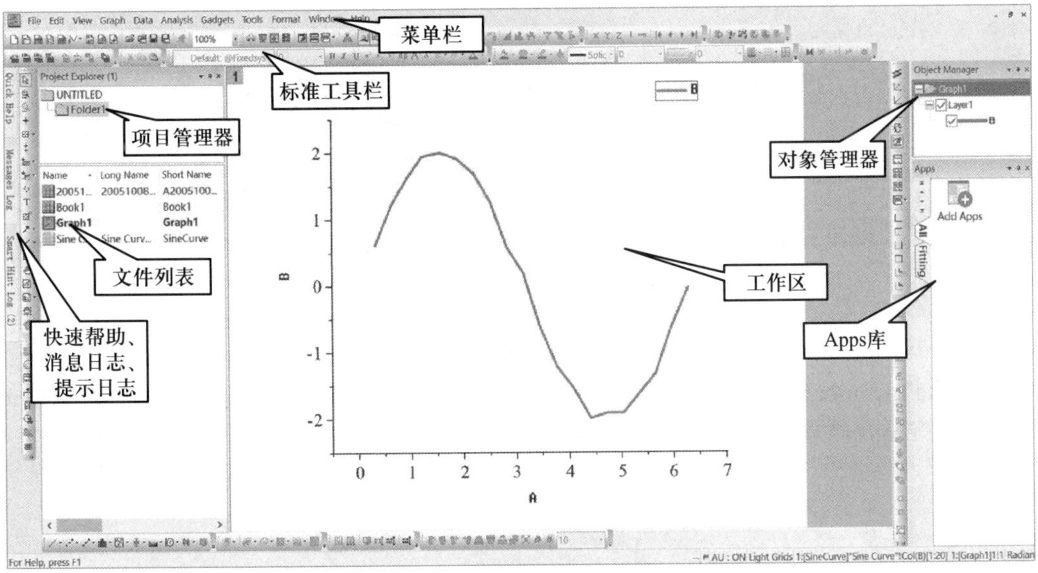

图 1-2　Origin 2018 工作界面

2. 线性拟合

线性拟合是标准曲线法中最常用的一种数据处理方法，本部分将以“邻二氮菲比色法测定水中微量铁含量”为例，介绍采用 Origin 2018 的线性拟合处理方法。见图 1-3~图 1-6。

（1）数据输入。打开 Origin 2018 软件后，项目管理器中将自动新建一个工作簿“Book1”，同时在工作区显示该工作簿的工作表 Sheet1。在 Sheet1 中的 A（X）列中输入浓度数据、B（Y）列中输入吸光度的数据，其中每一列的前四行以黄底显示部分为列类型设置，后面的白底显示区域为数据输入单元格。在 A（X）列的“Longname”中输入“Concentration”，“Units”中输入“μg/mL”，在 B（Y）列的“Longname”中输入“Absorbance”，然后输入浓度和对应的吸光度数据。如图 1-3 所示。

background of each column are the type of the column, including Long Name, Units, Comment, and F(X)=. Meanwhile, the table cell with a white background is for inputting data. For example, enter "concentration" and "μg/mL" in the Long Name and Units of column A(X), respectively, enter "absorbance" in the Long Name of column B(Y). Then, the concentration and absorbance of the standard curve solution are entered into the table cell of column A(X) and column B(Y). As shown in Figure 1–3.

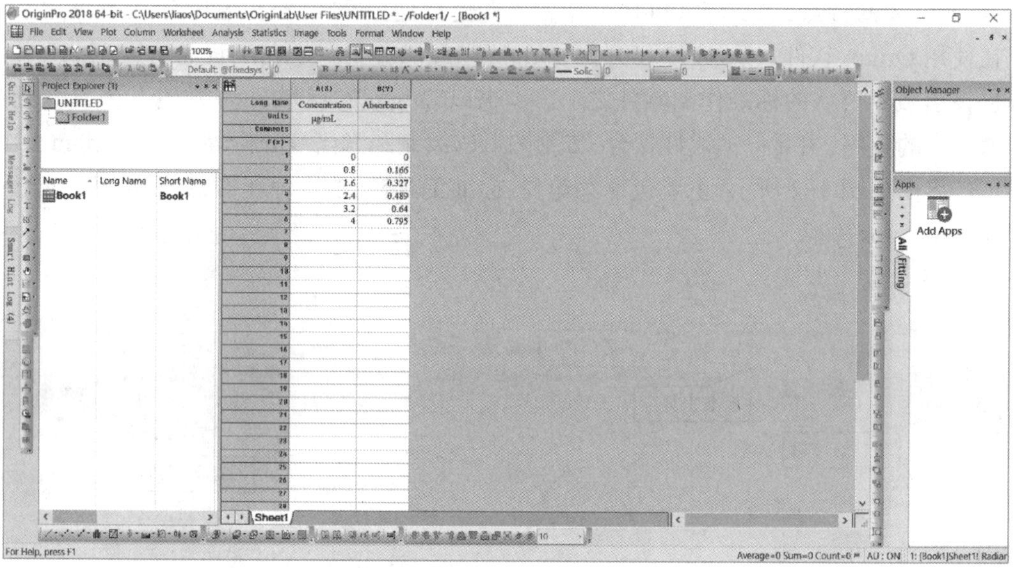

Figure 1–3 Importing data

(2) Plotting a 2D scatter graph. Select columns A(X) and B (Y), and then click "Plot" → "2D Scatter" in the menu bar to plot a 2D scatter graph. At the same time, a graphic file named Graph1 appears in the Project Explorer.As shown in Figure 1–4.

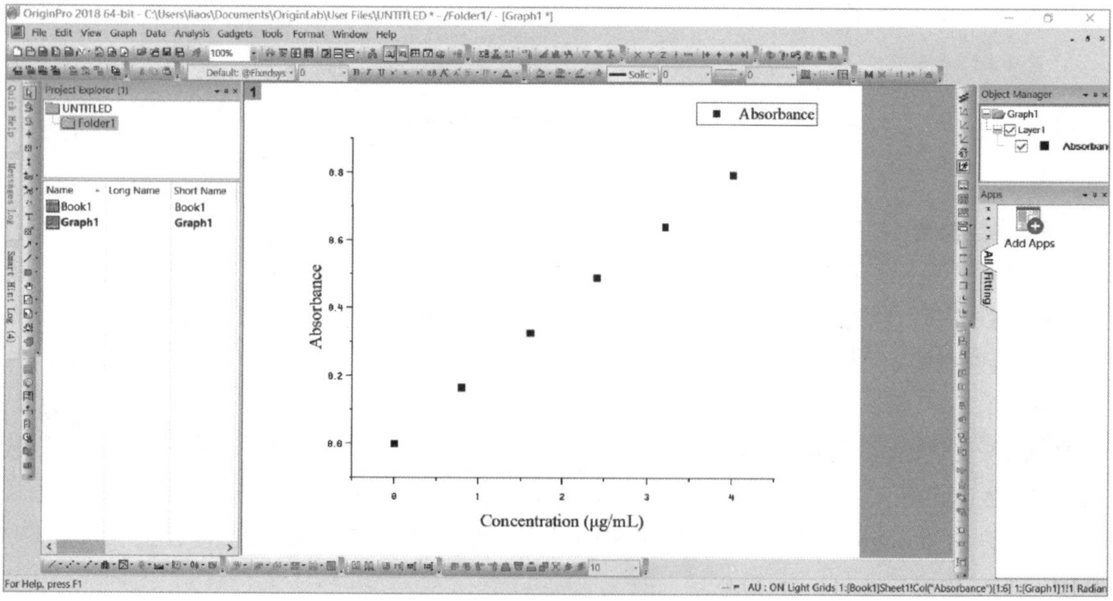

Figure 1–4 Plotting 2D scatter graph

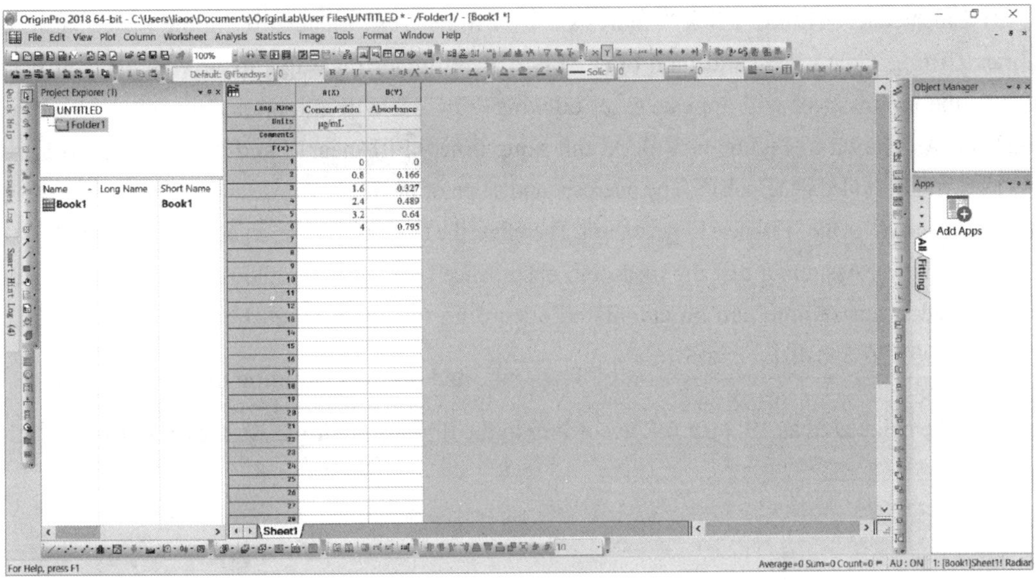

图 1-3　数据输入

（2）绘制散点图。选定 A（X）和 B（Y）列，然后单击菜单栏中“Plot”→“2D Scatter”，即可绘制二维散点图。同时在文件列表中出现“Graph1”文件。如图 1-4 所示。

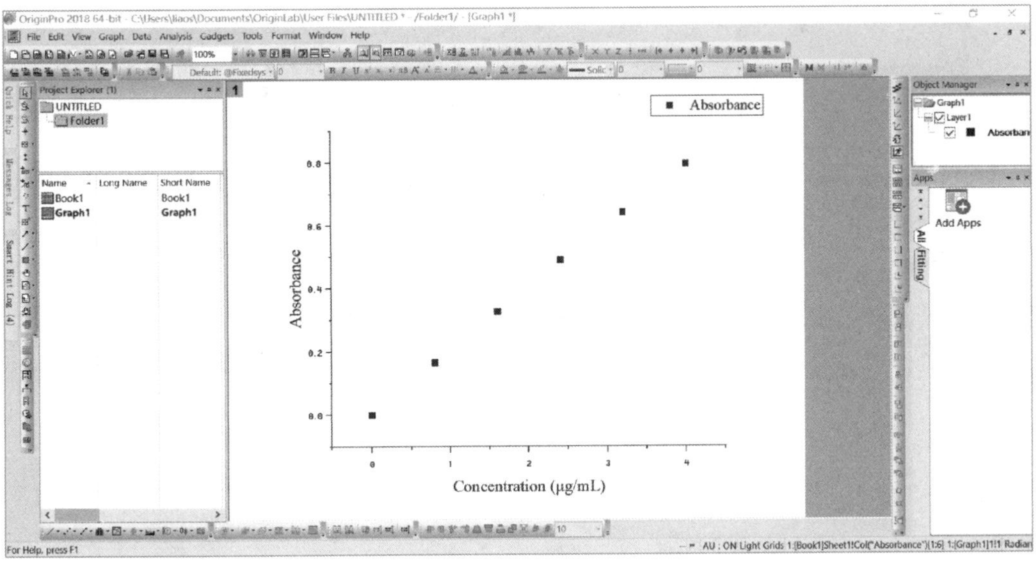

图 1-4　绘制散点图

(3) Linear curve fitting. Click "Analysis" → "Fitting" → "Linear Fit" in the menu bar to open the linear fitting dialog box, and then click "OK". A reminder message about whether you want to switch to the report sheet will appear. After clicking "OK", it will automatically switch to the report worksheet. As shown in Figure 1–5(a). At the same time, "FitLinear1" and "FitLinearCurve1" report worksheets will be added in "Book1". The intercept and slope of the linear regression equation can be obtained from the "Summary" of the "Fitlinear1" worksheet. Therefore, the linear regression equation is $A = 0.005\,76 + 0.198\,54c$ ($R^2 = 0.999\,7$). Assuming that the measured absorbance of a water sample is 0.401, the concentration of the diluted water sample can be calculated according to the obtained linear regression equation as: $c = \frac{A - 0.005\,76}{0.198\,54} = \frac{0.401 - 0.005\,76}{0.198\,54} = 1.99\ \mu g/mL$, and the concentration of trace iron in the water sample can be calculated as 19.9 μg/mL according to the dilution multiple. As shown in Figure 1–5(b).

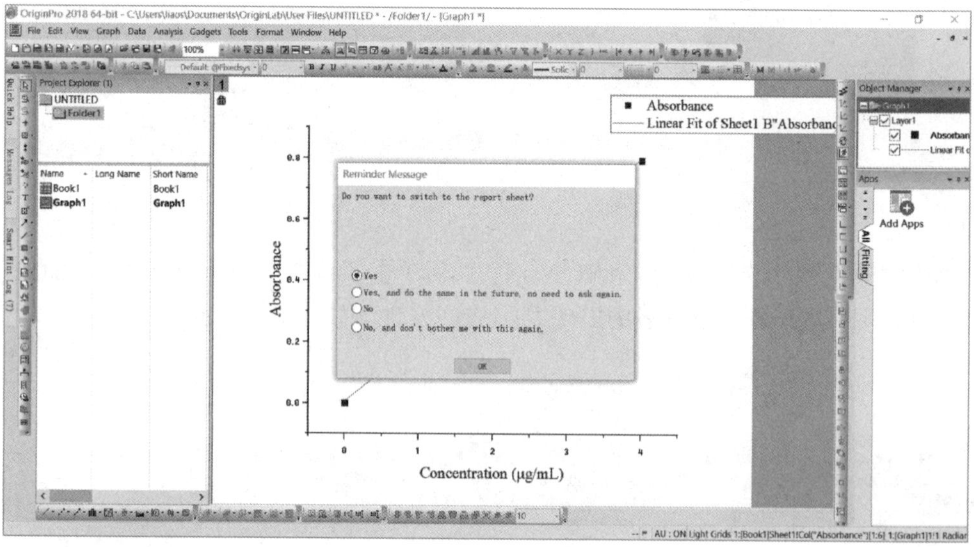

(a)

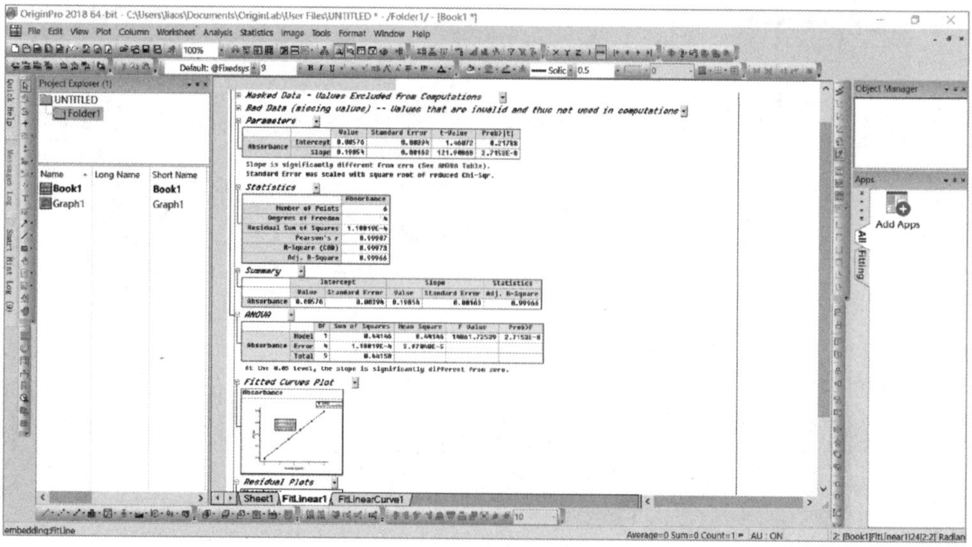

(b)

Figure 1–5 Linear curve fitting

（3）线性拟合。单击菜单栏中的“Analysis”→“Fitting”→“Linear Fit”，出现线性拟合对话框，然后单击“OK”，出现是否转换到报告工作表的提示信息，单击“OK”后，自动切换到报告工作表。如图 1–5（a）所示。同时在工作簿“Book1”中将新增“FitLinear1”和“FitLinearCurve1”报告工作表，从“FitLinear 1”工作表的“Summary”中可得到线性回归方程的截距和斜率。因此，可得本实验线性回归方程为：$A = 0.005\,76 + 0.198\,54c(R^2 = 0.999\,7)$。假设水样测得的吸光度为 0.401，代入该线性回归方程，可计算出稀释后的水样浓度为：$c = \dfrac{A - 0.005\,76}{0.198\,54} = \dfrac{0.401 - 0.005\,76}{0.198\,54} = 1.99\ \mu g/mL$，根据稀释倍数计算可得水样中微量铁的浓度为 19.9 μg/mL。如图 1–5（b）所示。

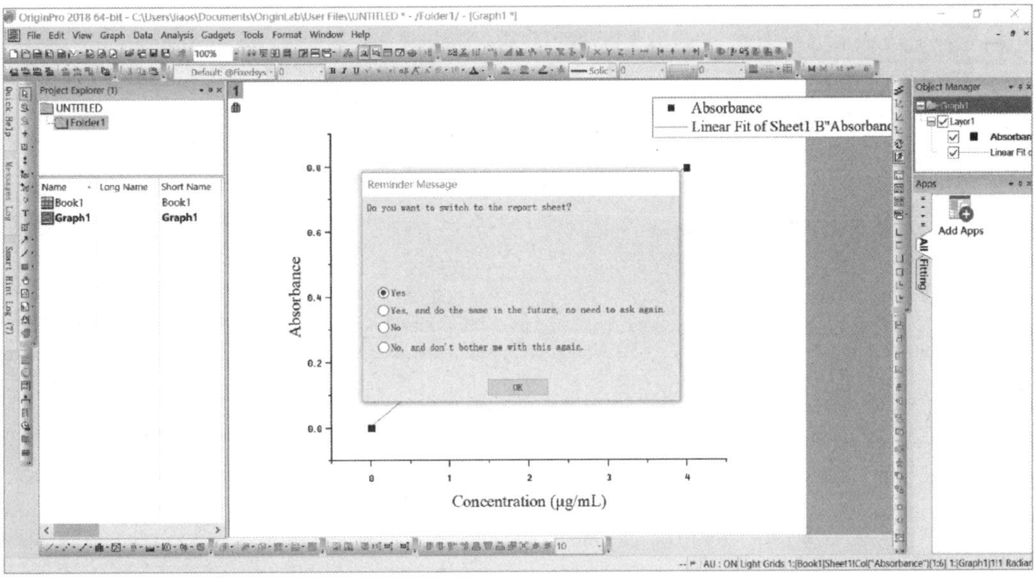

(a)

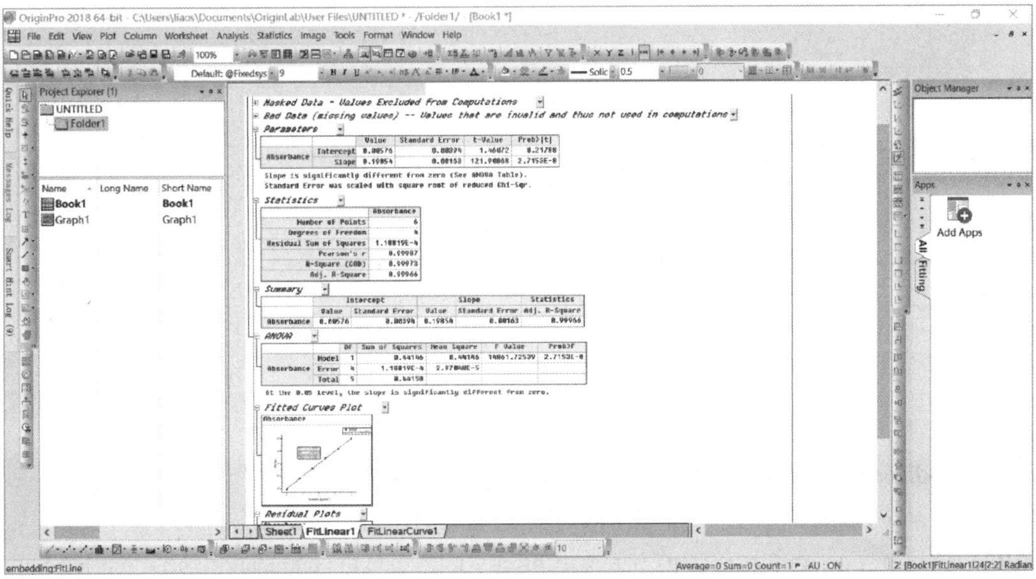

(b)

图 1–5　线性拟合

(4) Exporting graphs. In the "Graph1" file of the Project Explorer, click "Graph1" → "File" → "Export Graphs" → "Open Dialog" or directly use "Ctrl + G" to open the dialog box of Export Graphs, then select "image type" as jpeg, and set "File name" and "Path" for the target file.

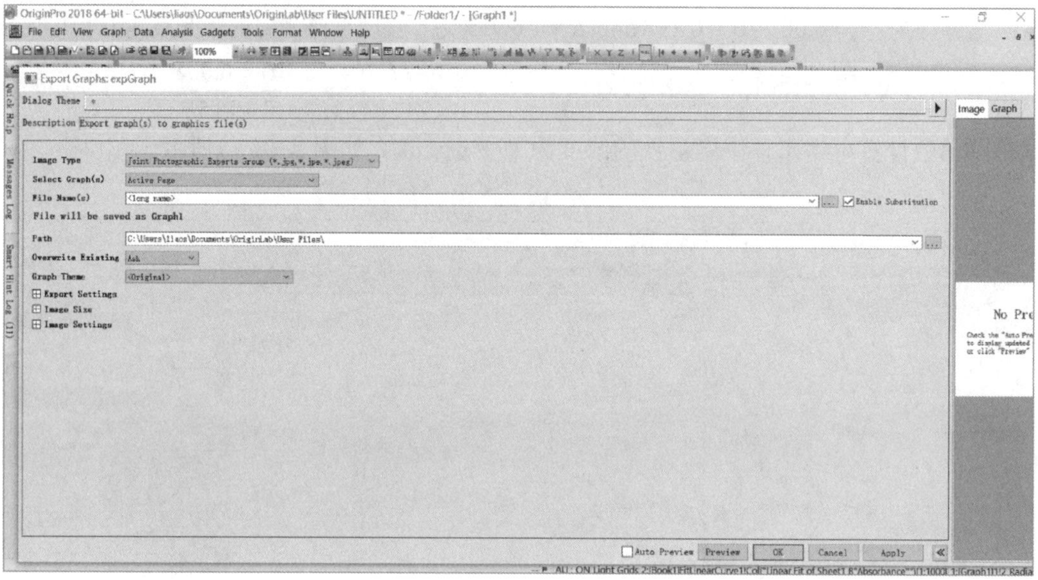

(a)

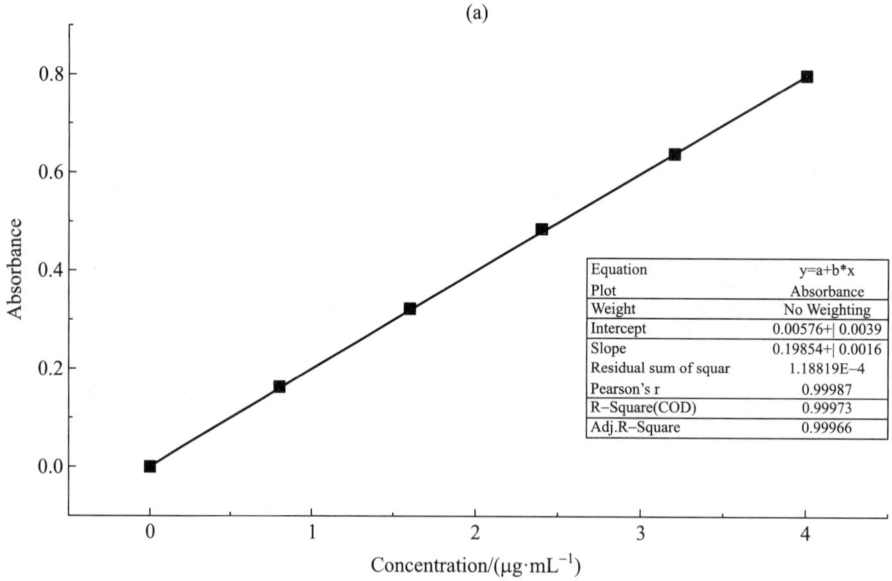

(b)

Figure 1-6 Exporting graphs

3. Two-dimensional Graphing

Plotting a two-dimensional graph is widely used in analytical chemistry, including titration curve and UV-Vis absorption spectrum. This part will briefly introduce the application of Origin in plotting a two-dimensional graph combined with the experimental data processing of "Potentiometric Titration Analysis of Phosphoric Acid and Determination of Dissociation Constant". As shown in Figure 1-7 to Figure 1-9.

（4）图形输出。线性拟合的图形在文件列表的“Graph1”文件中，单击“Graph1”→“File”→“Export Graphs”→“Open Dialog”或直接使用“Ctrl+G”快捷方式打开对话框，然后将“Image Type”选择为 jpeg，“File name”和“Path”设置为目标文件名和路径，如图 1-6（a）所示。所得线性拟合的图形如图 1-6（b）所示。

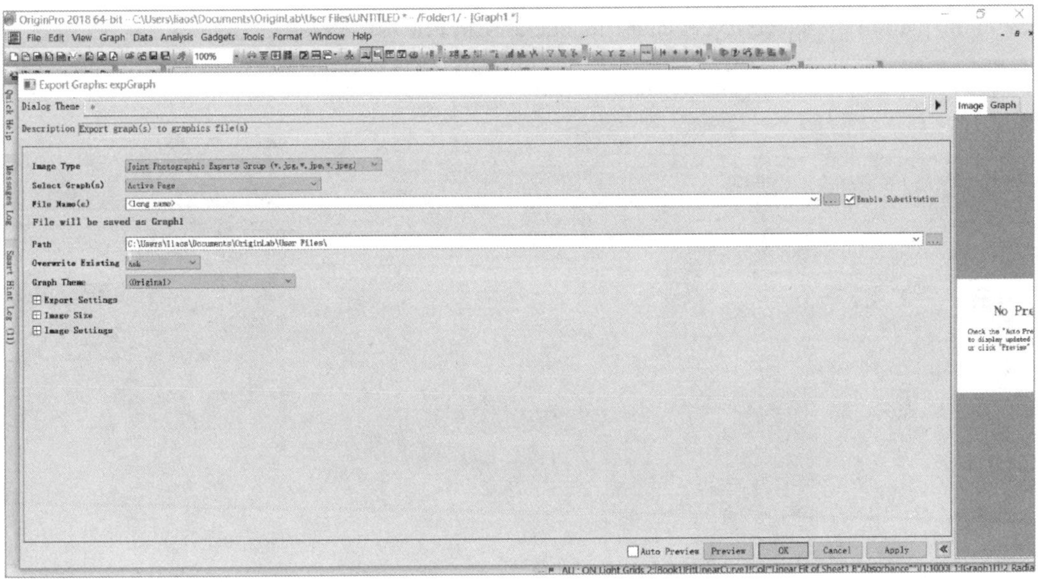

(a)

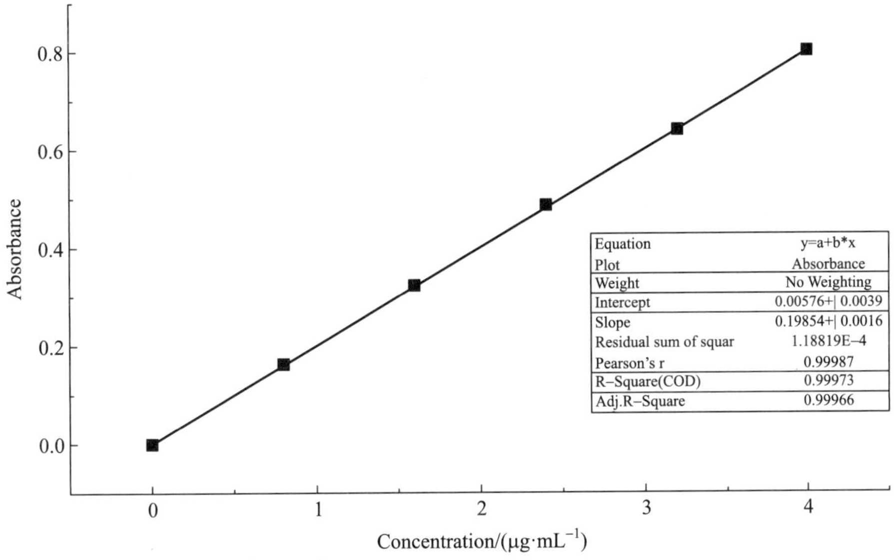

(b)

图 1-6　图形输出

3. 二维图形的绘制

二维图形的绘制在分析化学中具有非常广泛的用途，从滴定曲线到紫外－可见吸收光谱的绘制等均需使用二维图形，本部分将结合“磷酸的电位滴定分析及其解离常数的测定”实验数据的处理，简单介绍 Origin 在二维图形绘制中的应用。见图 1-7~ 图 1-9。

(1) Importing data. In Origin, in addition to entering data directly in the worksheet, the data obtained by some analytical instruments can be imported directly. The most common formats of data include ASCII format and Excel format. For example, when importing data of "Potentiometric Titration Analysis of Phosphoric Acid and Determination of Dissociation Constant" as Excel format, the operation is as follows: click "File" → "Import" → "Excel", and a dialog box will appear. After selecting the path of the saved Excel data file, click "Add File (s)" → "OK" .

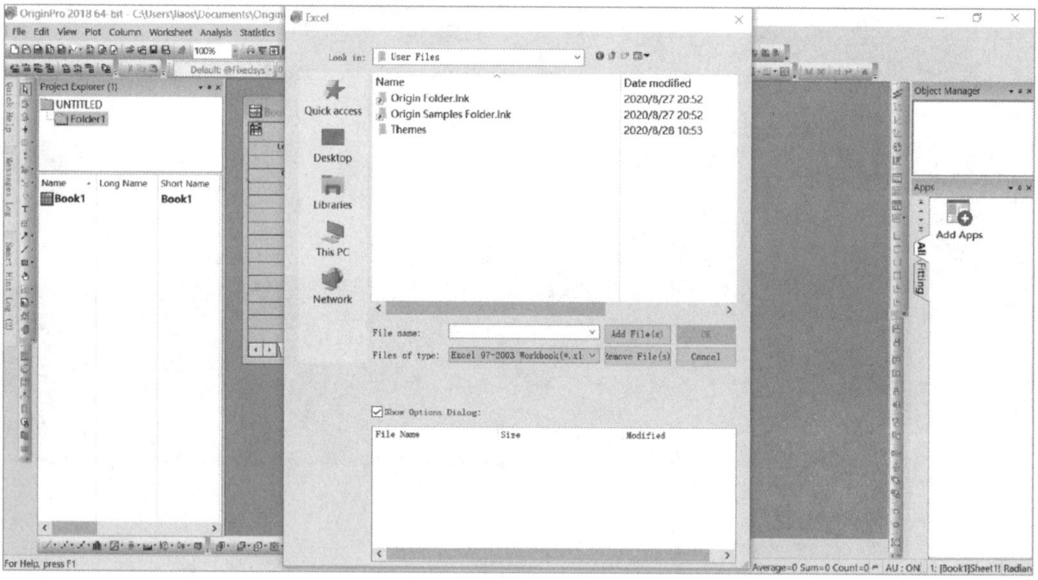

(a)

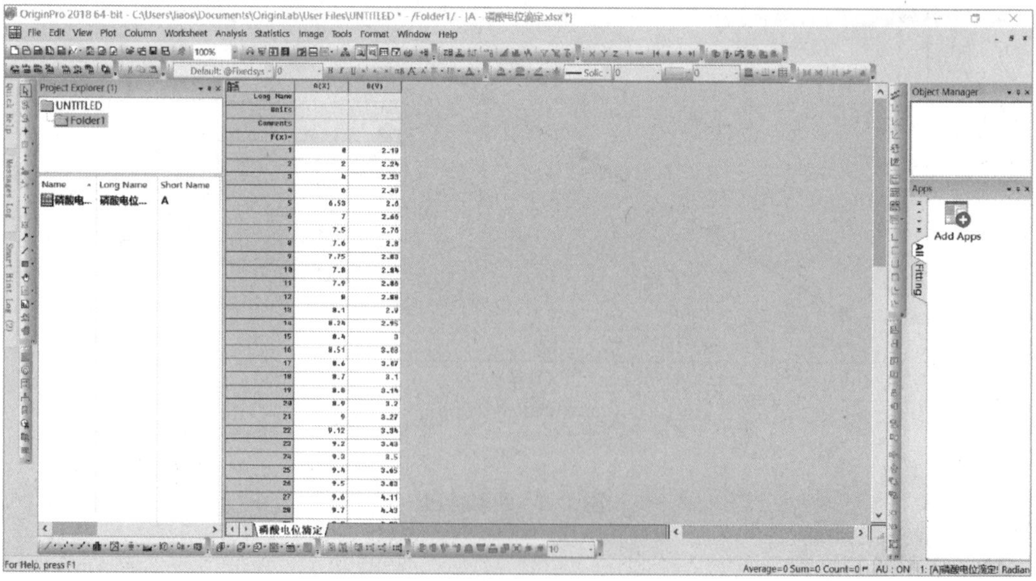

(b)

Figure 1-7　Importing data

（1）数据导入。在 Origin 中，除了前面所介绍的直接在工作表中输入数据外，还可以将某些分析仪器得到的数据直接进行导入，其中导入数据最常见的格式包括 ASCII 数据格式及 Excel 数据格式。例如，当导入“磷酸的电位滴定分析及其解离常数的测定”的 Excel 数据时，其操作如下：单击“File”→“Import”→“Excel”，出现数据导入对话框，如图 1-7（a）所示。选择保存的 Excel 数据文件路径后，单击“Add File(s)”→“OK”，如图 1-7（b）所示。

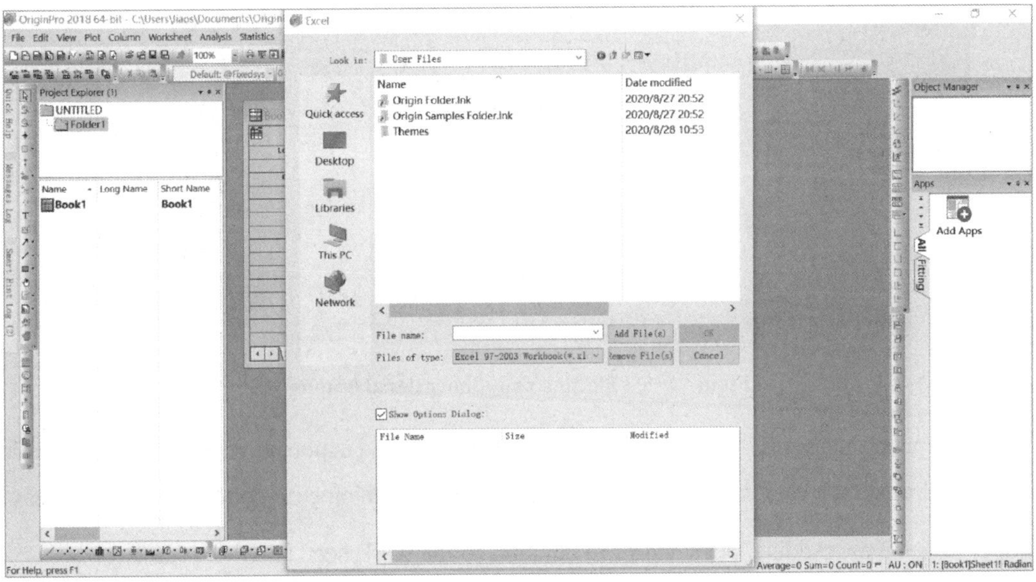

(a)

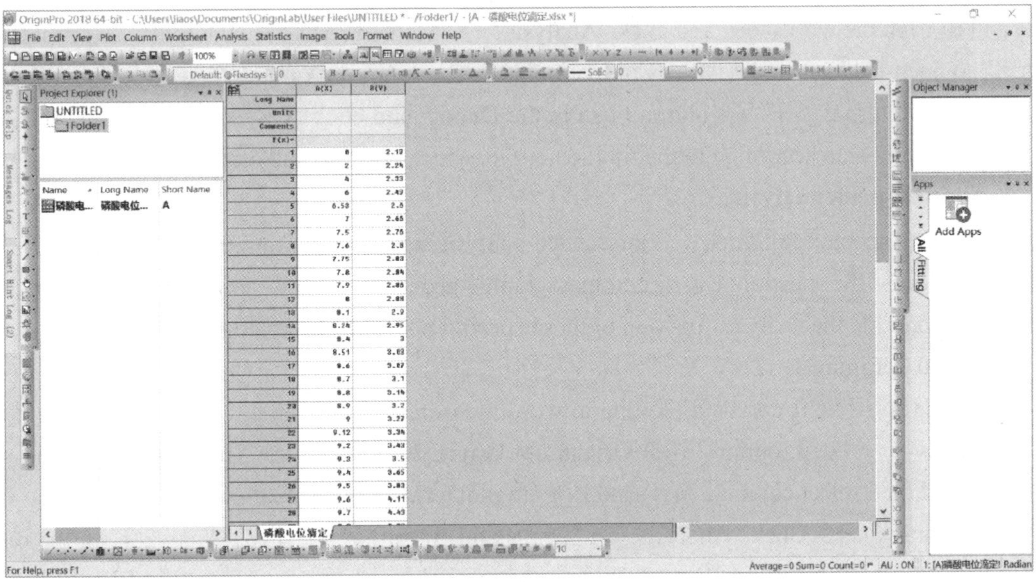

(b)

图 1-7　数据导入

(2) Plotting two-dimensional graph. Select columns A(X) and B(Y), then click "Plot" in the menu bar, and select "2D Line + Symbol" to plot a 2D point line graph. At the same time, the "Graph1" file appears in the Project Explorer.

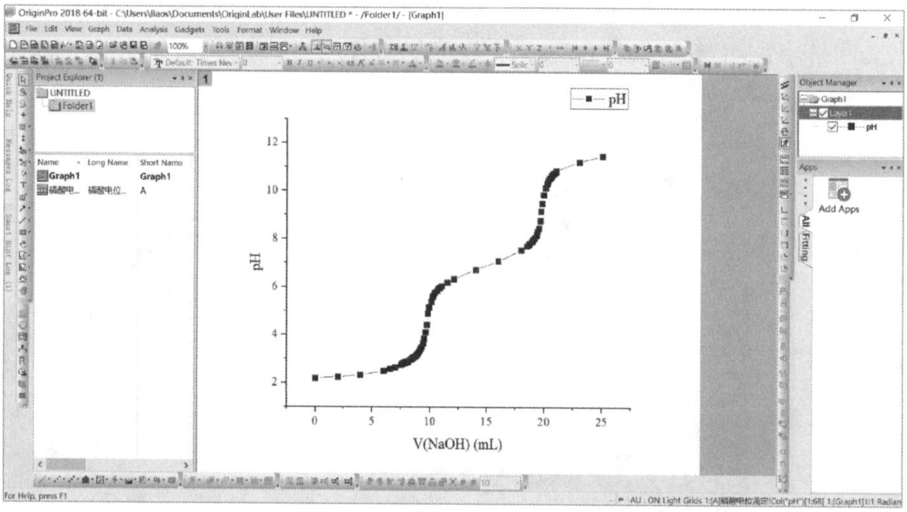

Figure 1-8 Plotting two-dimensional graphs

(3) Interpolate Y from X. According to the interpolation method in potentiometric titration, the volume of sodium hydroxide standard solution at the first and second stoichiometric points are calculated as V_{eq1} and V_{eq2}, respectively. Adding D(Y) and E(Y) columns to the worksheet, enter $\frac{V_{eq1}}{2}$ and $\frac{V_{eq1}+V_{eq2}}{2}$ in the D(Y) column of the worksheet. Assuming that the obtained V_{eq1} and V_{eq2} by interpolation methods are 9.74 mL and 19.67 mL, respectively, enter "4.87" and "14.70" in column D(Y). Select columns A(X) and B(Y) in the worksheet, and click "Analysis" → "Mathematics" → "Interpolate/Extrapolate Y from X" to open Dialog. Set "X Values to Interpolate" as column D (Y), "Method" as "Cubic Spline" and "Result of Interpolation" as column E(Y) in the Dialog, and click "OK" to calculate the pK_{a1} and pK_{a2} of phosphoric acid according to the titration curve, which are 2.36 and 6.86, respectively.

4. Spectral peak analysis

In UV-VIS spectrophotometry, fluorescence analysis, and chromatographic analysis, it is often necessary to locate the spectral peak or chromatographic peak and integrate the peak area. Origin 2018 software can provide the analysis function of these spectral peaks or chromatographic peaks. As shown is Figure 1-10 to Figure 1-12.

(1) Importing ASCII data and plotting a two-dimensional graph. Click "File" → "Import" → "Single ASCII" → "C:\Program Files\ OriginLab\ Origin 2018\ Samples\ Spectroscopy\ Peaks with Base.dat", and then select columns A(X) and B(Y) to plot a two-dimensional graph.

(2) Finding Peaks. Click "Analysis" → "Peaks and Baseline" → "Peak Analyzer" in the menu bar to open the Peak Analysis Wizard Dialog. After clicking " ▼ ", select "Find Peaks", click "Next", select "None" for "Baseline Mode", click "Next", check "Enable Auto Find", and then click "Finish".

（2）二维图形的绘制。选定 A（X）和 B（Y）列，然后单击菜单栏中“Plot”，选择“2D Line+Symbol”，即可绘制二维点线图，同时在文件列表中出现“Graph1”文件，如图 1-8 所示。

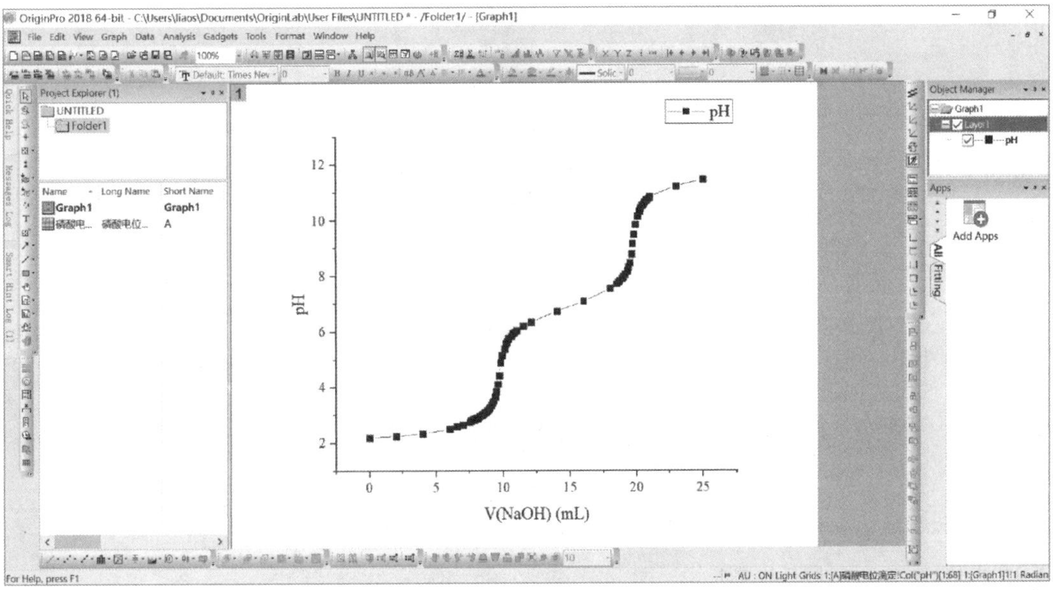

图 1-8　二维图形的绘制

（3）插值求 Y 值。根据电位滴定法中的内插法，求出磷酸第一个和第二个化学计量点时消耗的 NaOH 体积（V_{eq1}和V_{eq2}），然后在工作表中新增 D（Y）和 E（Y）列，将$\frac{V_{eq1}}{2}$和$\frac{V_{eq1}+V_{eq2}}{2}$值输入 D（Y）列。假设通过内插法求出的$V_{eq1}$和$V_{eq2}$分别为 9.74 mL 和 19.67 mL，则在 D（Y）列中输入“4.87”和“14.70”。选中工作表中的 A（X）和 B（Y）列，单击“Analysis”→“Mathematics”→“Interpolate/Extrapolate Y from X”，打开插值对话框。将对话框中的“X Values to Interpolate”设置为 D（Y）列，“Method”设置为“Cubic Spline”，“Result of Interpolation”设置为 E（Y）列，单击“OK”，就可根据滴定曲线的趋势求出磷酸的 pK_{a1} 和 pK_{a2} 分别为 2.36 和 6.86，如图 1-9 所示。

4. 光谱峰分析

在紫外－可见分光光度法、荧光分析法和色谱分析法中，常需对光谱峰或色谱峰的位置进行定位以及对其峰面积进行积分，而 Origin 2018 软件可提供这些光谱峰或色谱峰分析功能。见图 1-10～图 1-12。

（1）导入 ASCII 数据、绘制二维图形。单击“File”→“Import”→“Single ASCII”→“C:\Program Files\OriginLab\Origin 2018\Samples\Spectroscopy\Peaks with Base.dat”，然后选择 A（X）和 B（Y）列绘制二维图形。如图 1-10 所示。

（2）寻峰。单击菜单栏中的“Analysis”→“Peaks and Baseline”→“Peak Analyzer”，打开峰分析向导对话框。单击“▾”后，选择“Find Peaks”，单击“Next”；将“Baseline Mode”选择为“None”，单击“Next”；勾选“Enable Auto Find”后，然后单击“Finish”。如图 1-11 所示。

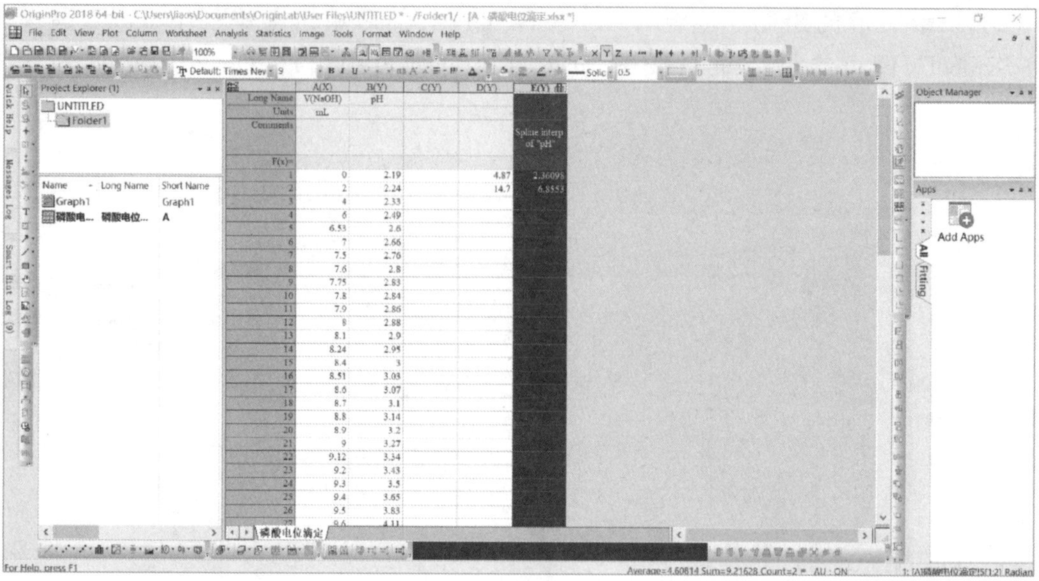

Figure 1-9 Interpolate Y from X

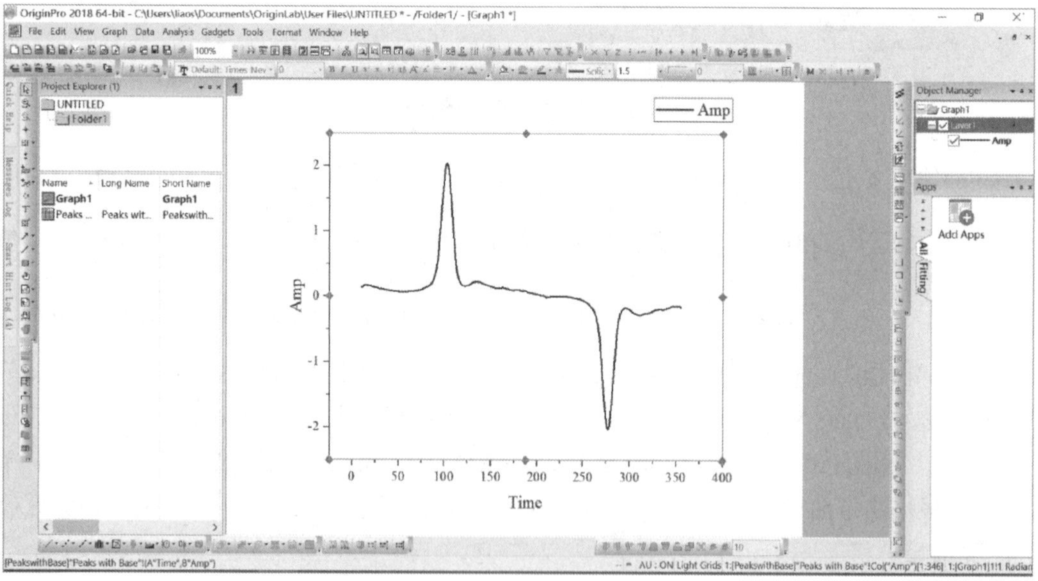

Figure 1-10 Importing ASCII data and plotting a two-dimensional graph

(3) Integrating Peaks. Click "Analysis" → "Peaks and Baseline" → "Peak Analyzer" in the menu bar to open the Wizard Dialog on peak analysis. After clicking " ▼ ", select "Integrate Peaks" and "Next"; select "Baseline Mode" as "None"; click "Next"; check "Enable Auto Find" and "Next"; select "Integration Window Width" as "Auto"; check "Show Integrated Area" and "Show Peak Index Tag", and then click "Finish", the peak area is shown in the sheet named "Integration Result1" of the "Peaks with Base" worksheet.

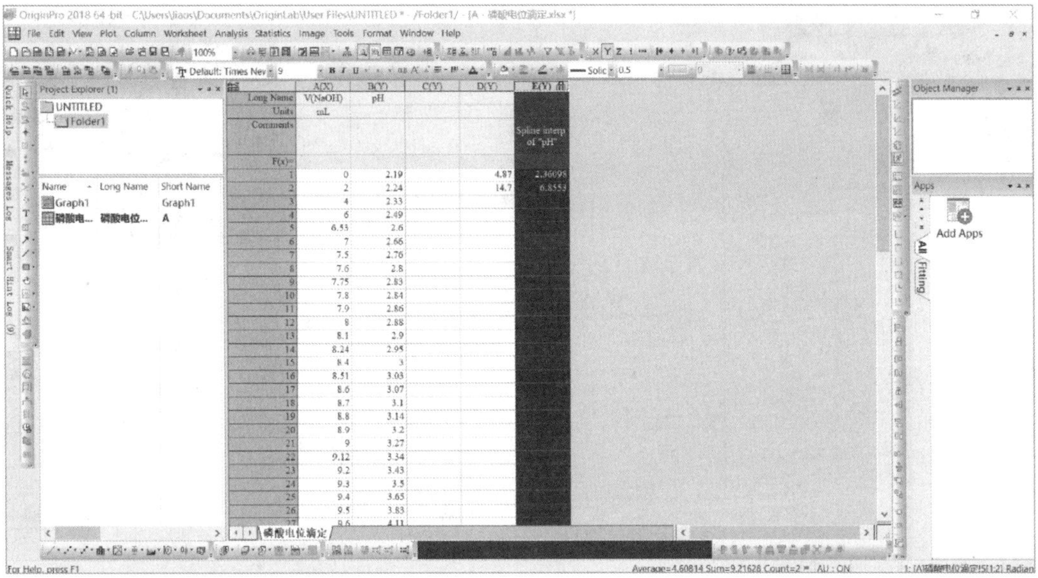

图 1-9　求值

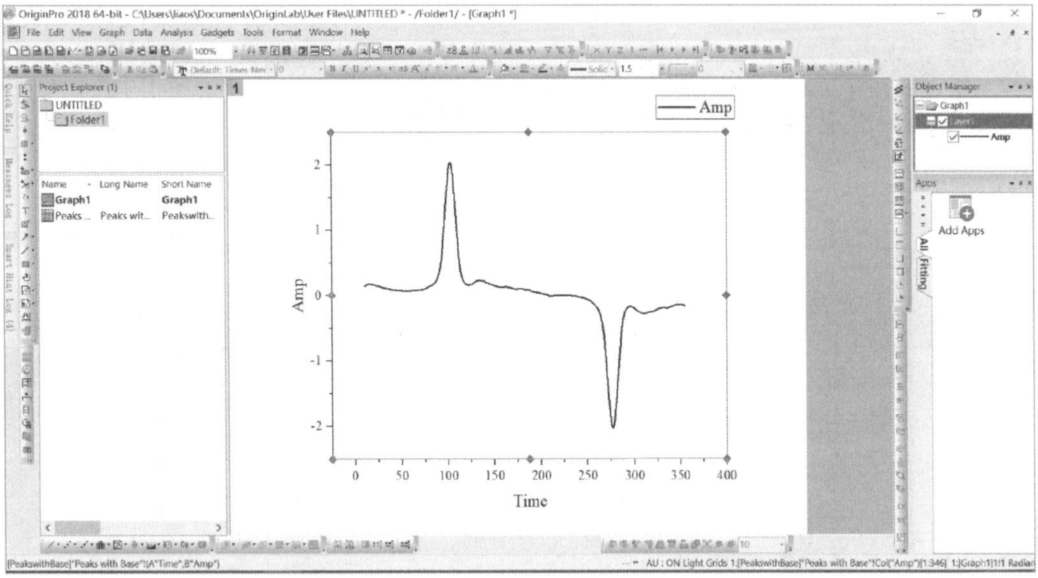

图 1-10　导入 ASCII 数据、绘制二维图形

（3）峰面积积分。单击菜单栏中的“Analysis”→“Peaks and Baseline”→“Peak Analyzer”，打开峰分析向导对话框。单击“▼”后，选择“Integrate Peaks”，单击“Next”；将“Baseline Mode”选择为“None”，单击“Next”；勾选“Enable Auto Find”后，单击“Next”；将“Integration Window Width”选择为“Auto”，勾选“Show Integrated Area”和“Show Peak Index Tag”，单击“Finish”，其峰面积值在“Peaks with Base”工作簿的“Integration Result1”工作表中。如图 1-12 所示。

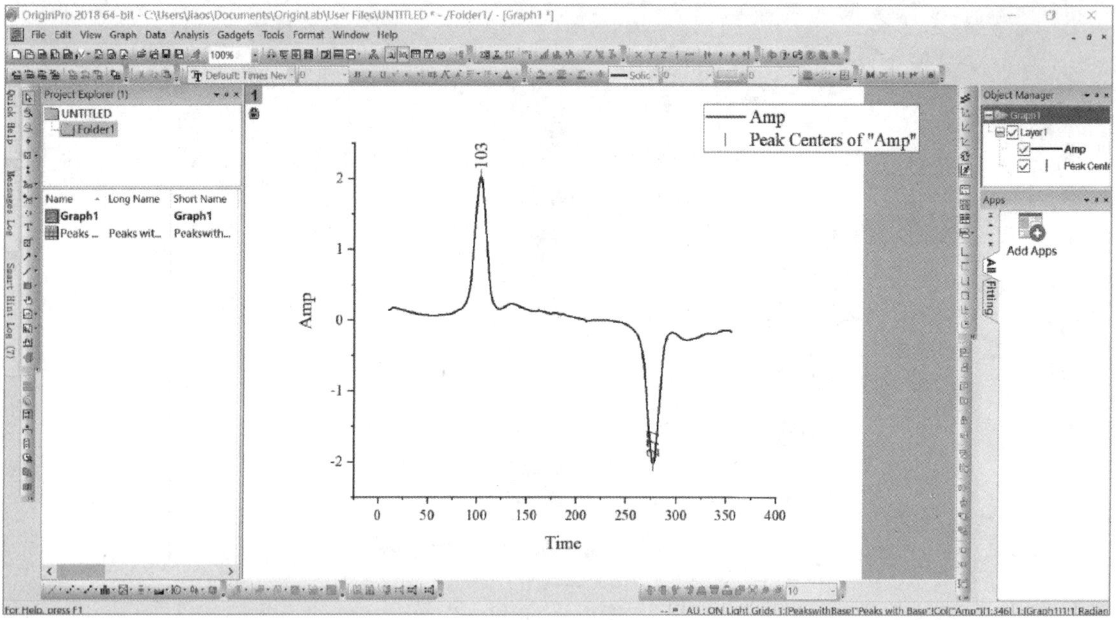

Figure 1-11 Finding peaks

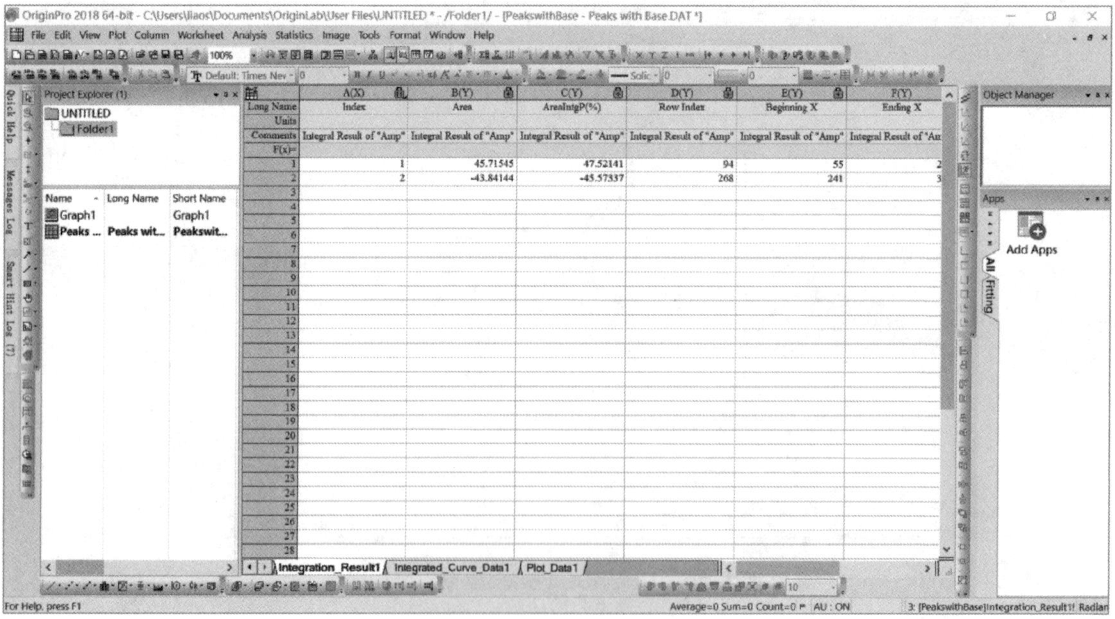

Figure 1-12 Integrating peaks

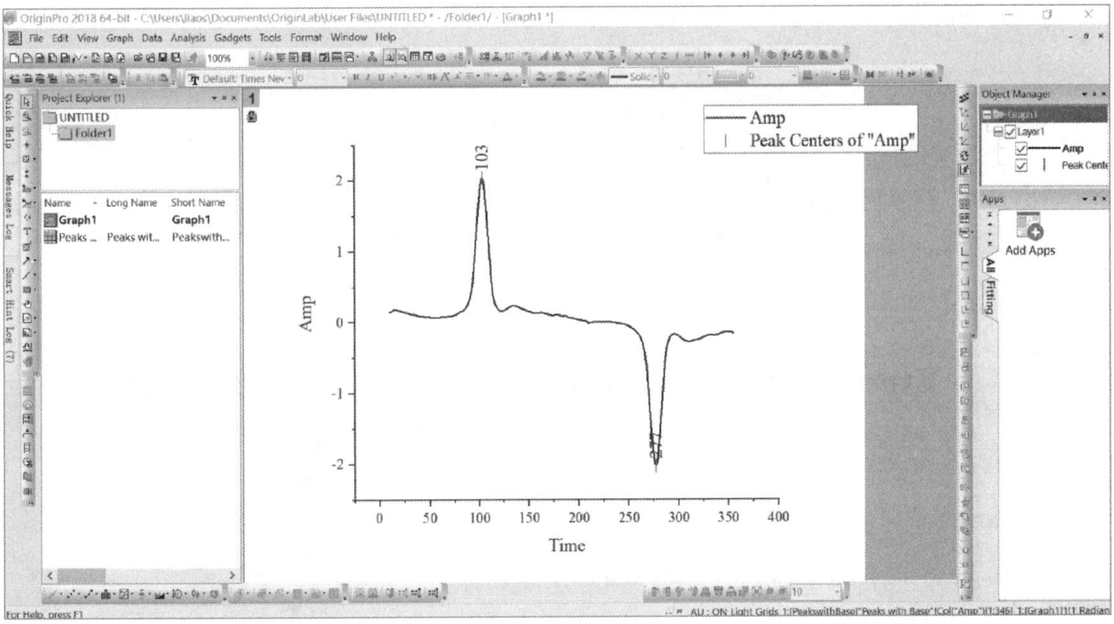

图 1-11　寻峰

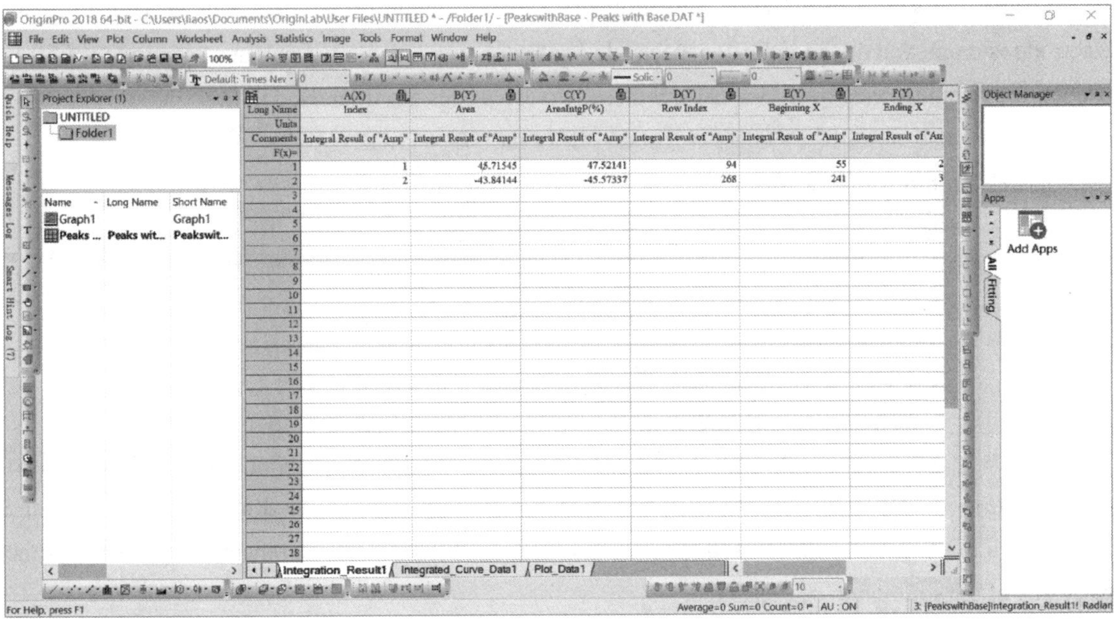

图 1-12　峰面积积分

Chapter 2 Electrochemical Analysis

Experiment 2.1 Determination of pH Values of Liquid Pharmaceutical Preparations

Purpose

(1) To grasp the principle of pH measurement.

(2) To grasp the method of pH measurements with pH meter.

Principle

The pH measurement by direct potentiometry usually constitutes galvanic cell, in which a glass electrode is employed as the indicator electrode (cathode), and a saturated calomel electrode (SCE) is used as the reference electrode (anode) and these two electrodes are immersed in the solution.

$$(-)\text{Glass electrode} \mid H^+ (x\ \text{mol}\cdot L^{-1}) \parallel \text{SCE}\ (+)$$

The electromotive force (E_x) of the cell is:

$$E_x = E_{SCE} - E_{glass}$$

$$E_x = E_{SCE} - (K'' - 0.0\,592\text{VpH}_x)(25℃)$$

$$E_x = E_{SCE} - K'' + 0.0\,592\text{VpH}_x$$

$$E_x = K + 0.0\,592\text{VpH}_x$$

$$(K = E_{SCE} - K'')$$

Where E_x is the electromotive force, V; E_{SCE} and E_{glass}, are the electrode potential of SCE and glass electrode respectively, V; K'' is the glass electrode constant, which is related to the pH value of the liquid filled in the glass electrode and the potential value of the internal reference electrode; pH_x is the pH value of the solution to be measured.

The above formula shows, the E_x is linear with the pH of the solution. As long as the glass electrode constant K'' is known and fixed, the E_x of the cell can be measured, and the pH_x of the solution to be tested can be obtained. In the experiment, since K'' changes slightly with the type of electrode, the composition of the solution to be tested and the electrode service time, its change value is not easy to accurately measured, the pH_x value of the solution is generally determined by comparison with the pH_s of the standard buffer solution.

That is, a galvanic cell composed of a standard buffer solution with a glass electrode and SCE is

第二章　电化学分析

实验 2.1　药物液体制剂的 pH 测定

一、实验目的

（1）掌握溶液 pH 测定的原理。

（2）掌握用 pH 计测定溶液 pH 的方法。

二、实验原理

直接电位法中测定溶液 pH，是以玻璃电极为指示电极（负极）；饱和甘汞电极（SCE）为参比电极（正极），插入待测溶液中，构成原电池。

$$(-)\ 玻璃电极\ |\ H^{+}\ (x\ mol \cdot L^{-1})\ \|\ SCE\ (+)$$

该电池的电动势（E_x）为

$$E_x = E_{SCE} - E_{glass}$$
$$E_x = E_{SCE} - (K'' - 0.059\,2VpH_x)(25℃)$$
$$E_x = E_{SCE} - K'' + 0.059\,2VpH_x$$
$$E_x = K + 0.059\,2VpH_x$$
$$(K = E_{SCE} - K'')$$

式中，E_x 为电池的电动势，V；E_{SCE}，E_{glass} 分别为饱和甘汞电极和玻璃电极的电极电位，V；K''为玻璃电极常数，与玻璃电极内充液的 pH 和内部参比电极电位值有关；pH_x 为待测溶液 pH。

上式表明，测得的电池电动势（E_x）与溶液的 pH 呈线性关系。只要玻璃电极常数 K'' 已知并固定不变，测得电池电动势 E_x，便可求得待测溶液的 pH_x。实验中，由于 K'' 随电极种类、待测溶液组成及电极使用时间而发生微小变化，其值不易准确测量，故 pH 测量常采用“两次测量法”。即先用标准缓冲溶液与玻璃电极和 SCE 组成原电池来校正（即“定位”），则

$$pH_s = \frac{E_s - K}{0.059\,2V}$$

校正后，再插入待测溶液中，则有

used for calibration (i.e., "positioning").

$$\mathrm{pH_s} = \frac{E_\mathrm{s} - K}{0.059\,2\mathrm{V}}$$

After calibration, insert it into the solution to be tested.

$$\mathrm{pH}_x = \frac{E_x - K}{0.059\,2\mathrm{V}}$$

Subtract the two formulas each other and we can obtain:

$$\mathrm{pH}_x = \mathrm{pH_s} + \frac{E_x - E_\mathrm{s}}{0.059\,2\mathrm{V}}$$

Where $\mathrm{pH_s}$ and pH_x are the pH values of standard buffer solution and sample solution respectively; E_s and E_x are the electromotive forces of standard buffer solution and sample solution with the glass electrode and SCE respectively, V.

Calculate the pH_x of the solution to be tested by comparison with the $\mathrm{pH_s}$ of the standard buffer solution, given the measured values of E_x and E_s, as well as $\mathrm{pH_s}$ of the standard buffer solution are known. Therefore, the error caused by the uncertainty of K'' can be eliminated.

When calibrating, in order to reduce the deviation caused by the residual liquid junction potential, we choose the standard buffer solution with the pH value similar to the target solution. To accurately determine the pH value of the solution to be tested, two different pH buffer solutions should be used for calibration. After positioning the buffer solution with a pH value of one, the pH of the other standard buffer solution with a difference of about 3 pH units should be determined within $\pm 0.1\mathrm{pH}$.

With the continuous development of electrochemical instruments, commonly used to determine the pH of the glass electrode has been widely be replaced by a typical pH combination electrode, incorporating both glass and reference electrodes (silver-silver chloride electrode) in one body. Thereafter, the operation is very simple and convenient, but the measurement principle is the same.

Instruments and Chemical Reagents

1. Instruments

Shanghai Leici PHS-25 pH meter; beaker (50 mL).

2. Chemical reagents

Potassium hydrogen phthalate standard buffer solution ($0.05\ \mathrm{mol \cdot L^{-1}}$); mixed phosphate standard buffer solution ($0.025\ \mathrm{mol \cdot L^{-1}}$); glucose solution for injection; physiological saline.

Procedure

(1) Install the pH meter according to the instructions.

(2) pH meter calibration: calibration with a standard buffer solution.

(3) Measurements: The pH values of glucose solution for injection and physiological saline are measured three times with a calibrated pH meter, respectively.

$$pH_x = \frac{E_x - K}{0.059\ 2V}$$

两式相减，得

$$pH_x = pH_s + \frac{E_x - E_s}{0.059\ 2V}$$

式中，pH_s，pH_x 分别为标准缓冲溶液和待测溶液的 pH；E_s 和 E_x 分别为标准缓冲溶液和待测溶液中的电池电动势，V。

按“两次测量”法计算待测溶液的 pH_x，已知 E_x 和 E_s 的测量值和标准缓冲溶液的 pH_s，无须知道 K'' 的数据。因此可以消除由于 K'' 的不确定性产生的误差。

在校正时，应选用与被测溶液的 pH 接近的标准缓冲溶液，以减少测定过程中由于残余液接电位而引起的误差。如要准确测定待测溶液的 pH，要用两种不同 pH 的缓冲溶液来进行校正，在用一种的 pH 的缓冲溶液定位后，测定相差约 3 个 pH 单位的另一种标准缓冲溶液的 pH 时，误差应在 ±0.1pH 之内。

随着电化学仪器的不断发展，现在常用的测定 pH 的玻璃电极已普遍制成复合 pH 电极，即玻璃电极作为指示电极，银－氯化银电极作为参比电极，二者整合为一，操作起来十分简单方便，但测量原理是相同的。

三、仪器和试剂

1. 仪器

上海雷磁 PHS–25 型 pH 计；烧杯（50 mL）。

2. 试剂

邻苯二甲酸氢钾标准缓冲溶液（$0.05\ mol \cdot L^{-1}$）；混合磷酸盐标准缓冲溶液（$0.025\ mol \cdot L^{-1}$）；注射用葡萄糖溶液；生理盐水。

四、实验步骤

（1）按照说明书对 pH 计进行安装。

（2）校正 pH 计：用标准缓冲溶液按 pH 计的使用方法定位。

（3）测定：用校正过的 pH 计测定注射用葡萄糖溶液和生理盐水的 pH，各测定 3 次。

（4）测定完毕，洗净擦干电极，放入电极帽中，最后关闭仪器电源。

五、数据处理

将多次测得的 pH 取平均值，得液体制剂的准确 pH。

4. After measuring, clean and dry the electrode, put it in the electrode cap, and turn off the power of the instrument.

Data Analysis

The accurate pH values of liquid preparations can be obtained by averaging the pH values measured several times.

Experiment Guidance

1. Preview instruction

(1) Understand the principle of measuring pH value of solution with glass electrode and the operation of double measurement methods.

(2) Be familiar with the use of conventional pH meter.

2. Notes

(1) The glass ball at the lower end of the glass electrode is very thin. Do not contact with hard objects. The plug and the jack of the electrode should be keep clear and dry, and pay attention to dust, moisture and corrosion prevention.

(2) When using glass electrode to determine the pH of alkaline solution, as quickly as possible, for pH > 9 solution, we should use high alkali glass electrode (such as type 231 glass electrode). The alkali difference should be corrected when using a sodium difference electrode. After the determination of colloid solution, protein and dye solution, the glass electrode should be carefully wiped gently with soft paper or cotton dipped in diethyl ether, then washed with alcohol, and finally washed with distilled water. If the electrode is stained with oil, it should be dipped in alcohol, then moved to CCl_4 or ether, then moved to alcohol, and finally soaked in distilled water.

(3) When calibrating the pH meter, the standard buffer solution ($\Delta pH \leqslant 3$) should be selected as close as possible to the pH value of the solution to be tested. The temperature difference between the two solutions should be less than 1℃. It is better to use a single alkaline salt or acid salt solution to calibrate the buffer solution of the instrument. The reagents used should be pure. Alkaline salts (such as borax) are easily weathered and absorb CO_2 from the air, and need to be recrystallized to be used. For a pH meter with a precision of 0.01, borax should be stored in a humidometer (70% humidity) made of saturated sodium chloride-sucrose solution. The buffer solution should be prepared with freshly boiled and cooled distilled water and be preserved with polyethylene plastic bottles, if the lid is not tight can be sealed with wax.

(4) For the determination of pH value of weak buffer solution (such as H_2O), the sample solution was calibrated with standard buffer solution of potassium hydrogen phthalate, and the sample solution was re-measured until the reading changed no more than 0.05pH value within 1min. Then calibrate the instrument with borax standard buffer solution, and then determine as above, the difference between the two readings does not exceed ± 0.1 pH. The average of the two readings is the pH of the solution.

(5) Three standard buffer solutions (25 ℃) with pH of 4.00, 6.86 and 9.18 were prepared as

六、实验指导

1. 预习要求

（1）理解玻璃电极测定溶液 pH 的原理及两次测量法的操作。

（2）熟悉常规 pH 计的使用。

2. 注意事项

（1）玻璃电极下端的玻璃球很薄，切忌与硬物接触，电极插头和电极插孔应保持清洁干燥，注意防尘、防潮和防腐蚀。

（2）用玻璃电极测定碱性溶液时，尽量快速测量。测定 pH>9 的溶液时，应使用高碱玻璃电极（如 231 型玻璃电极）。若使用有钠差的电极测定时，应校正钠差。在测定胶体溶液、蛋白质和染料溶液后，玻璃电极宜用软纸或棉花沾乙醚小心地轻轻擦拭，然后用酒精清洗，最后用蒸馏水洗净。如果电极上沾有油污，应先浸入酒精中，然后移到 CCl_4 或乙醚中，再移至酒精中，最后用蒸馏水浸泡。

（3）校准仪器时，应尽量选择与待测液 pH 接近的标准缓冲溶液（$\Delta pH \leqslant 3$）。两溶液温度差要小于 1 ℃。校准仪器的缓冲溶液，采用单一的碱性盐或酸性盐所配的溶液较好。所用试剂纯度要高，碱性盐（如硼砂）易风化和吸收空气中的 CO_2，需重结晶才能使用。对于精密度为 0.01 的 pH 计，硼砂应在恒湿器（湿度 70%，饱和氯化钠 – 蔗糖溶液）中保存。配制缓冲溶液时，宜用新煮沸且冷却的蒸馏水配制。保存时宜用聚乙烯塑料瓶，盖子若不严密可用蜡封口。

（4）对于弱缓冲溶液（如 H_2O）的 pH 测定，选用邻苯二甲酸氢钾标准缓冲溶液校准后，测定样品溶液 pH，并重取样品液再测，直至读数在 1 min 内的改变不超过 0.05pH 为止。然后再用硼砂标准缓冲溶液校正仪器，再如上进行测定，两次读数之差不超过 ±0.1pH。取两次读数的平均值即是该溶液的 pH。

（5）pH 分别为 4.00、6.86 和 9.18 的三种标准缓冲溶液（25 ℃），配制方法如下：

① 邻苯二甲酸氢钾溶液（$0.05\ mol \cdot L^{-1}$，pH=4.00）：邻苯二甲酸氢钾在（115 ± 5）℃下烘干 2~3 h，称取 10.21 g，溶于蒸馏水，在容量瓶中稀释定容至 1 000 mL。

② 磷酸二氢钾和磷酸氢二钠混合溶液（$0.025\ mol \cdot L^{-1}$，pH=6.86）：磷酸二氢钾和磷酸氢二钠分别在（115 ± 5）℃下烘干 2~3 h，分别称取磷酸二氢钾 3.40 g 和磷酸氢二钠 3.55 g，溶于蒸馏水，在容量瓶中稀释定容至 1 000 mL。

③ 硼砂溶液（$0.01\ mol \cdot L^{-1}$，pH=9.18）：称取 $Na_2B_4O_7 \cdot 10H_2O$ 3.81 g（注意勿烘干），溶于蒸馏水，在容量瓶中稀释定容至 1 000 mL。

（6）pH 玻璃电极在使用前必须在溶液中浸泡，其原因如下：

① pH 玻璃电极的敏感膜只有在其表面形成很薄的水合凝胶层时，才能正常对氢离子作出响应，电位与 pH 的关系才能遵循能斯特方程。

② pH 玻璃电极在水中浸泡后，其不对称电位会下降并趋于稳定，同时内阻降低。

③ 对于复合 pH 电极而言，应在饱和 KCl 溶液中浸泡，可使液接界保持润湿和畅通，液接界电位保持稳定。

活化：pH 玻璃电极一般可采用蒸馏水（或去离子水）、pH 为 4.00 的缓冲液或 $0.01\ mol \cdot L^{-1}$ 盐

follows:

① Potassium hydrogen phthalate solution(0.05 mol·L^{-1}, pH = 4.00) : Potassium hydrogen phthalate was dried at (115 ± 5) ℃ for 2–3 hours, weighed 10.21g, dissolved in distilled water, and diluted to 1 000 mL in volumetric flask;

② Mixed solution of potassium dihydrogen phosphate and disodium hydrogen phosphate(0.025 mol·L^{-1}, pH = 6.86) : Potassium dihydrogen phosphate and disodium hydrogen phosphate were dried at (115 ± 5) ℃ for 2–3 hours respectively. 3.40g of potassium dihydrogen phosphate and 3.55 g of disodium hydrogen phosphate were respectively weighed and dissolved in distilled water, then diluted to 1 000 mL in volumetric flask.

③ Borax solution(0.01 mol·L^{-1}, pH = 9.18) : weigh $Na_2B_4O_7 \cdot 10H_2O$ 3.81g (do not dry), dissolve in distilled water, dilute to 1 000 mL in volumetric flask.

(6) The pH glass electrode must be immersed in solution before use for the following reasons:

① The sensitive film of the pH glass electrode can respond to hydrogen ions normally only when a very thin hydrated gel layer is formed on its surface. The relationship between the response potential and pH value follow the Nernst equation.

② After the pH glass electrode is immersed in the aqueous solution, its asymmetric potential will decrease and tend to be stable, and its internal resistance will decrease.

③ For the pH combination electrode, immersion in the saturated potassium chloride solution can keep the liquid interface moist and smooth, and the liquid injunction potential stable.

Activation: The pH glass electrode can be soaked in distilled water (or deionized water), buffer solution with pH value of 4.00 or hydrochloric acid solution of 0.01 mol·L^{-1}. The soaking time depends on the thickness of the sensitive film, the shape of the sensitive film and the aging degree of the electrode. Thick sensitive film, pH electrode use time is longer, its immersion time is also longer, generally 8–24 h. The cone type pH electrode has longer soaking time because of its structural characteristics. Generally speaking, the solution temperature is higher than the low temperature immersion effect, but by all means do not soak in alkaline solution.

After long-term use of the pH combination electrode, if the slope is found to be slightly reduced, the lower end of the electrode can be soaked in 4% HF solution for 3–5 s, washed with distilled water, and then soaked in 0.1 mol·L^{-1} HCl solution to activate it.

3. Discussion

(1) What factors affect the pH of the standard buffer solution? How to keep the pH constant?

(2) Why should the pH meter be calibrated by the standard buffer solution which pH is close to the pH value of the solution to be measured?

(3) Usually, a kind of buffer solution means a mixture of the conjugated acid and alkali, then why potassium hydrogen phthalate and sodium borate also can be regarded as buffer solutions?

酸浸泡。浸泡时间根据敏感膜的厚薄、形状及电极老化程度而定。敏感膜较厚，pH 电极使用时间较长，其浸泡时间也较长，一般为 8~24 h。锥形 pH 电极由于其结构特点，浸泡时间更长。一般来说，溶液温度高比温度低浸泡效果好，但切忌浸泡在碱性溶液中。

复合 pH 电极经长期使用后如发现斜率略有降低，则可把电极下端浸泡在 4%HF 溶液中 3~5 s，用蒸馏水洗净，然后在 0.1 $mol \cdot L^{-1}$ HCl 溶液中浸泡，使之复新。

3. 讨论

（1）标准缓冲溶液的 pH 受哪些因素影响？如何保证其 pH 不变？

（2）为什么校正 pH 计要用与待测溶液 pH 相近的标准缓冲溶液？

（3）缓冲溶液常为共轭酸碱的混合物。邻苯二甲酸氢钾、硼砂为什么也可看作一种缓冲溶液？

Experiment 2.2 Potentiometric Titration Analysis of Phosphoric Acid and Determination of Dissociation Constant

Purpose

(1) To master the principle and method of potentiometric titration of phosphoric acid.

(2) To learn to plot the potentiometric titration curve and calculate the ending-point with the curve or a second derivative method.

(3) To learn to measure of the ionization constants of phosphoric acid by potentiometric titration.

Principle

Potentiometric titration is a method to determine the end point of titration according to the sudden change of electromotive force in the process of titration. The potentiometric titration of phosphoric acid is performed by using sodium hydroxide standard solution as titrant to determine the concentration of phosphoric acid and the values of K_{a1} and K_{a2}.

1. Determination of pK_a

Phosphoric acid ionizes in aqueous solution as follows:

$$H_3PO_4 + H_2O = H_3O^+ + H_2PO_4^-$$
$$H_2PO_4^- + H_2O = H_3O^+ + HPO_4^{2-}$$
$$HPO_4^{2-} + H_2O = H_3O^+ + PO_4^{3-}$$

When the first hydrogen of phosphoric acid is half-titrated, namely at half of the first neutral point, $[H_2PO_4^-] = [H_3PO_4]$ and $[H_3O^+] = K_{a1}$ (pH=pK_{a1}). In the same manner, when the second hydrogen of phosphoric acid is half-titrated, $[HPO_4^{2-}] = [H_2PO_4^-]$ and $[H_3O^+] = K_{a2}$ (pH=pK_{a2}). The values of pK_{a1} and pK_{a2} can be obtained by the titration curve as Figure 2-1.

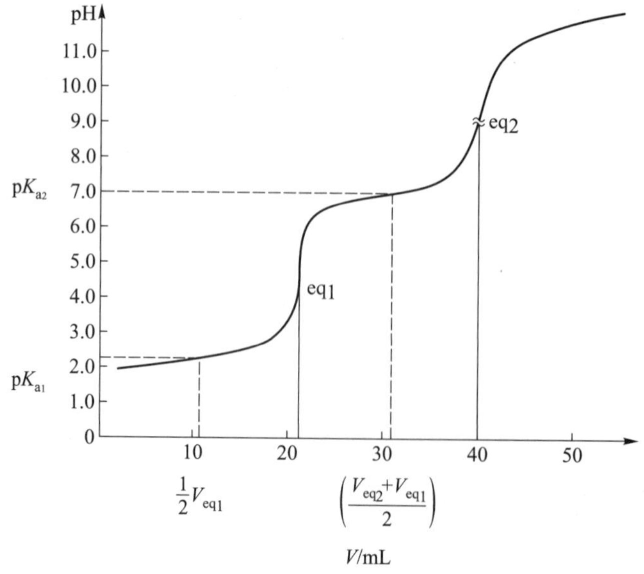

Figure 2-1 Potentiometric titration curve of standard NaOH solution (0.1 mol·L^{-1}) for H_3PO_4(0.1 mol·L^{-1})

实验 2.2　磷酸的电位滴定分析及其解离常数的测定

一、实验目的

（1）掌握磷酸电位滴定的原理和方法。

（2）学会绘制电位滴定曲线，并由滴定曲线或二级微商法确定滴定终点的方法。

（3）学会电位滴定法测定磷酸解离常数的方法。

二、实验原理

电位滴定法是根据滴定过程中电池电动势的突变来确定滴定终点的方法。磷酸的电位滴定是以氢氧化钠标准溶液为滴定剂，测定磷酸的浓度和 K_{a1}，K_{a2} 的值。

1. 解离常数测定

磷酸在水溶液中有如下解离：

$$H_3PO_4 + H_2O \longrightarrow H_3O^+ + H_2PO_4^-$$

$$H_2PO_4^- + H_2O \longrightarrow H_3O^+ + HPO_4^{2-}$$

$$HPO_4^{2-} + H_2O \longrightarrow H_3O^+ + PO_4^{3-}$$

当磷酸的第一个氢被滴定一半时，即第一个半中和点，$[H_2PO_4^-]=[H_3PO_4]$，$[H_3O^+]=K_{a1}$（$pH=pK_{a1}$）。同样，当磷酸的第二个氢被滴定一半时，即第二个半中和点，$[HPO_4^{2-}]=[H_2PO_4^-]$，$[H_3O^+]=K_{a2}$（$pH=pK_{a2}$）。磷酸的 pK_{a1}，pK_{a2} 可以从滴定曲线上得到。滴定曲线见图 2-1。

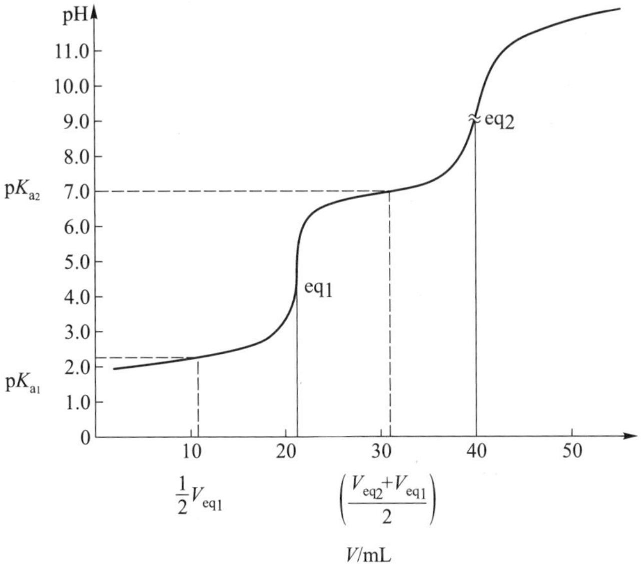

图 2-1　NaOH 标准溶液（0.1 mol·L^{-1}）滴定磷酸（0.1 mol·L^{-1}）电位滴定曲线

2. Determination of end point

Potentiometric titration is used to determine the end point of titration by plotting of pH or *E vs* the volume of titrant and determination the point with the maximum slope on the graph, that is, the end point of titration. When the slope of the titration curve is very steep near the end point, the maximum slope point is easy to determine accurately. However, when the slope of the curve is not steep, a derivative method may offer less error in locating the end point. Additionally, the end point can also be obtained by plotting the graph of $\Delta pH / \Delta V - \bar{V}$ which is the highest point of the graph. The end point can also be calculated when the value of $\Delta^2 pH/\Delta V^2$ is zero, which is accurate and often used.

3. Measurement of pH

When measuring pH, the pH meter must be calibrated with standard buffer solution. The calibrated pH meter can determine the pH value of the solution system while titrating during titration.

Instruments and Chemical Reagents

1. Instruments

A pH meter with a combination electrode made of a glass and a silver-silver chloride electrode; magnetic stirrer with a Teflon-coated stirring bar; burette (25 mL); beaker (100 mL); pipette (10 mL).

2. Chemical reagents

Standard NaOH solution (0.1 $mol \cdot L^{-1}$); phosphoric acid (0.1 $mol \cdot L^{-1}$); potassium hydrogen phthalate solution (0.05 $mol \cdot L^{-1}$, pH=4.00).

Procedure

(1) Calibrate the pH meter using a potassium hydrogen phthalate solution (0.05 $mol \cdot L^{-1}$, pH=4.00). Wash the electrode thoroughly, and blot with absorbent paper.

(2) Pipette a 10.00 mL portion of 0.1 $mol \cdot L^{-1}$ phosphoric acid into a 100 mL flask, and dilute with 20 mL distilled water. Place the combination electrode and a magnetic stirring bar into the beaker. Add 0.1 $mol \cdot L^{-1}$ NaOH standard solution from burette and record volume readings after each addition. In the beginning (<10.00 mL) add 2.00 mL at a time, but reduce the additions to 0.05 mL closing of stoichiometric points. It is preferable to add the same volume of NaOH standard solution each time for data processing. Continue titration until passing the second stoichiometric point with excess of about 5 mL. Repeat the titration to check the results obtained above.

Data Analysis

(1) Record the volumes of NaOH and pH values and calculate the V_{eq1} and V_{eq2} when the value of $\Delta^2 pH/\Delta V^2$ is 0 in the following table. And based on V_{eq1} and V_{eq2} , the half of the first and second neutral points are obtained.

2. 滴定终点确定

电位滴定法通过以 pH 或电位对滴定剂体积（V）作图，找到图上斜率最大点，即为滴定终点。当终点附近滴定曲线很陡时，斜率最大点很容易确定。曲线不陡时，使用偏微分的方法可使终点确定的误差减小一些。也可以用 $\Delta pH/\Delta V-\bar{V}$ 曲线，即曲线的最高点对应的体积为滴定终点体积。以上两种均为作图法。最常用的、最准确的是用二级微商内插法计算求得滴定终点体积，即 $\Delta^2 pH/\Delta V^2-V$ 曲线，当 $\Delta^2 pH/\Delta V^2=0$ 时对应的体积即为滴定终点体积。

3. pH 的测定

测定 pH 时，pH 计须先用标准缓冲溶液校正。校正后的 pH 计即可在滴定过程中测定溶液体系的 pH。

三、仪器和试剂

1. 仪器

pH 计；复合 pH 电极（含玻璃电极和银 – 氯化银电极）；电磁搅拌器；Teflon 搅拌子；烧杯（100 mL）；滴定管（25 mL）；移液管（10 mL）。

2. 试剂

氢氧化钠标准溶液（0.1 mol·L^{-1}）；磷酸（约 0.1 mol·L^{-1}）；邻苯二甲酸氢钾溶液（0.05 mol·L^{-1}，pH=4.00）。

四、实验步骤

（1）用邻苯二甲酸氢钾标准缓冲溶液（0.05 mol·L^{-1}，pH=4.00）校正 pH 计。将电极彻底冲洗干净，用吸水纸吸干待用。

（2）用移液管精密吸取 10.00 mL 磷酸样品溶液，置于 100 mL 烧杯中，加蒸馏水 20 mL，插入复合 pH 电极。用氢氧化钠标准溶液（0.1 mol·L^{-1}）滴定，边滴定边用电磁搅拌器搅拌。滴定剂体积未达 10.00 mL 前，每加 2.00 mL 标准溶液，记录 pH。在接近化学计量点时，每次加入标准溶液逐渐减少。以每次加入 1 滴（0.05 mL）测量并记录一次 pH。每次滴加的氢氧化钠标准溶液最好体积相等，以便于数据处理。继续滴定，至第二个计量点后 5 mL 左右。重复滴定一次检验。

五、数据处理

（1）按下表记录氢氧化钠标准溶液体积及相应的 pH，并按 $\Delta^2 pH/\Delta V^2-V$ 曲线法（二级微商法）求出第一、第二滴定终点体积，由此求得第一、第二半中和点体积。

V_{NaOH}/mL	pH	ΔpH	ΔV	ΔpH/ΔV	$\bar{V}$	Δ(ΔpH/ΔV)	ΔV	Δ^2pH/ΔV^2

(2) Plot pH–V and determine pK_{a1} and pK_{a2} from the titration curve (see Figure 2-1).

(3) Calculate the concentration of H_3PO_4 as follow.

$$c_{H_3PO_4} = \frac{c_{NaOH} \times V_{eq1}}{10.00\ \text{mL}}$$

Where V_{eq1} is the volume of NaOH standard solution consumed at the first stoichiometric point, mL; $c_{H_3PO_4}$ is the concentration of H_3PO_4, mol·L^{-1}; c_{NaOH} is the concentration of NaOH, mol·L^{-1}.

Experiment Guidance

1. Preview instruction

(1) Review the determination principle and method of dissociation constant of acid and base.

(2) Understand the drawing of potentiometric titration curve and the method to judge the end point.

(3) Review the basic operation of pipette and burette.

2. Notes

(1) After each addition of NaOH standard solution, record the data till the reading of pH is stable.

(2) The distribution of measuring points in potentiometric titration should be controlled closer before and after stoichiometric points and sparser farther away from stoichiometric points. Add exactly 0.05 mL of NaOH standard solution near the measuring point, with the help of a thin glass rod.

(3) Choose a proper speed of stirring to avoid the splash of titrate.

(4) The pH value of the standard buffer should be close to the measured value.

(5) The new pH combination electrodes must be immersed in a buffer solution for 3 h and then stored in water. Keep electrodes in the saturated KCl solution at all times when not in use. If it is observed that the electrode response is not linearly related to pH, treate the electrade briefly with dilute HF.

3. Discussion

(1) Phosphoric acid is a ternary acid. Can the K_{a3} of phosphoric acid be obtained from the titration curve?

V_{NaOH}/mL	pH	ΔpH	ΔV	ΔpH/ΔV	$\bar{V}$	Δ(ΔpH/ΔV)	ΔV	Δ^2pH/ΔV^2

（2）绘制pH–V曲线，第一、第二半中和点体积所对应的pH，即分别为磷酸pK_{a1}，pK_{a2}的值（参见图2–1）。

（3）计算磷酸的浓度。

$$c_{H_3PO_4}=\frac{c_{NaOH}\times V_{eq1}}{10.00\ mL}$$

式中，V_{eq1}为第一计量点所消耗的氢氧化钠标准溶液体积，mL；$c_{H_3PO_4}$为磷酸的浓度，mol·L^{-1}；c_{NaOH}为氢氧化钠的浓度，mol·L^{-1}。

六、实验指导

1. 预习要求

（1）复习酸碱解离常数的测定原理及方法。

（2）理解电位滴定曲线的绘制及判断终点的方法。

（3）回顾移液管及滴定管的基本操作。

2. 注意事项

（1）每次加入氢氧化钠标准溶液后，等到读数稳定再记录pH。

（2）电位滴定中的测量点分布，应控制在计量点前后密些，远离计量点疏些。在计量点附近，准确加入0.05 mL的氢氧化钠标准溶液，并使用细玻璃棒搅拌。

（3）选择合适搅拌速率，以防溶液溅出。

（4）标准缓冲液的pH应与被测值接近。

（5）新的复合pH电极须将其浸入缓冲液3 h，然后储存于水中。长期不使用时，要使电极始终保存于饱和KCl溶液中。如果观察到电极响应与pH不呈线性关系，将其用稀HF溶液快速处理一下。

3. 讨论

（1）磷酸是三元酸，其K_{a3}可以从滴定曲线上求得吗？

(2) In all types of potentiometric titration, can E value be used to replace of pH?

(3) If potentiometric titration is used for other titrations, such as redox titration, precipitation titration and complexometric titration, what kinds of indicator electrodes and reference electrodes should be selected?

（2）在各类电位滴定中，是否均可用 E 的变化代替 pH 的变化？

（3）若以电位滴定法进行其他滴定，如氧化还原滴定、沉淀滴定和络合滴定，应各选择什么指示电极和参比电极？

Experiment 2.3 Determination of Procaine Hydrochlorid by Dead–Stop Titration

Purpose

(1) To master the principle and procedure of dead-stop titration.

(2) To study the operating conditions and key points of the assay of procaine hydrochoride.

Principle

Procaine hydrochloride, 2-diethylaminoethy 4-aminobenzoate hydrochloride, ($C_{13}H_{20}N_2O_2 \cdot HCl$, FW =272.77) is widely used in clinical anesthesia. It possesses good local anesthesia, low toxicity and no addiction. It is classified as the para-aminobenzoic esters anesthesia drugs. There is an aromatic primary amine in the molecular structure, which could react with sodium nitrite in acidic solution. In Chinese Pharmacopoeia (2020th edition), procaine hydrochloride and procaine hydrochloride for injection are determined by nitrite titration.

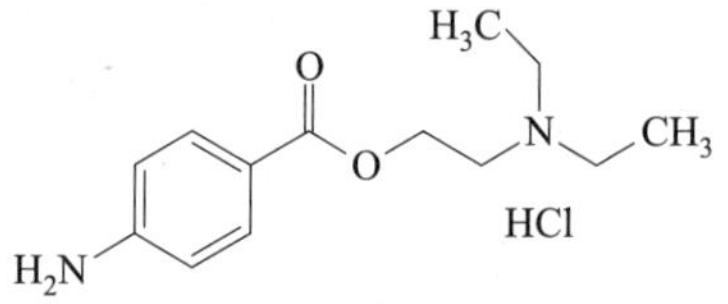

Procaine hydrochloride

Nitrite titration (diazotization) is used in the analysis of aromatic compounds containing an amino group in the molecules structure, which belongs to volumetric analysis method. Sodium nitrite is generally used in direct method of diazotization, and it gives nitric acid in acidic solution. This is based on the reaction between aromatic primary amine and sodium nitrite, in presence of excessive mineral or inorganic acids. Accordingly, many aromatic primary amines with free amino group can be analyzed quantitatively by measuring the volume of sodium nitrite standard solution required to convert them into diazonium salts, in which the end point is confirmed by dead-stop titration. The typical reaction of diazotization reaction in presence of HCl is given as follows.

$$\mathrm{Ar{-}NHCOR{+}H_2O \xrightarrow{H^+} Ar{-}NH_2{+}RCOOH}$$

$$\mathrm{Ar{-}NH_2{+}NaNO_2{+}2HCl \longrightarrow Ar{-}N_2^+Cl^- + NaCl{+}2H_2O}$$

Dead-stop titration belongs to amperometric titration which can be used for the confirmation of end point of nitrite titrations. In the dead-stop titration, a low voltage of about 50 mV is applied across two same platinum electrodes. Before the end point, there is no current or only a very weak background current since there is no reversible electric pair in the solution. When the end point is reached and there is a little excess titrant, there is HNO_2/NO reversible electric pair in the solution and the current is generated. The galvanometer pointer shows that the deflection does not return to zero, indicating that the end point has been reached.

实验 2.3　永停滴定法测定盐酸普鲁卡因的含量

一、实验目的

（1）掌握永停滴定法的方法与原理。

（2）熟悉测定盐酸普鲁卡因的操作条件及要点。

二、实验原理

盐酸普鲁卡因，即 4-氨基苯甲酸-2-（二乙氨基）乙酯盐酸盐（$C_{13}H_{20}N_2O_2 \cdot HCl$，相对分子质量 272.77），是临床广泛使用的局部麻醉药，具有良好的局部麻醉作用，毒性低，无成瘾性。该药物属于对氨基苯甲酸酯类局麻药物，分子结构中的芳伯氨基在酸性溶液中可与亚硝酸钠反应。《中国药典》2020 年版规定，采用亚硝酸钠滴定法测定盐酸普鲁卡因及其注射用无菌粉末的含量。

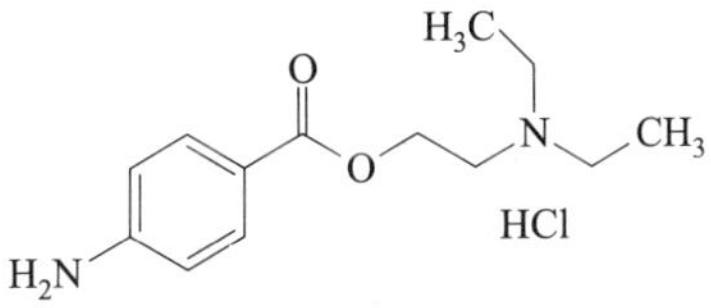

盐酸普鲁卡因

以亚硝酸钠溶液为滴定液的容量分析法称为重氮化法，又称亚硝酸钠法。亚硝酸钠是重氮化反应最常用试剂，它在酸性环境中能够释放亚硝酸根。芳伯氨基或水解后生成芳伯氨基的药物在酸性溶液中能定量与亚硝酸钠产生重氮化反应，生成重氮盐。依此，用已知浓度的亚硝酸钠滴定液采用永停滴定法指示终点，根据消耗的亚硝酸钠滴定剂的浓度和体积，可计算出芳伯胺类药物的含量。反应式如下：

$$Ar—NHCOR+H_2O \xrightarrow{H^+} Ar—NH_2+RCOOH$$

$$Ar—NH_2+NaNO_2+2HCl \longrightarrow Ar—N_2^+Cl^- + NaCl+2H_2O$$

永停滴定法属于电流滴定法，可用于重氮化法反应的终点指示。采用两支相同的铂电极，在电极间外加一小电压（约为 50 mV）时，反应达到终点前溶液中不存在可逆电对，电流指针停留在零位（或接近零位）不动。当达到终点并稍有过量的滴定液时，溶液中有 HNO_2/NO 可逆电对，电路中有电流产生，电流计指针显示偏转并不回至零位，指示终点到达。

三、仪器和试剂

1. 仪器

永停滴定仪；酸度计；分析天平；滴定管（25 mL，10 mL）；量筒（100 mL）；烧杯（100 mL）。

2. 试剂

盐酸普鲁卡因（原料药）；溴化钾（分析纯）；亚硝酸钠（分析纯）；对氨基苯磺酸（基准物）；无水碳酸钠（分析纯）；浓氨试液；盐酸（1→2）；淀粉-KI 试纸（淀粉水溶液中加入等量的 5% KI 溶液）；

Instruments and Chemical Reagents

1. Instruments

Dead-stop titration apparatus; pH meter; analytic balance; burette (25 mL, 10 mL), graduated cylinder (100 mL), beaker (100 mL).

2. Chemical reagents

Procaine hydrochloride (raw material), potassium bromide (A.R.), sodium nitrite (A.R.) ; 4-aminobenzene sulfonic acid (primary standard substance); concentrated ammonia solution (TS); hydrochloric acid (1→2); starch potassium iodine indicator paper (the starch solution containing equivalent volume of 5% KI solution in water); distilled water.

Procedure

1. Sodium nitrite (0.1 mol·L^{-1}) VS (volumetric solution)

Preparation: weigh about 6.9 g of $NaNO_2$, then add 0.1 g of non-aqueous sodium carbonate, dissolve in water and dilute to 1 000 mL, shake well.

Standardization: Weigh accurately about 0.5 g of 4-aminobenzene sulfonic acid, previously dried to constant weight at 120 ℃, and dissolve it in 30 mL water and 3 mL concentrated ammonia TS. Add 20 mL hydrochloric acid solution (1→2) with stirring, plunge the burette into the solution so that about 2/3 of the tip is under the liquid surface, titrate with sodium nitrite VS quickly with stirring at a temperature below 30 ℃. Withdraw the burette tip towards the end point of titration, rinse it with water and add the washings to the solution, continue the titration slowly, and adopt the dead-stop titration method for end point determination. When the galvanometer pointer has a large deflection and does not turn again for 1 min, it is the end point. Each 1 mL of sodium nitrite (0.1 mol·L^{-1})VS is equivalent to 17.32 mg of 4-aminobenzene sulfonic acid.

2. Determination of procaine hydrochloride

Weigh accurately about 0.6 g procaine hydrochloride in a beaker on a magnetic stirrer, add distilled water 40 mL and HCl (1→2) 15 mL, unless otherwise specified, stir to dissolve it at the temperature of 15–25 ℃. Then add 2g KBr and dip the platinum electrodes into the solution. Plunge the burette into solution and make it that about 2/3 of the tip under the liquid surface, and titrate with sodium nitrite standard solution (0.1 mol·L^{-1}) quickly with stirring. Withdraw the burette tip when the end point is nearly reached, rinse it with water and add the washings to solution, and continue the titration slowly until the end point is reached (the galvanometer pointer is permanently deflected and does not turn again for 1 min). When the end point is nearly reached, take a little solution from the beaker with a glass rod to the starch-KI indicator paper. When the paper turns blue, record the volume of sodium nitrite VS consumed. Compare the two methods to determine the end point.

Data Analysis

The content of procaine hydrochloride can be calculated according to the following formula:

蒸馏水。

四、实验步骤

1. 亚硝酸钠滴定液（0.1 mol·L^{-1}）

配制：称取亚硝酸钠 6.9 g，加无水碳酸钠 0.1 g，加适量水溶解，定容至 1 000 mL，摇匀。

标定：取在 120 ℃干燥至恒重的基准物对氨基苯磺酸约 0.5 g，精密称定，加水 30 mL 与浓氨试液 3 mL，溶解后加盐酸（1→2）20 mL，搅拌，在 30 ℃以下用亚硝酸钠滴定液迅速滴定，滴定时将滴定管尖端插入液面下约 2/3 处，边滴边搅拌，至近终点时，将滴定管尖端提出液面，用少量水洗涤尖端，洗液并入溶液中，继续缓慢滴定，用永停滴定法指示终点。当检流计指针发生较大偏转，持续 1 min 不复转时，即为终点。每毫升亚硝酸钠滴定液（0.1 mol·L^{-1}）相当于 17.32 mg 对氨基苯磺酸。根据滴定液的消耗量与对氨基苯磺酸的取用量算出本溶液的浓度，即得。

2. 盐酸普鲁卡因的含量测定

取本品约 0.6 g，精密称定，置于烧杯中，在 15~25 ℃，除另有规定外，加水 40 mL 与盐酸（1→2）15 mL，而后置于电磁搅拌器上，搅拌使之溶解，再加溴化钾 2 g，插入双铂电极后将滴定管的尖端插入液面下约 2/3 处，用亚硝酸钠滴定液（0.1 mol·L^{-1}）迅速滴定，边滴边搅拌，临近终点，将滴定管的尖端提出液面，用少量水淋洗尖端，洗液并入溶液中，继续缓慢滴定，至电流计指针突然偏转，并不再恢复，即为滴定终点。每毫升亚硝酸钠滴定液（0.1 mol·L^{-1}）相当于 27.28 mg $C_{13}H_{20}N_2O_2 \cdot HCl$。在终点附近，同时用细玻璃棒蘸取溶液少许，点在淀粉 -KI 试纸上，观察是否变色。比较两种方法确定终点的情况。

五、数据处理

盐酸普鲁卡因的百分含量按下式计算：

$$w_{C_{13}H_{20}N_2O_2 \cdot HCl}(\%)=\frac{c_{NaNO_2} \cdot V_{NaNO_2} \times \dfrac{M_{C_{13}H_{20}N_2O_2 \cdot HCl}}{1\,000}}{m_{样品}} \times 100\%$$

式中，c_{NaNO_2}为亚硝酸钠的浓度，mol·L^{-1}；V_{NaNO_2}为亚硝酸钠标准溶液体积，mL；$m_{样品}$为样品的质量，g；$M_{C_{13}H_{20}N_2O_2 \cdot HCl}$为盐酸普鲁卡因的摩尔质量，g·mol^{-1}。

取平行操作 3 次的数据，分别计算百分含量，求百分含量平均值及相对平均偏差。

六、实验指导

1. 预习要求

（1）复习重氮化反应的基础知识。

（2）掌握永停滴定法的原理及判断终点的方法。

（3）复习亚硝酸钠滴定液的标定方法。

2. 注意事项

（1）加入适量溴化钾，加快反应速率。

（2）酸度一般在 1~2 mol·L^{-1} 为宜。

$$w_{C_{13}H_{20}N_2O_2\cdot HCl}(\%)=\frac{c_{NaNO_2}\cdot V_{NaNO_2}\times\frac{M_{C_{13}H_{20}N_2O_2\cdot HCl}}{1\,000}}{m_{sample}}\times 100\%$$

Where c_{NaNO_2} is the concentration of sodium nitrite VS, mol·L^{-1}; V_{NaNO_2} is the volume of sodium nitrite VS, mL; m_{sample} is the weight of sample, g; $M_{C_{13}H_{20}N_2O_2\cdot HCl}$ is the molar mass of procaine hydrochlorid, g·mol^{-1}.

Calculate the content of sample by averaging three portions of parallel data and give the *RAD*.

Experiment Guidance

1. Preview instruction

(1) Review the basic knowledge of diazotization.

(2) Grasp the principle of dead-stop titration and the method to judge the end point.

(3) Review the standardization method for sodium nitrite VS.

2. Notes

(1) Adding suitable amount of KI to speed up the reaction.

(2) Acidity: 1–2 mol·L^{-1}.

(3) Reaction temperature: The reaction may be performed at room temperature (10–30 ℃). Results obtained below 15 ℃ are relative accurate, because the diazotization reaction should be carried out at the temperature of 0–15 ℃ to prevent the decomposition of nitrite.

(4) When all aromatic amine has reacted with $NaNO_2$ then next portion (slightly excessive) of $NaNO_2$ VS is added to the solution, converted to HNO_2 that remain in the solution and can be detected by the starch-KI indicator paper as an external indicator. The reaction is as follows.

$$KI+HCl \longrightarrow HI+KCl$$

$$2HI+2HNO_2 \longrightarrow I_2+2NO+2H_2O$$

$$\text{Excessive of } I_2+\text{Starch}\longrightarrow\text{End point (blue)}$$

(5) The surface of the platinum electrode should be thoroughly cleaned before use. It can be polished with polishing powder, cleaned with ultrasonic wave or soaked with diluted nitric acid and then rinsed with deionized water.

3. Discussion

(1) What is the purpose of adding potassium bromide when determining the content of the sample?

(2) What type of compounds may be assayed with the dead-stop titration by sodium nitrite?

(3) What are the conditions for diazotization?

（3）反应温度：室温（10~30 ℃）下进行，其中 15 ℃以下结果较准确，因为重氮化反应宜在 0~15 ℃温度下进行，常温下实验，须防止亚硝酸的分解。

（4）反应到终点时加入稍过量的亚硝酸钠滴定液，即可产生亚硝酸，使得外指示剂淀粉-KI 试纸变色。指示终点反应如下：

$$KI+HCl \longrightarrow HI+KCl$$

$$2HI+2HNO_2 \longrightarrow I_2+2NO+2H_2O$$

$$\text{过量(碘)} + \text{淀粉} \longrightarrow \text{蓝色(指示终点)}$$

（5）金属指示电极在使用前应对其表面做彻底清洗，抛光粉抛光、超声波清洗或用稀硝酸浸泡后再用去离子水冲洗即可使用。

3. 讨论

（1）测定样品含量时，加溴化钾的目的是什么？

（2）具有何种结构的药物可以用亚硝酸钠法进行测定？

（3）重氮化反应的条件是什么？

Experiment 2.4 Determination of Caffeine by Potentiometric Titration

Purpose

(1) To master the principle and method of non-aqueous titration of very weak base.

(2) To master the method of potentiometric titration to determine the end point.

Principle

Caffeine ($C_8H_{10}N_4O_2$, as shown in the figure below) has a very weak alkalinity (K_b =4.0×10^{-14}), which is still slightly alkaline even in glacial acetic acid, so it can't be titrated directly with the standard solution of perchloric acid. By adding appropriate amount of acetic anhydride into glacial acetic acid, the cationic acid of acetic anhydride acetyl produced with the dissociation of acetic anhydride is greater than the cationic acid of acetic acid and proton acid, which enhances the alkalinity of caffeine and increases the range of titration jump, and can be titrated with the standard solution of perchloric acid.

$$2(CH_3CO)_2O \rightleftharpoons (CH_3CO)_3O^+ + CH_3COO^-$$

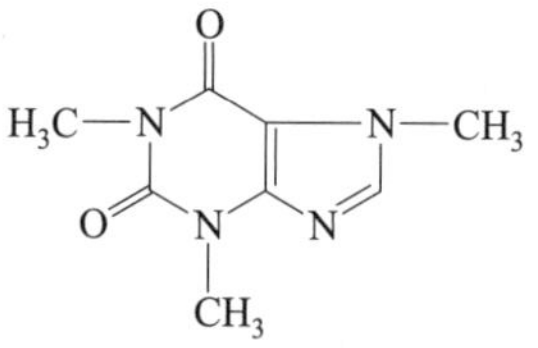

Caffeine

Non-aqueous titration is a method of titration analysis performed in a non-aqueous solvent. Non-aqueous titration can use indicator to determine the end point, but in the titration process, the color of the indicator will undergo a series of changes, the end point is not easy to determine, if the potential titration method to indicate the end point will be more accurate. Potentiometric titration method is a titration method in which the end point is determined by monitoring the potential change of indicator electrode of the analyte (or titrant) in the titration process to be measured with standard solution. It usually uses two electrodes, one as an indicator electrode, the other as a reference electrode, to form a galvanic cell. It can determine the end point by plotting method or second derivative method. Compared with the titration method using the indicator, the potentiometric titration method is objective and reliable, with high accuracy, and is not limited by the color and turbidity of the solution.

In this experiment, the mixed solution of acetic anhydride and glacial acetic acid is used as the solvent, and perchloric acid standard solution is used as the titrant, the content of caffeine is determined by potentiometric titration.

Instruments and Chemical Reagents

1. Instruments

Microburette (10 mL); burette (25 mL); conical flask (50 mL); graduated cylinder (25 mL, 100 mL);

实验 2.4　电位滴定法测定药用咖啡因的含量

一、实验目的

（1）掌握极弱碱非水滴定的原理和方法。

（2）掌握电位滴定法确定终点的方法。

二、实验原理

咖啡因（$C_8H_{10}N_4O_2$，结构式见下图）的碱性极弱（$K_b=4.0\times10^{-14}$），即使在冰醋酸中仍显较弱碱性，不能用高氯酸标准溶液直接滴定。而在冰醋酸中加入适量醋酸酐，利用醋酸酐解离产生的醋酐合乙酰阳离子酸性大于醋酸合质子酸性的特性，增强咖啡因的碱性，增大滴定突跃范围，可实现高氯酸标准溶液滴定。

$$2(CH_3CO)_2O \rightleftharpoons (CH_3CO)_3O^+ + CH_3COO^-$$

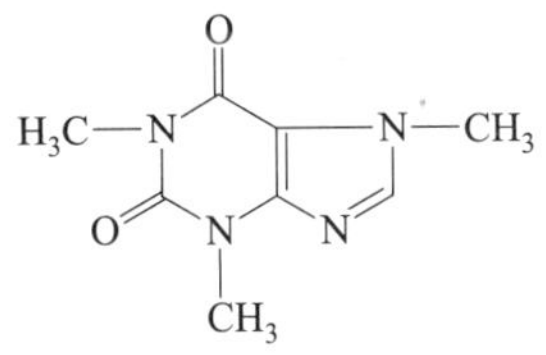

咖啡因

非水滴定即在非水溶剂中进行的滴定分析方法。非水滴定可以用指示剂确定终点，但是在滴定过程中，指示剂的颜色会发生一系列的变化，终点不易掌握，若以电位滴定法指示终点就会更加准确。

电位滴定法是在用标准溶液滴定待测溶液的滴定过程中，借助监测待测物（或滴定剂）指示电极的电位变化确定终点的滴定分析法。电位滴定法通常采用两根电极，一根为指示电极，另一根为参比电极，组成原电池。该方法可以通过作图法或二阶微商内插法确定终点。相比指示剂滴定法，电位滴定法客观可靠，准确度高，不受溶液颜色、浑浊程度的限制。

本实验以醋酐－冰醋酸混合溶液为溶剂，用高氯酸标准溶液为滴定剂，采用电位滴定法确定终点来测定药用咖啡因的含量。

三、仪器和试剂

1. 仪器

微量滴定管（10 mL）；滴定管（25 mL）；锥形瓶（50 mL）；量筒（25 mL，100 mL）；电炉；pHS-25 型酸度计；玻璃电极；217 型双盐桥甘汞电极；电磁搅拌器；铁芯搅拌棒。

2. 试剂

咖啡因（药用）；醋酸（分析纯）；醋酐（分析纯）：浓度为 97%，密度 1.08 mg·mL^{-1}；邻苯二甲酸氢钾（基准物）；高氯酸（分析纯）：质量百分浓度为 70%~72%，密度 1.75 mg·mL^{-1}；结晶紫指示剂

electric furnace; pHS-25 pH meter; glass electrode; 217 double salt bridge calomel electrode; electromagnetic stirrer; iron core stirrer.

2. Chemical reagents

Caffeine (medicinal); acetic acid (A.R.); acetic anhydride (A.R.): 97%, density 1.08 mg·mL^{-1}; potassium hydrogen phthalate (primary standard substance); perchloric acid (A.R.): 70%–72% (g/g), density 1.75 mg·mL^{-1}; crystal violet IS (indicating solution): dissolved in 0.5% glacial acetic acid.

Procedure

(1) Preparation and standardization of 0.1 mol·L^{-1} perchloric acid solution.

Preparation: Take 750 mL of glacial acetic acid, add 8.5 mL of perchloric acid (70%–72% g/g) and shake well. At room temperature, add 24 mL of acetic anhydride dropwise with shaking, cool and dilute with dehydrated glacial acetic acid to 1 000 mL, mix well and allow standing for 24 hours. If the sample is susceptible to acetylation, the water content of perchloric acid solution should be determined by the water determination. Then add water or acetic anhydride to make sure the water content between 0.01% and 0.2%.

Standardization: Weigh accurately about 0.16 g of potassium acid phthalate primary standard, previously dried to constant weight at 105–110 ℃, dissolve it in 10 mL of solvent of acetic anhydride-acetic acid (1:4). Add 1 drop of crystal violet IS and titrate slowly with perchloric acid (0.1 mol·L^{-1}) to a blue end point. Correct the results with blank test.

The following equation can be used for calculating the concentration of perchloric acid solution:

$$c_{HClO_4} = \frac{m_{KHC_8H_4O_4}}{V_{HClO_4}\dfrac{M_{KHC_8H_4O_4}}{1\,000}}$$

$$M_{KHC_8H_4O_4} = 204.2\ g\cdot mol^{-1}$$

Where c_{HClO_4} is the concentration of $HClO_4$ standard solution, mol·L^{-1}; V_{HClO_4} is the volume of $HClO_4$ standard solution after blank correction, mL; $m_{KHC_8H_4O_4}$ is the mass of the primary standard substance, g; $M_{KHC_8H_4O_4}$ is the molar mass of primary standard substance, g·mol^{-1}.

(2) Adjust the pH meter according to the instructions and use mV for the experiment. Connect calomel electrode with positive and glass electrode with negative.

(3) The sample was dried at 80℃ to a constant weight of about 0.15 g, accurately weighed, and 25 mL of the mixture of acetic anhydride and glacial acetic acid (5:1) was added. The mixture was dissolved by mild heat, and then cooled. The two electrodes were inserted into the solution and the electromagnetic stirrer was powered. Fill a 25 mL burette with perchloric acid standard solution and start the titration. Additional titrant may be added each time at the beginning of the titration and at the end of the titration, but near the end point, drop by drop. Record the volume and electrode potential (mV) consumed by one drop. The volume of consumed perchloric acid standard solution should be calibrated by blank test.

（0.5% 的冰醋酸溶液）。

四、实验步骤

（1）0.1 mol·L^{-1} $HClO_4$ 标准溶液的配制与标定。

配制：取无水冰醋酸 750 mL，加入高氯酸（70%~72%）8.5 mL，摇匀，在室温下缓缓加入醋酐 24 mL，边加边摇，加完后再振摇均匀，冷却。加适量的无水冰醋酸使溶液体积达到 1 000 mL，摇匀，放置 24 h。若所测样品易乙酰化，则须用水分滴定法测定本溶液的含水量，再用水和醋酐反复调节至本溶液的含水量为 0.01%~0.2%。

标定：取 105~110 ℃干燥至恒重的基准物邻苯二甲酸氢钾约 0.16 g，精密称定。加醋酐－冰醋酸（1∶4）混合溶剂 10 mL 使之溶解，加结晶紫指示液 1 滴，用高氯酸标准溶液（0.1 mol·L^{-1}）滴定至蓝色，即为终点。将滴定结果用空白试验校正。

$HClO_4$ 标准溶液的浓度按下式计算：

$$c_{HClO_4}=\frac{m_{KHC_8H_4O_4}}{V_{HClO_4}\dfrac{M_{KHC_8H_4O_4}}{1\,000}}$$

$$M_{KHC_8H_4O_4}=204.2\ g\cdot mol^{-1}$$

式中，c_{HClO_4} 为高氯酸溶液的浓度，mol·L^{-1}；V_{HClO_4} 为空白校正后高氯酸标准溶液体积，mL；$m_{KHC_8H_4O_4}$ 为基准物的质量，g；$M_{KHC_8H_4O_4}$ 为基准物的摩尔质量，g·mol^{-1}。

（2）按酸度计使用说明调好仪器，实验用 mV 挡。将甘汞电极接正极，玻璃电极接负极。

（3）取在 80 ℃干燥至恒重的样品约 0.15 g，精密称定，加醋酐－冰醋酸（5∶1）的混合液 25 mL，微热使其溶解，冷却，加入搅拌子，插入电极，开启电磁搅拌器，测定电极电位。

在 25 mL 滴定管内装入高氯酸的冰醋酸溶液，开始滴定。在滴定开始和滴定结束前滴定剂体积可适当大些，但在终点附近，要一滴一滴地加。滴加一次，记录一次滴剂消耗的体积及电极电位（mV）。同时应做空白试验。

五、数据处理

对滴定咖啡因消耗的高氯酸标准溶液和测得的电极电位值进行处理，作 $\Delta^2E/\Delta V^2-V$ 曲线，用二阶微商法计算确定终点，扣除空白体积，求出样品的含量。

咖啡因的百分含量按下式计算：

$$w_{C_8H_{10}N_4O_2}(\%)=\frac{c_{HClO_4}\cdot V_{HClO_4}\times\dfrac{M_{C_8H_{10}N_4O_2}}{1\,000}}{m_{样品}}\times 100\%$$

$$M_{C_8H_{10}N_4O_2}=194.19\ g\cdot mol^{-1}$$

Data Analysis

Plot the $\Delta^2 E / \Delta V^2 - V$ curve based on the original data, and the end point was determined by the second derivative method. The content of the sample was obtained by deducting the blank volume.

The content of caffeine is calculated as follows:

$$w_{C_8H_{10}N_4O_2}(\%) = \frac{c_{HClO_4} \cdot V_{HClO_4} \times \frac{M_{C_8H_{10}N_4O_2}}{1\,000}}{m_{sample}} \times 100\%$$

$$M_{C_8H_{10}N_4O_2} = 194.19\ g \cdot mol^{-1}$$

Where c_{HClO_4} is the concentration of $HClO_4$ standard solution, $mol \cdot L^{-1}$; V_{HClO_4} is the volume of $HClO_4$ standard solution after blank correction, mL; m_{sample} is the mass of the sample, g; $M_{C_8H_{10}N_4O_2}$ is the molar mass of sample, $g \cdot mol^{-1}$.

Experiment Guidance

1. Preview instruction

(1) Review the basic knowledge of non-aqueous titration and common standard solution standardization method.

(2) Master the principle of potentiometric titration and the method to determine the end point.

2. Notes

(1) Glassware should be cleaned and dried in advance.

(2) The caffeine sample is not easy to dissolve at room temperature, so it is slightly dissolved in water bath, and then titrated after cooling.

(3) Non-aqueous solvents are used in this experiment. Therefore, it is best to use the 217 type double-salt bridge calomel electrode as the reference electrode of the pH meter, and the outer tube is filled with anhydrous methanol solution of contacting KCl.

(4) The solvent should be recycled after the experiment.

(5) Double bridge type electrode, when in use, must remove the rubber plug and rubber cap, the second salt bridge is put into the appropriate inert electrode solution and then is installed.

3. Discussion

(1) Why can't caffeine in glacial acetic acid be titrated directly with $HClO_4$ standard solution?

(2) What principles should be used to select the appropriate solvent for non-aqueous titration of organic weak acids or bases of different strengths?

(3) What's the aim of blank test?

式中，c_{HClO_4}为高氯酸溶液的浓度，$mol \cdot L^{-1}$；V_{HClO_4}为空白校正后高氯酸标准溶液体积，mL；$m_{样品}$为样品的质量，g；$M_{C_8H_{10}N_4O_2}$为样品的摩尔质量，$g \cdot mol^{-1}$。

六、实验指导

1. 预习要求

（1）复习非水滴定的基础知识及常见的标准溶液的标定方法。

（2）掌握电位滴定法原理及确定终点的方法。

2. 注意事项

（1）使用的玻璃器皿需预先洗净、烘干。

（2）样品在常温下不易溶解，置水浴中微热溶解，放冷后再进行滴定。

（3）本实验使用非水溶剂，因此，酸度计的参比电极最好使用217型双盐桥甘汞电极，外套管内盛储KCl的无水甲醇溶液。

（4）实验结束后应回收溶剂。

（5）双桥式的电极，在使用的时候一定要拔去橡皮塞和橡皮帽，第二节盐桥装入适当的惰性电极溶液后再使用。

3. 讨论

（1）为什么咖啡因在冰醋酸中不能用$HClO_4$标准溶液直接进行滴定？

（2）不同强度的有机弱酸或弱碱，它们在非水滴定中应根据什么原则来选择适当的溶剂？

（3）为何要做空白试验？

Experiment 2.5 Determination of Fluoride Ion in Drinking Water by Fluoride Ion Selective Electrode

Purpose

(1) To master the method and data processing of fluoride ion determination with fluoride ion selective electrode.

(2) To understand the basic properties of fluoride ion selective electrode and its application method.

Principle

Fluorine content in drinking water has a certain influence on people's health. If the fluorine content is too low, the dental caries will be easily occurred, otherwise the fluorosis will happen. The suitable content is 0.5–1.0 mg·L^{-1}.

At present, the determination methods of fluorine are colorimetric method and direct potential method. The colorimetric method has a wide measurement range, but there are many interference factors, and the sample must be pretreated. Although the measurement range of direct potential method is not as wide as that of colorimetric method, it can meet the requirements of environmental monitoring. Moreover, it is simple to operate and has fewer interference factors. Generally, it is not necessary to pretreat the samples. Therefore, the potentiometric method gradually replace the colorimetric method to become the conventional method to measure the content of fluoride ion.

Fluorine ion selective electrode (Fluorine electrode) uses LaF_3 single wafer as sensitive membrane and has good selectivity to fluorine ion in solution. The galvanic cell composed of fluorine electrode, saturated calomel electrode (SCE) and the solution to be tested can be expressed as:

Ag | AgCl, NaCl, NaF | LaF_3 membrane | tested solution || KCl (saturated), Hg_2Cl_2 | Hg

Generally, the fluorine electrode on the pH/mV meter is connected to "–", and the SCE is connected to "+". The electromotive force of the galvanic cell is measured as:

$$E = \varphi_{\mathrm{SCE}} - \varphi_{\mathrm{F^-}}$$

Where E is electromotive force, V; φ_{SCE} and $\varphi_{\mathrm{F^-}}$ are the potential values of SCE and fluorine electrode respectively, V.

The following formula is obtained in the certain condition:

$$\varphi = K + 0.059\,2\mathrm{V}\lg \alpha_{\mathrm{F^-}} \quad (25\,℃)$$

Where K is the constant; 0. 059 2 is the theoretical response slope of electrode at 25℃; $\alpha_{\mathrm{F^-}}$ is F^- activity in the liquid to be tested, mol·L^{-1}.

Ion activity is measured with an ion-selective electrode, whereas ion concentration is usually required for quantitative analysis.

实验 2.5　氟离子选择性电极测定饮用水中氟离子含量

一、实验目的

（1）掌握用氟离子选择性电极测定氟离子的实验方法及数据处理。

（2）了解氟离子选择性电极的基本性能及其使用方法。

二、实验原理

饮用水中氟含量的高低对人的健康有一定的影响。氟含量太低，易得牙龋病，过高则会发生氟中毒，适宜含量为 0.5~1.0 $mg \cdot L^{-1}$。目前，测定氟的方法有比色法和直接电位法。比色法测量范围较宽，但干扰因素多，并且要对样品进行预处理；直接电位法，即用离子选择性电极进行测量，其测量范围虽不如比色法宽，但已能满足环境监测的要求，而且操作简便，干扰因素少，一般不必对样品进行预处理。因此，电位法逐渐取代比色法成为测量氟离子含量的常规方法。

氟离子选择性电极（简称氟电极）以 LaF_3 单晶片为敏感膜，对溶液中的氟离子具有良好的选择性。氟电极、饱和甘汞电极（SCE）和待测溶液组成的原电池可表示为

Ag | AgCl，NaCl，NaF | LaF_3 膜|试液 || KCl（饱和），Hg_2Cl_2 | Hg

一般 pH/mV 计上氟电极接“–”，饱和甘汞电极接“+”，测得原电池的电动势为

$$E = \varphi_{SCE} - \varphi_{F^-}$$

式中，E 为电动势，V；φ_{SCE} 和 φ_{F^-} 分别为饱和甘汞电极和氟电极的电位，V。当其他条件一定时：

$$\varphi = K - 0.059\,2V \lg \alpha_{F^-} \quad (25℃)$$

式中，K 为常数；0. 059 2 为 25℃时电极的理论响应斜率；α_{F^-} 为待测溶液中 F^- 活度，$mol \cdot L^{-1}$。

用离子选择性电极测量的是离子活度，而通常定量分析需要的是离子浓度。若加入适量惰性电解质作为总离子强度调节缓冲剂（TISAB），使离子强度保持不变，则电位可表示为

$$\varphi = K + 0.059\,2V \lg c_{F^-}$$
$$= K - 0.059\,2V \lg(-c_{F^-}) = K - 0.059\,2V pF$$

式中，c_{F^-} 为待测溶液中 F^- 浓度，$mol \cdot L^{-1}$。

φ 与 pF 呈线性关系，因此根据 φ–pF 标准曲线和测定水样的 φ_x 值，可求得水中氟离子含量。

用氟电极测量 F^- 时，最适宜 pH 范围为 5.0~5.5。pH 过低，易形成 HF、HF_2^- 等，降低了 c_{F^-}；pH 过高，OH^- 浓度增大，OH^- 在氟电极上与 F^- 产生竞争响应。由于 OH^- 能与单晶膜中 LaF_3 产生如下反应：

$$LaF_3 + 3OH^- \longrightarrow La(OH)_3 + 3F^-$$

反应产物 F^- 为电极本身响应而造成的干扰。故通常用柠檬酸盐缓冲溶液来控制溶液的 pH。氟电极只对游离氟离子有响应，而 F^- 非常容易与 Al^{3+}、Fe^{3+} 等离子配位。因此，在测定时必

If an appropriate amount of inert electrolyte is added as the total ionic strength adjustment buffer (TISAB) to keep the ionic strength unchanged, the potential can be expressed as:

$$\varphi = K + 0.059\,2\text{V}\lg c_{\text{F}^-}$$
$$= K - 0.059\,2\text{V}\lg(-c_{\text{F}^-}) = K - 0.059\,2\text{VpF}$$

Where c_{F^-} is the concentration of F^- of the tested solution, mol·L^{-1}.

The relationship between φ and pF is linear, so the content of fluorine can be obtained according to the standard curve of φ- pF and the measured φ_x value of water sample.

Theoretically, the optimum pH range for F^- measurement with fluorine electrode is 5.0–5.5.

When the pH value is too low, it is easy to form HF, HF^-_2, etc., and reduced the value of α_{F^-}. When the pH value is too high, the concentration of OH^- increases, and OH^- produces a competitive response with F^- on the fluorine electrode. Additionally, OH^- can react with LaF_3 in the single crystal film as follows:

$$LaF_3 + 3OH^- \longrightarrow La(OH)_3 + 3F^-$$

The reaction product F^- is the interference caused by the response of the electrode itself. Therefore, citrate buffer solution is usually used to control the pH value of the solution. Since the fluorine electrode only responds to free fluorine ion, and free fluorine ion is easily coordinated with Al^{3+} and Fe^{3+}, therefore, the ligand with strong coordination ability must be added. For example, citrate is a strong coordination agent, and the interference of Al^{3+} and Fe^{3+} can be eliminated, so as to obtain reliable and accurate results.

Instruments and Chemical Reagents

1. Instruments

pH meter; electromagnetic stirrer; fluorine ion selective electrode; saturated calomel electrode (SCE); volumetric flask (50 mL, 100 mL).

2. Chemical reagents

NaF (A.R.); NaCl (A.R.); sodium citrate (A.R.); glacial acetic acid (A.R.); NaOH (A.R.); redistilled water.

Procedure

1. Preparation of solutions

F^- stock solution (1 mg·mL^{-1}) : NaF was dried at 120℃, accurately weighted 2.210 5 g, dissolved in distilled water, then moved into a 1 L volumetric flask, diluted to the scale, 1 mg·mL^{-1} stock solution was obtained, stored in a polyethylene flask.

F^- standard solution (0.01 mg·mL^{-1}) : Pipe 1.00mL of 1mg·mL^{-1} F^- stock solution, transfer it in a 100 mL volumetric flask and dilute it to volume with buffer solution (TISAB).

TISAB solution: weigh 58 g NaCl and 0.357g sodium citrate and dissolve in redistilled water, add 60 mL acetic acid, adjust the pH value of 5.1–5.5 with 50% (*V*/*V*) sodium oxide solution, cool down to

须加入配位能力较强的配体(如柠檬酸盐是较强的配位剂),消除 Al^{3+}、Fe^{3+} 等离子的干扰,才能测得可靠准确的结果。

三、仪器和试剂

1. 仪器

pH 计;电磁搅拌器;氟离子选择性电极;饱和甘汞电极(SCE);容量瓶(50 mL,100 mL)。

2. 试剂

NaF(分析纯);NaCl(分析纯);柠檬酸钠(分析纯);冰乙酸(分析纯);氢氧化钠(分析纯);二次蒸馏水。

四、实验步骤

1. 溶液配制

氟离子标准储备液($1\ mg\cdot mL^{-1}$):将分析纯 NaF 在 120 ℃烘干,准确称取 2.210 5 g 溶于二次蒸馏水中,移入 1 L 容量瓶中,稀释至刻度,即得到 $1\ mg\cdot mL^{-1}$ 氟离子标准溶液,然后储存在聚乙烯瓶中备用。

氟离子标准稀释液($0.01\ mg\cdot mL^{-1}$):吸取 1.00 mL $1\ mg\cdot mL^{-1}$ 氟离子标准储备液,置于 100 mL 容量瓶中,用缓冲溶液(TISAB)稀释至刻度。

缓冲溶液(TISAB):称取 58 g NaCl 及 0. 357 g 柠檬酸钠溶于二次蒸馏水中,加冰乙酸 60 mL,用 50%(体积分数)氢氧化钠调节 pH 为 5.1~5.5,冷却至室温,转入 1 L 容量瓶中,用二次蒸馏水稀释至刻度,摇匀,转入洗净、干燥的试剂瓶中。

2. 开机

将氟电极和 SCE 分别与 pH 计上的接口正确相接(氟电极接测量电极,饱和甘汞电极接参比电极,用 mV 挡测量),开启仪器,预热仪器。

3. 清洗电极

于 50 mL 的烧杯中,加入 40~50 mL 的二次蒸馏水,放入搅拌磁子,插入氟电极和 SCE 至合适位置,开启搅拌器,调节搅拌速率适中($200\sim300\ r\cdot min^{-1}$),使之保持较慢而稳定的转速(注意:在整个实验过程中保持该转速不变),清洗电极。若读数(仪器显示值绝对值,后同)小于 350 mV,更换蒸馏水,继续清洗,直至该数大于 350 mV。

4. 标准曲线的绘制

分别取 0.50 mL、1.00 mL、1.50 mL、2.00 mL、3.00 mL F^- 标准稀释溶液于 5 只 50 mL 容量瓶中,加缓冲溶液 10.00 mL,用二次蒸馏水稀释至刻度,摇匀。将全部溶液倒入烧杯中,放入搅拌磁子,插入前面清洗好的两电极,开启搅拌器,待读数稳定后,读取电位值。按浓度从低至高依次测量,记录测量结果。

room temperature, transfer them into 1 L volumetric flask, dilute with redistilled water to scale, shake well, and transfer them into cleaned and dried reagent flask.

2. Boot the pH meter

Connect the fluorine electrode and SCE with the interface on the pH meter respectively and correctly (fluorine electrode is connected to the measuring electrode, saturated calomel electrode is connected to the reference electrode, measuring with mV), power on the instrument, and preheat the instrument.

3. Clean the electrode

Add 40–50 mL of redistilled water into a 50 mL beaker, add a stirring magneton, place fluorine electrode and SCE to the appropriate position, turn on the mixer, adjust stirring speed (200–300 $r \cdot min^{-1}$), keep the speed slow and stable (note: keep the speed constant throughout the experiment), and clean the electrode. If the reading (absolute value of the displayed value of instrument) is less than 350 mV, replace distilled water and continue cleaning until the reading is greater than 350 mV.

4. Drawing of a standard curve

Pipe 0.50 mL, 1.00 mL 1.50 mL, 2.00 mL, 3.00 mL F^- standard solution into five volumetric flasks of 50 mL, add TISAB solution 10.00 mL respectively, dilute it with redistilled water to the scale, and shake well. Pour all the solution into the beaker, put the agitator magneton, place the two electrodes which were cleaned before, turn on the agitator, and record the potential value after the reading is stable, with the concentration from low to high. Record the results in the Table below.

5. Determination of water sample

Pipe 25.00 mL of water sample, put it into 50 mL volumetric flask, add 10.00 mL TISAB solution, dilute it with distilled water to scale, and shake well. Pour all the solution into the beaker, put the agitator magneton, place the two electrodes which were cleaned before, turn on the agitator, and read the potential value after the reading is stable. Record the results in the Table below.

Data Analysis

(1) The concentration of F^- standard solution and its corresponding potential value are filled in the table below. According to the concentration of F^-, calculate $\lg c_{F^-}$ and pF, and fill in the table.

No.	1	2	3	4	5	6
$c_{F^-}/(mg \cdot L^{-1})$						
$\lg c_{F^-}$						
pF						
φ/mV						

(2) Plot the standard curve with pF as the abscissa and the potential value (φ) as the ordinate, and

5. 水样的测定

取自来水样 25.00 mL，置 50 mL 容量瓶中，加 10. 00 mL 缓冲溶液，用二次蒸馏水稀释至刻度，摇匀。将全部溶液倒入烧杯中，放入搅拌磁子，插入前面清洗好的两电极，开启搅拌器，待读数稳定后，读取电位值。记录测量结果。

五、数据处理

（1）将氟离子标准系列溶液的浓度与其对应的电位值填写在下表中。根据氟离子的浓度，计算出 $\lg c_{F^-}$ 和 pF。

编号	1	2	3	4	5	6
$c_{F^-}/(mg\cdot L^{-1})$						
$\lg c_{F^-}$						
pF						
φ/mV						

（2）以 pF 为横坐标、电位值（φ）为纵坐标绘制标准工作曲线，得到标准工作曲线方程（校正曲线）及相关系数。根据待测样品的电位值 φ_x 和稀释倍数，利用标准曲线求出所测自来水样中氟离子的含量。氟离子的浓度用科学记数法记录，保留 3 位有效数字。

六、实验指导

1. 预习要求

（1）复习离子选择性电极的工作原理及测量方法。

（2）学习饮用水中氟离子含量的测定方法。

（3）了解氟离子选择性电极测定氟离子的实验方法。

2. 注意事项

（1）氟离子选择性电极的活化：将氟电极在含 1.0×10^{-4} mol·L^{-1} 或更低浓度的氟离子溶液中浸泡 1 h 左右，然后用二次蒸馏水清洗至读数在 350 mV 左右。连续使用间隔应浸入二次蒸馏水中。电极若暂不使用宜干燥保存。电极晶片要小心保护，切勿与尖硬物碰撞。如电极沾有油污，应用脱脂棉依次涂酒精和丙酮轻拭，再以二次蒸馏水洗净。

（2）电极在接触浓的含氟溶液后再测稀溶液时，往往伴有迟滞效应，测定顺序应由稀到浓进行。

（3）电极电位的平衡时间会随着氟离子浓度降低而延长。测定时，若电位在 1 min 变化不超过 1 mV，即可读取平衡电位值。

（4）氟离子标准溶液建议存放在聚乙烯的塑料瓶中，对使用过的容量瓶、移液管和其他的玻璃器皿要及时清洗。

curve equation (correction curve) and correlation coefficient were obtained. According to the potential φ_x and dilution ratio of the sample to be tested, the content of fluoride ion in the water sample was obtained by using the standard curve. Fluoride concentration is recorded by scientific enumeration, with 3 significant figures.

Experiment Guidance

1. Preview instruction

(1) Review the principle and measuring method of ion selective electrode.

(2) Learn the method for determination of fluoride ion content in drinking water.

(3) Understand the method for fluoride ion determination with fluoride ion selective electrode.

2. Notes

(1) Activation of fluoride ion selective electrode: The fluoride electrode was immersed in a fluoride ion solution containing 1.0×10^{-4} mol·L^{-1} or lower concentration for about 1 h, and then cleaned with redistilled water until the reading was about 350 mV. And it should be immersed in redistilled water at intervals of continuous use. If the electrode is not used temporarily, it should be dry and stored. Additionally, the electrode wafer should be carefully protected from collision with sharp hard objects. If the electrode surface is stained with oil, apply absorbent cotton with alcohol and acetone to wipe it gently, and then rinse with redistilled water.

(2) The hysteresis effect often occurs when the electrodes contact the concentrated fluorinated solution and then measure the diluted solution. The order of measurement should be from diluted solution to concentrated one.

(3) The equilibrium time of electrode potential will be prolonged with the decrease of fluoride ion concentration. When measuring, if the potential change within 1 min is not more than 1 mV, the equilibrium potential value can be read.

(4) Fluorine standard solution is recommended to be stored in polyethylene plastic bottles, and the used volumetric flasks, pipettes and other glassware should be cleaned after use.

3. Discussion

(1) What's the reason for using the TISAB?

(2) What should be paid attention to using of fluorine electrode?

(3) How does the pH value of the solution affect the determination?

3. 讨论

（1）为什么要加入总离子强度调节缓冲剂（TISAB）？

（2）氟电极在使用时应注意哪些问题？

（3）溶液的 pH 对测定有何影响？

Experiment 2.6 Determination of Water Content in Antibiotic Drugs

Purpose

(1) To master the principle and experimental technique of Karl Fischer method for measuring trace water.

(2) To be familiar with preparation method of Fischer test solution.

Principle

Karl Fischer method for the determination of trace water is an application of iodimetry in non-aqueous titration. The titrant of Karl Fischer method is be composed of iodine, sulfur dioxide and anhydrous pyridine dissolved in a solution of anhydrous methanol in a certain proportion, also known as Fischer test solution. The total reaction of titrant with water can be expressed as:

$$I_2 + SO_2 + 3C_5H_5N + CH_3OH + H_2O \longrightarrow 2C_5H_5N \cdot HI + C_5H_5N \cdot HSO_4—CH_3$$

The end point of the reaction can be determined by self-indicator method or dead-stop titration method. In the dead-stop titration, there is no reversible electric pair in the solution before the end point, so the galvanometer pointer stops at zero value. When the end point is reached with a slight excess of I_2, I_2 / I^- reversible electric pair are present in the solution, and the following electrode reactions occur on the two electrodes:

$$\text{Anode: } 2I^- \longrightarrow I_2 + 2e^-$$

$$\text{Cathode: } I_2 + 2e^- \longrightarrow 2I^-$$

There is a current passing through the circuit, and the pointer of the galvanometer shows that the deflection will not return to zero, which is the end point of the titration.

Instruments and Chemical Reagents

1. Instruments

Analytical balance; tray balance; microburette (minimum indexing value 0.05 mL); electromagnetic stirrer; automatic water determination apparatus; desiccator; erlenmeyer flask with stopper. All the items and glass instruments that are in direct contact with the reagent or Fischer test solution must be dry at 120 ℃ for at least 2 h, and the rubber plug shall be dry baked at 80 ℃ for 2 h. Then, they shall be taken out and placed in a dryer prior to use.

2. Chemical reagents

Antibiotic drugs; redistilled water; I_2 (A.R.); anhydrous methanol (A.R.), moisture content<0.1%; pyridine (A.R.), water content <0.1%; sulfur dioxide (usually uses compressed sulfur dioxide gas, which is dehydrated by sulfuric acid when used); concentrated sulfuric acid (A.R.); anhydrous calcium oxide (C.P.).

实验 2.6 抗生素药物中含水量的测定

一、实验目的

（1）掌握 Karl Fischer 法测定微量水分的原理和实验技术。

（2）熟悉 Fischer 试液的配制方法。

二、实验原理

Karl Fischer（卡尔·费歇尔）法测定微量水是碘量法在非水滴定中的一种应用。Karl Fischer 法的滴定剂为碘、二氧化硫和无水吡啶按一定比例溶于无水甲醇的溶液，也称为 Fischer 试液。滴定剂与水的总反应可表示为

$$I_2 + SO_2 + 3C_5H_5N + CH_3OH + H_2O \longrightarrow 2C_5H_5N \cdot HI + C_5H_5N \cdot HSO_4\text{—}CH_3$$

终点的确定可采取自身指示剂法或永停滴定法。永停滴定法中，终点前溶液中不存在可逆电对，故电流计指针停止在零位不动。当达到终点并稍有过量的 I_2 存在时，则溶液中便有 I_2/I^- 可逆电对存在，两个电极上发生如下的电极反应：

$$\text{阳极：} 2I^- \longrightarrow I_2 + 2e^-$$

$$\text{阴极：} I_2 + 2e^- \longrightarrow 2I^-$$

电路中有电流通过，电流计指针显示偏转不再回至零位，即为滴定终点。

三、仪器和试剂

1. 仪器

分析天平；托盘天平；微量滴定管（最小分度值 0.05 mL）；电磁搅拌器；自动水分测定仪；干燥器；具塞锥形瓶；凡与试剂或 Fischer 试液直接接触的物品、玻璃仪器须在 120℃至少烘干 2 h，橡胶塞在 80℃烘干 2 h，取出置于干燥器内备用。

2. 试剂

抗生素类药物；二次蒸馏水；碘（分析纯），含水量 <0.1%；吡啶（分析纯），含水量 <0.1%；二氧化硫（一般使用压缩的二氧化硫气体，用时通过硫酸脱水）；浓硫酸（分析纯）；无水氧化钙（化学纯）。

四、实验步骤

1. Fischer 试液制备

称取碘（置硫酸干燥器内 48 h）110 g，置于干燥的具塞锥形瓶中，加无水吡啶 160 mL，注意冷却，振摇至碘全部溶解后加无水甲醇 300 mL，称定质量，将锥形瓶置冰浴中冷却，在避免空气中水分侵入的情况下，通入干燥的 SO_2 至质量增加 72 g，再加无水甲醇至 1 000 mL，密塞，摇匀，在暗处放置 48 h。试液应遮光，密封，置阴凉干燥处保存，用前标定浓度。也可以购买市售的 Fischer 试液，市售的试液可以是不含吡啶的其他碱化剂，或不含甲醇的其他醇类等，可以是单一

Procedure

1. Preparation of Karl Fischer test solution

Place 110 g of iodine, previously dried in a desiccator over sulfuric acid for more than 48 h, in a dry stoppered erlenmeyer flask, add 160 mL of anhydrous pyridine and cool, and shake to effectively complete dissolution. Add 300 mL of anhydrous methanol and weigh the flask. Keep the flask cold in an ice bath, pass dry sulfur dioxide into the flask until the increase of weigh is 72 g, and add anhydrous methanol to produce 1 000 mL. Stopper tightly, mix well, and allow to stand for 24 h away from light. This solution should be preserved in tightly closed containers, protected from light and stored in a cool and dry place, and standardized before using. The Karl Fischer test solution is also commercially available.

2. Standardization of Karl Fischer test solution

Accurately weigh redistilled water (10–30 mg) (according to Fischer test titer and burette volume), place in a dry stoppered erlenmeyer flask, add appropriate amount of anhydrous methanol unless otherwise specified under the condition of avoiding the invasion of water in the air. Titrate with Karl Fischer test solution until the color changes from pale yellow to reddish brown. The end point may also be determined by dead-stop titration. Perform a blank titration and calculate the water equivalent of the test solution in mg of water per mL by the formula as follows.

$$F = \frac{W}{A - B}$$

Where F is the weight of redistilled water equivalent of the solution, mg; W is the weight of redistilled water, mg; A is the volume of the test solution consumed in the titration of redistilled water, mL; B is the volume of the test solution consumed in the blank titration, mL.

3. Determination of sample

Accurately weigh a quantity of sample examined which is estimated to consume 1–5 mL of Karl Fischer test solution to a dry stoppered erlenmeyer flask, add a quantity of absolute methanol and titrate with Karl Fischer test solution until the color changes from pale yellow to reddish brown, while shaking or stirring continuously. The end point may also be determined by dead-stop titration. Perform a blank titration and calculate the water equivalent of the test solution in mg of water per mL by the formula as follows.

$$w_{\text{water}}(\%) = \frac{(A - B)F}{W} \times 100\%$$

Where A is the volume of the test solution consumed in the titration of redistilled water, mL; B is the volume of the test solution consumed in the blank titration, mL; F is the weight of redistilled water equivalent of the solution, mg; W is the weight of sample examined, mg.

After the titration, the Fischer test solution is moved to the storage flask for sealed storage. The titration apparatus are washed with methanol to prevent the precipitation of crystals between the burette, the grinding mouth and the piston from blocking.

的溶液或由两种溶液混合而成。

2. Fischer 试液的标定

准确称取二次蒸馏水 10 ~ 30 mg（据 Fischer 试液滴定度和滴定管体积而定），置干燥的具塞锥形瓶中，除另有规定外，加入适量无水甲醇，在避免空气中水分侵入的情况下，用 Fischer 试液滴定至溶液由浅黄色变为红棕色，或用永停滴定法指示终点。另做空白试验，按下式计算：

$$F=\frac{W}{A-B}$$

式中，A 为滴定所消耗费 Fischer 试液体积，mL；B 为空白所消耗费 Fischer 试液容积，mL；F 为每毫升 Fischer 试液相当于二次蒸馏水的质量，mg；W 为称取重蒸馏水的质量，mg。

3. 供试品的测定

准确称取供试品适量，除另有规定外，溶液为无水甲醇，用水分测定仪直接测定。准确称取供试品适量（消耗 Fischer 试液 1~5 mL），置于干燥的具塞锥形瓶中，加适量无水乙醇，在不断振摇下用 Fischer 试液滴定至溶液由浅黄色变为红棕色，或用永停滴定法指示终点。另做空白试验，按下式计算：

$$w_{H_2O}(\%)=\frac{(A-B)F}{W}\times 100\%$$

式中，A 为供试品所消耗 Fischer 试液的体积，mL；B 为空白所消耗 Fischer 试液的体积，mL；F 为每毫升 Fischer 试液相当于二次蒸馏水的质量，mg；W 为供试品的质量，mg。

滴定完毕后，将 Fischer 试液移入贮存瓶中密闭保存，滴定装置用甲醇洗涤，以防滴管间及磨口和活塞处析出结晶以致堵塞。

五、实验指导

1. 预习要求

（1）复习碘量法的基础知识。

（2）掌握 Karl Fischer 法的基本原理、Fischer 试液的制备及标定。

（3）掌握永停滴定法的基本原理。

（4）了解自动水分测定仪的操作。

2. 注意事项

（1）取 3 份以上 Fischer 试液进行标定，3 次标定结果 RAD 应在 ±1% 以内，以平均值作为标准浓度。

（2）Fischer 试液应密封，避光，并于干燥处保存，滴定装置中的干燥剂应定期更换。

（3）水分测定中所用的容器均应干燥，所用的试剂均应无水。

（4）每次水分测定前，Fischer 试液应重新标定。

（5）避免搅拌棒碰撞电极。如果电极钝化，终点指示不灵敏，应用丙酮浸洗。

（6）Karl Fischer 法能够测定绝大多数有机化合物和无机化合物中的微量水分。以合适的溶剂溶解样品，用已知滴定度的 Fischer 试液直接滴定样品，滴定终点判断用永停滴定法或外指

Experiment Guidance

1. Preview instruction

(1) Review the basic knowledge of iodimetry.

(2) Grasp the basic principle of Karl Fischer method, preparation and standardization of Fischer test solution.

(3) Master the basic principle of dead-stop titration.

(4) Understand the operation procures of automatic water determination apparatus.

2. Notes

(1) The standardization of Fischer test solution should be carried out more than 3 times, and the RAD of the three results should be within 1%, and the average value should be used as the standard concentration.

(2) The Fischer test solution should be sealed, protected from light, and kept in a dry place. The desiccant in the titration apparatus should be replaced periodically.

(3) All containers used in the water determination should be dry and all reagents used should be anhydrous.

(4) The Fischer test should be re-standardized before each measurement.

(5) Avoid mixing bar colliding with electrode. If the electrode is passivated and the end point indication is insensitive, immerse it with acetone.

(6) Karl Fischer method is capable of determining trace amounts of water in most organic and inorganic compounds. Dissolve the sample in a suitable solvent, and titrate the sample directly with Fischer test solution with known titer. The end-point of titration can be determined by dead-stop titration method or indicator method.

(7) The reference of sample amount is shown in the Table 2-1.

Table 2-1 The reference of sample amount according to estimated water content

Estimated water content /%	Sample amount/mg	Estimated water content /%	Sample amount/mg
0.1~0.5	500~1 000	5~10	100
0.5~2	200	10~25	100
2~5	100	>25	100

3. Discussion

(1) Please explain the principle of determining the end point of titration by the dead-stop titration method.

(2) To discuss the principle of determining the end point by solution color and the difference of the accuracy between the volumetric analysis and the dead-stop titration.

(3) What should be paid attention to when using Fischer test solution?

示剂法均可。

（7）供试品取样量的参考见表 2-1。

表 2-1　供试品取样量的参考表

预计的样品含水量 /%	取样量 /mg	预计的样品含水量 /%	取样量 /mg
0.1~0.5	500~1 000	5~10	100
0.5~2	200	10~25	100
2~5	100	>25	100

3. 讨论

（1）请说明永停滴定法判断滴定终点的原理。

（2）分析本实验用溶液颜色判断终点的原理及其与永停滴定法判断终点准确度的差异性。

（3）使用 Fischer 试液应注意哪些问题？

Chapter 3 Spectral Analysis

Experiment 3.1 Solvent Effect of Ultraviolet Absorption Spectra of Organic Compounds

Purpose

(1) To be familiar with the use of ultraviolet-visible spectrophotometer.

(2) To understand the effect of different polar solvents on the position, shape and intensity of ultraviolet absorption band of organic compounds.

Principle

Hexane, water, ethanol and other solvents are commonly used in scanning ultraviolet-visible (UV-Vis) absorption spectrum. Some solvents, especially polar solvents, may affect the wavelength, intensity and shape of the solute absorption peak. Because hydrogen bonds are often formed between solvent and solute and the polarity of solute would be enhanced by solvent dipole, the $n-\pi^*$ and $\pi-\pi^*$ absorption bands shift. With the increase of solvent polarity, the $n-\pi^*$ absorption band has a blue shift, and the $\pi-\pi^*$ absorption band has a red shift.

Solvent not only affects the absorption wavelength, but also affects the absorption intensity and fine structure. For example, the fine structure of B absorption band is clear in non-polar solvent, but not clear in polar solvent, sometimes even disappear and a wide peak appears. Therefore, in the determination of UV-Vis absorption spectrum, the solvent cannot be absorbed in the measurement spectral region, and should have smaller polarity as far as possible within the range of solubility.

Instruments and Chemical Reagents

1. Instruments

Spectrophotometer; volumetric flask (100 mL); micropipettor (100 μL); quartz cuvette; dropper.

2. Chemical reagents

Benzene; ethanol; *n*-hexane; isopropylidene acetone. All are analytical pure reagents. deionized water.

Procedure

1. Preparation of solutions

第三章 光 谱 分 析

实验 3.1 有机化合物紫外吸收光谱的溶剂效应

一、实验目的

（1）熟悉紫外可见分光光度计的使用。

（2）了解不同极性溶剂对有机化合物紫外吸收带位置、形状及强度的影响。

二、实验原理

紫外吸收光谱中的常用的溶剂有正己烷、水、乙醇等。有些溶剂，特别是极性溶剂，对溶质吸收峰的波长、强度和形状可能产生影响。这是因为溶剂和溶质间常形成氢键，或溶剂的偶极作用使溶质的极性增强，引起 $n-\pi^*$，$\pi-\pi^*$ 吸收带的迁移，随溶剂极性的增强，$n-\pi^*$ 吸收带发生蓝移，$\pi-\pi^*$ 吸收带发生红移。

此外，溶剂除了对吸收波长有影响外，还影响吸收强度和精细结构。例如，苯环 B 吸收带的精细结构在非极性溶剂中较清楚，但在极性溶剂中则较弱，有时甚至消失而出现一个宽峰。因此，在进行紫外可见吸收光谱测定时，溶剂除了不能在样品的测量光谱区域内有吸收外，在溶解度允许的范围内还应尽量选择极性较小的溶剂。

三、仪器和试剂

1. 仪器

紫外可见分光光度计；石英比色皿；容量瓶（100 mL）；移液枪（100 μL）；滴管。

2. 试剂

苯；乙醇；正己烷；异丙叉丙酮。均为分析纯。去离子水。

四、实验步骤

1. 溶液配制

苯的正己烷溶液、乙醇溶液（约 0.1 $mg \cdot mL^{-1}$）的配制：取两只 100 mL 容量瓶，分别注入 10 μL 苯，然后分别用正己烷和乙醇稀释到刻度，摇匀。

异丙叉丙酮的正己烷溶液、水溶液（约 0.1 $mg \cdot mL^{-1}$）的配制：取两只 100 mL 容量瓶，各注入 10 μL 的异丙叉丙酮，然后分别用正己烷和去离子水稀释到刻度，摇匀。

2. 苯蒸气的紫外吸收光谱的绘制

Preparation of *n*-hexane solution and ethanol solution of benzene (about 0.1 $mg \cdot mL^{-1}$): pipet 10 μL benzene into two 100 mL volumetric flasks, then dilute them to volume with *n*-hexane and ethanol, respectively, and mix well.

Preparation of *n*-hexane solution and aqueous solution of isopropylidene acetone (about 0.1 $mg \cdot mL^{-1}$): pipet 10 μL isopropylidene acetone into two 100 mL volumetric flasks, dilute to volume with *n*-hexane and deionized water, respectively, and mix well.

2. Plot of the UV absorption spectra of benzene vapor

Take two drops of benzene with a dropper into a 1 cm quartz cuvette, cover it, stand for 2–3 min. Scan the UV absorption spectrum in the wavelength range of 200–320 nm.Take the empty quartz cuvette as the reference.

3. Plot of the UV absorption spectra of benzene in *n*-hexane and ethanol solution

The UV absorption spectra of benzene in different polar solvents are obtained in the wavelength range of 200–320 nm by using corresponding solvents as blank reference.

4. Plot of the UV absorption spectra of isopropylidene acetone in *n*-hexane and aqueous solution

The UV absorption spectra of isopropylidene acetone in different polar solvents are obtained in the wavelength range of 200–320 nm by using corresponding solvents as blank reference.

Data Analysis

(1) Compare the UV absorption curves of benzene vapor and benzene ethanol solution, and discuss the effect of solvent on the fine structure of absorption spectrum.

(2) Compare the effects of non-polar solvent and polar solvent on the maximum absorption wavelength of the UV absorption spectrum of isopropylidene acetone, and determine the maximum absorption wavelengths of K-band and R-band of isopropylidene acetone.

Experiment Guidance

1. Preview instruction

(1) Review the basic principle of UV-Vis absorption spectrum.

(2) Understand the factors affecting UV absorption bands.

(3) Be familiar with composition and absorbance measurement of UV-Vis spectrophotometer.

2. Notes

(1) After scanning the UV-Vis absorption spectrum of benzene, clean the cuvette with absolute ethanol for several times.

(2) The factors affecting the UV-Vis absorption spectrum of organic compounds include internal influences (conjugation effect, trans-ring effect, etc.) and external influences (polarity and acidity of solvent).

3. Discussion

(1) How to distinguish $n \rightarrow \pi^*$ and $\pi \rightarrow \pi^*$ electron transition with UV-Vis absorption spectrum?

(2) What are the common absorption bands in UV-Vis spectrum? What are their characteristics?

用滴管取两滴苯加入 1 cm 石英比色皿中，加盖，放置 2~3 min 后置于样品光路中，以空石英比色皿为参比，在 200~320 nm 波长范围内扫描其紫外吸收光谱。

3. 苯的正己烷溶液、乙醇溶液紫外吸收光谱的绘制

用 1 cm 石英比色皿，分别以各自溶剂为参比溶液，在 200~320 nm 波长范围内扫描紫外吸收光谱，得到苯在不同极性溶剂中的紫外吸收光谱。

4. 异丙叉丙酮的水溶液、正己烷溶液的紫外吸收光谱的绘制

用 1 cm 石英比色皿，分别以各自溶剂为参比溶液，在 200~320 nm 波长范围内扫描紫外吸收光谱，得到异丙叉丙酮在不同极性溶剂中的紫外吸收光谱。

五、数据处理

（1）比较苯蒸气和苯的正己烷溶液、乙醇溶液的紫外吸收曲线，讨论溶剂对吸收光谱精细结构的影响。

（2）比较非极性溶剂和极性溶剂对异丙叉丙酮紫外吸收光谱中最大吸收波长的影响，并确定异丙叉丙酮 K 带和 R 带的最大吸收波长。

六、实验指导

1. 预习要求

（1）复习紫外可见吸收光谱的基础知识。

（2）理解影响紫外光谱吸收带的因素。

（3）熟悉紫外可见分光光度计的组成和吸光度测量方法。

2. 注意事项

（1）做完苯溶液的紫外吸收光谱后，要用少许无水乙醇多次清洗比色皿。

（2）影响有机化合物的紫外可见吸收光谱的因素有：内因（共轭效应，跨环效应等）和外因（溶剂的极性和酸碱性）。

3. 讨论

（1）如何使用紫外可见吸收光谱区别 $n \rightarrow \pi^*$ 和 $\pi \rightarrow \pi^*$ 两种不同跃迁类型？

（2）紫外可见光谱中常见的吸收带有哪些？它们分别有什么特点？

Experiment 3.2 Determination of the Absorption Coefficient of API

Purpose

(1) To learn the definition of API's absorption coefficient.

(2) To master the method for determination of the API's absorption coefficient.

Principle

The absorption coefficient of compounds which absorb ultraviolet-visible (UV-Vis) light can be measured by spectrophotometry. The absorption coefficient of a drug is achieved by averaging the results on five spectrophotometers of different types, and the relative standard deviation must be not more than 1%. Drugs must be purified by recrystallization or other methods to achieve acute melting point and dried to constant weight before use. Spectrophotometers, balance, volumetric flask and suction pipets must be calibrated.

Dissolve a drug to prepare a solution which has the absorbance of 0.7–0.8 and dilute it to prepare a solution of exact half concentration, which has the absorbance of 0.3–0.4. The relative deviation between the two coefficients must be less than 1%.

Instruments and Chemical Reagents

1. Instruments

752 Spectrophotometer; volumetric flask (50 mL,100 mL); suction pipet (5 mL,10 mL).

2. Chemical reagents

Sulfuric acid solution (0.05 $mol \cdot L^{-1}$); chlorphenamine (standard substance); double-distilled water.

Procedure

1. Preparation of solutions

Chlorphenamine stock solution:Weigh accurately about 0.015 g of chlorphenamine into a 100 mL volumetric flask, and dilute to the mark with 0.05 $mol \cdot L^{-1}$ sulfuric acid solution, mix well.

Pipet 5.00 mL and 10.00 mL portions of chlorphenamine stock solution into two 50 mL volumetric flasks, respectively, dilute to the mark with 0.05 $mol \cdot L^{-1}$ sulfuric acid solution, mix well.

2. Determination of absorption coefficient

Using the blank as the reference, measure the absorbance of any one of the chlorphenamine solutions at different wavelength near 264 nm by taking 2 nm apart. Select the wavelength of maximum absorbance for the determination. At the selected wavelength, measure the absorbance of each of the solutions.

Data Analysis

实验 3.2　原料药吸收系数的测定

一、实验目的

（1）了解原料药吸收系数的定义。

（2）掌握测定原料药吸收系数的方法。

二、实验原理

有紫外吸收的物质可用分光光度计测定其吸收系数。药品的吸收系数经 5 台以上不同型号的紫外分光光度计测定，所得结果再经数理统计方法处理，相对偏差在 1% 以内，最后确定吸收系数。药品应事先干燥至恒重(或测定干燥失重，在计算中扣除)。分光光度计及天平、容量瓶、移液管都必须按鉴定标准经过校正。

溶解药物配成溶液使其吸光度在 0.7~0.8，稀释一倍使其吸光度在 0.3~0.4。按浓溶液和稀溶液计算的吸收系数之间的相对误差值也应在 1% 以内。

三、仪器和试剂

1. 仪器

752 型分光光度计；容量瓶（100 mL，50 mL）；移液管（10 mL，5 mL）。

2. 试剂

H_2SO_4 溶液（0.05 mol·L^{-1}）；扑尔敏(标准品)；二次蒸馏水。

四、实验步骤

1. 溶液的配制

扑尔敏储备液：取扑尔敏纯品约 0.015 g，精密称定，置于 100 mL 容量瓶中，用 H_2SO_4 溶液（0.05 mol·L^{-1}）溶解并稀释至刻度，摇匀。

取两只 50 mL 容量瓶，用移液管分别加入 5.00 mL 和 10.00 mL 扑尔敏储备液，用 H_2SO_4 溶液（0.05 mol·L^{-1}）稀释至刻度，摇匀，作为扑尔敏样品溶液。

2. 吸收系数的测定

使用空白溶液（0.05 mol·L^{-1} H_2SO_4 溶液）作为参比，测定任一扑尔敏溶液在 264 nm 附近不同波长处的吸光度，以 2 nm 为间隔记录读数。选择吸光度最大的波长作为检测波长，以选定的波长测定稀、浓样品溶液的吸光度。

五、数据处理

计算稀、浓样品溶液的吸收系数，其相对偏差值应在 1% 以内。

六、实验指导

1. 预习要求

（1）掌握吸收系数的概念、表示方法及测量方法。

Calculate the absorption coefficient of each solution. The relative deviation between the two results should not be more than 1%.

Experiment Guidance

1. Preview instruction

(1) Grasp the concept, representation and measurement of absorption coefficient.

(2) Understand the factors affecting absorption coefficient.

(3) Be familiar with the operation of UV-Vis spectrophotometer.

2. Notes

(1) The loss of weight on dryness must be calibrated if not heated to constant weight.

(2) Dilute the concentrated solution with solvent in the same batch number.

3. Discussion

(1) Why the relative deviation between the coefficients of thick and dilute solution must be not more than 1%?

(2) Why are there so many requirements to meet in determining the absorption coefficient of a drug? Under what conditions, the absorption coefficient of a drug can be cited as a physical constant?

（2）理解吸收系数的影响因素。

（3）熟悉紫外可见分光光度计的操作方法。

2. 注意事项

（1）样品若非干燥至恒重，应先扣除干燥失重，即样品质量 = 称量值 ×（1- 干燥失重 %）。

（2）将浓溶液稀释一倍时，应用同一批号溶剂稀释。

3. 讨论

（1）测定药品吸收系数时先配制某一浓度的溶液并测其吸收度，然后稀释一倍再测其吸光度。根据稀、浓两溶液吸光度计算所得的吸收系数的相对误差值不得大于 1%，为什么？

（2）为什么要用多台仪器来确定药物的吸收系数？在什么条件下吸收系数才能用作物理常数？

Experiment 3.3 Identification and Determination of Vitamin B_{12} Injection by Ultraviolet-visible Spectrophotometry

Purpose

(1) To master the basic configuration and the operation of ultraviolet-visible spectrophotometer.

(2) To master the method of identification and determination of vitamin B_{12} injection.

Principle

1. The basic configuration of ultraviolet-visible spectrophotometer

Ultraviolet-visible (UV-Vis) spectrophotometer is mainly composed of light sources, monochromator, sample cell, detector and signal processor. Light sources usually employ deuterium lamp for ultraviolet and tungsten lamp for visible light, while prism and grating are the most commonly used monochromators. Commonly, quartz and glass are used to make sample cells. Photovoltaic cell, phototube and photomultiplier tube have been used as detector successively. The configuration and operational principle of single-beam spectrophotometer are shown in Figure 3-1.

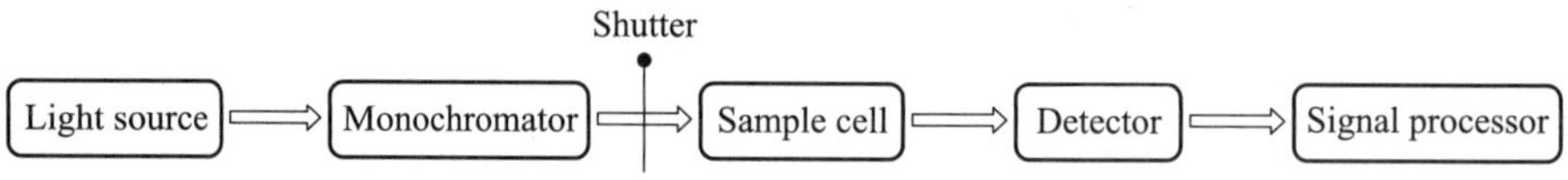

Figure 3-1 The Configuration of UV-Vis Spectrophotometer

2. Identification of vitamin B_{12} in samples

When electromagnetic radiation passes through a substance such as solid, liquid and gas, which can selectively absorb frequencies of radiation because of its structure and properties. The ultraviolet absorption spectrum of vitamin B_{12} reveals its characteristic in chemical structure, thus three absorption peaks appear at 278 nm, 361 nm and 550 nm, respectively. Accordingly, based on characteristic of the spectrum, vitamin B_{12} can be identified by measuring the ratios of absorbances (i.e. A_{361}/A_{278} and A_{361}/A_{550}), respectively. According to the values authorized by Chinese Pharmacopoeia,the ratios of A_{361}/A_{278} and A_{361}/A_{550} must be between 1.70–1.88 and 3.15–3.45, respectively.

实验 3.3　紫外－可见分光光度法鉴别和测定维生素 B_{12} 注射液

一、实验目的

（1）掌握紫外－可见分光光度计的基本结构及使用方法。

（2）掌握维生素 B_{12} 注射液的鉴别及含量测定方法。

二、实验原理

1. 紫外－可见分光光度计的组成与结构

紫外－可见分光光度计主要由光源（氘灯、钨灯）、单色器（棱镜、光栅、滤光片）、样品池、检测器（光电管、光电倍增管、光电池）以及信号处理和显示系统等部分组成，其基本结构和工作流程如图 3-1 所示。

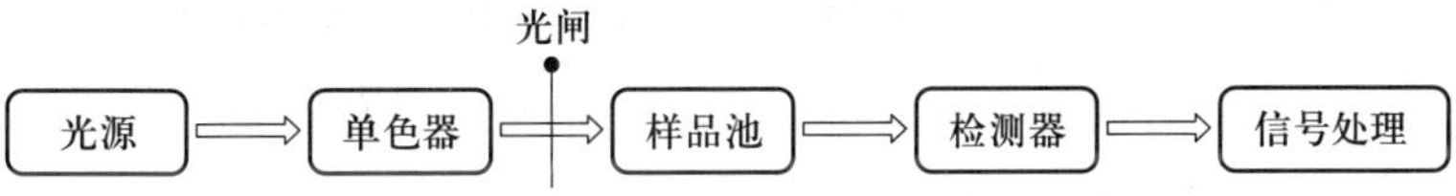

图 3-1　紫外－可见分光光度计示意图

2. 维生素 B_{12} 的定性鉴别

由于物质的性质和结构不同，物质对光的吸收具有选择性。维生素 B_{12} 的吸收曲线反映了其化学结构的基本特征，分别在 278 nm、361 nm 和 550 nm 波长处有三个吸收峰，因此可利用其特征吸收值之间的比值 A_{361}/A_{278} 和 A_{361}/A_{550} 进行定性鉴别。《中国药典》规定，维生素 B_{12} 的 A_{361}/A_{278} 和 A_{361}/A_{550} 的值应分别在 1.70~1.88 和 3.15~3.45。

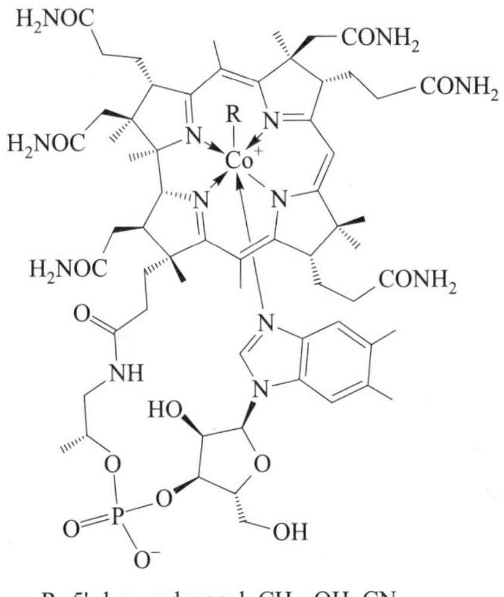

R=5'-deoxyadenosyl, CH_3, OH, CN

维生素 B_{12}

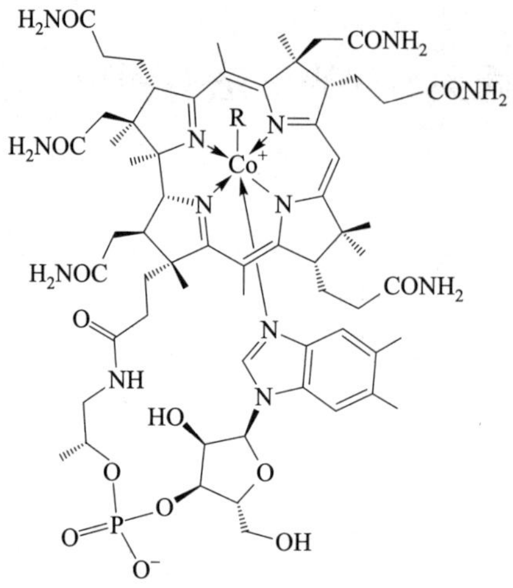

R=5'-deoxyadenosyl, CH_3, OH, CN

Vitamin B_{12}

3. Determination of vitamin B_{12} in samples

Vitamin B_{12} can be determined directly by using absorption coefficient method because of the maximum absorption ($E_{1cm}^{1\%}$ =207) and less interference at 361 nm. Through measured the absorbance at the wavelength, the content of vitamin B_{12} can be calculated as follows:

$$A= E_{1cm}^{1\%}\ cl \ \Rightarrow c=\frac{A}{E_{1cm}^{1\%}l}=\frac{A}{207}\times 10^4 = A\times 48.31\,(\mu g\cdot mL^{-1})$$

$$w_{VB_{12}}(\%)=\frac{A\times 48.31\times n}{0.5}\times 100\ \%$$

Where A is absorption; c is concentration of solution, $\mu g\cdot mL^{-1}$; l is the length of cell, cm; n is the dilution factor.

Instruments and Chemical Reagents

1. Instruments

TU1810 spetrophotometer; quartz cell (1 cm); volumetric flask (10 mL); pipet (1 mL).

2. Chemical reagents

Vitamin B_{12} reference; vitamin B_{12} injection (labeled amont 0.5 $mg\cdot mL^{-1}$); double-distilled water.

Procedure

1. Preparation of standard solution and sample solution

Weigh accurately a certain quantity of vitamin B_{12} reference subsatance, dissolve it with distilled water, and dilute to the concentration of 25 $\mu g\cdot mL^{-1}$.

Pipet precisely 0.5 mL of the vitamin B_{12} injection into 10 mL volumetric flask, dilute it to volume with distilled water and mix well (the concentration of vitamin B_{12} is about 25 $\mu g\cdot mL^{-1}$).

2. Identification of vitamin B_{12} injection

Transfer a certain volume of standard solution in quartz cell carefully, and put it in a

3. 维生素 B_{12} 注射液的定量分析

由于维生素 B_{12} 在 361 nm 处的吸收最强（$E_{1cm}^{1\%}=207$），且干扰因素少，因此以 361 nm 为测定波长，在此波长下测量其吸光度 A，采用吸收系数法可直接按下式计算维生素 B_{12} 的百分含量：

根据 $A=E_{1cm}^{1\%}cl$　则 $c=\dfrac{A}{E_{1cm}^{1\%}l}=\dfrac{A}{207}\times10^4=A\times48.31\,(\mu g\cdot mL^{-1})$

$$w_{VB_{12}}(\%)=\frac{A\times48.31\times n}{0.5}\times100\,\%$$

式中，A 为吸光度；c 为溶液浓度，$\mu g\cdot mL^{-1}$；l 为吸收池厚度，cm；n 为稀释倍数。

三、仪器与试剂

1. 仪器

TU1810 紫外－可见分光光度计；石英比色皿（1 cm）；容量瓶（10 mL）；吸量管（1 mL）。

2. 试剂

维生素 B_{12} 对照品；维生素 B_{12} 注射液（标示量为 0.5 $mg\cdot mL^{-1}$）；二次蒸馏水。

四、实验步骤

1. 维生素 B_{12} 对照品溶液和样品溶液的配制

准确称取维生素 B_{12} 对照品适量，加水稀释成 25 $\mu g\cdot mL^{-1}$ 的溶液。

精密吸取维生素 B_{12} 注射液 0.5 mL 于 10 mL 容量瓶中，用水稀释至刻度，摇匀，得到待测样品溶液（按标示含量稀释成含维生素 B_{12} 约 25 $\mu g\cdot mL^{-1}$ 的溶液）。

2. 吸收光谱的绘制与注射液的鉴别

取对照品溶液进行光谱扫描（200~600 nm），得到维生素 B_{12} 的吸收曲线，观察在 278 nm、361 nm 和 550 nm 波长附近的 3 个吸收峰。然后在以上三个吸收峰处测量维生素 B_{12} 样品溶液的吸光度。

3. 维生素 B_{12} 的定量测定

根据吸收曲线，选择在 361 nm 附近的最大吸收波长作为测定波长，测量维生素 B_{12} 样品溶液的吸光度。

五、数据处理

（1）计算 A_{361}/A_{278} 和 A_{361}/A_{550} 的值，鉴别维生素 B_{12} 的真伪。

（2）利用 361 nm 附近最大吸收波长处的吸光度值，计算维生素 B_{12} 的标示量含量（含量为 90%~110% 视为合格）。

六、实验指导

1. 预习要求

（1）复习紫外－可见吸收光谱法定性和定量方法。

spetrophotometer. Then scanning is performed from 200 nm to 600 nm to draw the absorption spectrum of vitamin B_{12}. Find out the wavelengths of absorption peaks near 278 nm, 361 nm and 550 nm, respectively. Next, measure the absorbances of sample solution at three wavelengths selected.

3. Determination of vitamin B_{12} injection

According to the spectrum of vitamin B_{12}, the maximum absorption wavelength near 361 nm is selected to measure the absorbance of the sample solution.

Data Analysis

(1) Calculate the absorption ratio of A_{361}/A_{278} and $A_{361}/A_{550,}$ respectively, and then identify vitamin B_{12}.

(2) Calculate the content of vitamin B_{12} using the absorbance value at the maximum absorption wavelength near 361 nm, which is certificated between 90% and 110% according to Chinese Pharmacopoeia.

Experiment Guidance

1. Preview instruction

(1) Review the qualitative and quantitative methods of UV-Vis absorption spectroscopy.

(2) Be familiar with the use of UV-Vis spectrophotometer.

2. Notes

(1) Pay attention to the place of sample cells in the instrument when you measure.

(2) Don't open the cover of sample chamber when you measure.

3. Discussion

(1) What requirement must be met in the determination of content in a sample by absorption coefficient method?

(2) Compare experiment results with other group of students through the shape of absorption spectra, the location of maximum absorption wavelength and the absorbance for the same solution in different instrument, and explain why they are same or different.

(3) Compare the absorption coefficient method with the calibration curve method, which is better? Explain it.

（2）熟悉紫外可见分光光度计的使用。

2. 注意事项

（1）使用五联池时要注意比色皿在样品池中的位置不可混淆。

（2）测定时不要打开仪器的样品池盖。

3. 讨论

（1）采用吸收系数法直接测定样品含量有何要求？

（2）利用其他组学生的实验结果，比较同一溶液在不同仪器上测得的吸收曲线的形状、吸收峰波长及吸光度有无不同，并作出解释。

（3）比较吸收系数法和标准曲线法，你认为哪种方法好？为什么？

Experiment 3.4 Condition Optimization for Colorimetric Determination of Iron with 1,10-Phenanthroline

Purpose

(1) To be familiar with the operation of the 752 spectrophotometer.

(2) To be familiar with the condition optimization in spectrophotometry.

Principle

The reaction of Fe^{2+} with 1,10-phenanthroline can produce a very stable orange-red complex ($\lg K$ = 21.3, 20 ℃), which is a good method for the quantitative determination of trace iron ions.

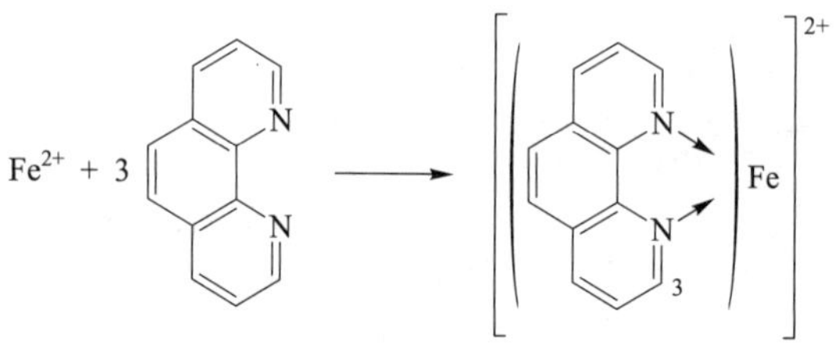

In addtion to the λ_{max} selection, conditions such as the concentration, stability, acidity, composition of complex will be studied in this experiment. The effect of interfering substances, temperature, range of determination and suitability of the method, etc. will also be discussed.

Instruments and Chemical Reagents

1. Instruments

752 spectrophotometer; 25 pH meter (or pHS-25 pH meter); volumetric flask (50 mL); pipet (1 mL, 2 mL, 5 mL, 10 mL); beaker (10 mL), rubber suction bulb.

2. Chemical reagents

1 $mol \cdot L^{-1}$ NaOH solution; 0.15% 1,10-phenanthroline solution (freshly prepared); 10% hydroxylamine hydrochloride solution (freshly prepared); 1 $mol \cdot L^{-1}$ sodium acetate solution; $NH_4Fe(SO_4)_2 \cdot 12H_2O$ (primary standard substance); 6 $mol \cdot L^{-1}$ hydrochloride acid solution; double-distilled water.

Procedure

1. Preparation of solutions

Standard iron solution (1×10^{-3} $mol \cdot L^{-1}$): Weigh accurately 0.482 2 g $NH_4Fe(SO_4)_2 \cdot 12H_2O$ into a beaker. Add 10 mL hydrochloride acid solution (6 $mol \cdot L^{-1}$) and a little distilled water to dissolve. Transfer the solution quantitively to a 1 L volumetric flask, dilute exactly to the mark with distilled water, and mix well.

2. Effect of the concentration of 1,10-phenanthroline

Pipet 2 mL standard iron solution (1×10^{-3} $mol \cdot L^{-1}$) into eight 50 mL volumetric flasks, add 1 mL

实验 3.4　邻二氮菲比色法测定铁的显色条件优化

一、实验目的

（1）熟悉 752 型分光光度计的操作。

（2）熟悉分光光度法测定条件的优化。

二、实验原理

Fe^{2+} 与邻二氮菲反应能生成极稳定的橙红色配合物（$\lg K_{稳}$=21.3，20℃）。此反应灵敏度高，是定量测定微量铁离子的良好方法。

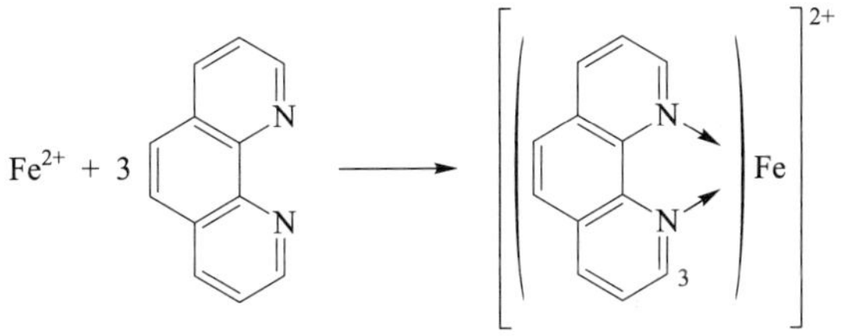

从邻二氮菲 –Fe（Ⅱ）吸收曲线中找出最大吸收波长 λ_{max} 后，还需进一步研究在 λ_{max} 处显色剂的浓度、有色溶液的稳定性、溶液的酸度、显色物的组成（通常是配合物）等。此外还要研究干扰物质的影响、反应温度、测定范围、方法适用范围等。本实验包含几个基本条件试验，从中学习吸收光度法测定条件的优化。

三、仪器和试剂

1. 仪器

752 型分光光度计；25型酸度计（或 pHS –25 型酸度计）；容量瓶（50 mL）；吸量管（1 mL，2 mL，5 mL，10 mL）；烧杯（10 mL）；洗耳球。

2. 试剂

1 $mol \cdot L^{-1}$ NaOH 溶液；0.15% 邻二氮菲溶液（新鲜配制）；10% 盐酸羟胺水溶液（新鲜配制）；1 $mol \cdot L^{-1}$ 醋酸钠溶液；$NH_4Fe(SO_4)_2 \cdot 12H_2O$（基准物）；6 $mol \cdot L^{-1}$ HCl 溶液；二次蒸馏水。

四、实验步骤

1. 溶液配制

铁标准溶液（1×10^{-3} $mol \cdot L^{-1}$）：准确称取 0.482 2 g $NH_4Fe(SO_4)_2 \cdot 12H_2O$ 置于烧杯中，加入 HCl 溶液（6 $mol \cdot L^{-1}$）10 mL 和少量水，溶解后，转移至 1 L 容量瓶中，以水稀释至刻度，摇匀。

2. 显色剂浓度的影响

取 8 只 50 mL 容量瓶，各加入铁标准溶液（1×10^{-3} $mol \cdot L^{-1}$）2 mL，10% 盐酸羟胺溶液

10% hydroxylamine hydrochloride solution, mix well. To each flask, add 0.15% 1,10-phenanthroline 0.00 mL, 0.30 mL, 0.80 mL, 1.00 mL, 1.20 mL, 1.50 mL, 2.00 mL and 4.00 mL, respectively, then add 5 mL NaAc solution (1 $mol \cdot L^{-1}$), dilute all the solutions with water to the marks and mix well.

Choose the blank solution without 1,10-phenanthroline as the reference, measure the absorbance of each solution at the selected wavelength in a 1 cm quartz cell, from the plot of the absorbance vs volume of 1,10-phenanthroline, suitable volume of 1,10-phenanthroline can be determined.

3. Stability of colored solutions

Pipet 2.00 mL standard iron solution (1×10^{-3} $mol \cdot L^{-1}$) into a 50 mL volumetric flask. Add 1 mL 10% hydroxylamine hydrochloride solution, 2 mL 0.15% 1,10-phenanthroline and 5 mL 1 $mol \cdot L^{-1}$ NaAc solution, dilute with water to marks and mix well.

Choose the blank solution without standard iron solution as the reference, measure the absorbance at the selected wavelength, then stand for 2 min, 5 min, 10 min, 30 min, 1 h, 2 h, 3 h, measure the absorbance at each time point. From the plot of absorbance vs time curve, the stability of the colored solution can be known.

4. Effect of the pH of solution

Into nine 50 mL volumetric flasks, pipet 2.00 mL standard iron solution (1×10^{-3} $mol \cdot L^{-1}$) and 1 mL 10% hydroxylamine hydrochloride solution, mix well, stand for 2 min then add 2 mL 0.15% 1,10-phenanthroline, mix well. To each flask, pipet 1 $mol \cdot L^{-1}$ NaOH solution 0.00 mL, 0.20 mL, 0.50 mL, 1.00 mL, 1.10 mL, 1.30 mL, 1.50 mL, 2.00 mL and 2.50 mL, respectively, then dilute with water to marks and mix well. Measure pH values with a pH meter.

Choose the solution without standard iron solution as the blank reference, measure the absorbance at the selected wavelength. From the plot of absorbance vs pH, suitable pH range can be determined.

Data Analysis

(1) The curve of absorbance vs volume of 1,10-phenanthroline is plotted, from which a suitable volume of 1,10-phenanthroline can be chosen.

(2) The curve of absorbance vs time is plotted, from which we can discuss the stability of complex.

(3) The curve of absorbance vs pH is plotted, from which we can choose the suitable pH range.

Experiment Guidance

1. Preview instruction

(1) Review the basic knowledge of visible spectrophotometry (colorimetry).

(2) Be familiar with the condition optimization content and selection principle of visible spectrophotometry.

(3) Understand the types of organic and inorganic chromogenic agents.

2. Notes

(1) It takes a long time to determine the stability of colored solutions, so it can be interspersed in other condition tests.

1 mL，摇匀。分别加入 0.15% 邻二氮菲溶液 0.00 mL、0.30 mL、0.80 mL、1.00 mL、1.20 mL、1.50 mL、2.00 mL 及 4.00 mL，然后加入 NaAc 溶液（1 mol·L^{-1}）5 mL，加水稀释至刻度，摇匀。以不含显色剂的溶液作为空白溶液，用 1 cm 比色皿，在选定波长下测定各浓度的吸光度。以邻二氮菲体积为横坐标，吸光度为纵坐标，绘制吸光度 - 显色剂用量曲线，从而确定测定过程中应加入显色剂的体积。

3. 有色溶液的稳定性

取 1 只 50 mL 容量瓶，加入铁标准溶液（1×10^{-3} mol·L^{-1}）2.00 mL，10% 盐酸羟胺溶液 1 mL，0.15% 邻二氮菲溶液 2 mL，NaAc 溶液（1 mol·L^{-1}）5 mL，加水稀释至刻度，摇匀。以不含铁的相应试剂溶液作空白溶液，用 1 cm 比色皿，立刻在选定波长下测定吸光度。然后放置 2 min、5 min、10 min、30 min、1 h、2 h、3 h，测定相应的吸光度。以时间为横坐标，吸光度为纵坐标绘出吸光度 - 时间曲线，从曲线观察有色溶液的稳定时间。

4. 溶液 pH 的影响

取 9 只 50 mL 容量瓶，每只加入标准铁溶液（1×10^{-3} mol·L^{-1}）2.00 mL，10% 盐酸羟胺溶液 1 mL，摇匀，放置 2 min。再加入 0.15% 邻二氮菲溶液 2 mL，摇匀，用吸量管分别加入 NaOH 溶液（1 mol·L^{-1}）0.00 mL、0.20 mL、0.50 mL、1.00 mL、1.10 mL、1.30 mL、1.50 mL、2.00 mL、2.50 mL，加水稀释至刻度，摇匀。用酸度计测定各溶液的 pH。然后，用 1 cm 比色皿，以不含铁的相应的试剂溶液作空白溶液，在所选定波长下测定吸光度。以 pH 为横坐标，吸光度为纵坐标，绘制吸光度 -pH 曲线。找出测定铁的适宜的 pH 范围。

五、数据处理

（1）记录显色剂用量与吸光度的关系，绘制相应曲线，并确定实验应选择的显色剂用量。

（2）记录吸光度随时间变化的曲线，根据曲线讨论该配合物的稳定性。

（3）记录不同 pH 溶液的吸光度，并绘制相应曲线，从中选择最适宜的 pH 范围。

六、实验指导

1. 预习要求

（1）复习可见分光光度法（比色法）的基础知识。

（2）熟悉可见分光光度法测定条件的内容及选择原则。

（3）了解有机及无机显色剂的种类。

2. 注意事项

（1）测定有色溶液稳定性所用时间较长，在进行此项条件试验时，可穿插在其他试验中进行。

（2）遵守平行原则。如配制标准系列溶液时，空白与标准系列溶液均应按相同的操作步骤进行操作，包括加入试剂的量、顺序、时间等应一致。

（3）注意吸收池（比色皿）的配对性。

（4）配制溶液时，必须先加盐酸羟胺溶液，后加邻二氮菲溶液，顺序不能颠倒。

(2) Obey parallel principle. For example, when preparing the standard solutions, the blank and standard solutions should be prepared according to the same steps, including the addition amount, sequence and time.

(3) Match the quartz cells.

(4) When preparing solution, add hydrolamine hydrochloride first, then 1,10-phenanthroline. The order cannot be reversed.

3. Discussion

(1) In this experiment, which reagents should be prepared and added accurately? Which reagent needn't be prepared accurately, but should be added accurately?

(2) Why is NaAc solution used? If we use NaOH solution instead of NaAc solution, what's a disadvantage of this?

(3) Discuss the results of the condition test, then select the proper conditions.

3. 讨论

（1）本实验中，哪些试剂需准确配制和准确加入？哪些试剂不需准确配制，但要准确加入？

（2）实验中，醋酸钠的作用是什么？若用氢氧化钠代替醋酸钠，有什么缺点？

（3）试根据所做的条件试验进行讨论，并选择适宜的测定条件。

Experiment 3.5 Colorimetric Determination of Trace Iron in Water with 1,10-Phenanthroline

Purpose

(1) To master the method of quantitive analysis with 752 spectrophotometer.

(2) To learn the parallel principle.

Principle

The reaction between iron (Ⅱ) and 1,10-phenanthroline to form a red complex serves as a good sensitive method for determining iron. The molar absorptivity of the complex, $[(C_{12}H_8N_2)_3Fe]^{2+}$, is 11 000 $L\cdot mol^{-1}\cdot cm^{-1}$ at 508 nm. The intensity of the color is independent of pH in the range 2 to 9. The complex is very stable and the color intensity doesn't change over very long periods of time. Beer's law is obeyed.

The iron must be in the +2 oxidation state, so a reducing agent is added before the color is developed. Hydroxylamine hydrochloride can be used, and the reaction is as follows:

$$2\,Fe^{3+} + 2NH_2OH + 2OH^- = 2\,Fe^{2+} + N_2 + 4H_2O$$

The pH is adjusted to a value between 6 and 9 by addition of ammonia or sodium acetate.

Instruments and Chemical Reagents

1. Instruments

752 spectrophotometer; volumetric flask (50 mL, 100 mL); pipet (1 mL, 2 mL, 5 mL, 10 mL); volumetric cylinder (100 mL); rubble suction bulb.

2. Chemical reagents

0.15% 1,10-Phenanthroline aqueous solution; 1 $mol\cdot L^{-1}$ sodium acetate solution; 10% hydroxylamine hydrochloride aqueous solution; 6 $mol\cdot L^{-1}$ hydrochloride acid solution; water sample; $NH_4Fe(SO_4)_2\cdot 12H_2O$ (primary standard substance); double-distilled water.

Procedure

1. The preparation of the standard curve

Standard iron solution (100 $\mu g\cdot mL^{-1}$): Weigh accurately 0.100 0 g $NH_4Fe(SO_4)_2\cdot 12H_2O$ to a beaker, add hydrochloride acid solution (6 $mol\cdot L^{-1}$) 10 mL and little distilled water. Dissolve and transfer quantitively to a 1 L volumetric flask, dilute exactly to the mark with distilled water and mix well.

Pipet 5.00 mL standard iron solution (100 $\mu g\cdot mL^{-1}$) into a 100 mL volumetric flask, add hydrochloride acid (6 $mol\cdot L^{-1}$) 2 mL, dilute to the mark with distilled water, mix well. The content of Fe^{2+} is 20.0 $\mu g\cdot mL^{-1}$.

Pipet 0.00 mL, 2.00 mL, 4.00 mL, 6.00 mL, 8.00 mL and 10.00 mL portions of the standard iron solution (20.0 $\mu g\cdot mL^{-1}$) into six 50 mL volumetric flasks. To each flask add 1 mL of the

实验 3.5　邻二氮菲比色法测定水中微量铁含量

一、实验目的

（1）掌握用 752 型分光光度计进行定量测定的方法。

（2）掌握平行测定的原则。

二、实验原理

Fe^{2+} 与邻二氮菲生成极稳定的橙红色配位离子 $[(C_{12}H_8N_2)_3Fe]^{2+}$，此反应灵敏度高，是用于定量测量微量铁离子的良好方法。生成的配合物在 508 nm 处的摩尔吸收系数为 11 000 $L \cdot mol^{-1} \cdot cm^{-1}$，在 pH 2~9 范围内，颜色深度与酸度无关。该配合物稳定，颜色深度在很长时间内不变化，适用于比尔定律。

反应中铁必须以二价离子形式存在，故于显色前加入还原剂盐酸羟胺，反应式如下：

$$2Fe^{3+} + 2NH_2OH + 2OH^- \xlongequal{} 2Fe^{2+} + N_2 + 4H_2O$$

用氨水或醋酸钠调节 pH 为 6~9。

三、仪器和试剂

1. 仪器

752 型分光光度计；容量瓶（50 mL，100 mL）；吸量管（10 mL，5 mL，2 mL，1 mL）；量筒（100 mL）；洗耳球。

2. 试剂

0.15% 邻二氮菲溶液（新鲜配制）；10% 盐酸羟胺溶液（新鲜配制）；1 $mol \cdot L^{-1}$ NaAc 溶液；6 $mol \cdot L^{-1}$ HCl 溶液；水样；$NH_4Fe(SO_4)_2 \cdot 12H_2O$（基准物）；二次蒸馏水。

四、实验步骤

1. 标准曲线的制作

铁标准溶液（100 $\mu g \cdot mL^{-1}$）：准确称取 0.100 0 g $NH_4Fe(SO_4)_2 \cdot 12H_2O$ 置烧杯中，加入 HCl 溶液（6 $mol \cdot L^{-1}$）10 mL 和少量水，溶解后，转移至 1 L 容量瓶中，以水稀释至刻度，摇匀。

用移液管吸取铁标准溶液（100 $\mu g \cdot mL^{-1}$）5.00 mL 于 100 mL 容量瓶中，加入 HCl 溶液（6 $mol \cdot L^{-1}$）2 mL，以水稀释至刻度，摇匀。此溶液含 Fe^{2+} 20.0 $\mu g \cdot mL^{-1}$。

在 6 只 50 mL 容量瓶中，用吸量管分别加入标准铁溶液（20.0 $\mu g \cdot mL^{-1}$）0.00 mL、2.00 mL、4.00 mL、6.00 mL、8.00 mL、10.00 mL，再分别加入 10% 盐酸羟胺溶液 1 mL，0.15% 邻二氮菲溶液 2 mL 和 NaAc 溶液（1 $mol \cdot L^{-1}$）5 mL，以水稀释至刻度，摇匀，静置 10 min。

以空白溶液为对照，用 1 cm 比色皿，在 400~600 nm 不同波长处测定显色后上述铁溶液的吸光度。在最大吸收波长（约 508 nm）附近每隔 2 nm 测一次，在其他波长处每隔 20 nm 测一次，记录不同波长处的吸光度。以波长对吸光度作图，并连成光滑曲线，选择最大吸收波长作为测定波长。

hydroxylamine hydrochloride solution (10%), 2 mL of the 1,10-Phenanthroline solution and 5 mL of the sodium acetate solution, dilute to the marks with distilled water, mix well and stand for 10 min.

Using the blank as the reference, measure the absorbance of one of solutions above at different wavelength from 400 to 600 nm. 1 cm quartze cell is used. Take readings at 20 nm intervals except near the absorbance maximum, where the 2 nm intervals are used. Plot the absorbance vs wavelength. Select the maximum absorbance wavelength for the determination of iron with 1,10-phenanthroline.

At the selected wavelength, measure the absorbance of each standard solution and the sample solution. Plot the standard curve with the absorbance of the standards vs concentration.

2. The determination of water sample

Pipet 5 mL of water into a 50 mL volumetric flask sample. Prepare the sample solution in the same manner as the standard solutions and measure its absorbance. From the absorbance of the unknown solution, calculate the concentration of iron in the original solution.

Data Analysis

Draw the standard curve with A vs c to get the linear equation. The A value of the water sample was substituted into the equation to calculate the iron content of the water sample.

$$A = a + bc(c\text{: } \mu g \cdot mL^{-1})$$

$$c_{Fe}(\mu g \cdot L^{-1}) = c \times 10 \times 1\,000$$

Experiment Guidance

1. Preview instruction

(1) Master the quantitative method of standard curve method.

(2) Be familiar with the preparation method of series standard solution.

(3) Be familiar with the content and significance of parallel principle.

(4) Review pipette and volumetric flask operation methods.

2. Notes

(1) When selecting the measurement wavelength, once the wavelength is changed, the absorbance should be measured after adjusting the 100% transmittance with a blank.

(2) When pipetting standard iron solution, pipetting error should be reduced as much as possible.

(3) Hydroxylamine hydrochloride is easy to be oxidized and cannot be left for a long time.

(4) The experimental conditions of sample and standard solutions should be consistent, and should be measured at the same time.

3. Discussion

(1) Why is the absorbance of the solution to be measured in the range of 0.2~0.7?

(2) When preparing the solutions, can the sequence of adding reagents be changed?

在所选定波长下，以试剂溶液为空白试验，测定各溶液的吸光度。以铁的浓度为横坐标，吸光度为纵坐标，绘制标准曲线。

2. 水样测定

准确吸取水样 5.00 mL（或适量），置于 50 mL 容量瓶中。按上述制备标准曲线的方法配制溶液并测定吸光度，根据测得的吸光度求出水中总铁量。

五、数据处理

以 A–c 绘制标准曲线，得线性方程。将水样的 A 值代入方程，计算水样含铁量：

$$A = a + bc\text{（}c \text{ 的单位为 } \mu g\cdot mL^{-1}\text{）}$$

$$c_{Fe}(\mu g\cdot L^{-1}) = c \times 10 \times 1\,000$$

六、实验指导

1. 预习要求

（1）掌握标准曲线法的定量方法。

（2）熟悉系列标准溶液的配制方法。

（3）熟悉平行原则的内容及意义。

（4）复习移液管的操作及容量瓶的定容方法。

2. 注意事项

（1）在选择测定波长时，每改变一次波长，均需用空白溶液调整 100% 透光率后，再测定吸光度。

（2）移取标准铁溶液时，应尽可能降低移取误差。

（3）盐酸羟胺易氧化，不能久置。

（4）样品和工作曲线测定的实验条件应保持一致，宜同时测定。

3. 讨论

（1）为什么待测溶液的吸光度最好控制在 0.2~0.7？

（2）配制溶液时，添加试剂的顺序可以变化吗？

Experiment 3.6 Determination of Sulfamethoxazol in the Compound Sulfamethoxazole Tablets by the Dual-Wavelength Method

Purpose

(1) To master the principle of the dual-wavelength method for the determination of drug components in compound formulation by spectrophotometry.

(2) To be familiar with the operation procedure of the dual-wavelength method by spectrophotometer.

Principle

In spectrophotometric measurement of a binary-component mixture, the spectra of two components usually overlap with each other. One of them will be interfered by another in spectrometry when it is determined. Based on the spectrum of the determined component, the maximum absorption wavelength is selected as measure wavelength λ_1. According to the absorbance of the interfered component at λ_1, another wavelength λ_2 which is the equal absorbance can be found out to use as reference wavelength (i.e. two equal-absorbance points). Then measure the absorbances of sample solution at two wavelengths, the absorbance difference ΔA of the determined component is directly proportional to its concentration, which can be calculated as follows:

$$\Delta A = A_1 - A_2 = (A_1^{a} + A_1^{b}) - (A_2^{a} + A_2^{b})$$

For $A_1^{b} = A_2^{b}$ at λ_1 and λ_2

$$\Delta A = A_1^{a} - A_2^{a} = (E_1^{a} - E_2^{a})\, c_a l$$

So

$$c_a = \frac{A_1^{a} - A_2^{a}}{(E_1^{a} - E_2^{a})\, l} = \frac{\Delta A}{\Delta E^{a} l}$$

Where A is absorbance; ΔA is the absorbance difference of a and b components; E is the absorption coefficient; ΔE is the absorption coefficient difference of a and b components; l is the cell length, cm; c is the concentration, $mg \cdot mL^{-1}$.

Here a is the determined component, b is the interfered component. Selecting measure wavelength λ_1 and reference wavelength λ_2 must make ΔA large enough for component a, and have equal absorbance for component b.

The given sample is a compound tablets that containing sulfamethoxazole (SMZ) and trimethoprim (TMP). The absorption spectra for two components in 0.1 $mol \cdot L^{-1}$ sodium hydroxide solution is shown in Figure 3–2. The maximum absorption for SMZ occurs at 257 nm, where minimum absorption for TMP locates, and then its equal absorbance also is near 304 nm. So the measure wavelength λ_1 is 257 nm, while the reference wavelength λ_2 is 304 nm.

实验 3.6　双波长法测定复方磺胺甲噁唑片中磺胺甲噁唑的含量

一、实验目的

（1）掌握等吸收双波长法测定复方片剂组分含量的原理及方法。

（2）熟悉利用单波长分光光度计进行双波长法测定。

二、实验原理

在二元混合组分的光度测定中，两组分的吸收光谱经常会相互重叠发生干扰。若要测定其中某一组分的含量，可根据吸收光谱选择被测组分的最大吸收波长作为测量波长 λ_1，利用在 λ_1 处干扰组分的吸光度寻找吸光度相等的另一波长作为参比波长 λ_2（即等吸收点），然后分别在 λ_1 和 λ_2 处测量被测组分的吸光度，根据被测组分在两波长处吸光度的差值 ΔA，通过下式计算可消除干扰组分的影响（即所谓的双波长法）：

$$\Delta A = A_1 - A_2 = (A_1^{a} + A_1^{b}) - (A_2^{a} + A_2^{b})$$

由于 $A_1^{b} = A_2^{b}$，则

$$\Delta A = A_1^{a} - A_2^{a} = (E_1^{a} - E_2^{a})\, c_{a} l$$

所以

$$c_{a} = \frac{A_1^{a} - A_2^{a}}{(E_1^{a} - E_2^{a})\, l} = \frac{\Delta A}{\Delta E^{a} l}$$

式中，A 为吸光度；ΔA 为 a、b 两组分的吸光度差值；E 为比吸收系数；ΔE 为 a、b 两组分的 E 差值；l 为吸收池厚度，cm；c 为溶液浓度，$mg \cdot mL^{-1}$。

此处设 a 为被测组分，b 为干扰组分，所选择的两个波长 λ_1 和 λ_2 应尽量使 a 组分的 ΔA 最大，b 组分在两波长处吸光度相等。

复方磺胺甲噁唑片是含磺胺甲噁唑（SMZ）和甲氧苄啶（TMP）的复方制剂。在 0.1 $mol \cdot L^{-1}$ 氢氧化钠溶液中，SMZ 和 TMP 的吸收光谱重叠如图 3–2 所示，SMZ 在 257 nm 波长处有最大吸收峰，TMP 在此波长吸收最小并在 304 nm 波长附近有一等吸收，故分别选择 λ_1=257 nm 作为测定波长，λ_2 =304 nm 作为参比波长进行测定。

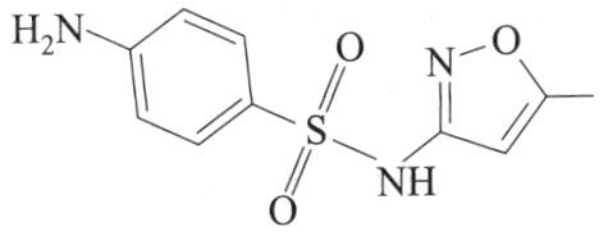

磺胺甲噁唑

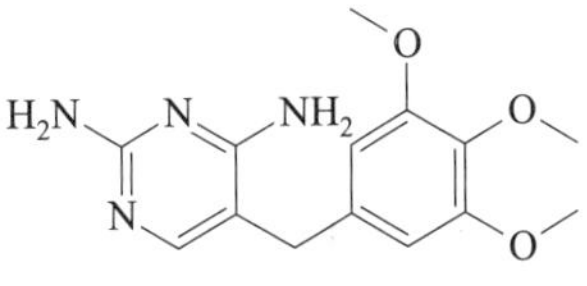

甲氧苄啶

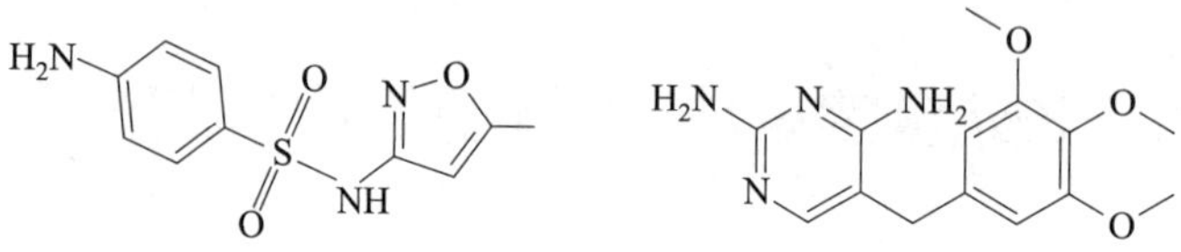

SMZ TMP

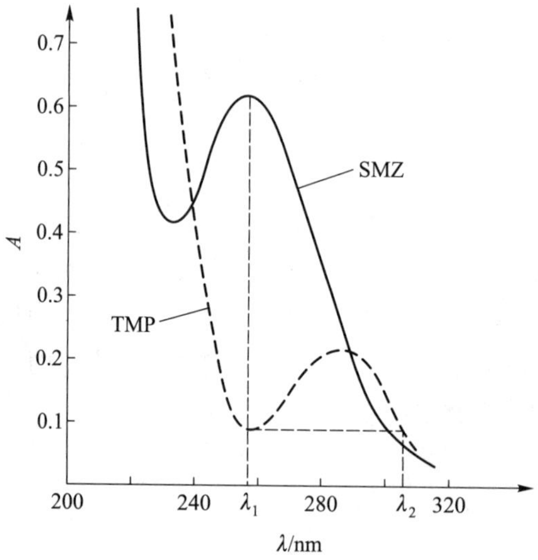

Figure 3-2 Ultraviolet absorption spectra of SMZ and TMP

Instruments and Chemical Reagents

1. Instruments

TU1810 spetrophotometer; 1 cm quartz cell; analytical balance; volumetric flask (100 mL); pipette (2 mL); mortar.

2. Chemical reagents

Sulfamethoxazole (SMZ) reference and trimethoprim (TMP) reference; Sulfamethoxazole tablets (each tablet contains SMZ 0.4 g and TMP 0.08 g); 0.1 mol·L^{-1} sodium hydroxide solution; double-distilled water.

Procedure

1. Preparation of standard solutions and sample solution

(1) TMP standard solution: Weigh accurately 10 mg of TMP previously dried to constant weight at 105 ℃, dissolve in ethanol and dilute to volume 100 mL, transfer 2.00 mL standard solution to 100 mL volumetric flask, dilute with 0.1 mol·L^{-1} sodium hydroxide solution to volume and mix well.

(2) SMZ standard solution: Weigh accurately 50 mg of SMZ previously dried to constant weight at 105 ℃, dissolve in ethanol and dilute to volume 100 mL, transfer 2.00 mL standard solution to 100 mL volumetric flask, dilute with 0.1 mol·L^{-1} sodium hydroxide solution to volume and mix well.

(3) Sample solution: Take 10 tablets, weigh accurately and grind. Weigh accurately a quantity of the powder equivalent to about 50 mg of SMZ and 10 mg of TMP into a 100 mL volumetric flask,

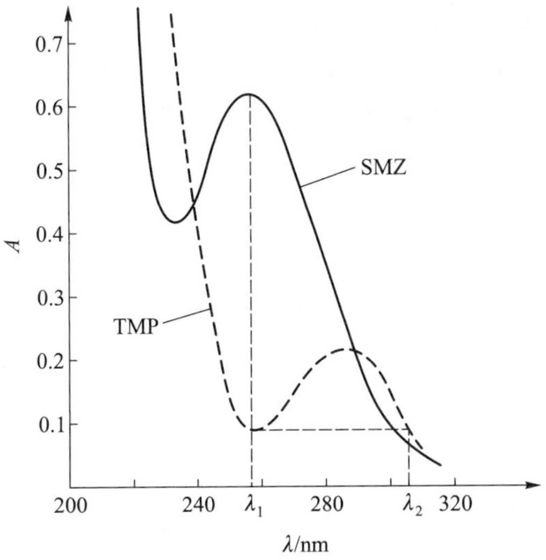

图 3-2　SMZ 和 TMP的紫外吸收光谱

三、仪器和试剂

1. 仪器

TU1810 紫外可见分光光度计；1 cm 石英比色皿；分析天平；容量瓶（100 mL）；移液管（2 mL）；研钵。

2. 试剂

磺胺甲噁唑（SMZ）、甲氧苄啶（TMP）对照品；复方磺胺甲噁唑片（每片含磺胺甲噁唑 0.4 g，甲氧苄啶 0.08 g）；0.1 mol·L^{-1} 氢氧化钠溶液；二次蒸馏水。

四、实验步骤

1. 对照品和样品溶液的配制

（1）TMP对照品溶液：精密称取 105℃干燥至恒重的 TMP 10 mg，用乙醇溶解定容到 100 mL，取上述溶液 2.00 mL 加 0.1 mol·L^{-1} 氢氧化钠溶液定容到 100 mL，摇匀。

（2）SMZ 对照品溶液：精密称取 105 ℃干燥至恒重的 SMZ 50 mg，乙醇溶解定容到 100 mL，取上述溶液 2.00 mL 加 0.1 mol·L^{-1} 氢氧化钠溶液定容到 100 mL，摇匀。

（3）样品溶液：取片剂 10 片，精密称定，研细，精密称取相当于 SMZ 50 mg 与 TMP 10 mg 的粉末，用乙醇溶解，定容到 100 mL，过滤，取出滤液 2.00 mL 加 0.1 mol·L^{-1} 氢氧化钠溶液定容到 100 mL。

2. SMZ、TMP 标准溶液吸收光谱绘制以及等吸收点的寻找和样品的测定

（1）以 0.4% 氢氧化钠溶液为参比溶液，分别取 SMZ、TMP 标准溶液进行波长扫描（220~320 nm），可得到 SMZ、TMP吸收光谱。根据 SMZ 吸收光谱寻找最大吸收波长作为测量波长 λ_1，然后在 λ_1 处分别测量 SMZ 标准溶液、TMP 标准溶液与样品溶液的吸光度，得到 $A_{SMZ}^{\lambda_1}$ 、$A_{TMP}^{\lambda_1}$ 、$A_{样}^{\lambda_1}$ 。

（2）根据测量得到的 $A_{TMP}^{\lambda_1}$ 值，按照 TMP 的吸收光谱在 304 nm 附近寻找 TMP 的等吸收点

dissolve in ethanol and dilute to 100 mL. Filter and transfer successive filtrate 2.00 mL to 100 mL volumetric flask, dilute with 0.1 $mol \cdot L^{-1}$ sodium hydroxide solution to volume and mix well.

2. Plot the absorption spectra of SMZ, TMP, find out the equal-absorbance points and determine the sample solution

(1) Use 0.4% sodium hydroxide solution as blank reference for measurement, transfer a certain volume of SMZ standard solution, TMP standard solution and sample solution in quartz cells, and take them in sample chamber of a spetrophotometer, respectively. Scan wavelengths from 220 nm to 320 nm for SMZ standard solution and TMP standard solution in turn, so as to draw the absorption spectra of SMZ and TMP. Select the maximum absorption wavelength as measure wavelength λ_1 according to SMZ spectrum. Then measure the absorbances of the SMZ standard solution, TMP standard solution and sample solution at λ_1, respectively to obtain $A_{SMZ}^{\lambda_1}$, $A_{TMP}^{\lambda_1}$, and $A_{sample}^{\lambda_1}$.

(2) According to SMZ spectrum and $A_{TMP}^{\lambda_1}$, find out the reference wavelength λ_2 near 304 nm which the absorbance of TMP ($A_{TMP}^{\lambda_2}$ is equal to $A_{TMP}^{\lambda_1}$), then measure the absorbances of the SMZ standard solution and sample solution at λ_2 respectively to obtain $A_{TMP}^{\lambda_2}$ and $A_{sample}^{\lambda_2}$.

Data Analysis

Based on absorbance measured, the content of SMZ can be calculated according to the following equation. The content is certified between 90% and 110% according to Chinese Pharmacopoeia.

$$w_{SMZ}(\%) = \frac{(A_{sample}^{\lambda_1} - A_{sample}^{\lambda_2}) \times m_{SMZ\ standard} \times \text{average weight / per tablet (g)}}{(A_{SMZ}^{\lambda_1} - A_{SMZ}^{\lambda_2}) \times m_{sample} \times 0.4} \times 100\ \%$$

Where $A_{sample}^{\lambda_1}$ and $A_{sample}^{\lambda_2}$ are the absorbance of samples at wavelength λ_1 and λ_2, respectively; $m_{SMZ,standard}$ is the mass of SMZ standard, g; $A_{SMZ}^{\lambda_1}$ and $A_{SMZ}^{\lambda_2}$ are the absorbance of SMZ standard solutions at wavelength λ_1 and λ_2, respectively; m_{sample} is the weight of sample, g.

Experiment Guidance

1. Preview instruction

(1) Review the quantitative method of multi-component by UV-Vis spectroscopy.

(2) Be familiar with the quantitative principle of dual-wavelength method.

(3) Understand the method of sample pretreatment in quantitative determination of drug tablets.

2. Notes

(1) Sample must be dissolved absolutely.

(2) Reference wavelength is confirmed by standard solution, because there are wavelength errors for different instruments.

3. Discussion

(1) How to select measure wavelength and reference wavelength?

(2) If determine the content of SMZ only, does the concentration of TMP need to prepare accurately?

(3) How to determine TMP in compound sulfamethoxazole tablets by the dual-wavelength method?

$A_{TMP}^{\lambda_2}$（$A_{TMP}^{\lambda_1} = A_{TMP}^{\lambda_2}$），以该波长作为参比波长 λ_2 然后在 λ_2 处分别测量 SMZ 标准溶液与样品溶液的吸光度，得到 $A_{SMZ}^{\lambda_2}$ 和 $A_{样}^{\lambda_2}$。

五、数据处理

根据测量得到的吸光度值，按以下公式计算复方磺胺甲噁唑中 SMZ 的标示量百分含量，SMZ 的标示量百分含量在 90%~110% 为合格。

$$w_{SMZ}(\%) = \frac{(A_{样}^{\lambda_1} - A_{样}^{\lambda_2}) \times m_{SMZ对照} \times 平均片重(g)}{(A_{SMZ}^{\lambda_1} - A_{SMZ}^{\lambda_2}) \times m_{样品} \times 0.4} \times 100\ \%$$

式中，$A_{样}^{\lambda_1}$，$A_{样}^{\lambda_2}$分别为波长 λ_1，λ_2 处样品的吸光度；$m_{SMZ对照}$为 SMZ 对照品质量，g；$A_{SMZ}^{\lambda_1}$，$A_{SMZ}^{\lambda_2}$分别为波长 λ_1，λ_2 处 SMZ 标准溶液的吸光度；$m_{样品}$为样品的质量，g。

六、实验指导

1. 预习要求

（1）复习紫外可见光谱法多组分定量方法。

（2）熟悉双波长法定量原理。

（3）了解药物片剂定量测定中的样品预处理方法。

2. 注意事项

（1）注意药物是否完全溶解。

（2）参比波长对测定影响较大，此波长可因仪器不同而异，故用对照品溶液来确定。

3. 讨论

（1）怎样选择适当的测定波长和参比波长？

（2）如果只测定磺胺甲噁唑，甲氧苄啶对照品溶液的浓度是否需准确配制？

（3）如何用双波长法测定复方磺胺甲噁唑片中的甲氧苄啶？

Experiment 3.7 Determination of Adrenalone in Adrenaline by Ultraviolet-visible Spectrophotometry

Purpose

(1) To master the method and principle of the determination of impurity limit by ultraviolet-visible spectrometry.

(2) To be familiar with the operation of ultraviolet-visible spectrophotometer.

Principle

When the ultraviolet absorption spectra of the compounds and impurities are different, the purity can be determined by ultraviolet-visible (UV-Vis) spectrophotometry.

Adrenaline is prepared from adrenalone by hydrogenation and reduction. If the hydrogenation is not complete, it is easy to introduce adrenalone impurities. According to the Chinese Pharmacopoeia (2020th Edition), it is necessary to carry out the limit test for adrenalone. The principle is that the adrenalone has the maximum absorption wavelength at 310 nm, while the main component of adrenaline almost has no absorption at this wavelength (shown in Figure 3-3). Therefore, the aim of limiting the content of corresponding adrenalone can be achieved by limiting the absorbance value at the wavelength of 310 nm. According to the Pharmacopoeia, the absorbance of adrenaline solution (containing 2.0 mg adrenaline per mL) at 310 nm should not exceed 0.05.

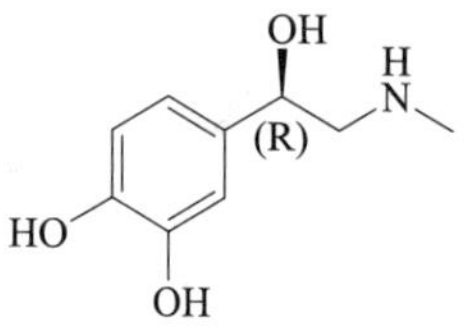

Adrenaline

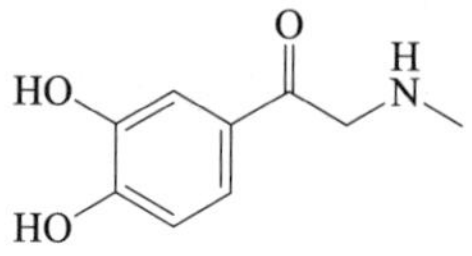

Adrenalone

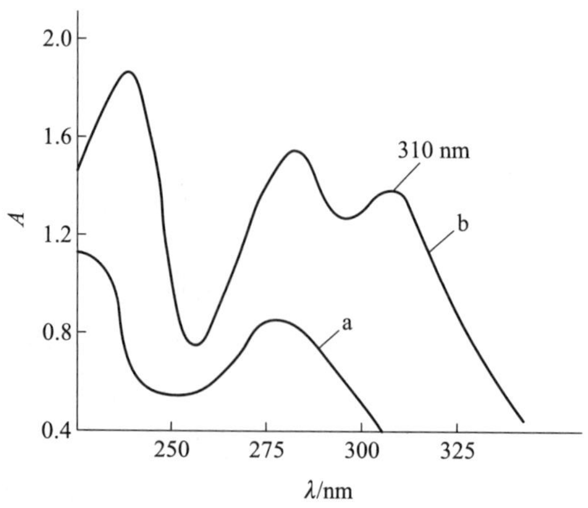

Figure 3-3 Ultraviolet absorption spectra of adrenaline (a) and adrenalone (b)

实验 3.7　紫外－可见分光光度法测定肾上腺素中杂质肾上腺酮的含量

一、实验目的

（1）掌握利用紫外－可见分光光度法测定杂质限量的方法和原理。

（2）熟悉紫外－可见分光光度计的使用。

二、实验原理

当化合物与所含杂质的紫外吸收曲线有差别时，可以利用紫外－可见分光光度法来测定纯度。

肾上腺素在生产中由其酮体经氢化还原制得。若氢化不完全，则易引入酮体杂质。《中国药典》（2020 年版）规定，须对酮体进行限量检查。检查原理是利用酮体在 310 nm 波长有最大吸收，而肾上腺素主成分在此波长几乎无吸收（图 3–3），因此通过限制在 310 nm 波长处的吸光度值，即可达到限制相应酮体含量的目的。《中国药典》规定，肾上腺素溶液（每 1 mL 中含 2.0 mg 肾上腺素）在 310 nm 波长处的吸光度不得超过 0.05。

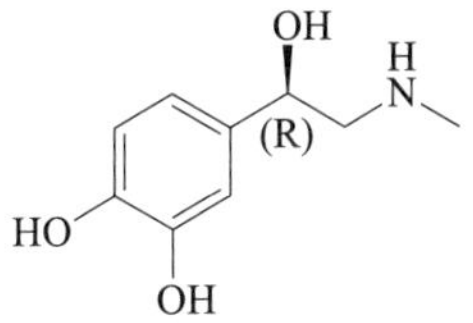

肾上腺素

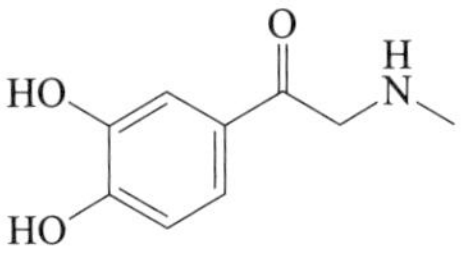

肾上腺酮

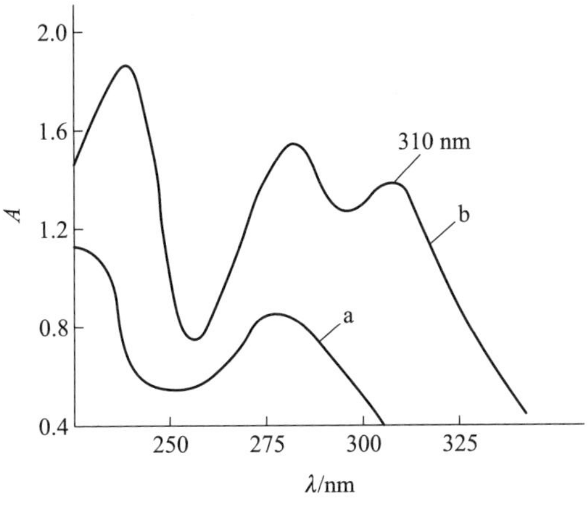

图 3–3　肾上腺素（a）和肾上腺酮（b）的紫外吸收光谱

三、仪器和试剂

1. 仪器

紫外－可见分光光度计；1 cm 石英比色皿；容量瓶（25 mL）；移液管（5 mL）。

Instruments and Chemical Reagents

1. Instruments

Spectrophotometer; volumetric flask (25 mL); pipet (5 mL); quartz cuvette.

2. Chemical reagents

Adrenaline sample; double-distilled water; Hydrochloric acid solution (9 → 2 000): Take 9 mL concentrated hydrochloric acid, dilute to 2 000 mL with distilled water, and mix well.

Procedure

1. Preparation of sample solution

Weigh accurately 0.25 g adrenaline sample into a 25 mL volumetric flask, dissolve and dilute with hydrochloric acid solution (9 → 2 000) to the volume, mix well. Transfer 5 mL of the above solution to a 25 mL volumetric flask, dilute with hydrochloric acid solution (9 → 2 000) to the volume, mix well.

2. Determination of the absorbance

The absorbance of sample solution at 310 nm is determined by using hydrochloric acid solution (9 → 2 000) as reference.

Data Analysis

(1) Determine whether the adrenone in the adrenaline sample meets the requirements.

(2) The specific absorption coefficient of adrenone at 310 nm is 453. Calculate the content of adrenone in the sample.

Experiment Guidance

1. Preview instruction

(1) Review the basic knowledge of purity detection by UV-Vis absorption spectrometry.

(2) Be familiar with the impurity limit measurement method.

2. Notes

(1) For impurities in drug products, a limit should be established, that is, impurities limit detection.

(2) The purity test of compound generally includes impurity test and impurity limit detection. When the absorption spectrum of a pure compound is different from that of the impurities contained in it, the impurities can be examined by UV-Vis absorption spectroscopy.

3. Discussion

(1) What is the impurity limit? According to the principle of this experiment, what is the impurity limit of adrenone in adrenaline according to Chinese Pharmacopoeia (2020 Edition)?

(2) How is adrenone produced? How does it differ from epinephrine in pharmacology?

2. 试剂

肾上腺素样品；二次蒸馏水；盐酸（9 → 2 000）：取浓盐酸 9 mL，用蒸馏水稀释至 2 000 mL，摇匀。

四、实验步骤

1. 溶液的配制

取肾上腺素样品 0.25 g，精密称定，置于 25 mL 容量瓶中，用盐酸（9 → 2 000）溶解并稀释至刻度，摇匀。精密量取上述溶液 5 mL，置于 25 mL 量瓶中，用盐酸（9 → 2 000）溶解并稀释至刻度，摇匀。

2. 吸光度的测定

以盐酸（9 → 2 000）为参比，测定肾上腺素溶液在 310 nm 处的吸光度。

五、数据处理

（1）判断该肾上腺素样品中的肾上腺酮是否符合要求。

（2）已知酮体在 310 nm 时的比吸光系数为 453，计算该样品中酮体的含量。

六、实验指导

1. 预习要求

（1）复习紫外 - 可见分光光度法进行纯度检测的基础知识。

（2）熟悉杂质限量测量方法。

2. 注意事项

（1）对于药品中的杂质，需制定一个允许其存在的限度，即杂质限量检测。

（2）化合物的纯度检测一般包括杂质检查和杂质限量检测。当某一纯化合物的吸收光谱与所含杂质的吸收光谱有差别时，可用紫外 - 可见分光光度法检查杂质。

3. 讨论

（1）什么是杂质限量检测？根据本实验的原理，《中国药典》（2020 年版）规定的肾上腺素中酮体的杂质限量是多少？

（2）肾上腺酮是如何产生的？其与肾上腺素的药理作用有何不同？

Experiment 3.8 Preparation and Spectral Determination of Samples with Different States in Infrared Spectrophotometry

Purpose

(1) To be familiar with the operation of infrared spectrometer.

(2) To master the preparation methods of different physical state samples in infrared spectrometry.

Principle

The advantage of infrared spectrometry is its wide applications. The test substance can be solid, liquid or gas. Different sample preparation techniques should be used for different samples. For the same sample, different sample preparation techniques also can be used and it is possible to obtain different spectra. Therefore, it is necessary to select the appropriate sample preparation method according to the test purpose and requirements in order to obtain accurate and reliable data.

The commonly used preparation methods for solid samples are KBr method, liquid paraffin paste method and film method. The film method is mainly used for the determination of polymer materials. Liquid cell is commonly used for liquid samples. For samples with high boiling point, the sample can also be directly dropped on the salt plate and covered with another salt sheet to form a liquid film between the two blank salt plates. Gas samples are determined by gas cell.

Equipment and Chemical Reagents

1. Equipment

Shimadzu FTIR-8400S infrared spectrophotometer; compression mold; infrared lamp; agate mortar; liquid cell; gas cell.

2. Chemical reagents

Potassium bromide (spectrum reagent); benzoic acid; methyl salicylate; absolute ethanol; polystyrene film; benzene (All are analytical reagents).

Procedure

1. Preparation of infrared samples with different states

(1) Preparation of solid samples

KBr method: take about 1 mg of benzoic acid in a clean agate mortar, add about 200 mg dry KBr powder, and fully grind (the particle size is less than 2 μm). Take out about 80 mg of the mixture, spread it evenly in the compression mold, and make a transparent slice.

Membrane method: the polystyrene film is sandwiched between two salt plates and fixed in the sample holder to determine its infrared spectrum. The polymer can also be dissolved in a suitable solvent (concentration is 1%–20%), and then the solution is dropped on the salt slice and evenly

实验 3.8 红外分光光度法中不同物态样品的制备及光谱测定

一、实验目的

（1）熟悉红外光谱仪的操作规程。

（2）掌握红外光谱分析时各种物态样品的制备方法。

二、实验原理

红外光谱的优点是应用范围非常广泛。测试的对象可以是固体、液体或气体。对不同的样品要采用不同的制样技术，对同一样品，也可以采用不同的制样技术，但得到的光谱可能也有差异。所以要根据测试目的和要求选择合适的制样方法，才能得到准确可靠的测试数据。

固体样品常用的制备方法有溴化钾压片法、液体石蜡研糊法和薄膜法，其中薄膜法主要用于高分子材料的测定。液体样品常用的是液体池法，对于高沸点的样品，也可将样品直接滴在盐片上，盖上另一盐片，使两盐片之间形成一定厚度的液膜，装入样品架固定后进行测定。气体样品采用气体池法测定。

三、仪器和试剂

1. 仪器

岛津 FTIR-8400S 红外光谱仪；压片模具；红外灯；玛瑙研钵；液体池；气体池。

2. 试剂

KBr（光谱纯）；苯甲酸；水杨酸甲酯；无水乙醇；聚苯乙烯薄膜；苯（均为分析纯）。

四、实验步骤

1. 不同物态红外样品的制备

（1）固体样品的制备

溴化钾压片法：取约 1 mg 苯甲酸于干净的玛瑙研钵中，再加约 200 mg 干燥 KBr 粉末，充分研磨（颗粒为 2 μm 以下）。取出约 80 mg 混合物均匀铺洒在干净的压模内，于压片机上制成透明薄片。

薄膜法：将聚苯乙烯薄膜夹在两盐片之间，放入样品架固定，测定其红外图谱。也可将聚合物溶于适当的溶剂中（浓度为 1%~20%），然后将溶液滴在盐片上摊匀，在红外灯下使溶剂逐渐挥发成膜后，盖上另一盐片，装入样品架固定。

（2）液体样品的制备　用氯化钠液体池测定水杨酸甲酯的红外光谱图，测试完毕后要用无水乙醇清洗液体池，并用镜头纸擦干，使用多次后，晶片会有划痕，而且样品中微量的水会溶解晶片，使之下凹，此时需要重新抛光。

（3）气体样品的制备　取出气体池，打开两活塞中任意一个，将其与真空泵相连接；打开真空泵，抽出空气槽内原有的空气，关闭抽气活塞及油泵开关。将气体样品苯接入样槽任意一个入

spread. After the solvent is gradually evaporated under the infrared lamp, another salt slice is covered and fixed in the sample holder.

(2) Preparation of liquid samples The infrared spectrum of methyl salicylate is determined by sodium chloride liquid cell. After the determination, the liquid cell should be cleaned with absolute ethanol and dried with lens paper. After being used for many times, the salt slice will have scratches, and the micro amount of water in the sample will dissolve the salt slice and make it concave. So it needs to be polished.

(3) Preparation of gas samples Take out the gas cell, open any one of the two pistons and connect it with the vacuum pump. Turn on the vacuum pump to extract the original air in the gas cell, and turn off the air extraction piston and pump switch. The benzene gas sample is connected to any inlet of the gas cell, and the piston is opened for injection, control the gas cell pressure within the required range for detection.

2. Plot of infrared spectrum

(1) Turn on the infrared spectrometer, click on the software in the computer to set the experimental parameters.

(2) Determine the air background.

(3) The prepared samples are inserted into the sample holder in turn, and the infrared spectra are measured between 4 000~400 cm^{-1}.

Data Analysis

(1) Correct the baseline and smooth the measured spectrum with the spectrum processing function, mark the wave numbers of the main absorption peaks.

(2) According to the IR spectrum, classify the functional groups.

Experiment Guidance

1. Preview instruction

(1) Review the theoretical knowledge of infrared spectroscopy.

(2) Be familiar with the preparation method of common sample of infrared spectroscopy.

(3) Be familiar with the composition and operation of infrared spectrophotometer.

2. Notes

(1) The concentration of the sample and the thickness of the KBr plate should be appropriate, and special attention should be paid to drying during the grinding, placing and testing process of the sample.

(2) Do not touch the surface of salt slices with hand; clean the salt slices with acetone, wipe them with lens paper or absorbent cotton, and then put them into the dryer for storage.

(3) The liquid sample should be dried and dehydrated before preparation. Common salt slices should not be used for corrosive sample preparation.

3. Discussion

(1) Why is the special sample preparation method used in infrared spectroscopy?

(2) What kind of sample is not suitable for KBr method?

口，打开活塞注样，使气体池压力控制在所需范围内进行检测。

2. 红外光谱的测绘

（1）打开红外光谱仪电源开关，点击计算机软件，设置实验参数。

（2）测定空气背景。

（3）将预先制备好的样品依次放入样品架，在 4 000~400 cm^{-1} 测定红外光谱图。

五、数据处理

（1）采用常规图谱处理功能，对所测图谱进行基线校正及适当的平滑处理，标出主要吸收峰的波数值，保存数据。

（2）根据所得红外光谱图，判别官能团的归属。

六、实验指导

1. 预习要求

（1）复习红外吸收光谱的理论知识。

（2）熟悉红外吸收光谱的常用样品的制备方法。

（3）熟悉红外分光光度计的组成及操作。

2. 注意事项

（1）溴化钾制样品时的浓度和片的厚度应适当，在样品研磨、放置和测试过程中应特别注意干燥。

（2）切不可用手触摸 NaCl、KBr 盐片表面；用丙酮清洗盐片，镜头纸或脱脂棉擦拭后，放入干燥器保存。

（3）液体样品制备前应干燥除水，腐蚀性样品切不可用常规盐片制备。

3. 讨论

（1）为什么红外光谱检测要采用特殊的制样方法？

（2）哪类样品不适宜采用溴化钾压片制样？

Experiment 3.9 Determination of the Drug Chemical Structure by Infrared Spectrophotometry

Purpose

(1) To grasp the method of plotting infrared spectrum and the operation of infrared spectrophotometer.

(2) To grasp the preparation method of solid sample.

Principle

The infrared absorption spectrum is caused by the energy level transition of molecular vibration and rotation. Every functional group in compound has several modes of vibration. These vibrations can absorb light of a particular frequency in middle infrared and has obvious characteristics. Except few special ones, each compound has its respective IR spectrum. So IR spectrophotometry is an important method for qualitative analysis. In this experiment, we will take acetylsalcylie acid as an example to learn the preparation of solid sample and the plotting of IR spectrum.

Instruments and Chemical Reagents

1. Instruments

Shimadzu FTIR-8400S infrared spectrophotometer; infrared lamp; compression mold; agate mortar.

2. Chemical reagents

Acetylsalicylie acid (medicinal); potassium bromide (spectral pure reagent); 95% ethanol (A.R.).

Procedure

Weigh 1~2 mg dry acetylsalicylie acid sample, mix it with 200 mg KBr (spectral pure reagent, dried and sieved by 200 mesh sieve) in an agate mortar and grind the mixture under the infrared lamp. Then pour it into the compression mold (ϕ13mm) and connect the mold with a vacuum pump. At first, pump for 5 min to eliminate moisture and air, and then add pressure to 2 t step by step while pumping and keep for 5 min. Release pressure, take out the mold, an even and transparent sample slice of KBr is obtained. Put it into the sample holder, plot the IR spectrum.

Data Analysis

(1) According to the IR spectrum of sample, find out the vibrational mode style causing characteristic absorption and deduce what functional group the compound may be composed of.

(2) Find out the absorption frequency of the primary functional group of compound in the IR spectrum of sample.

实验 3.9 红外分光光度法测定药物的化学结构

一、实验目的

(1) 了解红外光谱的测绘方法及红外光谱仪的使用方法。

(2) 了解固体样品的制样方法。

二、实验原理

红外吸收光谱是由分子的振动－转动能级跃迁产生的光谱。化合物中每个官能团都有几种振动形式,在中红外区产生相应的吸收峰,因而特征性强。除了极个别化合物外,每种化合物都有其特征红外光谱,所以,红外光谱是定性鉴别的有力手段。本实验以乙酰水杨酸为例,介绍固体样品的制样及红外光谱的测绘方法。

三、仪器与试剂

1. 仪器

岛津 FTIR-8400S 红外光谱仪;红外灯;压片模具;玛瑙研钵。

2. 试剂

乙酰水杨酸(药用);溴化钾(光谱纯);95% 乙醇(分析纯)。

四、实验步骤

称取干燥的乙酰水杨酸样品 1~2 mg 和 200 mg 光谱纯 KBr 粉末(事先干燥,过 200 目筛),置于玛瑙研钵中,在红外灯照射下,研磨均匀,倒入压片模具(ϕ13 mm)中,铺匀,装好模具,连接真空系统,置于油压机上,先抽气 5 min 以除去混在粉末中的湿气及空气,再边抽气边加压至 2 t 并维持约 5 min。除去真空,取下模具,冲出 KBr 样片,即得一均匀透明的薄片,置于样品架上,测绘红外光谱图。

五、数据处理

(1) 根据红外光谱图,找出特征吸收峰的振动形式,并从相关峰推测该化合物所含基团。

(2) 从红外光谱图上找出样品分子中主要基团的吸收峰。

六、实验指导

1. 预习要求

(1) 复习红外吸收光谱的理论知识。

(2) 熟悉红外吸收光谱的常用样品的制备方法,尤其是固体样品。

(3) 熟悉红外分光光度计的使用,掌握红外光谱解析方法。

2. 注意事项

(1) 样品研磨应在红外灯下进行,以防样品吸水。

Experiment Guidance

1. Preview instruction

(1) Review the theoretical knowledge of IR absorption spectrum.

(2) Be familiar with the preparation method of sample, especially solid sample in IR absorption spectrum.

(3) Be familiar with the use of infrared spectrophotometer and grasp its spectrum analysis method.

2. Notes

(1) Grind the sample under infrared light to avoid moisture.

(2) KBr slice with sample should be homogeneous. Otherwise there will be some pocks in the sample slice and the transmittance will be lower.

(3) In the process of sample slice preparation, the pumping time under pressure should not be too long and the vacuum eliminating process should be slow to avoid the crack-up of the sample slice.

(4) According to pharmacopoeia, the transmittance of the baseline should be above 90% and the strongest absorption peak should be below 10%.

(5) When another type infrared spectrophotometer is used, IR spectrum of polystyrene should be plotted firstly using this device so as to check whether its resolution is qualified or not. An infrared spectrophotometer with high resolution can distinguish 7 C—H stretching vibration peaks between 3 100–2 800 cm^{-1}.

3. Discussion

(1) Compare the device structure between IR spectrophotometer and UV spectrophotometer.

(2) Interpret the IR spectrum of acetylsalicylie acid.

(3) What kind of sample can be used to plot IR spectrum?

（2）KBr 压片法制样要均匀，否则制得的样片有麻点，使透光率降低。

（3）制样过程中，加压抽气时间不宜太长。除真空要缓缓除去，以免样片破裂。

（4）《中国药典》规定，测定红外光谱时，基线应控制在 90%透光率以上，最强吸收峰在 10%透光率以下。

（5）若使用不同型号的仪器，应首先用该仪器绘制聚苯乙烯红外光谱图，以检查其分辨率是否符合要求。分辨率高的仪器在 3 100~2 800 cm^{-1} 区间能分出 7 个碳氢伸缩振动峰。

3. 讨论

（1）比较红外光谱仪与紫外分光光度计部件上的差别。

（2）解析乙酰水杨酸的红外光谱图。

（3）测定红外光谱时对样品有什么要求？

Experiment 3.10 Determination of Magnesium in Tap Water by Atomic Absorption Spectrophotometry

Purpose

(1) To master the method of quantitive analysis with atomic absorption spectrometry.

(2) To learn the main performances and operation of atomic absorption spectrometry.

(3) To be familiar with the principle and method of standard curve.

Principle

Atomic absorption spectrophotometry (AAS) is a method for quantitative analysis of determined element using the absorption of ground state atom in vapor to the charactenstic spectral line. Under flame temperature (blow 3 000 K), low concentration of magnesium in tap water will be changed into atomic vapour, which can absorb powerfully the characteristic spectral line (285.2 nm) radiated from the hollow cathode lamp of magnesium. The relationship between the absorbed intensity and atomic vapour concentration for magnesium is as follows:

$$A = Kc$$

Where A is absorbance; K is absorption constant; c is the concentration of magnesium atom, $mg \cdot mL^{-1}$.

The absorbed intensity for the characteristic spectral line is proportional to the low concentration of magnesium in samples under certain conditions. The content of magnesium in sample is usually determined by standard curve method in AAS measurement.

Instruments and Chemical Reagents

1. Instruments

Shimadzu AA7000 atomic absorption spectrophotometer; magnesium element hollow cathode lamp; air compressor; acetylene cylinder; volumetric flask (250 mL, 100 mL); pipet (10 mL, 2 mL).

2. Chemical reagents

Magnesium oxide (A.R.) ; hydrochloric acid (A.R.); deionized water; tap water sample; 1% (V/V) HCl solution.

Procedure

1. Preparation of 0.05 $mg \cdot mL^{-1}$ standard magnesium solution

Magnesium oxide (0.021 g) is weighted accurately to a beaker, dissolved with 1% (V/V) HCl solution and transferred quantitatively to a 250 mL volumetric flask, then dilute to the mark with deionized water, finally mixed well.

2. Preparation of the standard curve

Pipet 10.00 mL standard magnesium solution (0.05 $mg \cdot mL^{-1}$) into a 100 mL volumetric flask,

实验 3.10 原子吸收分光光度法测定自来水中镁的含量

一、实验目的

(1) 掌握原子吸收分光光度法测定样品含量的方法。

(2) 了解原子吸收分光光度计的性能和操作方法。

(3) 熟悉标准曲线法的基本原理和方法。

二、实验原理

原子吸收分光光度法(atomic absorption spectrophotometry,AAS)是利用待测元素原子蒸气中的基态原子对该元素的特征谱线的吸收来测定待测元素的分析方法。自来水中的镁在火焰温度(低于 3 000 K)下通过原子化变成镁原子蒸气,由镁元素空心阴极灯辐射出镁的特征谱线(285.2 nm)被镁原子蒸气强烈吸收,其吸收的强度与样品中镁原子蒸气浓度的关系符合以下关系:

$$A = Kc$$

式中,A 为吸光度;K 为吸收常数;c 为镁原子蒸气浓度,$mg\cdot mL^{-1}$。

在一定实验条件下,可根据低浓度时镁原子蒸气吸收特征谱线的强度与样品中镁的浓度成正比,采用校正曲线法求待测溶液中镁的含量。

三、仪器和试剂

1. 仪器

岛津 AA7000 原子吸收分光光度计;镁元素空心阴极灯;空气压缩机;乙炔钢瓶,容量瓶(250 mL,100 mL);移液管(10 mL,2 mL)。

2. 试剂

氧化镁(分析纯);盐酸(分析纯);去离子水;自来水样品;盐酸(1%,V/V)。

四、实验步骤

1. 0.05 $mg\cdot mL^{-1}$ 镁标准溶液的配制

准确称取 0.021 g 氧化镁置于烧杯中,用 1%(V/V)盐酸溶解后,转移至 250 mL 容量瓶中,以去离子水稀释至刻度,摇匀。

2. 标准曲线的绘制

准确吸取镁标准溶液(0.05 $mg\cdot mL^{-1}$)10.00 mL 置于 100 mL 容量瓶中,用去离子水稀释至刻度,摇匀,此溶液含镁 5 $\mu g\cdot mL^{-1}$。再准确吸取此稀释溶液 0.00 mL、2.00 mL、4.00 mL、6.00 mL、8.00 mL、10. 00 mL 分别置于 6 只 100 mL 容量瓶中,用去离子水稀释至刻度,摇匀。按照选定的

dilute to the mark with deionized water, mix well. The content of magnesium is 5 μg·mL^{-1}. Then, into six 100 mL volumetric flasks, pipet this standard solution of 5 μg·mL^{-1} 0.00 mL, 2.00 mL, 4.00 mL, 6.00mL, 8.00mL and 10.00 mL, respectively, dilute to the marks with deionized water, mixed well, determine their absorbance under the selected operating conditions from low to high concentration. The standard curve of the absorbance versus concentration of the standards is plotted.

3. Determination of tap water sample

Pipet accurately 2.0 mL of tap water (or proper volume) into a 100 mL volumetric flask. Prepare the sample solution in the same manner as the standard solutions and measure its absorbance. Then, calculate the content of magnesium in tap water sample from the absorbance of the unknown solution under the same conditions of standard curve.

4. Operating conditions

The working electric current of hollow cathode lamp: 6.5 mA; slit width: 0.1 mm; wavelength: 285.2 nm; burner height: 9 cm; flow rate of acetylene: 1.0 L·min^{-1}.

5. Instrumentation

(1) Turn on the power switch and high pressure switch (about 500 V high voltage).

(2) Install hollow cathode lamp, accommodate location of the lamp to focus its brightest speckle on the slit and then pre heat it for 30 min.

(3) Adjust the slit-width, burner height and electric current of hollow cathode lamp as well as wavelength to the selected conditions.

(4) Switch on air compressor and acetylene cylinder, regulate flow rate according to the selected conditions, ignite above the burner, and preheat it for 5 min.

(5) Spray with blank solution for 2–3 min, and adjust transmittancy to 100%.

(6) After determination, spray with distilled water for 2–3 min. Close acetylene gas first then shut air switch, turn off the power and turn turnbutton to zero position at last.

Data Analysis

(1) Plot the standard curve, and measure the absorbance of magnesium in the tap water sample, then calculate the amount of magnesium based on standard curve.

(2) Calculate regression equation and correlation coefficient by least square method, and then calculate the concentration of magnesium in the tap water sample based on the absorbance of magnesium .

Experiment Guidance

1. Preview instruction

(1) Review the basic principle and quantitative analysis method of atomic absorption spectrophotometry (AAS).

(2) Be familiar with the composition and operation method of AAS spectrophotometer.

仪器操作条件，由稀到浓依次测定各标准溶液的吸光度。以标准溶液的浓度为横坐标，吸光度为纵坐标，绘制标准曲线。

3. 自来水样品的测定

准确量取自来水样 2.0 mL（或适量），置于 100 mL 容量瓶中。按上述制备标准曲线的方法配制溶液并测定吸光度，然后从标准曲线上求出镁的含量。

4. 仪器操作条件

空心阴极灯工作电流：6.5 mA；狭缝宽度：0.1 mm；波长：285.2 nm；燃烧器高度：9 cm；乙炔流量：1.0 $L \cdot min^{-1}$。

5. 仪器操作

（1）打开电源开关和高压开关（高压在 500 V 左右）。

（2）装上空心阴极灯，调节灯的位置，使灯的最亮斑点聚焦在狭缝上，并预热 30 min。

（3）将狭缝宽度、燃烧器高度、空心阴极灯电流及波长调至所选定的条件。

（4）接通空气压缩机和乙炔钢瓶，按照所选定的条件调节流量，并在燃烧器上方点火，预热 5 min。

（5）用空白溶液喷雾 2~3 min，调节透光率至 100%。

（6）测定完毕后，用蒸馏水喷雾 2~3 min，然后先关闭乙炔，后关闭空气开关，切断电源，将各旋钮转至零位。

五、数据处理

（1）绘制标准曲线。根据测得的标准溶液的吸光度绘制标准曲线，再依据测得的自来水样的吸光度，从标准曲线中查得水中镁的浓度。

（2）标准曲线的回归方程。根据测得的标准溶液的吸光度，用最小二乘法求出回归直线方程式及相关系数，再利用其计算出自来水中镁的浓度。

六、实验指导

1. 预习要求

（1）复习原子吸收分光光度法的基本原理和定量分析方法。

（2）熟悉原子吸收分光光度计的组成和操作方法。

2. 注意事项

（1）原子吸收分光光度法是一种灵敏的分析方法，实验中所使用的试剂纯度应符合要求，玻璃器皿应严格洗涤并用重蒸馏的去离子水充分冲洗。

（2）仪器使用前一般需要预热 10~30 min。

（3）点燃火焰时，应先开空气开关，后开乙炔开关。熄灭火焰时，应先关乙炔开关，后关空气开关，并检查乙炔钢瓶总开关关闭后压力表指针是否回到零位。

（4）因待测元素含量很低，要防止污染、挥发和吸附损失。

2. Notes

(1) AAS is an extremely sensitive method, therefore, reagent purity used in the experiment should meet analytical requirement, and glassware should be washed strictly and rinsed thoroughly with double distilled deionized water.

(2) The instrument should be preheated 10–30 min before operation.

(3) When flame is lighted, air switch should be opened first, then acetylene gas. But when flame is put out, acetylene gas switch should be closed at first, then air switch be shut off. Examine whether pressure gage pointer is back in zero position or not after master switch of acetylene gas cylinder is closed.

(4) Contamination, volatilization and adsorption loss should be prevented because of low content of the determined element.

3. Discussion

(1) Compare the different function of monochromator between AAS and UV-Vis spectrophotometer.

(2) What requirements must light source meet when different elements are determined in AAS?

(3) Which operating conditions are included in AAS measurement? How will they affect the experimental results?

3. 讨论

（1）原子吸收分光光度计与紫外分光光度计中单色器的作用有何不同？

（2）原子吸收分光光度法测定不同元素时，对光源有什么要求？

（3）原子吸收分光光度法操作中包括了哪些实验条件？这些条件是如何影响实验结果的？

Experiment 3.11 Determination of Calcium in Calcium Gluconate Oral Solution by Atomic Absorption Spectrometry

Purpose

(1) To be familiar with the operation of atomic absorption spectrometry.

(2) To master the method of determination of calcium by atomic absorption spectrometry.

Principle

Atomic absorption spectrophotometry (AAS) is a method for quantitative analysis of determined element using the absorption of ground state atom in vapor to the charactenstic spectral line. Under flame temperature (blow 3 000 K), low concentration of calcium in calcium gluconate oral solution will be changed into atomic vapour, which can absorb powerfully the characteristic spectral line radiated from the hollow cathode lamp of calcium. The relationship between the absorbed intensity and atomic vapour concentration for calcium is consistent with Beer's law:

$$A=Kc$$

Where A is absorbance; K is absorption constant; c is the concentration of calcium ion, $\mu g \cdot mL^{-1}$.

The absorbed intensity for the characteristic spectral line is proportional to the low concentration of calcium in samples under selected conditions. The content of calcium in sample is usually determined by standard curve method in AAS measurement.

Instruments and Chemical Reagents

1. Instruments

Shimadzu AA7000 atomic absorption spectrophotometer; calcium element hollow cathode lamp; air compressor; volumetric flask (10 mL, 100 mL); pipette (1 mL, 100 μL) .

2. Chemical reagents

Calcium standard solution (1 000 $\mu g \cdot mL^{-1}$); calcium gluconate oral solution (10 mL/tube which contains 100 mg calcium gluconate per milliliter, equivalent to 9 mg calcium); nitric acid (spectrally purity); ultrapure water.

Procedure

1. Preparation of solutions

Preparation of standard solutions: Pipet 1.00 mL calcium standard solution into a 10 mL volumetric flask, and dilute to the mark with 0.2% nitric acid, then mix well. Into six 10 mL volumetric flasks, pipet 0.000 mL, 0.200 mL, 0.400 mL, 0.600 mL, 0.800 mL, 1.000 mL of the diluted solution, respectively, dilute to the mark with 0.2% nitric acid, and mix well to obtain 0.00 $\mu g \cdot mL^{-1}$, 2.00 $\mu g \cdot mL^{-1}$, 4.00 $\mu g \cdot mL^{-1}$, 6.00 $\mu g \cdot mL^{-1}$, 8.00 $\mu g \cdot mL^{-1}$ and 10.00 $\mu g \cdot mL^{-1}$ solutions.

实验 3.11　原子吸收分光光度法测定葡萄糖酸钙口服液中钙的含量

一、实验目的

（1）进一步熟悉原子吸收分光光度计的性能和操作。

（2）掌握原子吸收分光光度法测定钙含量的方法。

二、实验原理

原子吸收分光光度法（atomic absorption spectrophotometry，AAS）是利用待测元素原子蒸气中的基态原子对该元素的特征谱线的吸收来测定待测元素的分析方法。葡萄糖酸钙口服液中的钙在火焰温度下通过原子化变成钙原子蒸气，由钙元素空心阴极灯辐射出钙的特征谱线被钙原子蒸气强烈吸收，其吸收的强度与样品中钙原子蒸气浓度的关系符合 Beer 定律：

$$A=Kc$$

式中 A 为吸光度；K 为吸收常数；c 为溶液中钙浓度，$\mu g \cdot mL^{-1}$。

在一定实验条件下，可根据低浓度时钙原子蒸气吸收特征谱线的强度与样品中钙的浓度成正比，采用标准曲线法求待测溶液中钙的含量。

三、仪器及试剂

1. 仪器

岛津 AA7000 原子吸收分光光度计；钙元素空心阴极灯；空气压缩机；容量瓶（10 mL，100 mL）；移液枪（1 mL，100 μL）。

2. 试剂

钙元素标准溶液（1 000 $\mu g \cdot mL^{-1}$）；葡萄糖酸钙口服液（规格为 10 mL/ 支，每 mL 含葡萄糖酸钙 100 mg，相当于钙 9 mg）；硝酸（光谱纯）；超纯水。

四、实验步骤

1. 溶液的配制

标准溶液的配制：准确吸取 1.00 mL 钙标准溶液置于 10 mL 容量瓶中，用 0.2% 硝酸稀释至刻度，摇匀。然后取此稀释溶液 0.000 mL、0.200 mL、0.400 mL、0.600 mL、0.800 mL、1.000 mL 置于 10 mL 容量瓶中，用 0.2% 硝酸定容，摇匀，得 0.00 $\mu g \cdot mL^{-1}$、2.00 $\mu g \cdot mL^{-1}$、4.00 $\mu g \cdot mL^{-1}$、6.00 $\mu g \cdot mL^{-1}$、8.00 $\mu g \cdot mL^{-1}$、10.00 $\mu g \cdot mL^{-1}$ 系列标准溶液。

样品溶液的配制：吸取葡萄糖酸钙口服液 2 mL，置 100 mL 容量瓶中，加 0.2% 硝酸定容得葡萄糖酸钙稀释液。吸取稀释液 10 mL，置 500 mL 容量瓶中，加 0.2% 硝酸定容。

Preparation of sample solution: Pipet 2.00 mL calcium gluconate oral solution into a 100 mL volumetric flask, and dilute with 0.2% nitric acid to the mark, then mix well. Into a 500 mL volumetric flasks, pipet 10.00 mL of the diluted solution, and dilute to the mark with 0.2% nitric acid, and mix well.

2. Operating conditions

Wavelength: 422.7 nm; slit width: 0.7 nm; the working electric current of hollow cathode lamp: 10 mA; flame type: air/acetylene; measurement mode: flame continuous method; flow rate of acetylene: 2.0 $L \cdot min^{-1}$; flow rate of air: 15.0 $L \cdot min^{-1}$.

3. Instrumentation

(1) Connect acetylene cylinder and air compressor.

(2) Install the hollow cathode lamp.

(3) Turn on the computer and set the parameters.

(4) Turn on the instrument and connect the instrument with the computer.

(5) Instrument initialization.

(6) Perform spectral line search.

(7) Ignite the fire.

(8) Zero-adjustment: Inlet ultrapure water into the instrument, and wait for about 10 min.

(9) Determination: Each sample is measured for 3 times.

(10) After the determination, rinse with ultrapure water for 5 min.

(11) Click "residual gas combustion", and carry out the operation of flameout, turn off acetylene gas and air according to the prompt. Turn off the computer and the instrument.

4. Determination of standard solutions

According to the working parameters set, the absorbance of the standard solutions is measured from low to high concentration. Each solution is measured for three times, and the average value is calculated.

5. Determination of the sample solution

The absorbance of the sample solution is determined for 3 times and the average value is calculated.

Data Analysis

Plot the standard curve, find out the calcium concentration in the sample solution, and then calculate the calcium content in calcium gluconate oral solution (expressed in $mg \cdot mL^{-1}$).

Experiment Guidance

1. Preview instruction

(1) Review the basic principle and quantitative analysis method of AAS.

(2) Be familiar with the composition and operation method of AA spectrophotometer.

2. 工作参数的设置

检测波长：422.7 nm；狭缝：0.7 nm；灯电流 Low（峰值）：10 mA；火焰类型：空气 / 乙炔；测量模式：火焰连续法；燃气流量：2.0 $L \cdot min^{-1}$；助燃气流量：15.0 $L \cdot min^{-1}$。

3. 仪器操作步骤

（1）接通乙炔钢瓶与空气压缩机。

（2）装上空心阴极灯。

（3）打开计算机，进行参数设定。

（4）打开仪器，在计算机端连接仪器。

（5）仪器自检。

（6）执行谱线搜索。

（7）点火。

（8）进行调零，将溶剂通入仪器中，等待约 10 min。

（9）进行测定，每个样品测定 3 次。

（10）测定完毕后，用超纯水冲洗 5 min。

（11）计算机端点击"余气燃烧"，并根据提示进行熄火、关乙炔气、关空气等操作。关闭计算机并关闭仪器。

4. 标准曲线的绘制

按照设置好的仪器工作参数，在原子吸收分光光度计上由低浓度到高浓度测定标准溶液的吸光度，每个浓度均测定 3 次，取其平均值。

5. 样品溶液的测定

按照设置好的仪器工作参数，在原子吸收分光光度计上测定样品溶液的吸光度，测定 3 次，取其平均值。

五、数据处理

根据测得的标准溶液的吸光度绘制标准曲线，再依据测得的样品溶液的吸光度，从标准曲线上查得样品溶液中钙的浓度，计算葡萄糖酸钙中钙的含量（以 $mg \cdot mL^{-1}$ 表示）。

六、实验指导

1. 预习要求

（1）复习原子吸收分光光度法的基本原理和定量分析方法。

（2）熟悉原子吸收分光光度计的组成和操作方法。

2. 注意事项

（1）原子吸收分光光度法常用定量方法包括标准曲线法、标准加入法和内标法等。当样品基体影响大，无纯净的基体空白，或测定纯物质中极微量元素时，常采用标准加入法。待测溶液的浓度可用计算法或作图法求得。

（2）样品的吸光度应在标准曲线的中部，否则可改变取样的体积。

2. Notes

(1) The quantitative methods commonly used in AAS include standard curve method, standard addition method and internal standard method. When the sample matrix has a great influence, there is no pure matrix blank, or the determination of trace elements in pure substances, the standard addition method is often used. The concentration of the solution to be measured can be calculated or plotted in this method.

(2) The absorbance of the sample should be in the middle of the standard curve, otherwise the volume of the sample can be adjusted.

3. Discussion

(1) What are the main experimental conditions that affect the results in flame atomization AAS?

(2) Why hollow cathode lamp of the element to be measured is used as light source in AAS? Can deuterium lamp or tungsten lamp be used instead? Explain it.

3. 讨论

（1）在火焰原子化法中，影响测定结果的实验条件主要有哪些？

（2）在原子吸收光度法中为什么要用待测元素的空心阴极灯作为光源？可否用氘灯或钨灯代替？为什么？

Experiment 3.12 Determination of Cadmium and Lead in Salvia miltiorrhiza by Inductively Coupled Plasma–Atomic Emission Spectrometry

Purpose

(1) To be familiar with the principle and characteristics of inductively coupled plasma-atomic emission spectrometry.

(2) To understand the operation of inductively coupled plasma atomic emission spectrometry.

Principle

Atomic emission spectrometry (AES) is a physical and chemical method, which is closely related to the structure of atoms. At room temperature, the atoms in the matter are in the ground state. When they are excited by the external energy, the outer electrons will get the energy and excited to the excited state. However, atoms in the excited state are very unstable. The average life of the atoms in the excited state atoms is only 10^{-8} seconds. They will revert to the low energy level or ground state quickly, emitting electromagnetic radiation of corresponding energy and generating emission spectrum.

Because there are many energy levels of atoms or ions and the structures of different elements are different, a series of characteristic spectra of different wavelengths can be generated by the atoms or ions of specific elements. Qualitative analysis is carried out by identifying the characteristic spectral lines of the elements.

The intensity of emission characteristic light is different when the content of elements is different. Based on this, quantitative analysis can be carried out. The quantitative relationship can be expressed by Lomakin–Scherbe formula:

$$I = Ac^{b} \qquad \text{or} \qquad \lg I = b\lg c + \lg A$$

Where A and b are two constants. b is the self-absorption coefficient and the value of b is related to the characteristics of light source, the content of elements to be measured in the sample, the properties of elements and the properties of spectral lines.

Inductively coupled plasma atomic emission spectrometry (ICP-AES) is an atomic emission spectrometry method using inductively coupled high frequency plasma (ICP) as a light source. It consists of high frequency plasma generator, plasma torch, sampling system, splitting system and data processing system. After the sample is brought into the atomization system by carrier gas for atomization, it enters the plasma torch flame in the form of aerosol. The sample is evaporated and excited, and the characteristic spectral lines of the contained elements are emitted. ICP light source has the characteristics of annular channel, high temperature and inert atmosphere, so the ICP-AES method has the advantages of high sensitivity, high precision, good stability, wide linear range, small matrix

实验 3.12　电感耦合等离子体发射光谱测定丹参中镉和铅的含量

一、实验目的

（1）熟悉电感耦合等离子体原子发射光谱定量分析的原理及特点。

（2）了解电感耦合等离子体原子发射光谱仪的基本操作技术。

二、实验原理

原子发射光谱法（atomic emission spectrometry，AES）分析是一种物理化学方法，与原子的结构密切相关。在室温下，物质中的原子处于基态，当受到外界能量作用时，其外层电子获得能量将向高能级跃迁而成为激发态，但激发态原子是很不稳定的，平均寿命一般只有 10^{-8} s，很快又向低能级或基态跃迁，发射出相应能量的电磁辐射，产生发射光谱。

由于原子或离子的能级很多并且不同元素的结构是不同的，因此对特定元素的原子或离子可产生一系列不同波长的特征光谱，可通过识别待测元素的特征谱线存在与否进行定性分析。元素的含量不同时，发射特征光的强弱也不同，据此可进行定量分析，其定量关系可用罗马金－赛伯（Lomakin-Scherbe）公式表示：

$$I = Ac^b \qquad 或 \qquad \lg I = b\lg c + \lg A$$

式中，A、b 是两个常数；b 是自吸系数，b 值与光源特性、样品中待测元素含量、元素性质及谱线性质等因素有关。

电感耦合等离子体原子发射光谱法（inductively coupled plasma-atomic emission spectrometry，ICP-AES）是利用电感耦合高频等离子体（ICP）作为光源的原子发射光谱分析方法。由高频等离子体发生器、等离子炬管、进样系统、分光系统和数据处理系统组成。样品由载气带入雾化系统进行雾化后，以气溶胶形式进入等离子体炬焰中，样品被蒸发和激发，发射出所含元素的特征谱线。ICP 光源具有环形通道、高温和惰性气氛等特点，因此 ICP-AES 法具有灵敏度高、精密度高、稳定性好、线性范围宽、基体效应小、分析速度快以及多元素同时测定等优点。

此外，ICP-AES 分析中自吸现象小，$b \approx 1$，强度与浓度呈线性关系。因此根据光谱线的强度可进行定量分析。

丹参为唇形科植物丹参（Salvia miltiorrhiza Bunge）的干燥根和根茎。具有活血祛瘀、通经止痛等疗效。重金属含量是中药材出口的重要指标之一，ICP-AES 以其独特的优势，已越来越多地用于中药材重金属及微量元素的检测。

三、仪器和试剂

1. 仪器

岛津 ICPE-9000 电感耦合等离子体发射光谱仪；消煮炉；容量瓶（25 mL，100 mL）；移液枪（1 mL）；吸量管（5 mL）。

effect, fast analysis speed and multi-element simultaneous determination.

In ICP-AES analysis, the self-absorption phenomenon is small, $b \approx 1$, and the intensity is linear to the concentration. Therefore, quantitative analysis can be carried out according to the intensity of spectral lines.

Salvia miltiorrhiza is the dry roots and rhizomes of a Salvia miltiorrhiza Bunge plant in the Labiaceae family.It has the effect of promoting blood circulation and removing blood stasis, relieving pain and so on. The content of heavy metals is one of the important indexes for the export of traditional Chinese medicinal materials (TCMs). ICP-AES has been used widely for the detection of heavy metals and trace elements in TCMs owing to its unique advantages.

Instruments and Chemical Reagents

1. Instruments

Shimadzu ICPE-9000 inductively coupled plasma emission spectrometer; digester oven; volumetric flask (25 mL, 100 mL); pipette (1 mL); pipet (5 mL).

2. Chemical reagents

Cd^{2+} standard solution (1 000 mg·L^{1}); Pb^{2+} standard solution (1 000 mg·L^{-1}); Salvia miltiorrhiza sample; HNO_3-$HClO_4$ (4:1) mixed acid solution, ultrapure water.

2% nitric acid solution: take 44 mL concentrated nitric acid, add 2 L ultrapure water, and mix well.

Procedure

1. Preparation of the standard solutions

Preparation of 1.00 μg·mL^{-1} Cd^{2+} standard solution: pipet 0.1 mL Cd^{2+} standard solution (1 000 μg·mL^{-1}) into a 100 mL volumetric flask, dilute to the volume with 2% nitric acid, and mix well.

Preparation of 1.00 μg·mL^{-1} Pb^{2+} standard solution: pipet 0.1 mL Pb^{2+} standard solution (1 000 μg·mL^{-1}) into a 100 mL volumetric flask, dilute to the volume with 2% nitric acid, and mix well.

Preparation of Cd^{2+} and Pb^{2+} standard curve solution: into six 50 mL volumetric flasks, pipet 1.00 μg·mL^{-1} Cd^{2+} standard solution 0.00 mL, 0.10 mL, 0.20 mL, 0.30 mL, 0.50 mL, 0.60 mL and 1.00 μg·mL^{-1} Pb^{2+} standard solution 0.00 mL, 0.50 mL, 1.00mL, 2.00 mL, 3.00 mL and 5.00 mL, respectively. Dilute to the volume with 2% nitric acid, and then mix well to obtain 0.000 μg·mL^{-1} Cd^{2+} + 0.000 μg·mL^{-1} Pb^{2+}, 0.002 0 μg·mL^{-1} Cd^{2+} + 0.010 μg·mL^{-1} Pb^{2+}, 0.004 0 μg·mL^{-1} Cd^{2+} + 0.020 μg·mL^{-1} Pb^{2+}, 0.006 0 μg·mL^{-1} Cd^{2+} + 0.040 μg·mL^{-1} Pb^{2+}, 0.010 0 μg·mL^{-1} Cd^{2+} + 0.060 μg·mL^{-1} Pb^{2+} and 0.012 0 μg·mL^{-1} Cd^{2+} + 0.100 μg·mL^{-1} Pb^{2+} series standard solutions.

2. Preparation of the sample solutions

Wet digestion: weigh accurately 1.0 g salvia miltiorrhiza, add 10 mL HNO_3: $HClO_4$ (4:1) mixed acid solution, soak overnight and shake for several times. Then the mixture is heated in the digester oven the next day. Boil it firstly at 100 ℃ for 1 h, and then at 250 ℃ for 4 h until there is no white smoke and the solution becomes colorless and transparent. Transfer the solution quantitatively into a

2. 试剂

Cd^{2+} 标准溶液（1 000 mg·L^{-1}）；Pb^{2+} 标准溶液（1 000 mg·L^{-1}）；丹参样品；HNO_3–$HClO_4$(体积比 4 ∶ 1）混合酸溶液；超纯水。

2% 稀硝酸：量取 44 mL 浓硝酸，加入 2 L 超纯水，搅拌均匀，即得。

四、实验步骤

1. 标准溶液的配制

1.00 μg·mL^{-1} 镉标准溶液的配制：准确吸取 0.1 mL 镉标准溶液（1 000 μg·mL^{-1}）置于 100 mL 容量瓶中，用 2% 的硝酸稀释至刻度，摇匀。

1.00 μg·mL^{-1} 铅标准溶液的配制：准确吸取 0.1 mL 铅标准溶液（1 000 μg·mL^{-1}）置于 100 mL 容量瓶中，用 2% 的硝酸稀释至刻度，摇匀。

镉及铅标准溶液的配制：在 6 只 50 mL 的容量瓶中，分别加入 1 μg·mL^{-1} 的镉标准溶液 0.00 mL、0.10 mL、0.20 mL、0.30 mL、0.50 mL、0.60 mL 和 1 μg·mL^{-1} 的铅标准溶液 0.00 mL、0.50 mL、1.00 mL、2.00 mL、3.00 mL、5.00 mL，用 2% 硝酸定容，摇匀，得到含 0.000 μg·mL^{-1} 镉 +0.000 μg·mL^{-1} 铅、0.002 0 μg·mL^{-1} 镉 +0.010 μg·mL^{-1} 铅、0.004 0 μg·mL^{-1} 镉 +0.020 μg·mL^{-1} 铅，0.006 0 μg·mL^{-1} 镉 +0.040 μg·mL^{-1} 铅，0.010 0 μg·mL^{-1} 镉 +0.060 μg·mL^{-1} 铅及 0.012 0 μg·mL^{-1} 镉 +0.100 μg·mL^{-1} 铅的系列标准溶液。

2. 样品溶液的配制

湿法消化：分别精密称取丹参样品约 1.0 g，加入 HNO_3:$HClO_4$（4 ∶ 1）混合酸 10 mL，先浸泡过夜，中间摇动数次，于第二天在消煮炉上进行消煮，先 100 ℃低温消煮 1 h，溶液变为澄清后，高温 250 ℃消煮 4 h，直到无白烟冒出，溶液变为无色透明，剩 1~2 mL 为止。将溶液定量转入 25 mL 容量瓶中，超纯水定容，摇匀。以不加样品同法操作的溶液作空白溶液。

3. 工作条件

RF 功率(高频入射功率)：1.2 kW；冷却气流量(等离子气)：10 L·min^{-1}；辅助气流量：0.6 L·min^{-1}；载气流量(雾化气)：0.7 L·min^{-1}。

4. 标准曲线的绘制

记录实验当天测得的六个不同浓度的标准溶液的发射强度 I。

5. 分析谱线的选择

选择分析元素的谱线时，要根据谱线的灵敏度和受干扰的情况来确定。尽量选择灵敏度高且干扰少的谱线作分析线。每次实验选择的分析线可能不同。

6. 样品的测定

在相同条件下记录空白和样品溶液的发射强度 I。

五、数据处理

分别绘制 Cd^{2+}、Pb^{2+} 标准曲线，从标准曲线上求出丹参样品中 Pb^{2+}，Cd^{2+} 的含量。根据《中国药典》（2020 年版）规定的重金属含量标准，Cd^{2+}≤0.3 mg·kg^{-1}，Pb^{2+}≤5.0 mg·kg^{-1}。判断本次实验测得的丹参中重金属 Pb^{2+}、Cd^{2+} 含量是否低于药典规定标准。

25 mL volumetric flask, fix the volume with ultrapure water, and shake well. The solution without sample prepared with the same method is used as the blank solution.

3. Working condition

RF power (high-frequency incident power): 1.2 kW; cooling gas flow (plasma gas): 10 $L \cdot min^{-1}$; auxiliary gas flow: 0.6 $L \cdot min^{-1}$; carrier gas flow (atomization gas): 0.7 $L \cdot min^{-1}$.

4. Determination of standard curve

Measure the intensity *I* of six different concentrations of standard solutions.

5. Selection of analytical spectral lines

When selecting the spectral lines of analytical elements, it is necessary to determine the spectral lines according to their sensitivity and interference. The spectral lines with high sensitivity and less interference should be selected as analytical lines. The analytical lines selected for each experiment may be different.

6. Determination of the sample

Under the same condition, record the intensity *I* of the blank solution and the sample solution.

Data Analysis

Plot the standard curves of Cd^{2+} and Pb^{2+}, respectively, and the contents of Cd^{2+} and Pb^{2+} in salvia miltiorrhiza were calculated from the standard curve. According to the standard for heavy metal content specified in Pharmacopoeia of the People's Republic of China (2020 Edtion), Cd^{2+} is less than 0.3 $mg \cdot kg^{-1}$, and Pb^{2+} is less than 5.0 $mg \cdot kg^{-1}$, respectively. Judge whether the content of Cd^{2+} and Pb^{2+} in salvia miltiorrhiza is lower than the national pharmacopoeia standard.

Experiment Guidance

1. Preview instruction

(1) Review the basic principle and qualitative and quantitative methods of ICP-AES.

(2) Be familiar with the composition and operation of ICP-AES.

(3) Understand the treatment method of Chinese medicinal materials samples by inductively coupled plasma emission spectrometry.

2. Notes

(1) Each element emits more or less characteristic lines. When qualitative analysis is carried out, only a few spectral lines need to be detected. The spectral lines used for analysis are called analytical lines. If only one spectral line of a certain element is observed, it cannot be concluded that the element does exist in the sample, because it may be the interference of other element spectral lines.

(2) Make sure the argon cylinder, water pump, air exhaust and air conditioning are turned on before the plasma can be ignited.

3. Discussion

(1) Summary the advantages and disadvantages of ICP light source.

(2) How is AES generated?

六、实验指导

1. 预习要求

（1）复习电感耦合等离子体发射光谱法的基本原理及定性定量方法。

（2）熟悉电感耦合等离子体发射光谱仪的组成和操作方法。

（3）了解电感耦合等离子体发射光谱法中的中药材样品处理方法。

2. 注意事项

（1）每种元素发射的特征谱线有多有少(多的可达几千条)。当进行定性分析时，只需检出几条谱线即可。进行分析时所使用的谱线称为分析线。如果只见到某元素的一条谱线，不可断定该元素确实存在于样品中，因为有可能是其他元素谱线的干扰。

（2）确保氩气钢瓶、水泵、排风、空调都打开后，才能点燃等离子体。

3. 讨论

（1）简述 ICP 光源的优缺点。

（2）原子发射光谱是如何产生的？

Experiment 3.13 Determination of Heavy Metals in Soil by Inductively Coupled Plasma–Atomic Emission Spectrometry

Purpose

(1) To be familiar with the operation of inductively coupled plasma-atomic emission spectrometry.

(2) To grasp the method of determination of heavy metals in soil by inductively coupled plasma-atomic emission spectrometry.

Principle

With the development of industry, heavy metal pollution in soil is becoming more and more serious. Qualitative and quantitative analysis of heavy metals in soil is of great significance to prevent and control heavy metal pollution, maintain ecological balance and protect people's health. Inductively coupled plasma-atomic emission spectrometry (ICP-AES) is the most widely used method in the determination of heavy metals in soil.

After pretreatment of soil samples with mixed acid solution, ICP-AES is used to simultaneously determine various heavy metals in soil samples. It has the advantages of simple operation, low injection volume and high accuracy.

Instruments and Chemical Reagents

1. Instruments

Shimadzu ICPE-9000 Inductively coupled plasma emission spectrometer; hot plate; Teflon beaker (50 mL); volumetric flask (10 mL, 100 mL); pipette (1 mL).

2. Chemical reagents

Cr, Cu, Ni, Pb and Zn standard solution (1 000 $mg \cdot L^{-1}$); soil sample; concentrated HCl solution (A.R.), concentrated HNO_3 solution (A.R.), $HClO_4$ (A.R.), HF (A.R.), ultrapure water.

Procedure

1. Preparation of the mixed standard solutions

Standard intermediate solution: pipet 1 mL Cr, Cu, Ni, Pb, Zn standard stock solution (1 000 $mg \cdot L^{-1}$) into a 100 mL volumetric flask to obtain the mixed standard intermediate solution with the concentration of 10.0 $mg \cdot L^{-1}$.

Add 0.00, 0.20, 0.40, 0.60, 0.80, 1.00 mL mixed standard intermediate solution (10.0 $mg \cdot L^{-1}$) into six 100 mL volumetric flasks, dilute to the volume with 2% nitric acid, and mix well. The mixed standard series solutions containing 0.000, 0.020, 0.040, 0.060, 0.080 and 0.100 $\mu g \cdot mL^{-1}$ of Cr, Cu, Ni, Pb and Zn are obtained.

2. Preparation of the sample solutions

Weigh accurately 0.2 g soil sample into a 50 mL teflon beaker, add some ultrapure water for

实验 3.13　电感耦合等离子体发射光谱法测定土壤中重金属的含量

一、实验目的

（1）进一步熟悉电感耦合等离子体原子发射光谱仪的操作技术。

（2）掌握电感耦合等离子体原子发射光谱测定土壤中重金属含量的方法。

二、实验原理

随着工业的发展，土壤重金属污染日益严重。对土壤中的重金属进行定性和定量分析，对于防治重金属污染，维持生态平衡，保护人民健康，有着重要意义。在土壤中重金属的分析方法中，目前应用最为广泛的是电感耦合等离子体原子发射光谱法（inductively coupled plasma atomic emission spectrometry，ICP-AES）。

本实验采用混酸溶液对土壤样品预处理后，使用 ICP-AES 同时测定土壤样品中多种重金属，具有操作简便、进样量少、准确度高等优点。

三、仪器和试剂

1. 仪器

岛津 ICPE-9000 电感耦合等离子体发射光谱仪；电子控温热台；聚四氟乙烯烧杯（50 mL）；容量瓶（10 mL，100 mL）；移液枪（1 mL）。

2. 试剂

Cr、Cu、Ni、Pb、Zn 标准溶液（1 000 $mg\cdot L^{-1}$）；土壤样品；浓 HCl 溶液（分析纯）；浓 HNO_3 溶液（分析纯）；$HClO_4$（分析纯）；HF（分析纯）；超纯水。

四、实验步骤

1. 混合标准溶液的配制

标准中间液：分别准确移取 Cr、Cu、Ni、Pb、Zn 标准储备液（1 000 $mg\cdot L^{-1}$）1 mL 于 100 mL 容量瓶中，得溶液浓度为 10.0 $mg\cdot L^{-1}$ 的混合标准中间溶液。

在六只 100 mL 容量瓶中，分别加入混合标准中间溶液（10.0 $mg\cdot L^{-1}$）0.00 mL、0.20 mL、0.40 mL、0.60 mL、0.80 mL、1.00 mL，用 2% 的硝酸定容，摇匀，得到含 Cr、Cu、Ni、Pb、Zn 浓度均为 0.000 $\mu g\cdot mL^{-1}$、0.020 $\mu g\cdot mL^{-1}$、0.040 $\mu g\cdot mL^{-1}$、0.060 $\mu g\cdot mL^{-1}$、0.080 $\mu g\cdot mL^{-1}$、0.100 $\mu g\cdot mL^{-1}$ 的混合标准系列溶液。

2. 样品溶液的配制

精确称取 0.2 g 的土壤样品于 50 mL 聚四氟乙烯烧杯中，加入少量超纯水润湿，再加入 5 mL 王水（$V_{HCl}:V_{HNO_3}=3:1$），1 mL $HClO_4$，5 mL HF，放置于电热板上加热至 180 ℃左右，待白烟冒尽溶液至呈黏稠状时，取下冷却，加入 2 mL HCl 溶液，定量转移至 10 mL 容量瓶中，用超纯水稀释至刻度，摇匀。以不加样品同法操作的溶液作空白溶液。

wetting, then add 5 mL nitrohydrochloric acid (V_{HCl} : V_{HNO_3}= 3 : 1), 1 mL $HClO_4$ and 5 mL HF. Heat the beaker on the hot plate to 180 ℃. When the white smoke is exhausted and the solution is viscous, remove from the hot plate and cool to the room temperature. Add 2 mL HCl solution into the beaker and quantitatively transfer to a 10 mL volumetric flask, dilute with ultrapure water to the volume and mix well. The solution prepared with the same method without sample was used as blank solution.

3. Working condition

RF power (high-frequency incident power): 1.2 kW; cooling gas flow (plasma gas): 15 $L \cdot min^{-1}$; auxiliary gas flow: 0.3 $L \cdot min^{-1}$; carrier gas flow (atomization gas): 0.8 $L \cdot min^{-1}$.

4. Determination of standard curve

Measure the intensity *I* of six different concentrations of the mixed standard solutions.

5. Selection of analytical spectral line

When selecting the spectral lines of analytical elements, it is necessary to determine the spectral lines according to their sensitivity and interference. The spectral lines with high sensitivity and less interference should be selected as analytical lines. The analytical lines selected for each experiment may be different.

6. Determination of the sample

Under the same condition, record the intensity *I* of the blank solution and the sample solution.

Data Analysis

Plot the standard curves of Cr, Cu, Ni, Pb and Zn, respectively, and the contents of the heavy metals in soil sample (expressed in $mg \cdot kg^{-1}$) are calculated from the standard curves.

Experiment Guidance

1. Preview instruction

(1) Review the basic principle and qualitative and quantitative methods of ICP-AES.

(2) Be familiar with the composition and operation of ICP-AES.

(3) Understand common pretreatment methods for soil samples.

2. Notes

(1) In ICP-AES, the sample introduction methods include liquid introduction method, solid introduction method and gas introduction method. Among them, the most commonly used one is liquid introduction method, by which more than 95% of samples introduced to ICP light source. Arc, electric spark, laser ablation and other methods are commonly used in solid introduction method. Hydride generation is commonly used for gas introduction.

(2) Common methods for sample converting to solution are atmospheric digestion, high pressure digestion, microwave digestion, dry ashing and melting.

3. Discussion

(1) Summary the principle of qualitivity and quantitativity of AES.

(2) What are the main interference factors in AES? How can these factors be reduced?

3. 工作条件

RF 功率(高频入射功率):1.2 kW;冷却气流量(等离子气):15 $L\cdot min^{-1}$;辅助气流量:0.3 $L\cdot min^{-1}$;载气流量(雾化气):0.8 $L\cdot min^{-1}$。

4. 标准曲线的绘制

记录六个不同浓度的混合标准系列溶液的强度 I。

5. 分析谱线的选择

选择分析元素的谱线时,要根据谱线的灵敏度和受干扰的情况来确定。尽量选择灵敏度高且干扰少的谱线作分析线。每次实验选择的分析线可能不同。

6. 样品的测定

在相同条件下记录空白和样品溶液的强度 I。

五、数据处理

分别绘制 Cr、Cu、Ni、Pb、Zn 标准曲线,从标准曲线上求出土壤样品中各重金属的含量(以 $mg\cdot kg^{-1}$ 表示)。

六、实验指导

1. 预习要求

(1) 复习电感耦合等离子体发射光谱法的基本原理及定性定量方法。

(2) 熟悉电感耦合等离子体发射光谱仪的组成和操作方法。

(3) 了解土壤样品的常见处理方法。

2. 注意事项

(1) ICP-AES 中,待测样品引入系统的形式有液体引入法、固体引入法和气体引入法。其中,最常用的引入方法为液体引入法,95% 以上的样品通过此法引入 ICP 光源。固体引入法中常用电弧、电火花、激光烧蚀等方法;气体引入常用氢化物发生法。

(2) 待测样品转化为溶液的常用方法:常压消解、高压消解、微波消解、灰化分解及熔融。

3. 讨论

(1) 简述发射光谱法定性和定量的原理。

(2) 原子发射光谱法中主要的干扰因素有哪些? 如何降低这些因素?

Experiment 3.14 Excitation and Emission Spectra of Anthracene by Fluorescence Spectroscopy

Purpose

(1) To understand the structural characteristics of fluorescent molecules.

(2) To master the definition of excitation spectrum and emission spectrum.

(3) To master the three characteristics of fluorescent emission spectrum.

(4) To understand the use of fluorescence spectrophotometer.

Principle

Fluorescence is the light emitted from the lowest vibrational energy level of the first excited singlet to each vibrational energy level of the ground state after the fluorescent molecule absorbs the energy of excitation light. Generally, organic molecules that can emit fluorescence have strong absorbance in UV-Vis range and certain fluorescent quantum efficiency.

Excitation spectrum refers to the spectrum with the fluorescent intensities at a certain wavelength of the organic fluorescent molecule radiated by the different wavelength of exciting light as ordinate and the wavelength of exciting light as abscissa. Emission spectrum refers to the spectrum with the fluorescent intensities at different wavelengths of organic fluorescent molecules irradiated by a certain wavelength of excitation light and the wavelength of the emitted light as abscissa. Excitation spectrum and emission spectrum are two major characteristic spectra in fluorescence analysis. In fluorescence analysis, the maximum excitation wavelength and maximum emission wavelength are often used for qualitative analysis, and the fluorescence intensity at the maximum emission wavelength can also be used for quantitative analysis.

Anthracene is a kind of polycyclic aromatic hydrocarbon, and its molecular structure is shown in the figure below. From the molecular structure, it can be seen that the organic molecule has a long conjugated π bond, which is easy to produce $\pi \rightarrow \pi^*$ electronic transition under UV irradiation. Moreover, the molecule has rigidity and a certain fluorescence quantum yield, so it can emit fluorescence under UV irradiation. In addition, anthracene is a colorless flake crystal, easy to sublimate, insoluble in water, insoluble in ethanol and ether, and soluble in hot benzene. In this experiment, anhydrous ethanol was used as a solvent to investigate the excitation and emission spectra of anthracene.

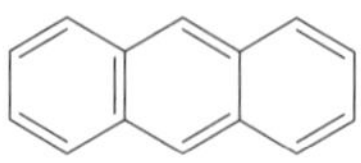

anthracene

Instruments and Chemical Reagents

1. Instruments

Shimadzu RF-6000 fluorescence spectrophotometer; fluorescence quartz cuvette; volumetric flask

实验 3.14　蒽的激发光谱和发射光谱

一、实验目的

（1）了解荧光物质分子的结构特点。

（2）掌握激发光谱和发射光谱的定义。

（3）掌握荧光发射光谱的三大特点。

（4）了解荧光分光光度计的使用方法。

二、实验原理

荧光是物质分子吸收激发光能量后，从第一电子激发单线态的最低振动能级返回至基态的各个振动能级时所发射的光。通常，能够产生荧光发射的有机分子具有强的紫外－可见吸收及一定的荧光效率。

激发光谱是指采用不同波长的激发光照射有机荧光分子，记录该有机荧光分子在某一波长处产生的荧光强度，以记录的荧光强度为纵坐标、激发光的波长为横坐标所绘制的谱图。发射光谱是指采用某一波长的激发光照射有机荧光分子，记录该有机荧光分子在不同波长处产生的荧光强度，以记录的荧光强度为纵坐标、有机荧光分子发射的荧光波长为横坐标所绘制的谱图。激发光谱和发射光谱是荧光分析法中两大特征光谱，在荧光分析法中常利用其最大激发波长和最大发射波长作为定性分析的依据，也可利用在最大发射波长处的荧光强度进行定量分析。

蒽是一种稠环芳烃类物质，其分子结构如下所示。从分子结构可知，该有机分子具有长共轭的 π 键，在紫外光的照射下，容易产生 π–π* 电子跃迁；并且该分子具有刚性和一定的荧光量子产率，因此在紫外光的照射下可产生荧光。此外，蒽是一种无色片状晶体，容易升华，不溶于水，难溶于乙醇和乙醚，易溶于热苯。因此本实验采用无水乙醇作为溶剂，绘制蒽的激发光谱和发射光谱。

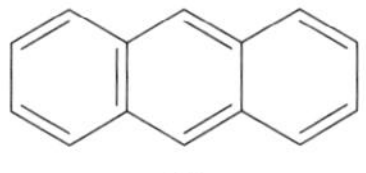

蒽

三、仪器和试剂

1. 仪器

Shimadzu RF-6000 荧光分光光度计；四面通透的石英吸收池；容量瓶（100 mL，50 mL）；移液管（5 mL）。

2. 试剂

蒽（分析纯）；无水乙醇（分析纯）。

(100 mL, 50 mL); pipette (5 mL).

2. Chemical reagents

Anthracene (A.R.); anhydrous ethanol (A.R.).

Procedure

1. Preparation of anthracene solution dissolved in anhydrous ethanol (0.5 mg·L^{-1})

Anthracene stock solution (10 mg·L^{-1}): accurately weigh about 10 mg of anthracene, dissolve with an appropriate amount of anhydrous ethanol. The obtained solution is quantitatively transfer to a 100 mL volumetric flask, dilute to the scale mark with anhydrous ethanol, and shake well. Then 5.00 mL of the above-mentioned solution is transferred into a 50 mL volumetric flask with a pipette and dilute to the mark with absolute ethanol for further use.

Accurately transfer 2.50 mL of anthracene stock solution to a 50 mL volumetric flask by a 5.0 mL pipette and be diluted to the mark with absolute ethanol. Shake it well.

2. Excitation spectra of anthracene

A fluorescence quartz cuvette is loaded with an appropriate amount of anthracene solution (0.5 mg·L^{-1}). Then the fluorescence quartz cuvette is placed into a fluorescence spectrophotometer. After the background signal of the fluorescent spectrophotometer is automatically adjusted to zero, the fluorescent intensities at the wavelength of 400 nm of anthracene solution under the excitation of light with a different wavelength in the range from 200 nm to 400 nm are recorded. The maximum excitation wavelength (λ_{ex}) of anthracene is found from the obtained excitation spectrum.

3. Emission spectrum of anthracene

A fluorescence quartz cuvette is loaded with an appropriate amount of anthracene solutions (0.5 mg·L^{-1}). Then the fluorescence quartz cuvette is placed into a fluorescence spectrophotometer. After the background signal of the fluorescent spectrophotometer is automatically adjusted to zero, the emission spectrum of anthracene is recorded in the range from 350 nm to 550 nm under the radiation of light with the wavelength of 365nm. The maximum emission wavelength (λ_{em}) of anthracene is found from the obtained emission spectrum. Finally, the wavelength of the exciting light source set at 355 nm or 360 nm or 370 nm or 375 nm, respectively, the above-mentioned procedures are carried out repeatedly.

Data Analysis

(1) Plot the excitation spectrum and the emission spectrum of anthracene dissolved in anhydrous ethanol solution (0.5 mg·L^{-1}). Carefully compare the shape of the excitation spectrum and the emission spectrum of anthracene dissolved in anhydrous ethanol.

(2) Plot the emission spectra of anthracene dissolved in anhydrous ethanol solution (0.5 mg·L^{-1}) under the excitation of light with different wavelengths. Investigate the effect of the excitation wavelength on the shape of the emission spectra of dissolved in anhydrous ethanol solution (0.5 mg·L^{-1}).

四、实验步骤

1. 蒽无水乙醇溶液（0.5 mg·L^{-1}）的制备

蒽储备液（10 mg·L^{-1}）：称取 10 mg 蒽置于烧杯中，用适量无水乙醇使其溶解后，定量转移至 100 mL 容量瓶中，并用无水乙醇稀释至刻度，摇匀。然后用移液管精密移取 5.00 mL，置于 50 mL 容量瓶中，并用无水乙醇稀释至刻度，摇匀，备用。

用 5.0 mL 移液管，精密移取 2.50 mL 蒽储备液，置于 50 mL 容量瓶中，用无水乙醇稀释至刻度后，摇匀，即得。

2. 蒽的激发光谱

取适量的蒽无水乙醇溶液（0.5 mg·L^{-1}）置于四面通透的石英吸收池中，然后将该吸收池放入荧光分光光度计的吸收池支架上，盖上暗箱盖。将荧光分光光度计的发射波长设定为 400 nm，经自动调零后，在激发波长为 200~400 nm 的范围内对其激发光谱进行扫描，并通过激发光谱找出蒽的最大激发波长 λ_{ex}。

3. 蒽的发射光谱

取适量的蒽无水乙醇溶液（0.5 mg·L^{-1}）置于四面通透的石英吸收池中，然后将该吸收池放入荧光分光光度计的吸收池支架上，盖上暗箱盖。将荧光分光光度计的激发波长设定为 365 nm，经自动调零后，在发射波长为 350~550 nm 的范围内对其发射光谱进行扫描，并通过其发射光谱找出其最大发射波长 λ_{em}。然后分别将激发波长设置在 355 nm、360 nm、370 nm 以及 375 nm，在 350~550 nm 的范围内对其发射光谱进行扫描。

五、数据处理

1. 绘制蒽无水乙醇溶液（0.5 mg·L^{-1}）的激发光谱以及发射光谱，并仔细对比其激发光谱和发射光谱的形状。

2. 绘制蒽无水乙醇溶液（0.5 mg·L^{-1}）在不同激发波长时的发射光谱，并比较激发光波长对蒽无水乙醇溶液（0.5 mg·L^{-1}）发射光谱的影响。

六、实验指导

1. 预习要求

（1）了解激发光谱和发射光谱的概念。

（2）掌握荧光发射光谱的三大特点。

（3）了解荧光分光光度计的使用方法。

2. 注意事项

（1）Shimadzu RF-6000 荧光分光光度计在使用之前须开机预热，测试样品之前要先打开氙灯。

（2）石英吸收池使用之前须采用蒽无水乙醇溶液（0.5 mg·L^{-1}）对其进行润洗，装溶液时溶液的体积不能超过石英吸收池体积的 3/4，装液后须用擦镜纸对吸收池擦拭干净。

（3）取吸收池时，手握住吸收池的一对棱或者上下底，不能用手直接接触吸收池的光面。

（4）测试完成后关闭氙灯和仪器，并清洗好吸收池。

Experiment Guidance

1. Preview instruction

(1) Understand the concepts of the excitation spectrum and the emission spectrum.

(2) Master the characteristics of the fluorescent emission spectrum.

(3) Understand the usage of a fluorescence spectrophotometer.

2. Notes

(1) Shimadzu RF-6000 fluorescence spectrophotometer should be turned on before use, and the xenon lamp should be turned on before testing samples.

(2) The fluorescence quartz cuvette must be rinsed with anthracene dissolved in absolute ethanol solution (0.5 $mg \cdot L^{-1}$). The volume of the solution filled in the fluorescence quartz cuvette should not exceed 3/4 of the volume of the cuvette. After filling, the cuvette should be wiped clean with lens paper.

(3) Handle the fluorescence quartz cuvette only at the top portions of the side plates. Never touch the optical surfaces of the cuvette with your hands because the leaving film will change the light transmission and reflection characteristics of the cell windows.

(4) After finishing the experiment, you should turn off the xenon lamp and instrument and clean the fluorescence quartz cuvette.

3. Discussion

(1) What are the three characteristics of fluorescent emission spectrum?

(2) Why is the shape of the fluorescent emission spectrum not affected by the wavelength of the excitation light?

(3) Please explain why the excitation and emission spectra of anthracene are mirror symmetry?

3. 讨论

（1）荧光发射光谱的三大特点是什么？

（2）为什么荧光发射光谱的形状与激发波长无关？

（3）请解释蒽的激发光谱和发射光谱为什么呈镜像对称关系。

Experiment 3.15 Determination of Acetylsalicylic Acid and Salicylic Acid in Aspirin Tablets by Fluorescence Analysis

Purpose

(1) To master the method for determining the content of acetylsalicylic acid and salicylic acid in aspirin tablets by fluorescence analysis.

(2) To understand the operation of Shimadzu RF-6000 fluorescence spectrophotometer.

Principle

Acetylsalicylic acid is the active ingredient in aspirin tablets and is easy to hydrolyze to form salicylic acid, so there is more or less salicylic acid in aspirin. Using chloroform as a solvent, the content of acetylsalicylic acid and salicylic acid can be measured by fluorescence analysis. Besides, acetylsalicylic acid and salicylic acid will emit more intense fluorescent in the presence of a small amount of acetic acid.

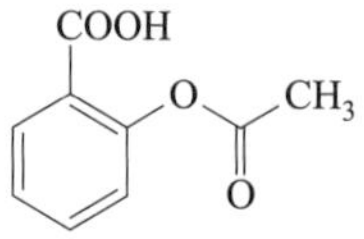

acetylsalicylic acid

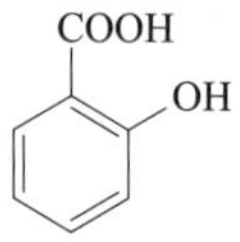

salicylic acid

The excitation and emission spectra of acetylsalicylic acid and salicylic acid in chloroform containing 1.0% acetic acid are shown in Figure 3-4. The fluorescence intensities are proportional to the concentration of molecules at low concentrations.

$$F=Kc$$

Where F represents the measured fluorescence intensity at a certain wavelength; K is a constant; c refers to the concentration of the fluorescent substance, $\mu g \cdot mL^{-1}$.

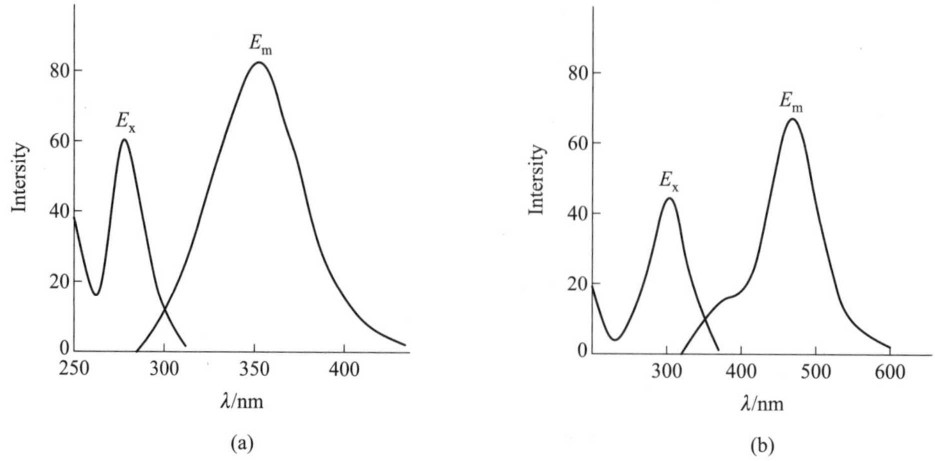

Figure 3-4 Excitation (E_x) and emission (E_m) spectra of acetylsalicylic acid (a) and salicylic acid (b)

实验 3.15　荧光分析法测定阿司匹林片中乙酰水杨酸和水杨酸的含量

一、实验目的

（1）掌握荧光分析法测定药物中乙酰水杨酸和水杨酸的方法。

（2）了解 Shimadzu RF-6000 荧光分光光度计的操作方法。

二、实验原理

阿司匹林片剂中的活性成分乙酰水杨酸水解后生成水杨酸，因此在阿司匹林中都或多或少地存在一些水杨酸。以三氯甲烷作为溶剂，用荧光分析法可测定它们的含量，加入少量醋酸可以增加两者的荧光强度。

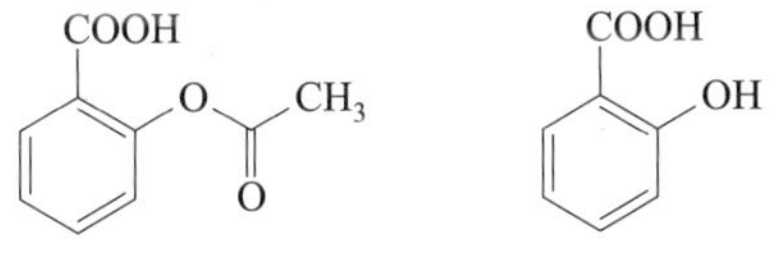

乙酰水杨酸　　水杨酸

在 1.0% 的醋酸－三氯甲烷中，乙酰水杨酸和水杨酸的激发光谱和发射光谱图如图 3-4 所示。在低浓度时，荧光强度与荧光物质的浓度成正比，故有

$$F=Kc$$

式中，F 为某一激发波长照射下测定的荧光物质在某一发射波长处的荧光强度；K 为常数；c 为荧光物质的浓度，$\mu g \cdot mL^{-1}$。

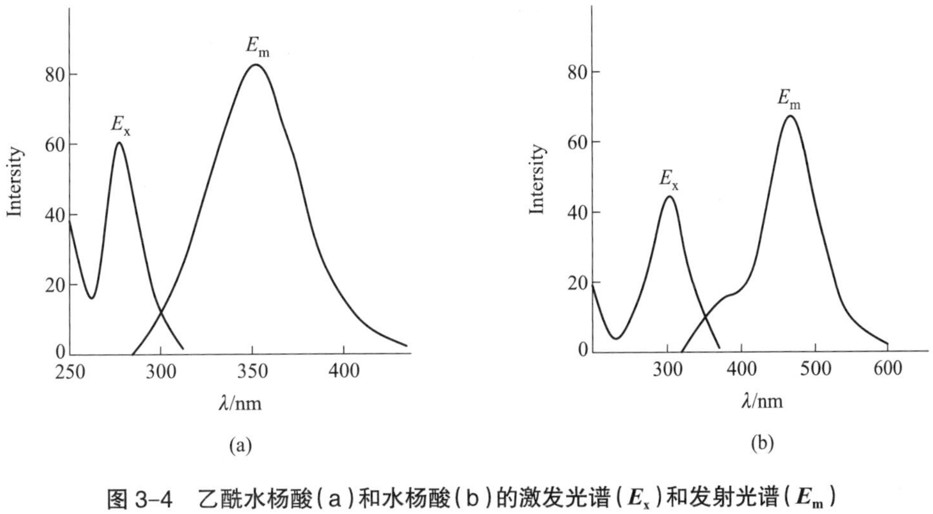

图 3-4　乙酰水杨酸（a）和水杨酸（b）的激发光谱（E_x）和发射光谱（E_m）

The standard curve between the fluorescence intensity and the concentration of analyte is obtained by measuring a series of standard solutions with known concentrations. Using the same method to prepare the sample solution, according to its fluorescence intensity, the content of the fluorescent substance in the sample can be calculated from the standard curve.

Instruments and Chemical Reagents

1. Instruments

Shimadzu RF-6000 fluorescence spectrophotometer; fluorescence quartz cuvette; volumetric flask (1 000 mL, 100 mL, 50 mL); pipette (10 mL); filter paper.

2. Chemical reagents

Acetylsalicylic acid (standard); salicylic acid (standard); aspirin tablet (commercially available); chloroform containing 1.0% acetic acid.

Procedure

1. Preparation of acetylsalicylic acid and salicylic acid stocking solutions

Acetylsalicylic acid stocking solution: weigh 0.4 g of acetylsalicylic acid, and completely dissolve with an appropriate amount of chloroform containing 1.0% acetic acid. The obtained solution is quantitatively transferred to a 1 000 mL volumetric flask, diluted to the scale mark with chloroform containing 1.0% acetic acid, and shake well.

Salicylic acid stocking solution: weigh 0.75 g of salicylic acid, and completely dissolve with an appropriate amount of chloroform containing 1.0% acetic acid. The obtained solution is quantitatively transferred to a 1 000 mL volumetric flask, diluted to the mark with chloroform containing 1.0% acetic acid, and shake well.

2. The excitation and emission spectra of acetylsalicylic acid and salicylic acid

The acetylsalicylic acid and salicylic acid stocking solution are diluted 100 times, respectively. The excitation spectrum and emission spectrum of acetylsalicylic acid and salicylic acid are recorded with the diluted solution by fluorescence spectrophotometer. The maximum excitation wavelength (λ_{ex}) and the maximum emission wavelength (λ_{em}) of acetylsalicylic acid and salicylic acid are found from their excitation and emission spectra, respectively.

3. Plot the standard curve of acetylsalicylic acid and salicylic acid

In five 50 mL volumetric flasks, add 2.00 mL, 4.00 mL, 6.00 mL, 8.00 mL, and 10.00 mL of 4.00 $\mu g \cdot mL^{-1}$ acetyl salicylic acid solution respectively with a pipette, and dilute to the mark with chloroform containing 1.0% acetic acid solvent. The fluorescence intensities the standard curve solutions under the radiation of light with the maximum excitation wavelength are measured at the maximum emission wavelength.

In five 50 mL volumetric flasks, add 2.00 mL, 4.00 mL, 6.00 mL, 8.00 mL, and 10.00 mL of 7.50 $\mu g \cdot mL^{-1}$ salicylic acid solution respectively with a pipette, and dilute to the mark with chloroform containing 1.0% acetic acid solvent. The fluorescence intensities of the standard curve solution under the radiation of light with the maximum excitation wavelength are measured at the maximum emission wavelength.

测定一系列已知浓度的标准溶液，即得到荧光强度－浓度的标准曲线。用相同的方法制备样品溶液，根据其荧光强度，可在标准曲线上求出样品中荧光物质的含量。

三、仪器和试剂

1. 仪器

Shimadzu RF-6000型荧光分光光度计；四面通透的石英吸收池；容量瓶（1 000 mL，100 mL，50 mL）；移液管（10 mL）；滤纸。

2. 试剂

乙酰水杨酸（对照品）；水杨酸（对照品）；阿司匹林片（市售）；1.0% 醋酸－三氯甲烷溶液。

四、实验步骤

1. 乙酰水杨酸、水杨酸储备液的配制

乙酰水杨酸储备液：称取0.4 g乙酰水杨酸，精密称定，置于1 000 mL容量瓶中，用适量的1.0% 醋酸－三氯甲烷溶液使其完全溶解后，并用1.0% 醋酸－三氯甲烷溶液稀释至刻度，摇匀，备用。

水杨酸储备液：称取0.75 g水杨酸，精密称定，置于1 000 mL容量瓶中，用适量的1.0% 醋酸－三氯甲烷溶液使其完全溶解后，并用1.0% 醋酸－三氯甲烷溶液稀释至刻度，摇匀，备用。

2. 绘制乙酰水杨酸和水杨酸的激发光谱和发射光谱

将乙酰水杨酸和水杨酸储备液分别稀释100倍，用稀释后的溶液分别绘制乙酰水杨酸和水杨酸的激发光谱曲线和荧光发射光谱曲线，并分别找出它们的最大激发波长（λ_{ex}）和最大发射波长（λ_{em}）。

3. 乙酰水杨酸和水杨酸标准曲线的绘制

在5只50 mL容量瓶中，用移液管分别加入4.00 $\mu g \cdot mL^{-1}$乙酰水杨酸溶液2.00 mL、4.00 mL、6.00 mL、8.00 mL、10.00 mL，用1.0% 醋酸－三氯甲烷溶液稀释至刻度。分别测量它们的荧光强度。

在5只50 mL容量瓶中，用移液管分别加入7.50 $\mu g \cdot mL^{-1}$水杨酸溶液2.00 mL、4.00 mL、6.00 mL、8.00 mL、10.00 mL，用1.0% 醋酸－三氯甲烷溶液稀释至刻度。分别测量它们的荧光强度。

4. 阿司匹林片中乙酰水杨酸和水杨酸的测定

精密称取0.4 g阿司匹林片粉末，用适量的1.0% 醋酸－三氯甲烷溶液使其完全溶解后，定量转移至100 mL容量瓶中，用1.0% 醋酸－三氯甲烷溶液稀释至刻度。取该溶液迅速通过定量滤纸过滤，取滤液与标准溶液在同样的条件下测定水杨酸的荧光强度。另将该滤液用1.0% 醋酸－三氯甲烷溶液稀释1 000倍，测定乙酰水杨酸的荧光强度。

五、数据处理

（1）分别绘制乙酰水杨酸和水杨酸的激发光谱和发射光谱，并从激发光谱和发射光谱中分别找出它们的最大激发波长和最大发射波长。

（2）分别绘制乙酰水杨酸和水杨酸的标准曲线，并采用最小二乘法求出它们的线性回归方程。

4. Determination of acetylsalicylic acid and salicylic acid in aspirin tablet

Accurately weigh about 0.4 g aspirin tablet powder, dissolve it completely with chloroform containing1.0% acetic acid solvent, transfer it to a 100mL volumetric flask quantitatively, and dilute it to the mark with chloroform containing1.0% acetic acid solvent. The solution is quickly filtered through quantitative filter paper, and the fluorescence intensity of salicylic acid is measured under the same conditions as the standard solution. Besides, the filtrate is diluted 1 000 times with chloroform containing 1.0% acetic acid solvent, and the fluorescence intensity of acetylsalicylic acid is measured.

Data Analysis

(1) Plot the excitation and emission spectra of acetylsalicylic acid and salicylic acid, respectively, and find out their maximum excitation wavelength and maximum emission wavelength from the excitation and emission spectra.

(2) The standard curves of acetylsalicylic acid and salicylic acid are drawn, respectively, and their linear regression equations are obtained by the least square method.

(3) Calculate the concentration of acetylsalicylic acid and salicylic acid in the sample, and calculate their percentage content in aspirin tablets, respectively, and compare the measured value of acetylsalicylic acid with the labeled amount.

Experiment Guidance

1. Preview instruction

(1) Review the basic principle and quantitative method of fluorescence analysis.

(2) Master the fluorescence characteristics and spectral characteristics of acetylsalicylic acid and salicylic acid.

(3) Be familiar with basic operation of fluorescence analyzer.

2. Notes

(1) After dissolving aspirin tablets, the measurement of fluorescent intensities of acetylsalicylic acid and salicylic acid should be completed within 1 hour. Otherwise, the content of acetylsalicylic acid will decrease.

(2) In order to ensure the stability of the light source, the instrument needs to be equipped with a voltage regulator. The xenon lamp needs thousands of volts of high voltage to turn on instantly, so it should be turned on away from the lamp power supply. The high pressure of the xenon lamp will produce ozone. Pay attention to ventilation.

3. Discussion

(1) Is the standard curve a straight line? If not, where to start bending? And explain the reason.

(2) From the excitation and emission spectra of acetylsalicylic acid and salicylic acid, explain the reason why the analytical method is feasible for determining the content of acetylsalicylic acid and salicylic acid in aspirin tablets.

(3) In fluorescence analysis, how to determine the maximum excitation wavelength and maximum emission wavelength? What are the factors that will affect the fluorescence intensities of a substance?

（3）计算样品中乙酰水杨酸和水杨酸的浓度，并求出阿司匹林片剂中乙酰水杨酸和水杨酸的百分含量，并将乙酰水杨酸的测定值与标示量对比。

六、实验指导

1. 预习要求

（1）复习荧光分析法的基本原理及定量方法。

（2）掌握乙酰水杨酸和水杨酸的荧光特性及光谱特点。

（3）熟悉荧光分析仪的基本操作。

2. 注意事项

（1）阿司匹林片溶解后，测定要在 1 h 内完成，否则乙酰水杨酸的含量将降低。

（2）为了保证光源的稳定性，仪器需要配备有稳压器。氙灯点亮瞬间需要上千伏的高压，所以开机时应远离氙灯电源。氙灯点亮瞬间的高压会产生臭氧，注意通风。

3. 讨论

（1）标准曲线是直线吗？若不是，从何处开始弯曲？解释其原因。

（2）从乙酰水杨酸和水杨酸的激发光谱和发射光谱，解释这种分析方法可行的原因。

（3）在荧光分析法中，如何确定待测物的最大激发波长和最大发射波长？影响荧光测定的因素有哪些？

Experiment 3.16 Determination of Aluminum Ion in Water by Fluorescence Analysis

Purpose

(1) To master the quantitative analysis method and experimental operation of standard curve method.

(2) To master the usage of separatory funnel.

Principle

Aluminum is a kind of silver-white light metal with ductility, which has a very wide range of applications in industrial production and daily life. Studies have shown that the abnormal level of aluminum ion (Al^{3+}) in the human body will cause damage to the human body, which may lead to Alzheimer's disease, Parkinson's disease, and other neurological diseases. For example, studies have shown that when the concentration of intracellular aluminum ion is 250-500 $\mu mol \cdot L^{-1}$, it will promote the hyperphosphorylation of tubulin and microtubule-related proteins in brain cells, which is one of the important pathological signals of Alzheimer's disease.

8-hydroxyquinoline is a white or light yellow crystals or crystalline powder, insoluble in water and ether, soluble in ethanol, acetone, chloroform, benzene or dilute acid or alkali. Therefore, Al^{3+} will complex with 8-hydroxyquinoline to form 8-hydroxyquinoline aluminum under weak alkaline conditions, and then 8-hydroxyquinoline aluminum was extracted from alkaline solution with dichloromethane as extraction solvent. Finally, the metal complex can emit green fluorescence under the excitation of ultraviolet light, and the content of Al^{3+} in water is quantitatively analyzed. The specific reaction process is as follows:

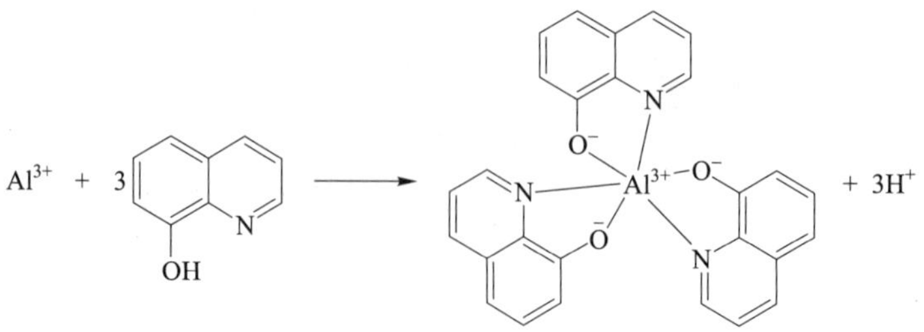

Instruments and Chemical Reagents

1. Instruments

Shimadzu RF-6000 fluorescence spectrophotometer; Fluorescence quartz cuvette; Separatory funnel (250 mL); volumetric flask (250 mL, 100 mL, 50 mL); pipette (10 mL).

2. Chemical reagents

Aluminum potassium sulfate dodecahydrate; 8-hydroxyquinoline; 10% (w/w) glacial acetic acid

实验 3.16 荧光分析法测定水中铝离子的含量

一、实验目的

（1）掌握标准曲线法的定量分析方法及其实验操作。

（2）掌握分液漏斗的使用方法。

二、实验原理

铝是一种银白色的轻金属，具有延展性，在工业生产以及日常生活中具有非常广泛的用途。研究表明人体中铝离子（Al^{3+}）浓度过高会对人体产生损伤，可能产生阿尔茨海默病（老年痴呆症）和帕金森病等神经性疾病。例如，有关研究表明细胞内铝离子的浓度为 250~500 μmol·L^{-1} 时，将促进脑细胞中的微管蛋白和与微管相关的蛋白产生过度磷酸化，而这是阿尔茨海默病的重要病变信号之一。

8- 羟基喹啉是一种白色或淡黄色结晶或结晶性粉末，不溶于水和乙醚，溶于乙醇、丙酮、氯仿、苯或稀酸、稀碱中。因此，本实验在弱碱性条件下将 Al^{3+} 与 8- 羟基喹啉发生络合反应，生成 8- 羟基喹啉铝，然后采用二氯甲烷作为萃取溶剂，将 8- 羟基喹啉铝从碱性溶液中萃取出来。最后利用该金属配合物在紫外光的激发下能够发射出绿色荧光，对水中 Al^{3+} 的含量进行定量分析。具体的反应过程如下：

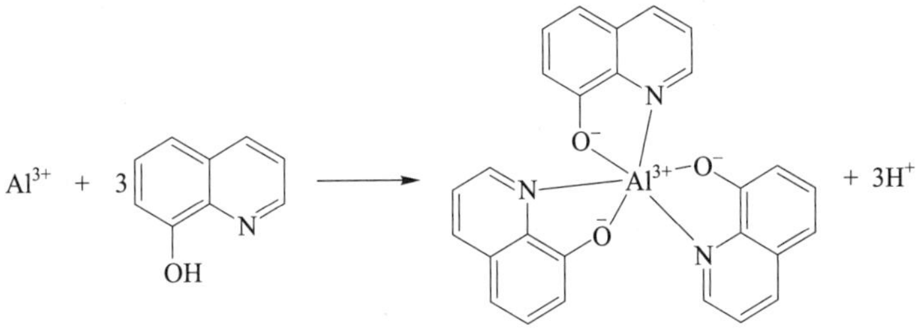

三、仪器和试剂

1. 仪器

Shimadzu RF-6000 荧光分光光度计；四面通透的石英吸收池；分液漏斗（250 mL）；容量瓶（250 mL，100 mL，50 mL）；移液管（10 mL）。

2. 试剂

十二水硫酸铝钾（基准物质）；8- 羟基喹啉（分析纯）；质量分数 10% 的冰醋酸水溶液；质量分数 8% 的氨试液；醋酸铵；二氯甲烷（分析纯）；二次蒸馏水。

四、实验步骤

1. 溶液配制

标准铝离子储备液（1.0 mg·L^{-1}）：取 0.44 g 十二水硫酸铝钾，精密称定，置于烧杯中，用适量

aqueous solution; dichloromethane; redistilled water.

Procedure

1. Preparation of solutions

Standard aluminum ion stocking solution (1.0 mg·L^{-1}): accurately weigh about 0.44 g aluminum potassium sulfate dodecahydrate, and completely dissolve with an appropriate amount of water, and is accurately transferred to a 250 mL volumetric flask. Then the obtained solution is diluted to the volume with water and shake it well. Finally, 1.00 mL of the solution above-mentioned is accurately transferred into a 100 mL volumetric flask with a pipette and is diluted with water to the scale mark and shake well.

8-hydroxyquinoline solution (2.0%): accurately weigh about 2.0 g of 8-hydroxyquinoline, completely dissolved with 60 mL of 10% (w/w) glacial acetic acid aqueous solution. Transfer the obtained solution to a 100 mL volumetric flask, dilute it with water to the volume, and shake it well.

Ammonium acetate buffer solution: weigh 4.5 g of ammonium acetate and put it in a beaker, then add 1.5 mL of 28% (w/w) ammonia test solution, dilute it with an appropriate amount of water, stir it evenly to make ammonium acetate completely dissolved, transfer it quantitatively to a 100 mL volumetric flask, dilute it with water to the volume, and shake it well.

Aluminum ion standard curve solution: to six 100 mL volumetric flasks, add 1.00, 2.00, 3.00, 4.00, 5.00, and 6.00 mL of standard aluminum ion stocking solution (1.0 mg·L^{-1}) into each volumetric flask, respectively, dilute with water to the volume, and shake it well. After the standard curve solution is transferred into a 250 mL separatory funnel, 2.00 mL of 8-hydroxyquinoline solution (2.0%) and 2.00 mL of ammonium acetate buffer solution is added accurately, shake it well. The obtained solution is extracted with 15 mL dichloromethane twice. The extracted dichloromethane solution is transferred into a 50 mL volumetric flask, and is diluted to the volume with dichloromethane, and shake it well.

Water sample solution to be tested: 100 mL of a water sample is transferred into 250 mL separatory funnel and is added by 2.00 mL of 8-hydroxyquinoline solution (2.0%) and 2.00 mL of ammonium acetate buffer solution accurately. After being shaken well, the solution is extracted with 15 mL of dichloromethane twice. The obtained extracted dichloromethane solution is quantitatively transferred into a 50 mL volumetric flask and is diluted to the volume by dichloromethane.

2. Emission spectra of 8-hydroxyquinoline aluminum

An appropriate amount of aluminum ion standard curve solution is loaded into a fluorescence quartz cuvette. Then the fluorescence quartz cuvette is placed into a fluorescence spectrophotometer. After automatically adjusting the background signal to zero, the emission spectrum of the aluminum ion standard curve solution from 400 nm to 600 nm is recorded under the radiation of the ultraviolet light with the wavelength of 365 nm by the fluorescence spectrophotometer. From the emission spectrum of the aluminum ion standard curve solution, the maximum emission wavelength (λ_{em}) is obtained.

3. Determination of fluorescent intensity of aluminum ion standard curve solution and water sample solution

The fluorescent intensities at the maximum emission wavelength of the aluminum ion standard

水使其溶解后，定量转移至 250 mL 容量瓶中，并用水稀释至刻度，摇匀。然后精密移取该溶液 1.00 mL 置于 100 mL 容量瓶中，用水稀释至刻度，摇匀，即得。

8- 羟基喹啉溶液（2.0%）：称取 2.0 g 8- 羟基喹啉，置于烧杯中，然后加入 60 mL 10% 冰醋酸水溶液使其完全溶解后，将该溶液定量转移至 100 mL 容量瓶中，并用于水稀释至刻度，摇匀，即得。

醋酸铵缓冲溶液：称取 4.5 g 醋酸铵置于烧杯中，然后加入 1.5 mL 28% 氨试液，并用适量水稀释后，搅拌均匀使醋酸铵完全溶解后，定量转移至 100 mL 容量瓶中，并用水稀释至刻度，摇匀，即得。

铝离子标准曲线溶液：取 6 个 100 mL 容量瓶，然后在每个容量瓶中分别精密加入 1.00 mL、2.00 mL、3.00 mL、4.00 mL、5.00 mL 和 6.00 mL 的标准铝离子储备液（1.0 $mg\cdot L^{-1}$），并用水稀释至刻度，摇匀。分别将该溶液置于 250 mL 分液漏斗中，并精密加入 2.00 mL 8- 羟基喹啉溶液（2.0%）和 2.00 mL 醋酸铵缓冲溶液，摇匀后，用 30 mL 二氯甲烷分两次萃取，每次 15 mL。萃取后的二氯甲烷溶液置于 50 mL 容量瓶中，并用二氯甲烷稀释至刻度，摇匀，即得铝离子标准曲线溶液。

水样待测溶液：取 100 mL 水样置于 250 mL 分液漏斗中，并精密加入 2.00 mL 8- 羟基喹啉溶液（2.0%）和 2.00 mL 醋酸铵缓冲溶液，摇匀后，用 30 mL 二氯甲烷分两次萃取，每次 15 mL。萃取后的二氯甲烷溶液置于 50 mL 容量瓶中，并用二氯甲烷稀释至刻度，摇匀即得水样待测溶液。

2. 8- 羟基喹啉铝的发射光谱

取一份铝离子标准曲线溶液置于四面通透的石英吸收池中，然后将该吸收池放入荧光分光光度计的吸收池支架上，盖上暗箱盖。将荧光分光光度计的激发波长设定为 365 nm，经自动调零后，在发射波长为 400~600 nm 的范围内对其进行发射光谱扫描，并通过其发射光谱找出其最大发射波长 λ_{em}。

3. 铝离子标准曲线溶液和水样待测溶液荧光强度的测定

分别取铝离子标准曲线溶液以及水样待测溶液，置于四面通透的石英吸收池中，然后将该吸收池放入荧光分光光度计的吸收池支架下，盖上暗箱盖。采用 365 nm 的激发波长，测定各溶液在其最大发射波长 λ_{em} 处的荧光强度。

五、数据处理

（1）绘制铝离子标准曲线溶液的荧光强度与其浓度的线性关系图，并采用最小二乘法求出其线性回归方程。

（2）采用作图法以及线性回归方程求出水样中铝离子的浓度。

六、实验指导

1. 预习要求

（1）了解标准曲线法的原理和计算方法。

（2）熟悉荧光分析法测定水样中铝离子浓度的原理和步骤。

2. 注意事项

（1）本实验所使用的容量瓶和分液漏斗较多，一定要记得编号。

curve solution and the water sample solution are measured under the excitation of the ultraviolet light with the wavelength of 365 nm, respectively by fluorescence spectrophotometer.

Data Analysis

1. Plot the standard curve between fluorescence intensity and concentration of the aluminum ion standard curve solution. Obtain the linear regression equation of the standard curve by the least-square method.

2. The concentration of the aluminum ion in the water sample can be calculated according to the obtained linear regression equation.

Experiment Guidance

1. Preview instruction

(1) Understand the principle and calculation of the standard curve method.

(2) Be familiar with the principle and procedures of determining aluminum ion in water sample by fluorescence analysis.

2. Notes

(1) There are many volumetric flasks and separatory funnels used in this experiment, so we must mark them.

(2) Pay attention to the use of separatory funnel.

(3) The Parallel Law, which means the addition order of reagents and the reaction condition must be consistent, should be obeyed during the experiment.

3. Discussion

(1) Why does the fluorescence intensity of 8-hydroxyquinoline increase after the aluminum ion is complex with 8-hydroxyquinoline?

(2) If tartrate or citrate anion exists in the aqueous solution, does it affect the experimental results? If so, will there be a positive error or a negative error? Why?

（2）注意分液漏斗的使用方法。

（3）实验过程中要遵守“平行原则”，试剂的加入顺序和反应时间要一致。

3. 讨论

（1）为什么铝离子与 8- 羟基喹啉发生络合反应后会使 8- 羟基喹啉的荧光强度增强？

（2）水溶液中如果存在酒石酸根或柠檬酸根阴离子时，对实验结果是否有影响？如有影响，将产生正误差还是负误差，为什么？

Experiment 3.17 Assay of Reserpine Tablets by Fluorescence Analysis

Purpose

(1) To master the quantitative analysis method of contrast method.

(2) To master the calculation method of the percentage content of labeled amount in drug.

(3) To understand the experimental method for determining the percentage content of labeled amount in reserpine tablets.

Principle

Reserpine tablets are colored tablets or sugar-coated tablets, which are white or light-brown after removing the coating. The active ingredient in reserpine tablets is reserpine, the chemical name, the molecular formula, and the relative molecular weight of which are Methyl 18*β*-hydroxy-11,17*α*-dimethoxy-3*β*,20*α*-yohimban-16*β*-carboxylate 3,4,5-trimethoxybenzoate, $C_{33}H_{40}N_2O_9$, and 608.69, respectively. Pharmacological studies have shown that reserpine has the effects of anti-hypertension, slowing heart rate and inhibiting the central nervous system by exhausting norepinephrine in peripheral cross-sensory nerve terminals, catecholamine, and 5-hydroxytryptamine in the heart, brain and other tissues. Therefore, reserpine tablets are mainly used as antihypertensive drugs in the clinic.

According to Chinese Pharmacopoeia (Volume Ⅱ, 2020 Edition), the percentage content of labeled amount in reserpine tablets was determined by fluorescence analysis. The principle is that the 2,3,4,9-tetrahydro-7-methoxy-1h-pyridoindole group in reserpine molecular structure can be oxidized by vanadium pentoxide to convert the non-fluorescent reserpine into 3,4-dihydroreserpine with yellow-green fluorescence emission.

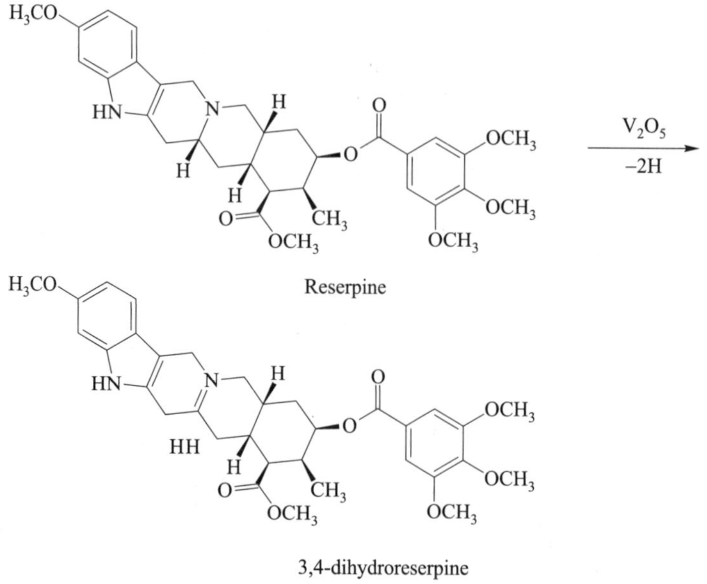

3,4-dihydroreserpine

实验 3.17　荧光分析法测定利血平片的含量

一、实验目的

（1）掌握对比法的定量分析方法。

（2）掌握标示量百分含量的计算方法。

（3）了解测定利血平片中标示量百分含量的实验方法。

二、实验原理

利血平片为着色片或糖衣片，除去包衣后显白色或淡褐色。其主要活性成分为利血平（化学名为 18*β*-（3，4，5- 三甲氧基苯甲酰氧基）-11，17*α*- 二甲氧基 -3*β*，20*α*- 育亨烷 -16*β*- 甲酸甲酯，分子式为 $C_{33}H_{40}N_2O_9$，相对分子质量为 608.69）。药理学研究表明利血平通过耗竭周围交叉感神经末梢的去甲肾上腺素，心、脑及其他组织中的儿茶酚胺和 5- 羟基色胺，具有抗高血压、减慢心率和抑制中枢神经系统的作用。因此，临床上利血平片主要作为抗高血压药物使用。

《中国药典》（2020 年版）二部规定，利血平片的标示量百分含量采用荧光分析法进行测定。其测定的原理是利用利血平分子结构中的 2，3，4，9- 四氢 -7- 甲氧基 -1*H*- 吡啶并吲哚官能团能被五氧化二钒氧化，将无荧光的利血平转换成具有黄绿色荧光发射的 3，4- 二去氢利血平，具体的反应过程如下：

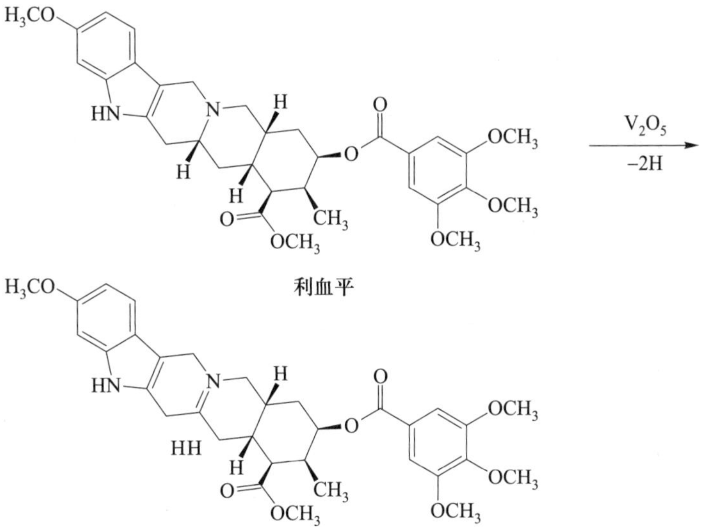

利血平

3，4- 二去氢利血平

此外，《中国药典》（2020 年版）二部中对于利血平片的含量测定采用对比法进行计算，规定利血平的含量应为标示量的 90.0%~110.0%，具体的计算公式如下：

$$
\text{标示量百分含量}(\%)=\frac{\dfrac{F_i}{F_s}\times c_s\times\dfrac{25\ \text{mL}}{10\ \text{mL}}\times 100\ \text{mL}}{0.25\ \text{mg}\times\dfrac{S}{\text{平均片重}}}\times 100\ \%
$$

Besides, the percentage content of labelled amount of reserpine tablets is calculated by the comparison method in the Chinese Pharmacopoeia (Volume Ⅱ , 2020 Edition), which stipulates that the percentage content of labelled amount in reserpine tablets should be 90.0%-110.0%. The specific calculation formula is as follows:

$$\text{The percentage content of labelled amount (\%)} = \frac{\dfrac{\dfrac{F_i}{F_s} \times c_s \times \dfrac{25\ \text{mL}}{10\ \text{mL}} \times 100\ \text{mL}}{S}}{0.25\ \text{mg} \times \dfrac{}{\text{the average weight of tablets}}} \times 100\ \%$$

Where F_i is the fluorescence intensity of the test solution; F_s is the fluorescence intensity of the reference solution; c_s is the concentration in of the reference solution, mg·mL^{-1}; S is the weight of the sample, g; the average weight of tablets is the average weight of 20 reserpine tablets, g / tablet.

Instruments and Chemical Reagents

1. Instruments

Shimadzu RF-6000 fluorescence spectrophotometer; fluorescence quartz cuvette; volumetric flask (100 mL, 25 mL); pipette (10 mL, 5 mL); stoppered tube (10 mL).

2. Chemical reagents

Reserpine Tablets (specification: 0.25 mg/tablet); reserpine (reference substance); chloroform (A.R.); ethanol (A.R.); deionized water.

Vanadium pentoxide test solution: an appropriate amount of vanadium pentoxide (A.R.) is dissolved in phosphoric acid and shaken for 2 hours to obtain the saturated solution of vanadium pentoxide. After being filtered, the filtrate is diluted with three times equal volume water.

Procedure

1. Preparation of test solutions

Calculate the average weight of tablets by weighing the weight of 20 reserpine tablets. If reserpine tablets are sugar-coated tablets, it is necessary to remove the coating. Then reserpine tablets are ground into powders. An appropriate amount (about equivalent to 0.5 mg of reserpine) of reserpine powders is accurately weighed and is placed into a 100 mL brown volumetric flask. After adding 10 mL of hot water and 10 mL of chloroform, the solution is diluted with ethanol to the scale mark, shake it well. Accurately transfer 10.00 mL of the filtrate to a 25 mL volumetric flask and dilute the volume with ethanol after the obtained solution is filtered.

2. Preparation of reference solutions

Accurately weigh about 10 mg of reserpine reference substance and put it in a 100 mL brown volumetric flask. After adding 10 mL of chloroform, the reserpine reference substance is completely dissolved and diluted to the mark with ethanol, and shake it well. Accurately transfer 2.00 mL of the solution above-mentioned to a 100 mL brown volumetric flask, dilute it with ethanol to the volume, and shake it well.

式中，F_i 为供试品溶液测得的荧光强度；F_s 为对照品溶液测得的荧光强度；c_s 为对照品溶液的浓度，$mg \cdot mL^{-1}$；S 为样品称取的质量，g；平均片重为 20 片利血平片的平均质量，g/ 片。

三、仪器和试剂

1. 仪器

Shimadzu RF-6000 荧光分光光度计；四面通透的石英吸收池；容量瓶（100 mL，25 mL）；移液管（10 mL，5 mL）；具塞试管（10 mL）。

2. 试剂

利血平片（规格：0.25 mg/ 片）；利血平对照品；三氯甲烷（分析纯）；乙醇（分析纯）；去离子水。

五氧化二钒试液：取五氧化二钒（分析纯）适量，加磷酸激烈振摇 2 h 后得其饱和溶液，用垂熔玻璃漏斗滤过，取滤液 1 份加水 3 份，混匀，即得。

四、实验步骤

1. 供试品溶液的制备

取利血平片 20 片，如为糖衣片应除去包衣，精密称定，研细，精密称取适量（约相当于利血平 0.5 mg），置于 100 mL 棕色容量瓶中，加热水 10 mL，摇匀，加三氯甲烷 10 mL，振摇，用乙醇稀释至刻度，摇匀，滤过，精密量取续滤液 10.00 mL 置于 25 mL 容量瓶中，并用乙醇稀释至刻度，摇匀后即制成每 1 mL 中约含利血平 2.0 μg 的供试品溶液。

2. 对照品溶液的制备

取利血平对照品 10 mg，精密称定，置于 100 mL 棕色容量瓶中，加三氯甲烷 10 mL 使利血平溶解后，用乙醇稀释至刻度，摇匀；精密量取 2.00 mL，置于 100 mL 棕色容量瓶中，用乙醇稀释至刻度，摇匀，即得。

3. 供试品和对照品溶液荧光强度的测定

精密量取供试品溶液与对照品溶液各 5.00 mL，分别置于具塞试管中，再精密加入五氧化二钒试液 2.00 mL，激烈振摇后于 30 ℃放置 1 h，在激发光波长 400 nm、发射光波长 500 nm 处分别测定其荧光强度。

五、数据处理

（1）精密称取 20 片利血平片的质量，如为糖衣片应除去包衣后精密称取 20 片利血平片的质量，计算其平均片重。

（2）按对比法的计算公式，计算利血平片标示量的百分含量。

六、实验指导

1. 预习要求

（1）掌握标示量百分含量的概念及其计算公式。

（2）了解对比法的原理及计算公式。

（3）掌握利血平片标示量百分含量测定的步骤。

3. Measurement of fluorescent intensity of test and reference solutions

5.00 mL of the test solution and 5.00 mL of the reference solution are accurately transferred into a stoppered tube, respectively. Then add 2.00 mL of vanadium pentoxide test solution accurately, the test solution and the reference solution are dramatically shaken and stood by for 1 hour at 30 ℃. The fluorescence intensity at the wavelength of 500 nm of the test solution and the reference are measured under the excitation of light with the wavelength of 400 nm.

Data Analysis

(1) Calculate the average weight of tablets by weighing the weight of 20 reserpine tablets. In the case of sugar-coated tablets, it is necessary to remove the coat of a reserpine tablet.

(2) Calculate the percentage content of labeled amount in reserpine tablets according to the formula of comparison method.

Experiment Guidance

1. Preview instruction

(1) Master the concept and the calculation of the percentage content of labeled amount in drugs.

(2) Understand the principle and the calculation of the comparison method.

(3) Be familiar with the procedures of determining the percentage content of labeled amount in reserpine tablets.

2. Notes

(1) In fluorescence analysis, the temperature has a great influence on the fluorescence intensity, so the temperature of the test solution and the reference solution should be controlled the same in this experiment.

(2) When the concentration of the test solution and the reference solution is too high, the fluorescence quenching will occur, resulting in the fluorescent intensity is not proportional to the concentration. Therefore, the concentration of the reserpine is low (2 $\mu g \cdot mL^{-1}$).

(3) Due to the high sensitivity of fluorescence analysis and the requirement of high purity of solvent, the blank experiment should be done first.

(4) The redox reaction time between reserpine and vanadium pentoxide should be moderate. If the reaction time is too short, reserpine may not be completely oxidized; if the reaction time is too long, the fluorescence intensity may decrease.

(5) If there are paramagnetic molecules such as dissolved oxygen in the solvent, it can cause fluorescence quenching. If necessary, inert gas can be introduced to remove dissolved oxygen molecules in the solvent before determination.

3. Discussion

(1) Whether the excipients in reserpine tablets have any influence on the determination of the percentage content of labeled amount in reserpine tablets, and if so, how to eliminate the influence?

(2) In the comparison method, why should the concentrations of the test solution and the reference solution be as close as possible?

2. 注意事项

（1）在荧光分析法中，温度对荧光强度具有较大的影响，因此在本实验中，供试品溶液和对照品溶液荧光强度测定时，其温度应控制一致。

（2）供试品溶液和对照品溶液浓度过大时可产生荧光猝灭，使发射光强度下降，导致发射光强度与浓度不成正比。因此，荧光分析法应在低浓度溶液中进行，故本品浓度配制为 $2\ \mu g \cdot mL^{-1}$。

（3）由于荧光分析法灵敏度高，要求溶剂纯度高，故应先做空白试验校正。

（4）利血平与五氧化二钒发生氧化还原反应的时间要适中，反应时间太短，可能导致利血平不能完全氧化；反应时间太长，可能导致荧光强度降低。

（5）溶剂中如存在溶解氧等顺磁性分子时，可导致荧光猝灭，必要时可在测定前通入惰性气体除去溶剂中溶解的氧分子。

3. 讨论

（1）利血平片中的辅料对利血平片的标示量百分含量测定是否有影响，如有影响如何消除？

（2）在对比法中，供试品溶液和对照品溶液的浓度为什么应该尽量接近？

Experiment 3.18 Determination of Quinine in Tonic Water by Standard Addition Method

Purpose

(1) To master the principle and experimental operation of standard addition method.

(2) To understand the determination method of quinine in Tonic water.

Principle

Tonic water is a kind of soft bubble beverage, which is often used to prevent and treat malaria. The earliest Tonic water only contains carbonated water and quinine, and the dosage of quinine is very high, so its taste is too hard to swallow. To improve the taste of Tonic water on the market, the content of quinine has been greatly reduced, and sugar, lemon, and other fruit flavoring ingredients have been added. It is often mixed with spirits to prepare various cocktails.

Quinine, an extract from the bark of Cinchona, has long been used by the Quechua Indians in Peru to treat malaria. In 1630, Princess Chinchon was infected with malaria during her visit to Peru, which was later cured by the bark of the Cinchona tree and introduced into Europe. In 1820, French scientists Pierre Joseph Pelletier and Joseph Bienaimé Caventou isolated quinine from the bark of Cinchona. The molecular formula of quinine is $C_{20}H_{24}N_2O_2$, the relative molecular weight is 324.417. When quinine is dissolved in 0.1 mol·L^{-1} H_2SO_4 solution, it can emit blue fluorescence under the irradiation of ultraviolet light. The excitation spectrum and emission spectrum of quinine are shown in Figure 3–5. The maximum excitation wavelength of quinine in 0.1 mol·L^{-1} H_2SO_4 is about 380 nm, and the

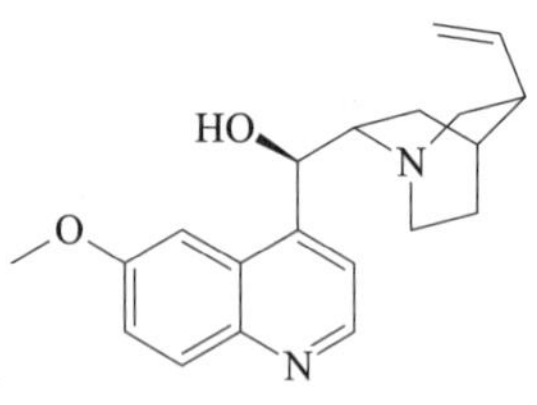

quinine

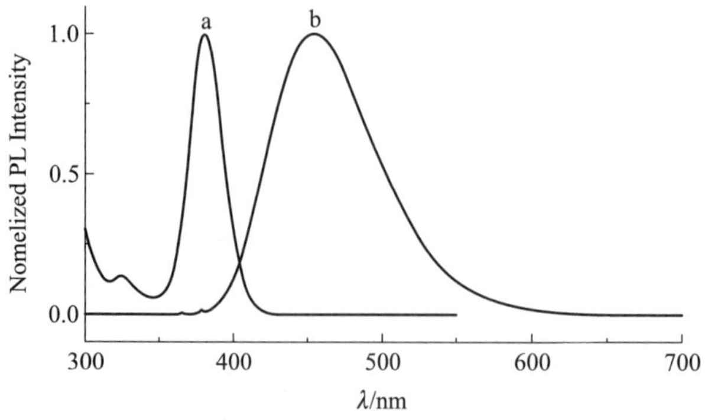

Figure 3–5 The excitation spectrum (a) and the emission spectrum (b) of quinine dissolved in 0.1 mol·L^{-1} H_2SO_4 solution

实验 3.18 标准加入法测定通宁水中奎宁的含量

一、实验目的

（1）掌握标准加入法的原理以及实验操作。

（2）了解通宁水中奎宁含量测定的方法。

二、实验原理

通宁水也被称为汤力水，是一种汽水类的软气泡饮料，常用于预防和治疗疟疾。最早的通宁水只含有碳酸水和奎宁两种主要成分，而且奎宁的剂量非常高，导致其味道太苦难以下咽。现在市面上的通宁水为了改善其口感，大幅降低了奎宁的含量，并加入了糖类、柠檬等水果气味成分在内，常与烈酒一起调配各种鸡尾酒。

奎宁是金鸡纳树（cinchona）树皮的一种提取物，长期以来被秘鲁的盖丘亚族印第安人用来治疗疟疾。1630 年，Chinchon 王妃参观秘鲁时感染疟疾，随后被金鸡纳树的树皮而治愈，从而被引入欧洲。1820 年，法国科学家 Pierre Joseph Pelletier 和 Joseph Bienaimé Caventou 从金鸡纳树皮中分离出奎宁。奎宁的分子式为 $C_{20}H_{24}N_2O_2$，相对分子质量为 324.417，其分子结构式如下所示。将奎宁溶于 0.1 $mol \cdot L^{-1}$ H_2SO_4 溶液时，在紫外光的照射下能产生蓝色的荧光。其激发光谱和发射光谱如图 3-5 所示，奎宁在 0.1 $mol \cdot L^{-1}$ H_2SO_4 溶液中最大激发波长大约为 380 nm，最大发射波长大约为 458 nm。

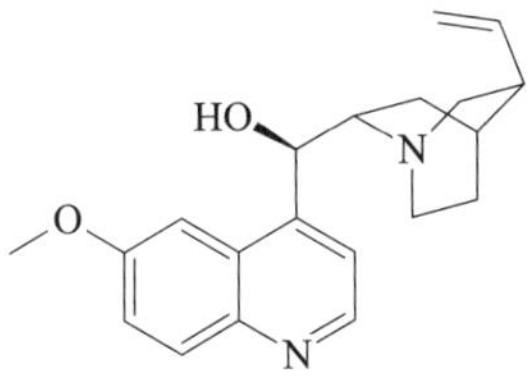

奎宁

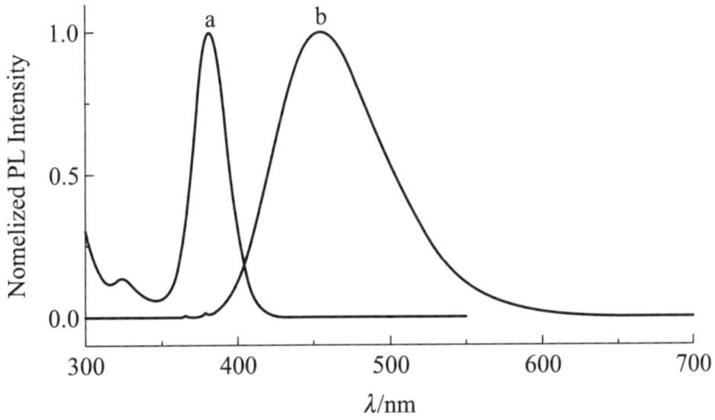

图 3-5 奎宁的 0.1 $mol \cdot L^{-1}$ H_2SO_4 溶液的激发光谱（a）和发射光谱（b） maximum emission wavelength is about 458 nm.

Because quinine dissolved in 0.1 mol·L^{-1} H_2SO_4 solution can emit strong blue fluorescence, and Tonic water contains corrigents and sweeteners, the standard addition method is often used in the determination of quinine content due to the complex background.

Instruments and Chemical Reagents

1. Instruments

Shimadzu RF-6000 fluorescence spectrophotometer; Fluorescence quartz cuvette; Volumetric flask (100 mL); Pipette (10 mL, 5 mL).

2. Chemical reagents

Tonic water (commercially avaible); Quinine (reference substance); 0.1 mol·L^{-1} H_2SO_4 solution; deionized water.

0.1 mol·L^{-1} H_2SO_4 solution: 6 mL of sulfuric acid is slowly dropped into an appropriate amount of water. After being cooled to room temperature, the solution is diluted to 1 000 mL with water, and shaked well.

Procedure

1. Preparation of solutions

Tonic water sample solution: 10.00 mL of Tonic water is transferred accurately into a 100 mL volumetric flask and diluted to the volume with 0.1 mol·L^{-1} H_2SO_4 solution, and shaked well.

Quinine reference stocking solution (10 mg·L^{-1}): accurately weigh about 0.1 g of quinine reference, place it in a 100 mL volumetric flask, dissolve it with an appropriate amount of 0.1 mol·L^{-1} H_2SO_4 solution, dilute it to the volume, and shake it well. Then 1.00 mL of the above-mentioned solution is quantitatively transferred into a 100 mL volumetric flask and diluted to the volume with 0.1 mol·L^{-1} H_2SO_4 solution, and shaked well.

Standard addition solution: 0.00, 1.00, 2.00, 3.00, 4.00, and 5.00 mL quinine reference stocking solution is added into six 100 mL volumetric flasks, containing 5.00 mL Tonic water sample solution respectively, and diluted to the volume with 0.1 mol·L^{-1} H_2SO_4 solution, and shaked well.

2. Determination of fluorescence intensity

A proper amount of the standard addition method solution is loaded into a fluorescence quartz cuvette. The fluorescence intensities at the emission wavelength of 485 nm of the standard addition method solutions are measured at the excitation of light with the wavelength of 380 nm with a fluorescence spectrophotometer.

Data Analysis

Plot the standard curve according to the fluorescent intensities and the concentration of the standard addition solution. Calculate the linear regressed equation of the standard curve by the least-square method. Calculate the concentration of quinine in Tonic water by extrapolation method.

由于奎宁的 H_2SO_4 溶液能够发射出强烈的蓝色荧光，而通宁水中含有矫味剂和甜味剂等，因此在进行奎宁含量测定时，由于背景复杂，常选用标准加入法。

三、仪器和试剂

1. 仪器

Shimadzu RF-6000 荧光分光光度计；四面通透的石英吸收池；容量瓶（100 mL）；移液管（10 mL，5 mL）。

2. 试剂

通宁水（市售）；奎宁（对照品）；0.1 mol·L^{-1} H_2SO_4 溶液；去离子水。

0.1 mol·L^{-1} H_2SO_4 溶液：取浓硫酸 6 mL，缓缓注入适量水中，冷却至室温，加水稀释至 1 000 mL，摇匀，即得。

四、实验步骤

1. 溶液配制

通宁水样品溶液：精密量取 10.00 mL 通宁水，置于 100 mL 容量瓶中，并用 0.1 mol·L^{-1} H_2SO_4 溶液稀释至刻度，摇匀，即得。

奎宁对照品储备液（10 mg·L^{-1}）：取奎宁对照品 0.1 g，精密称定，置于 100 mL 容量瓶中，用适量 0.1 mol·L^{-1} H_2SO_4 溶液溶解后并稀释至刻度，摇匀。然后精密量取该溶液 1.00 mL 置于 100 mL 容量瓶中，并用 0.1 mol·L^{-1} 的 H_2SO_4 稀释至刻度，摇匀，即得。

标准加入法溶液的制备：分别精密量取 5.0 mL 通宁水样品溶液，置于 6 个 100 mL 的容量瓶中，然后分别准确加入 0.00 mL、1.00 mL、2.00 mL、3.00 mL、4.00 mL、5.00 mL 的奎宁对照品储备液，并用 0.1 mol·L^{-1} H_2SO_4 溶液稀释至刻度，摇匀即可。

2. 荧光强度的测定

取适量的标准加入法溶液置于四面通透的石英吸收池中，然后将石英吸收池放入荧光分光光度计中，在激发光波长 380 nm、发射光波长 485 nm 处分别测定其荧光强度。

五、数据处理

以测得的荧光强度为纵坐标、加入的奎宁储备液浓度为横坐标作图，并将这些数据点利用最小二乘法进行线性回归，采用外推法计算出通宁水中奎宁的浓度。

六、实验指导

1. 预习要求

（1）复习荧光法的基本原理及定量方法。

（2）了解标准加入法的原理和溶液配制方法。

2. 注意事项

（1）在进行荧光强度测定前，进行空白对照实验。

（2）标准加入法溶液中奎宁的浓度不能太高，因此在实验前需将通宁水进行稀释。

Experiment Guidance

1. Preview instruction

(1) Review the basic principle and quantitative method of fluorescence method.

(2) Understand the principle of standard addition method and its solution preparation method.

2. Notes

(1) Before the fluorescence intensity measurement, the blank control experiment was carried out.

(2) The concentration of quinine in the solution of the standard addition method should not be too high, so Tonic water should be diluted before the experiment.

3. Discussion

(1) Why do we use a standard addition method to determine the content of quinine in Tonic water instead of a standard curve method?

(2) Please briefly describe the advantages and disadvantages of standard addition method.

3. 讨论

（1）本实验中为什么采用标准加入法测定通宁水中奎宁的含量，而不用标准曲线法？

（2）请简述标准加入法的优点和缺点。

Experiment 3.19 Structure Elucidation of Aspirin by ^{1}H Nuclear Magnetic Resonance Spectroscopy

Purpose

(1) To master the basic principle of ^{1}H nuclear magnetic resonance spectroscopy and the relationship between the structure and the spectrum.

(2) To master the elucidation of nuclear magnetic resonance spectrum.

(3) To be familiar with the operation of Nuclear Magnetic Resonance spectrum instrument and data analysis.

Principle

According to the principle of quantum mechanics, like a negatively charged electron, a positively charged nucleus also has a spin angular momentum (P). The specific value of the spin angular momentum is determined by the spin quantum number (I) of the nucleus, and the spin quantum number depends on the composition of the nucleus:

(1) For nuclei with even mass number and even proton number, the spin quantum number is 0;

(2) The mass number is odd, the proton number is odd or even, and the spin quantum number is half integer (1/2, 3/2, 5/2,···);

(3) The mass number is even, the proton number is odd, and the spin quantum number is integer (1, 2, 3,···).

When a charged nucleus spins, it will produce a nuclear magnetic moment (μ). The direction of the nuclear magnetic moment is the same as the spin direction of the nucleus, and its magnitude is directly proportional to the spin angular momentum of the nucleus ($\mu = \gamma P$, γ is the magnetic spin ratio, and γ is a fixed value for a given nucleus). If the nucleus is placed in an external magnetic field, the nuclear magnetic moment of the nucleus with spin quantum number I has $2I + 1$ direction, and the direction of the nuclear magnetic moment can only change between adjacent direction, thus forming a series of energy levels. When the nucleus in the magnetic field receives the energy input from external sources, the energy level transition will occur, that is, the angle between the nuclear magnetic moment and the external magnetic field will change.

In the external magnetic field, if the nuclear magnetic moment is different from the direction of the external magnetic field, the nuclear magnetic moment will rotate around the direction of the external magnetic field. This phenomenon is similar to the swing of the rotation axis of the gyroscope in the process of rotation, which is called precession. The precession of the nucleus has certain energy and frequency, which is determined by the Lamor equation ($\nu_0 = \gamma H_0/2\pi$, H_0 is the intensity of the external magnetic field). At this time, if an electromagnetic wave with frequency $\nu = \nu_0$ is used to irradiate the nucleus, the spin energy level of the nucleus will transit from ground state to excited state,

实验 3.19　^{1}H 核磁共振波谱法测定阿司匹林的结构

一、实验目的

（1）掌握利用 ^{1}H核磁共振波谱法测定简单化合物结构的基本原理。

（2）掌握核磁共振波谱图的解析方法。

（3）熟悉核磁共振波谱仪的操作步骤和数据处理方法。

二、实验原理

根据量子力学原理，与带负电的电子一样，带正电的原子核也具有自旋角动量（P），其自旋角动量的具体数值由原子核的自旋量子数（I）决定，而自旋量子数又取决于原子核的组成，规则如下：

（1）质量数为偶数，质子数也为偶数的原子核，自旋量子数为 0；

（2）质量数为奇数，质子数为奇数或偶数，自旋量子数为半整数（1/2，3/2，5/2，…）；

（3）质量数为偶数，质子数为奇数，自旋量子数为整数（1，2，3，…）。

带电的原子核自旋时会产生核磁矩（μ），核磁矩的方向与原子核的自旋方向相同，大小与原子核的自旋角动量成正比（$\mu = \gamma P$，γ 为磁旋比，对于给定的原子核，γ 为定值）。若将原子核置于外加磁场中，自旋量子数为 I 的原子核的核磁矩有 $2I+1$ 个不同的取向，核磁矩的方向只能在相邻的取向间变化，从而形成一系列能级。当原子核在外加磁场中接受其他来源的能量输入后，就会发生能级跃迁，也就是原子核的核磁矩与外加磁场的夹角会发生变化。

在外加磁场中，若原子核磁矩与外加磁场方向不同，则原子核磁矩会绕外磁场方向旋转，这一现象类似陀螺在旋转过程中转动轴的摆动，称为进动。原子核的进动具有能量也具有一定的频率，该频率由 Lamor 方程（$\nu_0 = \gamma H_0/2\pi$，H_0 为外磁场强度）确定。此时若用频率 $\nu = \nu_0$ 的电磁波照射原子核，原子核的自旋能级就会发生跃迁，从而产生核磁共振信号。

由于 H 和 C 是有机化合物的主要组成元素，且 ^{1}H 和 ^{13}C 核仅有两个自旋能级，因而是核磁共振波谱的主要研究对象。对于 ^{1}H 原子核，由于相邻质子核磁矩的互相干扰，会导致峰的分裂，对于一级谱图来说，裂分峰的数目符合 $n+1$ 规律，即取决于与其相邻的质子数目 n，由此可推测基团之间的连接关系。

对于简单的有机化合物，仅采用核磁共振氢谱（^{1}H nuclear magnetic resonance，^{1}H-NMR）即可推测其可能的结构。推测的主要依据来自 ^{1}H-NMR 波谱采集的信息：①波谱中总氢的数目与化合物分子总氢的数目相同；②出峰的位置可初步判断含氢的基团类型，积分峰面积与氢的数目成正比；③峰的裂分数目可判断相邻质子之间的耦合关系。根据以上信息即可推断简单化合物的结构。

核磁共振波谱仪一般包含磁场、射频发生器、射频接收器、样品管、仪器控制及数据处

resulting in a nuclear magnetic resonance signal.

Because H and C are the main elements of organic compounds, and there are only two spin levels in ^{1}H and ^{13}C nuclei, they are the main research objects of nuclear magnetic resonance spectrum. For the ^{1}H nucleus, the mutual interference of the magnetic moments of adjacent proton nuclei will lead to the splitting of the peaks. The number of splitting peaks conforms to the $n + 1$ rule, which depends on the number of adjacent protons n, therefore, the relationship between groups can be inferred.

For simple organic compounds, ^{1}H nuclear magnetic resonance spectrum (^{1}H-NMR) can be used to infer their possible structures. The main basis for the inference is the information collected from the ^{1}H-NMR spectrum: ① the number of total hydrogens in the spectrum is the same as that of the compound molecule; ② The area of the integral peak is proportional to the number of hydrogen; ③ The number of splitting peaks can be used to judge the coupling relationship between protons. Based on the above information, the structure of simple compounds can be deduced.

NMR spectrometer generally includes magnetic field, RF generator, RF receiver, sample tube, instrument control and data processing system, as shown in the Figure 3–6. The ^{1}H-NMR spectra of aspirin are determined by benchtop nuclear magnetic resonance spectrometer.

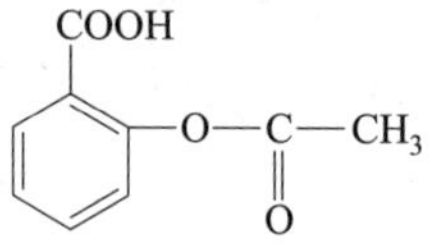

Aspirin

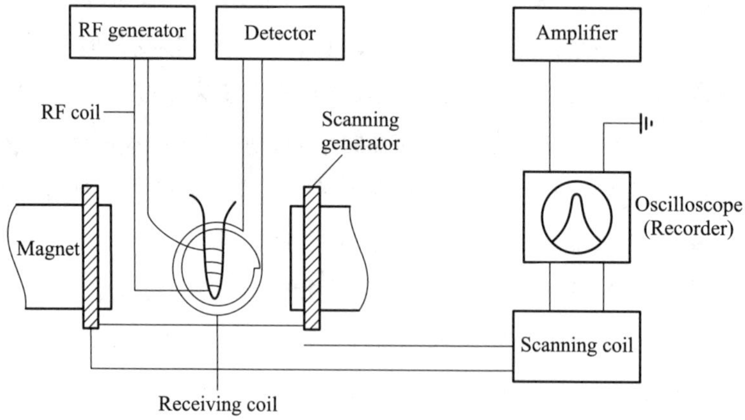

Figure 3–6 Schematic diagram of nuclear magnetic resonance spectrometer

Instruments and Chemical Reagents

1. Instruments

Thermo Picospin 80 NMR spectrometer; injector; 5 mm quartz glass NMR tube; MestReNova NMR software.

2. Chemical reagents

TMS (internal standard); aspirin (purity>99.0%); D-DMSO (deuterium substitution >99.8%).

理系统等几个部分，如图 3-6 所示。本实验采用桌面小型核磁共振波谱仪测定阿司匹林的 ^{1}H-NMR 谱。

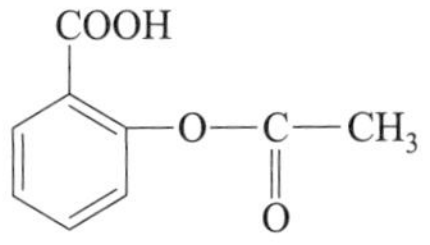

阿司匹林

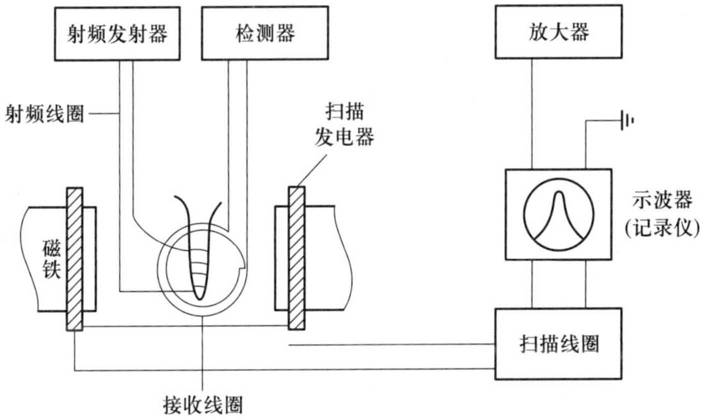

图 3-6　核磁共振波谱仪结构示意图

三、仪器和试剂

1. 仪器

Thermo Picospin 80 核磁共振波谱仪；注射器；5 mm 石英玻璃核磁管；MestReNova NMR 数据处理软件。

2. 试剂

TMS（内标）；阿司匹林（纯度 >99.0%）；氘代二甲亚砜（氘代度 >99.8%）。

四、实验步骤

（1）配制样品溶液：取阿司匹林适量，溶于氘代二甲亚砜中，浓度约为 5 mg·mL^{-1}。

（2）打开仪器和计算机，输入仪器的 IP 地址，联机。

（3）核磁共振波谱采集自 Picospin 80 NMR 核磁共振波谱仪。Picospin 80 核磁共振波谱仪采用 82 MHz 脉冲，傅里叶变换 ^{1}H-NMR 永久磁体，配有毛细管整体探头。波谱采用 90°激发脉冲、750 ms 采集时间和 8 s 循环延迟。纯净样品扫描 16 次，将所采集的谱图平均得到最终谱图。谱图处理采用 MestReNova NMR 软件，采用软件标准谱图处理参数，包括零点调整、相位校正、峰检测和积分。

Procedure

(1) Preparation of sample solution: Dissolve aspirin in D-DMSO to prepare a 5 $mg \cdot mL^{-1}$ solution.

(2) Power on the NMR instrument and the computer, input IP address of instrument, connect the instrument and computer.

(3) The NMR spectra were collected using picospin 80 NMR spectrometers. The spectrometers were 82 MHz pulsed, Fourier transform ^{1}H-NMR permanent magnet instruments equipped with a capillary cartridge probe. All spectra were acquired using a 90° excitation pulse, 750 ms acquisition time and 8 second recycle delay. Each final spectrum resulted from an average of co-added scans; 16 scans for neat samples and 64 scans for dissolved solids. Data was processed in the software using a standard set of processing parameters, including zero filling, phase correction, peak picking and integration.

Data Analysis

According to the collected ^{1}H-NMR spectrum of aspirin (Figure 3-7), correspond the proton in the spectrum to the structure of aspirin.

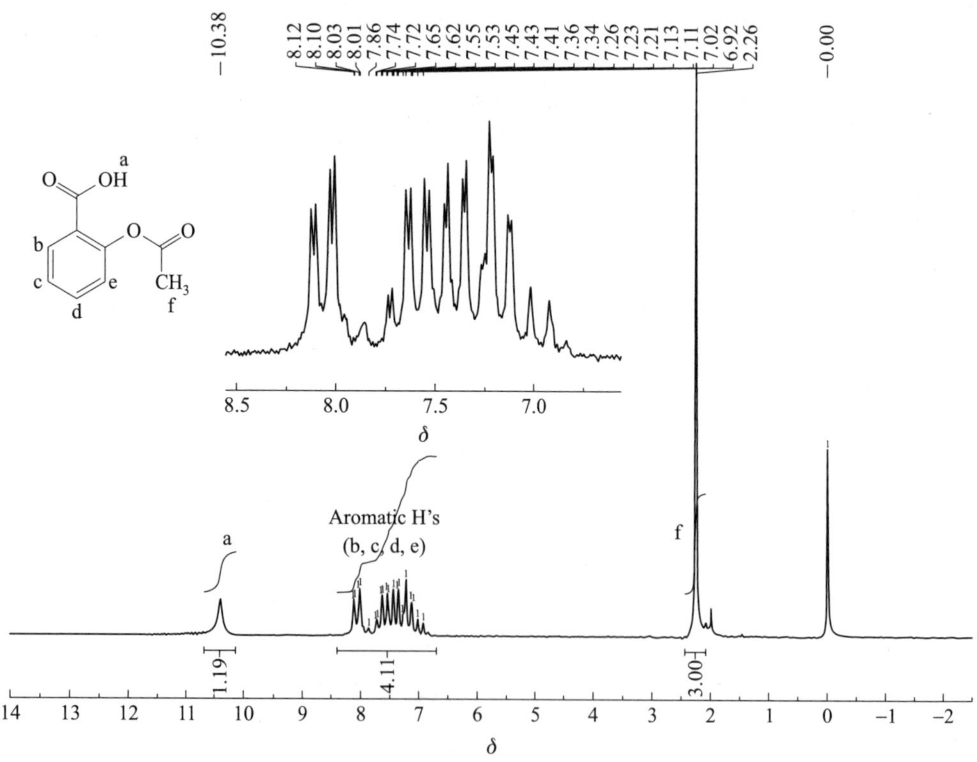

Figure 3-7 ^{1}H-NMR spectrum of aspirin by Picospin 80 NMR spectrometer

五、数据处理

典型的阿司匹林 ^{1}H–NMR 谱图见图 3–7，请对图中质子进行归属。

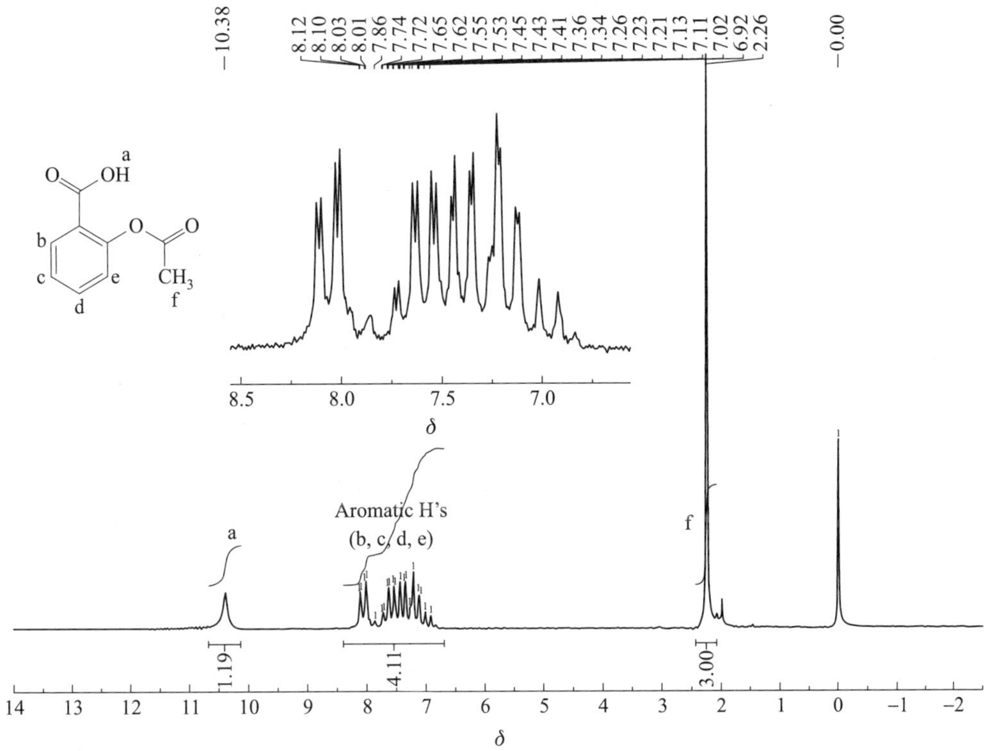

图 3–7　Picospin 80 核磁共振波谱仪上获得的阿司匹林 ^{1}H–NMR 谱图

六、实验指导

1. 预习要求

（1）复习核磁共振波谱法的基础知识。

（2）了解核磁共振波谱仪的结构及操作方法。

（3）掌握核磁共振氢谱的一级谱图解析方法。

2. 注意事项

（1）测试人员在进入实验室操作前，应对随身携带物品进行检查，可磁化物如机械手表、手机、镊子、磁卡、银行卡、钥匙、硬币等不得带入或靠近磁体，应在远离磁 5 高斯线圈外的地方。

（2）严禁心脏起搏器和金属假肢佩戴者进入核磁共振实验室。

（3）使用仪器过程中应防止溶液泄漏造成仪器不能正常工作。

（4）仅允许使用合格的核磁共振样品管。核磁管内溶液应澄清透明，无悬浮物，管内液面高度为 3.5 cm。

Experiment Guidance

1. Preview instruction

(1) Review the basic knowledge of NMR spectroscopy.

(2) Understand the structure and operation of NMR spectrometer.

(3) Master the analytical method of first-order ^{1}H-NMR spectrum.

2. Notes

(1) Before entering the laboratory, personnel should check the items they carry with them. Magnetized objects such as mechanical watches, mobile phones, tweezers, magnetic cards, bank cards, keys, coins, should not be carried into or near the magnet, but should be far away from the magnetic 5 Gaussian coil.

(2) Cardiac pacemakers and metal prosthesis wearers are strictly prohibited from entering the NMR laboratory.

(3) When using the instrument, the solution leakage should be avoided, or else the instrument will work abnormally.

(4) Only qualified NMR sample tubes are allowed. The solution in the NMR tube should be clear and transparent, without suspended matter, and the liquid level in the tube should be 3.5 cm.

(5) Before the experiment, check whether the air compressor has been started.

3. Discussion

(1) Does the chemical shift of proton in ^{1}H-NMR change with the intensity of applied magnetic field? Why?

(2) What structural information can be obtained from the ^{1}H-NMR spectra of compounds?

（5）实验前需查看空气压缩机是否已开。

3. 讨论

（1）^{1}H-NMR 中质子的化学位移是否随外加磁场强度改变而改变？为什么？

（2）从化合物的 ^{1}H-NMR 谱中可以得到哪些结构信息？

Chapter 4 Chromatographic Analysis

Experiment 4.1 Activity Determination of Silica Gel Adhesive Thin Layer

Purpose

(1) To master the preparation of silica gel thin layer plate.

(2) To master the relationship between silica gel activity, activity order and water content.

(3) To be familiar with the determination method of silica gel activity.

Principle

Thin layer chromatography (TLC) is a method that the adsorbent or other stationary phase is uniformly coated on the plane carrier to form a thin layer. After the sample is developed, it is compared with the chromatogram obtained by the same method with the corresponding reference substance or reference medicinal material to carry out drug identification, impurity inspection and content determination. The parameter used in TLC for the identification of compounds is the retardation factor of single component spot, that is, R_f value, which means the ratio of the migration distance of the spot to the migration distance of the solvent front, if TLC chromatogram is as shown in Figure 4–1, R_f of analyte can be calculated as:

$$R_f = \frac{\text{distance between the center of start spot and the center of the solute spot}}{\text{distance between the center of the start spot and the solvent front}} = \frac{b}{a}$$

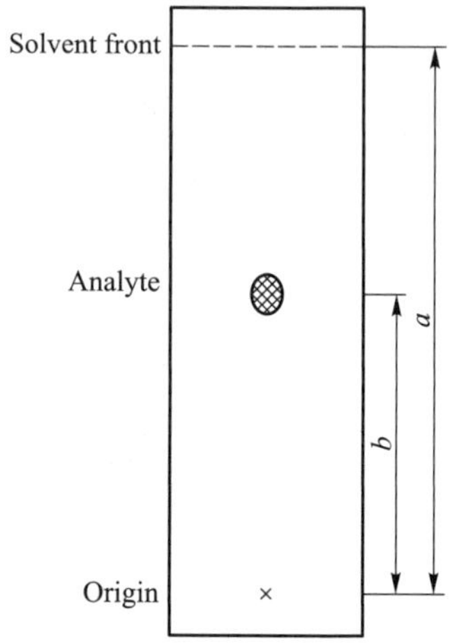

Figure 4–1 Schematic diagram of TLC

Silica gel is commonly used as adsorbent in TLC. According to the different substances added in silica gel, silica gel is divided into silica gel H (without additives), silica gel HF_{254} (adding inorganic substances with fluorescence at 254 nm in silica gel H), silica gel G (adding 15% calcined gypsum in silica gel H) and silica gel GF_{254} (adding inorganic substances with fluorescence at 254 nm in silica gel G). The adsorption capacity of silica gel thin layer is related to its water content, and the relationship between its water content and activity, activity order is shown in the Table 4–1.

第四章　色 谱 分 析

实验 4.1　硅胶黏合薄层的活度测定

一、实验目的

（1）掌握硅胶薄层板的制备方法。

（2）掌握硅胶的活度、活度级数与含水量之间的关系。

（3）熟悉硅胶活度的测定方法。

二、实验原理

薄层色谱法（thin layer chromatography，TLC）是指将吸附剂或其他固定相均匀地涂布于平面载体上形成薄层，待点样展开后与相应的对照品或对照药材按同法所得的色谱图对比，用以进行药物的鉴别、杂质检查和含量测定的方法。TLC 中用于化合物鉴别的参数为单个组分斑点的比移值，即 R_f 值，其含义为斑点的移行距离与溶剂前沿的移行距离的比值，若展开后的色谱如图 4–1，则被测物质斑点的 R_f 为

$$R_f = \frac{\text{原点中心至斑点中心的距离}}{\text{原点中心至溶剂前沿的距离}} = \frac{b}{a}$$

TLC 中常用的吸附剂为硅胶和氧化铝。根据硅胶中所添加的物质不同，又将硅胶分为硅胶 H（无添加物）、硅胶 HF_{254}（硅胶 H 中添加 254 nm 下有荧光的无机物）、硅胶 G（硅胶 H 中加 15% 煅石膏）、硅胶 GF_{254}（硅胶 G 中添加 254 nm 下有荧光的无机物）。硅胶薄层的吸附能力与其含水量有关，其含水量与活度和活性级数的关系见表 4–1。

因此测定硅胶薄层板的活度对保证实验结果的重复性非常重要。

目前一般都采用 Stahl 活度测定法测定硅胶黏合薄层的活度。具体方法为取二甲黄、苏丹红 G、靛酚蓝三种染料，用挥发性溶剂配制成各含 0.4 mg·mL^{-1} 的混合溶液，点于待测定活度的硅胶薄层上，用石油醚展开 10 cm，斑点应不移动，如改用苯展开 10 cm，则应分成三个斑点，合格的硅胶薄层的 R_f 值分别应为：二甲黄 0.58，苏丹红 G 0.19，靛酚蓝 0.08，展开时间为 30~40 min，经本法测定合格的硅胶薄层的活度与柱色谱法所定活度的Ⅱ–Ⅲ级相当。

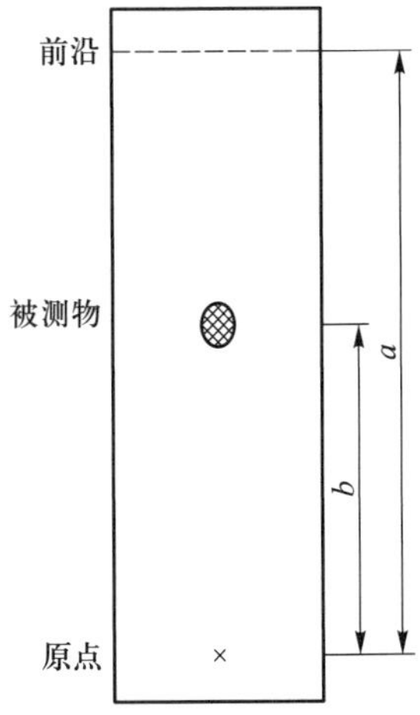

图 4–1　薄层色谱示意图

Table 4–1 Relationship between water content of silica gel and alumina, activity, activity order

Water content of silica gel/%	Water content of alumina/%	Activity order	Adsorption capacity
0	0	Ⅰ	↑
5	3	Ⅱ	
15	6	Ⅲ	
25	10	Ⅳ	
38	15	Ⅴ	

Therefore, it is very important to determine the activity of silica gel thin layer plate to ensure the repeatability of experimental results.

At present, Stahl method is generally used to determine the activity of silica gel thin layer. The method is to prepare a mixed solution of 0.4 mg·mL^{-1} of dimethylyellow, Sudan G and indophenol blue with volatile solvent, and sample it on the thin layer of silica gel whose activity is to be determined. The spots should not move when they are developed with petroleum ether for 10 cm. If they are developed with benzene for 10 cm, three spots should be shown on chromatogram. The R_f values of qualified thin layer of silica gel should be 0.58 for dimethylyellow, 0.19 for Sudan G and 0.08 for Indophenol blue, the development time is about 30–40 min. The activity of qualified silica gel thin layer determined by this method is equivalent to that of Ⅱ-Ⅲ activity determined by column chromatography.

Instruments and Chemical Reagents

1. Instruments

Chromatographic tank; sampling capillary; volumetric flask; electronic balance.

2. Chemical reagents

Mixed solution of 0.4 mg·mL^{-1} of dimethyl yellow, Sudan G and indophenol blue (A.R.); sodium carboxymethylcellulose; petroleum ether (A.R.); benzene (A.R.); distilled water.

Procedure

1. Laying of thin layer plate

Weigh 0.75 g of CMC–Na, add 100 mL of water, heat to dissolve, cool, and then add 50 g of silica gel below 250 mesh to make paste. Pour the paste on the clean glass plate. Because the paste has certain fluidity, the glass plate can be shaken or rotated to make it flow evenly on the whole glass plate to obtain a uniform liquid layer. Put the glass flat and dry naturally, then activate it at 110 ℃ for half an hour to 1 h, and store it in a desiccator.

2. Sampling and developing

Take a piece of silica gel plate (2.5 cm × 12 cm), at 1 cm from one end of the plate, gently draw a straight line with a pencil as the starting line, mark symbol × with a pencil at the middle point of the starting line, add the mixed solution with capillary with an inner diameter of about 1 mm, and the diameter of the spot should be 2–3 mm. After the solvent volatilizes, place the plate in the chromatographic tank containing the developing agent petroleum ether (boiling point 60–90 ℃), and wait until the front of the

表 4-1　硅胶和氧化铝的含水量与活度、活性级数的关系

硅胶含水量 /%	氧化铝含水量 /%	活性级数	吸附能力
0	0	Ⅰ	↑
5	3	Ⅱ	
15	6	Ⅲ	
25	10	Ⅳ	
38	15	Ⅴ	

三、仪器和试剂

1. 仪器

色谱缸；点样毛细管；容量瓶；电子天平。

2. 试剂

二甲黄、苏丹红 G、靛酚蓝（均为分析纯，配制成每毫升各含 0.4 mg 的混合溶液）；羧甲基纤维素钠（分析纯）；石油醚（分析纯）；苯（分析纯）；蒸馏水。

四、实验步骤

1. 黏合薄层板的铺制

称取羧甲基纤维素钠（CMC–Na）0.75 g，加入 100 mL 水中加热使溶解，放冷，放置后再分次加入 250 目以下的硅胶 50 g，调成糊状。将调成糊状的吸附剂混悬液倒在清洁的玻璃板上，由于糊状物有一定的流动性，可晃动或转动玻璃板，使其均匀流布于整块玻璃板上，而获得均匀的液层。将玻璃板平放自然晾干，然后于 110 ℃活化 0.5~1 h，置干燥器中贮存备用。

2. 点样与展开

取羧甲基纤维素硅胶板一块（2.5 cm × 12 cm）在距板一端 1 cm 处，用铅笔轻轻画一直线作为起始线，在起始线中点用铅笔作一标记（×），用内径约 1 mm 的平口毛细管点加混合溶液，其直径应为 2~3 mm，待溶剂挥发后，将板置于盛有展开剂石油醚（沸点 60~90 ℃）的色谱缸中，待展开剂前沿离起始线约 10 cm 处，混合物应不移动，取出硅胶板，待石油醚挥发后，再按同法以苯为展开剂，展开时间为 30~40 min，取出薄层板立即画出前沿线，待苯挥发，观察斑点的位置测量并计算 R_f 值，判断其活度。

五、数据处理

溶剂前沿距离	原始数据/cm	R_f	参比 R_f	硅胶板活度
		—	—	
二甲黄斑点			0.58	
苏丹红 G 斑点			0.19	
靛酚蓝斑点			0.08	

developing agent is about 10 cm from the starting line, the mixture should not move. Take out the plate, after the petroleum ether volatilizes, use benzene as the developing agent. The developing time is about 30–40 min. Take out the thin plate and immediately draw the front line. After the benzene volatilizes, observe the spot position, measure and calculate R_f value to determine its activity.

Data Analysis

Distance of solvent front	Original data /cm	R_f	Reference R_f	Activity of plate
		—	—	
Dimethyl yellow			0.58	
Sudan G			0.19	
Indophenol blue			0.08	

Experiment Guidance

1. Preview instruction

(1) Review the basic knowledge of thin layer chromatography.

(2) Be familiar with the laying method of thin layer plate.

(3) Be familiar with TLC operation and R_f calculation.

2. Notes

(1) The activated thin layer plate should be stored in a desiccator to avoid absorbing moisture and reducing the activity.

(2) The sample quantity should not be too much, otherwise the sample will not be separated well and forming a tailing spot.

(3) The content of water in the developer benzene will affect R_f value, so dry benzene and tanks are needed.

(4) Do not add too much developing solvent, and start line should not be immersed in the solvent.

(5) In qualitative analysis, the R_f value is commonly used parameter to identify various substances by TLC. But there are many factors affecting R_f value, among which the most important factors are the nature of adsorbent, polarity of the developing solvent and solubility of the substance. When the same adsorbent and the same solvent system are used, the R_f value of the tested material is affected by the thickness of the thin layer plate, the developing distance, the saturation of the developing solvent vapor in the chromatographic tank, the sample quantity, the water content of the thin layer plate and the experimental temperature. In order to solve the problem of poor reproducibility of R_f value, relative specific shift value can be used to identify substance.

(6) The proportion of various adhesives used in the preparation of thin-layer plates

① Using calcined gypsum as adhesive:The amount of calcined gypsum in silica gel calcined gypsum (silica gel G) is 5%–15%, and 10%–13% is commonly used. Calcined gypsum ($CaSO_4 \cdot 1/2H_2O$ is dried at 140 ℃ for 4 hours) and mixed with a small amount of silica gel, and then added silica gel in several times to fully grind. When making plate, add 2–3 parts of water to each mixture, and mix it

六、实验指导

1. 预习要求

（1）复习薄层色谱法的基础知识。

（2）熟悉黏合薄层板的铺制方法。

（3）熟悉薄层色谱法的操作过程及 R_f 的计算。

2. 注意事项

（1）活化后的薄层板应贮存于干燥器中，以免吸收湿气而降低活性。

（2）点样量不宜太多，否则会拖尾，分离不好。

（3）展开剂苯中含水量的多少会影响 R_f 值，故需用干燥的苯和器皿。

（4）展开剂不要加得过多，起始线切勿浸入展开剂中。

（5）薄层色谱法中 R_f 值的影响因素较多，其中最重要的是吸附剂的性质与展开剂的极性和对物质的溶解能力。当使用同一吸附剂和同一溶剂系统时，被测物质的 R_f 值受薄层板厚度、展开距离、层析容器内溶剂蒸气的饱和度、点样量、薄层板含水量及实验温度等因素的影响。为了解决 R_f 值重现性差的问题，可采用相对比移值进行定性。

（6）铺制黏合薄层板所用各种黏合剂的比例

① 用煅石膏为黏合剂：硅胶-煅石膏（硅胶 G）薄层含煅石膏量 5%~15%，常用的为 10%~13%。先将煅石膏（$CaSO_4 \cdot 1/2H_2O$ 在 140 ℃下烘 4 h）和少量硅胶研匀，再分次加入硅胶，充分研匀。制板时，每份上述混合物加水 2~3 份，调成糊状，至石膏开始凝固时铺板。氧化铝-煅石膏（氧化铝 G）薄层一般含石膏 5%。制板时，取 1 份氧化铝 G 加 2 份水调成糊状，依法铺制。

② 用 CMC-Na 为黏合剂：硅胶-CMC-Na 薄层：取 1 g CMC-Na，溶于 100 mL 水中，加热煮沸直至完全溶解（浓度为 1%）。取 180~200 目硅胶约 50 g，加 1%CMC-Na 溶液 100 mL，搅匀，即可铺板。如硅胶为 200~250 目，则将 CMC-Na 配成 0.75% 溶液，静置后，取上清液使用。氧化铝-CMC-Na 薄层：取过 200 目筛孔的氧化铝 60~80 g，加入 100 mL 1% CMC-Na 溶液中，按同法铺制。

（7）黏合薄层制备方法

① 倾注法　用倾注法铺板时，吸附剂糊中的水分要适当增加。根据所需铺制薄层的厚度及玻璃板的大小，取一定容量的吸附剂糊均匀铺成一薄层。铺成的薄层需在水平台面上自然晾干，再置烘箱中于 110 ℃活化 1 h，置于干燥器中备用。

② 平铺法　在水平玻璃台面上，放上 2 mm 厚的玻璃板，两边用 3 mm 厚的长条玻璃板作边，根据所需薄层的厚度（一般控制在 0.25~1 mm），可在中间的玻璃板下面垫塑料薄膜。将调好的吸附剂糊倒在中间玻璃板上，用有机玻璃尺（或边缘磨光的玻璃片）沿一定方向，均匀地一次将糊刮平，使成一薄层，去掉两边的玻璃，轻轻振动薄层板，即得均匀的薄层。自然晾干，依法活化。

③ 涂铺器法　涂铺器的种类较多，一般用金属或塑料制成，适用于制备一定规格（20 cm × 20 cm）的定量薄层板。涂铺器的构造有一个填装吸附剂的给料槽，由电机带动皮带轮驱动给料槽从玻璃板表面上经过时，即将吸附剂糊均匀地涂布于玻璃板上，成为一均匀的薄层。使用涂铺器铺制的薄层，厚度比较均匀一致，操作也较方便。目前市售的硅胶薄层板均采用涂铺器铺制，

into paste until the gypsum starts to become solid. The thin layer of alumina calcined gypsum (alumina G) generally contains 5% gypsum. When making the plate, take 1 part of alumina G and add 2 parts of water to make paste, and lay it according to the method above.

② Using CMC–Na as adhesive:Silica gel CMC–Na thin layer plate: take CMC–Na 1 g, dissolve in 100 mL of water, heat and boil until fully dissolved (concentration is 1%). Take about 50 g of 180–200 mesh silica gel, add 1% CMC–Na 100 mL, mix well, and then pave the plate. If the silica gel is 200–250 mesh, CMC–Na is prepared about 0.75% solution. After standing for some time, take the supernatant for use. Alumina CMC–Na thin layer: 60–80 g of alumina with 200 mesh sieves was taken, added to 100 mL of 1% CMC–Na aqueous solution, and prepared according to the same method.

(7) The preparation method of adhesive thin layer

① Pouring method:When the plate is laid by pouring method, the moisture in the paste of adsorbent should be increased appropriately. According to the thickness of the required layer and the size of the glass plate, a certain amount of adsorbent paste is evenly spread into a thin layer. The thin layer shall be dried naturally on the horizontal table, and then activated in the oven for 1 hour at 110 ℃ and put in the desiccator for later use.

② Tiling method:On the horizontal table, 2 mm thick glass plate is placed, and 3 mm thick long glass plates are used as the edge on both sides. According to the thickness of the required thin layer (generally controlled between 0.25–1 mm), plastic film can be padded under the middle glass plate. Paste the adjusted adsorbent on the middle glass plate, and scrape the paste evenly in a certain direction with an organic glass ruler (or glass sheet polished by the edge), so as to make the paste into a thin layer, remove the glass on both sides, and gently vibrate the thin layer, which forming a uniform thin layer. Dry naturally and activate according to the method above.

③ Applicator method:There are many kinds of applicators, which are made of metal or plastic. They are suitable for preparation of certain specifications (20 cm × 20 cm) of quantitative thin plate. Generally, there is a feeding tank filled with adsorbent. When the feeding trough is driven by the belt pulley driven by the motor, it will be evenly coated on the glass plate to form a uniform thin layer. The thin layer made by the applicator is uniform and uniform in thickness and convenient to operate. At present, the thin layer of silica gel is made by applicator. The thickness of thin layer plate for analysis is generally 0.2–0.3 mm, and the thickness of thin layer plate for preparation and separation is generally 1–3 mm.

3. Discussion

(1) What are the factors influencing R_f values in TLC?

(2) Why should thin layer plate be activated? And how should the activated ones be preserved?

(3) What are the applications of TLC?

分析用薄层板厚度一般在 0.2~0.3 mm，制备分离用薄层板厚度一般在 1~3 mm。

3. 讨论

（1）薄层色谱法中 R_f 值的影响因素有哪些？

（2）薄层板为何要活化？活化后的薄层板应该如何保存？

（3）薄层色谱法有哪些应用？

Experiment 4.2 Identification of Buguzhi (Fructus Psoraleae) by Thin Layer Chromatography

Purpose

(1) To know the application of thin layer chromatography in the identification of chemical drugs, traditional Chinese medicine and compound Chinese medicine.

(2) To learn to calculate the R_f value and resolution.

Principle

In thin layer chromatography (TLC) method, R_f is usually used as parameter to identify the single substance. R_f is defined as the ratio between distance moving by the spot and distance moving by the solvent. If a sample contained component A and B shows TLC chromatogram as in Figure 4–2 after development, R_f can be calculated as

$$R_{f,A} = \frac{a}{l} \qquad R_{f,B} = \frac{b}{l}$$

Where $R_{f,A}$ and $R_{f,B}$ are the retardation values of A and B components, respectively; a and b are distances between the center of spot and start line, cm; l is the distance between the solvent front and the start line, cm.

Resolution has been used to evaluate the separation capability of TLC, for component A and B in Figure 4–2, resolution is defined as the ratio of distance difference between A, B and half the sum of width of A and B, resolution can be calculated as:

$$R = \frac{a-b}{\frac{1}{2}\left(w_a + w_b\right)}$$

Where R is the resolution of A and B; a and b are the distances from the center of spots to the start line, cm; w_a and w_b are the vertical diameters of sample spots respectively, cm.

Buguzhi (Fructus Psoraleae) is a commonly used traditional chinese medicine, originated from leguminous plant Psoralea corylifolia L. dried maturated seeds; it has the effects of reinforcing the kidney and supporting yang. Various chemical constituents were contained in Buguzhi, such as oils, coumarins, flavones. In coumarins, psoralen and isopsoralen are characteristic compounds of Buguzhi, thus can be used to identify Buguzhi.

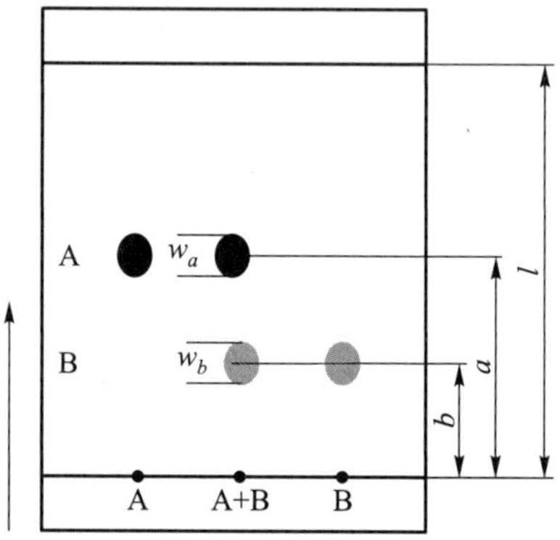

Figure 4–2 Typical diagrammatic drawing of TLC chromatogram by ascending development

实验 4.2　薄层色谱法鉴别补骨脂药材的真伪

一、实验目的

（1）了解薄层色谱法在化学药品鉴别、中药材鉴别及中药复方制剂鉴别中的应用。

（2）掌握 R_f 值及分离度的计算方法。

二、实验原理

薄层色谱法（TLC）中用于鉴别的参数为单个组分斑点的比移值，即 R_f 值，其含义为斑点的移行距离与溶剂前沿的移行距离的比值，若含有 A、B 两组分的样品经 TLC 分离后获得薄层色谱如图 4-2，则

$$R_{f,A}=\frac{a}{l} \qquad R_{f,B}=\frac{b}{l}$$

式中，$R_{f,A}$，$R_{f,B}$ 分别为 A，B 两组分的比移值；a，b 分别为组分 A，B 斑点中心点到样品起始线的距离，cm；l 为溶剂前沿到起始线的距离，cm。

衡量 TLC 分离能力的参数为相邻斑点的分离度，A、B 两组分的分离度定义为两个斑点移行距离的差值与两个斑点在展开方向上宽度和的一半的比值，如图 4-2 所示，R 的计算公式为

$$R=\frac{a-b}{\frac{1}{2}\left(w_a+w_b\right)}$$

式中，R 为 A，B 两组分的分离度；a，b 分别为组分 A，B 斑点中心点到样品起始线的距离，cm；w_a，w_b 分别为样品斑点的垂直直径，cm。

补骨脂为常用中药，来源于豆科植物补骨脂（Psoralea corylifolia L.）的干燥成熟果实，有

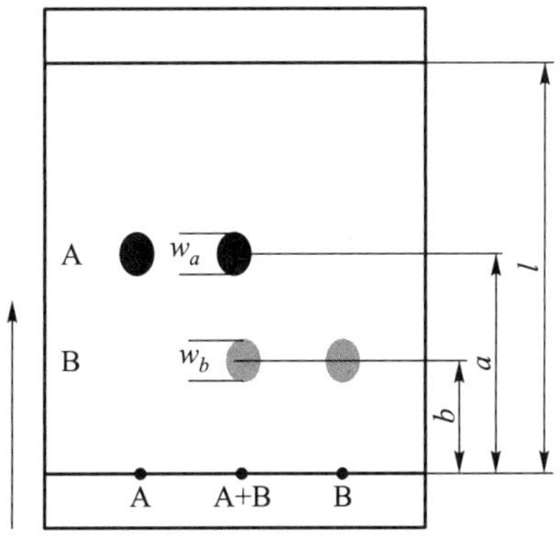

图 4-2　上行展开获得的典型薄层色谱示意图

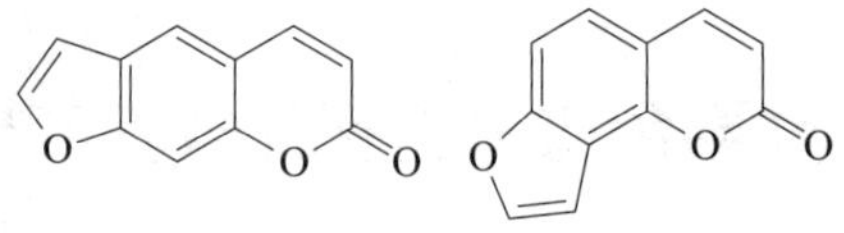

Psoralen Isopsoralen

Instruments and Chemical Reagents

1. Instruments

Chromatographic tank (suitable size for the TLC plate with frosted cover); ultraviolet lamp (365 nm); micro-syringe (or glass capillary); mortar; horn spoon; triangle flask (50 mL); ultrasonic cleaner; triangular funnel; filter paper; evaporating dish; water bath pot; commercial silicone G plate.

2. Chemical reagents

Psoralen (standard); Isopsoralen (standard); Buguzhi (herb); hexane (A.R.); acetyl acetae (A.R.); silica gel reagent (commercial); CMC–Na(A.R.); distilled water.

Procedure

1. Preparation of TLC plate

Dissolve 0.75 g CMC-Na in 100 mL distilled water, warmed if necessary, mix well, standing for a week until the solution is transparent. Measure 30 mL clear CMC-Na solution and put into the mortar, weigh 10 g silica gel G, put into mortar in several times, grind well and remove the bubbles. Pour the pasty silica gel on clean glass plate, vibrate or rotate the plate to make the silica paste flat uniformly, dry it at room temperature. Then activate the plate at 110 ℃ for an hour, store in the desiccator for later use. Commercial silica G plate is also an option.

2. Preparation of solutions

Psoralen standard solution: Dissolve psoralen in acetyl acetate to prepare a 2 $mg \cdot mL^{-1}$ solution.

Isopsoralen standard solution: Dissolve isopsoralen in acetyl acetate to prepare a 2 $mg \cdot mL^{-1}$ solution.

Buguzhi test solution: Add 20 mL acetyl acetate to 0.5 g Buguzhi powder, extracted by ultrasonic for 15 min, filter, drying the filtrate, then dissolve the residue with 1 mL acetyl acetate.

Developing reagent: hexane : acetyl acetae (4 ∶ 1, *V/V*), 10 mL.

3. Spotting

Mark the starting line with a pencil at 1 cm away from the bottom of the thin layer plate, and mark the sample location. The distance between each point is about 1 cm, and the distance between point and the side is at least 1 cm. Use a micro syringe to sample 3 μL psoralen reference solution, isopsoralen reference solution and the test solution respectively, and the spot diameter is not more than 2–3 mm.

4. Development

Place the thin layer plate in the chromatographic tank with 30 mL developer for 15 min, and then immerse the side with sample into the tank for about 0.3–0.5 cm to develop.

5. Coloration

When the solvent front moves about 8 cm, take out the thin plate and draw the front line with

补肾助阳的作用。补骨脂中主要含有挥发油、香豆素类化合物、黄酮类化合物等化学成分，其中香豆素类化合物补骨脂素和异补骨脂素为其特征化学成分，因此可以用来鉴别补骨脂药材的真伪。

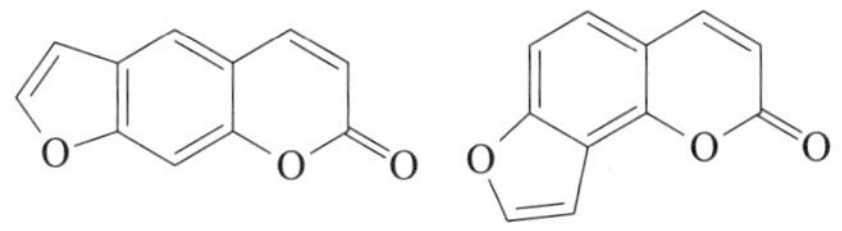

补骨脂素　　异补骨脂素

三、仪器和试剂

1. 仪器

色谱缸（适合薄层板大小的玻璃缸，并带有磨砂玻璃盖）；紫外灯（365 nm）；微量注射器（或点样毛细管）；乳钵；牛角匙，三角烧瓶（50 mL）；超声波清洗器；三角漏斗；滤纸；蒸发皿；水浴锅；商品化硅胶 G 板。

2. 试剂

补骨脂素对照品；异补骨脂素对照品；补骨脂药材；正己烷（分析纯）；乙酸乙酯（分析纯）；硅胶；羧甲基纤维素钠（CMC-Na，分析纯）；蒸馏水。

四、实验步骤

1. 黏合薄层板的铺制

称取 CMC-Na 0.75 g，置于 100 mL 水中，加热使其溶解，混匀，放置一周待澄清后备用。取上述 CMC-Na 上清液 30 mL（或适量），置于乳钵中。取 10 g 硅胶，分次放入研钵中，待充分研磨均匀后，取糊状的吸附剂适量置于清洁的玻璃板上。由于糊状物具有一定的流动性，可晃动或转动玻璃板，使其均匀地涂布于整块玻璃板上而获得均匀的薄层板。将其平放晾干，再在 110 ℃下活化 1 h，贮于干燥器中备用。或购买商品化硅胶 G 板。

2. 溶液配制

补骨脂素对照品溶液：取补骨脂素对照品，加乙酸乙酯制成每 1 mL 含 2 mg 的溶液，作为对照品溶液。

异补骨脂素对照品溶液：取异补骨脂素对照品，加乙酸乙酯制成每 1 mL 含 2 mg 的溶液，作为对照品溶液。

补骨脂药材供试品溶液：取补骨脂粉末 0.5 g，加乙酸乙酯 20 mL，超声处理 15 min，过滤，滤液蒸干，加乙酸乙酯 1 mL 溶解残渣。

展开剂：正己烷-乙酸乙酯（4 : 1，体积比），10 mL。

3. 点样

在距薄层板底边 1 cm 处用铅笔轻轻画一起始线，并标注点样位置，各点之间相距 1 cm，两侧点距侧边至少 1 cm，用微量注射器分别点补骨脂素对照品溶液、异补骨脂素对照品溶液、补骨脂药材供试品溶液各 3 μL，斑点直径不超过 2~3 mm。

pencil immediately. After the solvent is completely volatilized, spray 10% potassium hydroxide methanol solution, dry it with hot air, and inspect it with ultraviolet lamp (365 nm) to mark the position and appearance of each spot.

Data Analysis

Find out the center of each spot, measure the migration distance of each spot and the solvent front distance with a ruler, and calculate the R_f value of each spot respectively. By comparing the R_f value, the two components in Psoralea corylifolia were qualitatively identified to explain the authenticity of the drug, and calculate the resolution of psoralen and isopsoralen in Psoralea corylifolia.

Experiment Guidance

1. Preview instruction

(1) Review the basic knowledge of thin layer chromatography.

(2) Be familiar with TLC operation and R_f calculation.

(3) Understand the extraction method of Psoralea corylifolia.

2. Notes

(1) The uniformity of thin layer should be checked before use (by transmitted light and reflected light).

(2) When spotting, the micro syringe needle must not damage the surface of the thin layer.

(3) At the end of the experiment, the developer used in the experiment cannot be poured into the sink. And it must be poured into the designated waste liquid barrel for unified recycling treatment.

(4) The chromatography tank must be sealed; otherwise the solvent is volatile, thus changing the proportion of developing agent, affecting the separation effect.

3. Discussion

(1) What are the main coloration methods of thin layer chromatography?

(2) In this experiment, what is the reason for sample spots appearing on the thin plate when viewed by UV lamp under 365 nm?

4. 展开

待溶剂挥发后，将薄层板置于盛有 30 mL 展开剂的色谱缸中饱和 15 min，再将点有样品的一侧浸入展开剂 0.3~0.5 cm，展开。

5. 显色

待展开剂移行约 8 cm 时，取出薄层板，立即用铅笔画出前沿线，待展开剂完全挥发尽后，喷以 10% 氢氧化钾甲醇溶液，热风吹干，置于紫外灯（365 nm）下检视，标出各斑点的位置和外形。

五、数据处理

找出各斑点中心，用直尺量出各斑点移行距离及溶剂移行距离，分别计算各斑点的 R_f 值，通过比较 R_f 值对补骨脂药材中的两组分进行定性，说明药材的真伪，并计算补骨脂药材中补骨脂素和异补骨脂素的分离度。

六、实验指导

1. 预习要求

（1）复习薄层色谱法的基础知识。

（2）熟悉薄层色谱法的操作过程及 R_f 的计算。

（3）了解补骨脂药材的提取方法。

2. 注意事项

（1）薄层板使用前应先检查其均匀度(可通过透射光及反射光检视)。

（2）点样时，微量注射器针头切不可损坏薄层板表面。

（3）在实验结束后，实验中所用的展开剂，不可倒入水槽，须倒入专用的废液桶中，统一回收处理。

（4）色谱缸必须密封，否则溶剂易挥发，从而改变展开剂比例，影响分离效果。

3. 讨论

（1）薄层色谱法的主要显色方法有哪些？

（2）本实验中，将展开后的薄层板在紫外灯（365 nm）下检视出现样品斑点的原因是什么？

Experiment 4.3 Separation and Identification of Methionine and Glycine by Paper Chromatography

Purpose

(1) To grasp the basic principle of paper chromatography.

(2) To grasp the operation of paper chromatography.

Principle

According to the mechanism of separation, paper chromatography (PC) is one of partition chromatography. Filter paper is regarded as the inert carrier. The stationary phase is the water absorbed on the paper fiber (20%–25%), 6% of which combines with the cellulose's hydroxy group through the hydrogen bonds. Mobile phase is organic solvent. The substances to be separated are distributed between the stationary phase and mobile phase. Generally, the R_f is used to describe the position of each component on filter paper, as follows:

$$R_f = \frac{\text{distance between the center of start spot and the center of the solute spot}}{\text{distance between the center of the start spot and the solvent front}}$$

Under the same experiment condition, the R_f of each component is constant. So, R_f value can be used as the parameter to identify the substance.

In this experiment, the mixture of *n*-butyl alcohol-ice acetic acid-water (4 : 1 : 1, *V/V/V*) is used as mobile phase. Methionine [$CH_3SCH_2CH_2CH\ (NH_2)\ COOH$] and glycine NH_2CH_2COOH will be developed and separated. The structure of these two compounds is very similar, but the length of their carbon chain is different. So, their combination ability with water on the filter paper is different. Glycine has stronger polarity than methionine, and moves more slowly on the filter paper. So glycine's R_f is smaller than the methionine's. After development, make them react with ninhydrin under 60 ℃ and then magenta spots will appear on the paper. The color reaction between *α*-amino acid and ninhydrin is as follows:

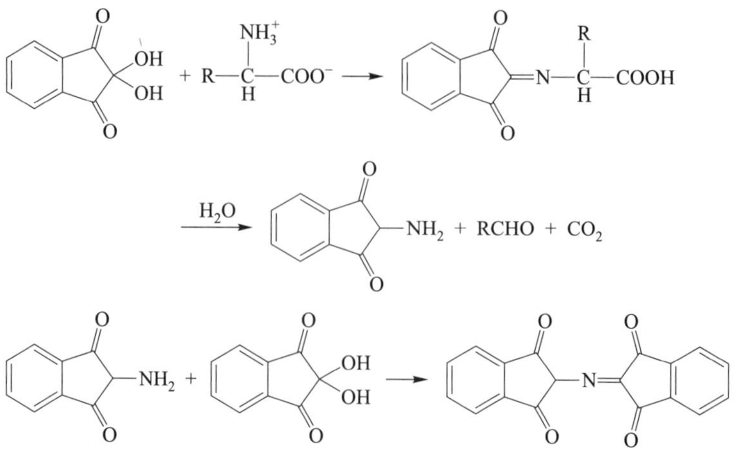

实验 4.3 纸色谱法分离鉴定蛋氨酸和甘氨酸

一、实验目的

（1）掌握纸色谱法分离鉴定的原理。

（2）掌握纸色谱法的基本操作方法。

二、实验原理

纸色谱法（paper chromatography，PC）属于分配色谱，滤纸被看作是一种惰性的载体，固定相为吸附于纸纤维上的水（20%~25%），其中 6% 左右的水通过氢键与纤维素上的羟基结合成复合物，流动相为有机溶剂，被分离物质在固定相和流动相之间进行分配。各组分在色谱中的位置，一般用比移值 R_f 表示，其定义为

$$R_f=\frac{\text{原点中心至斑点中心的距离}}{\text{原点中心至溶剂前沿的距离}}$$

在相同的实验条件下，物质的 R_f 值是一定的，因而由比移值可以进行物质的定性分析。

本实验中流动相为正丁醇–冰醋酸–水（4∶1∶1，体积比），以上行法展开分离蛋氨酸［$CH_3SCH_2CH_2CH(NH_2)COOH$］和甘氨酸（$NH_2CH_2COOH$）。两化合物虽然结构相似，但碳链长短不同，故与滤纸上的水形成氢键的能力不同。甘氨酸极性大于蛋氨酸，在滤纸上移行速度较慢，因而甘氨酸的 R_f 值小于蛋氨酸。展开后，在 60 ℃下与茚三酮发生显色反应，层析纸上出现红紫色斑点。α–氨基酸与茚三酮的显色反应如下：

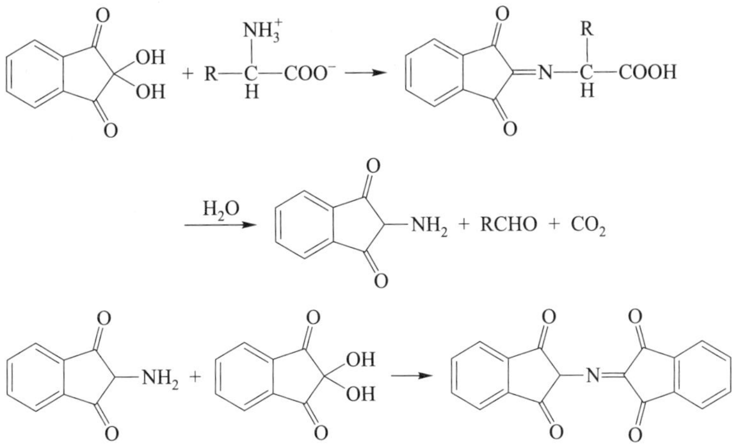

最后生成物为蓝色、紫色或红紫色。

三、仪器和试剂

1. 仪器

色谱缸（或标本缸）；中速色谱滤纸；毛细管（或微量注射器）；喷雾器；烘箱（或电炉）。

The product color is blue, purple or magenta.

Instruments and Chemical Reagents

1. Equipments

Chromatography cylinder (or sample tank); middle speed chromatographic paper;capillary (or micro-syringe); vaporizer; oven (or electric stove).

2. Chemical reagents

n-butyl alcohol (A.R.); glacial acetic acid (A.R.); methionine (standard); glycine (standard); ninhydrin (A.R.); acetone (A.R.); distilled water.

Procedure

1. Solution preparation

Developing solvent: *n*-butyl alcohol-ice acetic acid-water (4 : 1 : 1, *V*/*V*/*V*);

Coloration reagent: ninhydrin solution (0.15 g ninhydrin + 30 mL acetic acid + 50 mL acetone);

Methionine standard solution: 0.4 $mg \cdot mL^{-1}$ aqueous solution;

Glycine standard solution: 0.4 $mg \cdot mL^{-1}$ aqueous solution;

Mixed solution of methionine and glycine.

2. Spotting

Take a strip of middle speed chromatographic paper which is 15 cm long and 6 cm wide, using pencil draw a light starting line 1–2 cm above the bottom, spot three "×"on the line and make the space between "×" 1.5 cm. Spot standard solution and sample solution using capillary (or micro-syringe) for 3–4 times to make the spots' diameter smaller than 2 mm and dry them with blowing (or use cold wind).

3. Development

Add 35 mL developing solvent into the dry chromatographic tank, and hang the spotted filter paper in the tank and cover it to saturate the paper for 10 min. Then dip the paper's bottom edge into the solvent about 0.3–0.5 cm and develop it.

4. Coloration

After the solvent front reaches proper position above starting line (nearly 8 cm), take out paper and draw the solvent front line by pencil immediately. Dry the developed paper and spray the ninhydrin solution on it. Put the paper in the oven and let coloration last 5 min at 60 ℃ , or heat it on the electric stove carefully, and then the magenta spots appear.

5. Qualitative analysis

Circle the edge of spots with pencil and find the center of spots, then measure the distance between the center of spots and the start line, and the distance between the start line and the solvent front respectively.

Data Analysis

Calculate the R_f of each spot in the mixture and standard substances, respectively, then the components of mixture are identified. Calculate the resolution of spots in the mixture sample.

2. 试剂

正丁醇(分析纯);冰醋酸(分析纯);蛋氨酸(标准品);甘氨酸(标准品);茚三酮(分析纯);丙酮(分析纯);蒸馏水。

四、实验步骤

1. 溶液配制

展开剂:正丁醇-冰醋酸-水(4∶1∶1,体积比);

显色剂:茚三酮溶液(0.15 g 茚三酮 +30 mL 冰醋酸 +50 mL 丙酮溶解);

蛋氨酸标准溶液:0.4 mg·mL^{-1} 水溶液;

甘氨酸标准溶液:0.4 mg·mL^{-1} 水溶液;

蛋氨酸、甘氨酸混合样品液。

2. 点样

取长 15 cm、宽 6 cm 的中速色谱纸一张,在距底边约 2 cm 处用铅笔轻画起始线,在起始线上记 3 个“×”号,间距约为 1.5 cm,用毛细管(或微量注射器)分别点加上述标准溶液及样品混合液 3~4 次,斑点直径约 2 mm,晾干(或用冷风吹干)。

3. 展开

在干燥的色谱缸中加入 35 mL 展开剂,把点样后的滤纸垂直悬挂于色谱缸内,盖上缸盖,饱和 10 min。然后使滤纸底边浸入展开剂内 0.3~0.5 cm,进行展开。

4. 显色

待溶剂前沿展开至合适的部位(约 8 cm),取出色谱纸,立即用铅笔画下溶剂前沿的位置。晾干后,喷茚三酮显色剂,再置色谱纸于 60 ℃烘箱内显色 5 min,或在电炉上方小心加热,即可看出红紫色斑点。

5. 定性分析

用铅笔将各斑点的范围标出,找出各斑点的中心点,用米尺量出各斑点的中心到起始线的距离及起始线至溶剂前沿的距离。

五、数据处理

分别求出混合物及标准品中各斑点 R_f 值,对混合样品组分进行定性,计算混合物中甘氨酸和蛋氨酸的分离度,考察分离效果。

六、实验指导

1. 预习要求

(1)复习纸色谱法的基础知识。

(2)掌握纸色谱法的一般操作。

(3)了解氨基酸的显色原理。

2. 注意事项

(1)在选用滤纸型号时,应结合分离对象加以考虑。对 R_f 值相差很小的化合物,宜改用慢速滤纸,以利于分离。对 R_f 值相差较大的化合物,可用快速或中速滤纸。在选用薄型或厚型滤

Experiment Guidance

1. Preview instruction

(1) Review the basics of paper chromatography.

(2) Master the general operation of paper chromatography.

(3) Understand the coloration principle of amino acids in paper chromatography.

2. Notes

(1) In the selection of filter paper type, it should be combined with the separation of the analyte to be considered. For compounds with very small difference in R_f values, slow filter paper should be used for better separation. Fast or medium speed filter paper can be used for compounds with large difference in R_f values. When selecting thin or thick filter paper, it should be decided according to the analysis purpose. The thick paper has a large load for preparation or quantitative use, and the thin one is for general qualitative use.

(2) Each spot must be dry before another spotting and the spot diameter must be 2 mm around. Spotting times vary according to the concentration of sample solution.

(3) Since ninhydrin, the coloration reagent for amino acid, can react with body fluid, for example sweat, take the edge when pick up the filter paper to avoid impurity in paper.

(4) Ninhydrin solution should be prepared before use or stored in refrigerator.

(5) The spotted filter paper should not be dipped into the developing solvent during saturation (for 10 min). Carefully dip the paper into the solvent to develop it and avoid the solvent going beyond the starting line.

(6) Spray the coloration reagent equably and properly to avoid paper being too wet at local site.

3. Discussion

(1) Compare the R_f of the following three acid (a, b and c) when the mixed solution of *n*-butyl alcohol:formic acid:water (10 : 4 : 1) was used as developing solvent.

(2) How to get the chromatogram with concentrated spots and straight solvent front in paper chromatography?

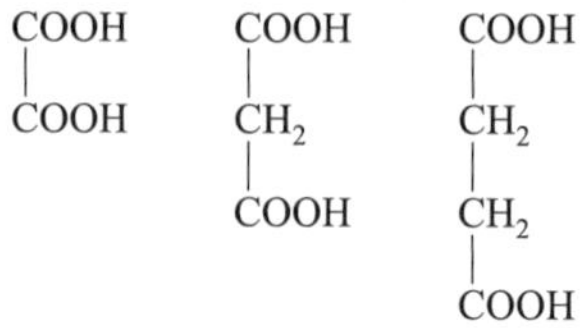

(a) (b) (c)

(3) Why should the filter paper be placed in the chromatographic tank to saturate before contacting the developing solvent? What are the requirements for saturation time and developing temperature?

纸时，应根据分析目的来决定，厚纸载量大，供制备或定量用，薄纸供一般定性用。

（2）点样时，每点一次一定要待吹干后再点第二次，斑点直径约为 2 mm。点样次数视样品溶液浓度而定。

（3）氨基酸的显色剂茚三酮对体液（如汗液）均能显色，在拿取滤纸时，应注意拿滤纸的顶端或边缘，以保证色谱纸上无杂质（如手纹印等）。

（4）茚三酮显色剂应临用前配制，或置冰箱中冷藏备用。

（5）点样后的滤纸在色谱缸内饱和 10 min 时，不可浸入展开剂内。开始展开时，要小心地将滤纸浸入展开剂中，勿使溶剂浸过起始线。

（6）喷显色剂要均匀、适量，不可过分集中，使局部太湿。

3. 讨论

（1）若有下列 3 种酸（a,b,c）在正丁醇-甲酸-水（10∶4∶1，体积比）的溶剂系统中展开，推断三者的 R_f 值从大到小的顺序。

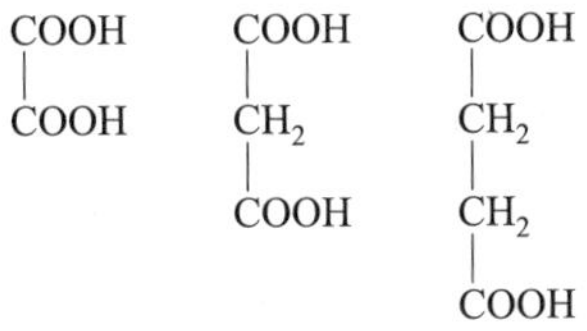

(a)　　(b)　　(c)

（2）怎样才能得到层析斑点集中、溶剂前沿整齐一致的图谱？

（3）滤纸在接触展开剂之前为什么要先置于色谱缸中进行饱和？对饱和的时间及温度有何要求？

Experiment 4.4 Determination of Dead Time and Content of Alkane Mixture with Normalization Method by Gas Chromatography

Purpose

(1) To master the determination method of dead time in gas chromatography.

(2) To master the quantitative analysis method of normalization.

(3) To be familiar with the basic parts and usage of gas chromatograph.

Principle

In chromatography, dead time refers to the time when the unreserved components pass through the column to reach the detector from the beginning of injection, which is used to calculate the retention factor (k) to optimize the experiment conditions. In gas chromatography (GC), air (for TCD, thermal conductivity detector) or methane (for FID, hydrogen flame ionization detector) are often used to determine dead time. However, due to the little distribution of air or methane in the stationary phase, this method can only be used for rough determination. Peterson Hirsch method is a more accurate method to determine the dead time of GC system. According to the linear relationship between the number of carbon atoms of homologues and the logarithm of the adjusted retention time, the dead time is calculated by using the retention time of homologues. If three homologues with the same difference number of carbon atoms Z are used, there are:

$$n - Z = a + b\lg t'_{R(n-Z)}$$

$$n = a + b\lg t'_{R(n)}$$

$$n + Z = a + b\lg t'_{R(n+Z)}$$

It can be concluded that: $$t'^2_{R(n)} = t'_{R(n-Z)} t'_{R(n+Z)}$$

Put $t'_R = t_R - t_0$ into above-mentioned formula, thus

$$t_0 = \frac{t_{R(n-Z)} t_{R(n+Z)} - t^2_{R(n)}}{t_{R(n-Z)} + t_{R(n+Z)} - 2t_{R(n)}}$$

Where Z is the difference number of carbon atoms of homologues; n is the number of carbon atoms in the homologue; a and b are constants; t'_R, t_R and t_0 are adjusted retention time, retention time and dead time respectively, min.

In this experiment, the mixture of n-hexane, n-heptane and n-octane with an interval of one carbon atom is used to determine the dead time.

实验 4.4　气相色谱法中死时间的测定和归一化法测定烷烃混合物的含量

一、实验目的

（1）掌握气相色谱法中死时间的测定方法。

（2）掌握归一化法的定量分析方法。

（3）熟悉气相色谱仪的基本结构和使用方法。

二、实验原理

色谱法中的死时间是指不保留组分从进样开始通过色谱柱到达检测器的时间，用于计算保留因子（k）以优化实验条件。气相色谱法中常用空气（对热导检测器，TCD）或甲烷（对氢火焰离子化检测器，FID）测定死时间，但由于空气或甲烷在固定相中也有极少的分配，因此该方法只能用于粗略测定。较准确的死时间测定方法是 Peterson-Hirsch 法，根据同系物的碳原子数与其调整保留时间的对数呈线性关系，利用同系物的保留时间来计算死时间。若使用的三个同系物间隔相同的碳原子数 Z，则有

$$n - Z = a + b\lg t'_{\mathrm{R}(n-Z)}$$

$$n = a + b\lg t'_{\mathrm{R}(n)}$$

$$n + Z = a + b\lg t'_{\mathrm{R}(n+Z)}$$

推导可得

$$t'^{2}_{\mathrm{R}(n)} = t'_{\mathrm{R}(n-Z)} t'_{\mathrm{R}(n+Z)}$$

将 $t'_{\mathrm{R}} = t_{\mathrm{R}} - t_0$ 代入，即得

$$t_0 = \frac{t_{\mathrm{R}(n-Z)} t_{\mathrm{R}(n+Z)} - t^2_{\mathrm{R}(n)}}{t_{\mathrm{R}(n-Z)} + t_{\mathrm{R}(n+Z)} - 2t_{\mathrm{R}(n)}}$$

式中，Z 为同系物间隔的碳原子数；n 为同系物的碳原子数；a，b 为常数；t'_{R}，t_{R}，t_0 分别为调整保留时间、保留时间和死时间，min。

本实验采用间隔一个碳原子的正己烷、正庚烷、正辛烷的混合物测定死时间。

在色谱分析中各组分的量与色谱峰面积成正比，归一化法是根据各组分在试样中所占的百分比，利用色谱峰面积来进行定量分析的方法。由于检测器对各组分的响应不同，需用校正因子进行校正，故各组分的含量可由下式计算：

$$w_i(\%) = \frac{m_i}{m_1 + m_2 + \cdots + m_n} \times 100\% = \frac{f_i A_i}{\sum_{i=0}^{n} f_i A_i} \times 100\%$$

式中，m_i 为各组分的质量，mg；f_i 和 A_i 分别为组分的校正因子和色谱峰面积。

In chromatographic analysis, the amount of each component is directly proportional to the chromatographic peak area. Normalization method is a quantitative analysis method based on the percentage of each component in the sample. Because the response of the detector of each component is different, the calibration factor is needed for accurate determination, so the content of each component can be calculated by the following formula:

$$w_i(\%) = \frac{m_i}{m_1 + m_2 + \cdots + m_n} \times 100\% = \frac{f_i A_i}{\sum_{i=0}^{n} f_i A_i} \times 100\%$$

Where m_i is the mass of components, mg; f_i and A_i are the calibration factor and peak area of components respectively.

The normalization method is simple and accurate, and does not need reference substance. The small change of injection volume and operating conditions has little effect on the experimental results, but it requires that all components must be eluted and the corresponding chromatographic peaks can be detected, which is not suitable for the analysis of trace components.

Instruments and Chemical Reagents

1. Instruments

Shimadzu GC-14A gas chromatograph; DB-5 capillary GC column (30 m × 0.53 mm, 0.25 μm); micro syringe (10 μL); sample bottle.

2. Chemical reagents

n-hexane (A.R.); *n*-heptane (A.R.); *n*-octane (A.R.).

Procedure

1. Preparation of sample solutions

Take a certain volume of *n*-hexane, *n*-heptane and *n*-octane into 5 mL sample bottle and mix them well.

2. Experimental conditions

Detector: hydrogen flame ionization detector (FID);

Column: DB-5 (30 m × 0.53 mm, 0.25 μm);

Carrier gas: N_2; flow rate: 18–35 mL/min; injector temperature: 110 ℃; detector temperature: 250 ℃; column temperature: 40 ℃; injection volume: 0.5 μL. Split ratio is 10 : 1.

3. Gas chromatograph operation

According to the experimental conditions, operate following the process: turn on the gas → power on the instrument → set the temperature (column temperature, detector, injector) → ignite the detector → open the chromatographic workstation to establish the file → view the baseline → injection for analysis.

4. Sample determination

Under the above experimental conditions, 0.5 μL of the sample is injected with a syringe. Record the chromatogram and save the data, repeat the determination for 3 times.

归一化法简便、准确，不需要对照品，进样量和操作条件的微小变动对实验结果影响不大，但要求所有组分必须全部能被洗脱和检测出相应的色谱峰，不适合微量组分的分析。

三、仪器和试剂

1. 仪器

岛津 GC-14A型气相色谱仪；DB -5 毛细管色谱柱（30 m ×0.53 mm，0.25 μm）；微量注射器（10 μL）；样品瓶。

2. 试剂

正己烷（分析纯）；正庚烷（分析纯）；正辛烷（分析纯）。

四、实验步骤

1. 样品溶液配制

分别精密移取一定体积的正己烷、正庚烷、正辛烷于 5 mL 样品瓶中，混匀。

2. 实验条件

检测器：氢火焰离子化检测器（FID）；

毛细管色谱柱：DB-5（30 m ×0.53 mm，0.25 μm）

载气：N_2；流速：18~35 mL·min^{-1}；气化室温度：110 ℃；检测器温度：250 ℃；柱温：40 ℃；进样量：0.5 μL，分流比 10∶1。

3. 气相色谱仪操作

根据实验条件，按照流程操作：开气→开机→设置温度（柱温、检测器、气化室）→打开检测器→点火→打开色谱工作站建立文件→查看基线→进样分析。

4. 样品测定

在上述实验条件下，用注射器进样 0.5 μL，记录色谱图并保存数据，重复测定 3 次。

五、数据处理

打开保存的数据文件进行离线数据分析，获取色谱图中各色谱峰的保留时间、峰面积，填入下表，用保留时间计算死时间，用峰面积归一化法计算各组分的含量，报告死时间和各组分含量的平均值。

进样次数	色谱峰	保留时间/min	峰面积	t_0/min	归一化含量 /%
1	正己烷				
	正庚烷				
	正辛烷				
2	正己烷				
	正庚烷				
	正辛烷				
3	正己烷				
	正庚烷				
	正辛烷				

Data Analysis

Open the saved data file for offline data analysis on computer, obtain the retention time and peak area of each chromatographic peak in the chromatogram, fill in the following table, calculate the dead time with retention time, calculate the content of each component with peak area normalization method, and report the dead time and the average content of each component.

No. of injection	Peaks	Retention time/min	Peak area	t_0/min	Content/%
1	*n*-hexane				
	n-heptane				
	n-octane				
2	*n*-hexane				
	n-heptane				
	n-octane				
3	*n*-hexane				
	n-heptane				
	n-octane				

Experiment Guidance

1. Preview instruction

(1) Review the basic knowledge of gas chromatography.

(2) Master the common quantitative methods of chromatography.

(3) Understand the use of gas chromatograph operating software.

2. Notes

(1) Turn on the gas first, and then turn on the power supply of the instrument; when shutting down, set the temperature first, turn off the power after the column temperature, injector temperature and detector temperature are all cooled to 50 ℃ , and finally turn off the carrier gas.

(2) The detector temperature should be above the column temperature to prevent the sample or the lost stationary phase from condensing in the detector.

(3) If the chromatographic peak is too small or too large, the injection volume can be adjusted appropriately.

3. Discussion

(1) What is the selection principle of column temperature? What happens if the detector temperature is lower than the column temperature?

(2) Why is the normalization method not suitable for the analysis of trace components?

(3) What factors are related to t_0?

六、实验指导

1. 预习要求

（1）复习气相色谱法的基础知识。

（2）掌握色谱法的常用定量方法。

（3）了解气相色谱仪操作软件的使用。

2. 注意事项

（1）先开气，后开仪器电源；关机时，先设置温度，待柱温、进样器温度、检测器温度均降至50 ℃后再关电源，最后关闭载气。

（2）检测器温度应高于柱温，以防样品溶液或流失的固定液冷凝在检测器里。

（3）如果色谱峰太小或太大，可适当调整进样量。

3. 讨论

（1）色谱柱温的选择原则是什么？检测器温度低于柱温会产生什么影响？

（2）为什么归一化法不适合微量组分的分析？

（3）死时间与哪些因素有关？

Experiment 4.5 Effect of Mobile Phase Velocity on Column Efficiency in Gas Chromatography

Purpose

(1) To master the concept and calculation method of theoretical plate number and height equivalent to the theoretical plate.

(2) To master the meaning of Van Deemeter equation, and the relationship between the column efficiency and the velocity of the carrier gas.

Principle

Gas chromatography (GC) is a powerful and widely used tool for the separation, identification, and quantitation of components in a mixture. In this technique, a sample is converted to the vapor state and a flowing streaming of carrier gas (helium in this experiment) sweeps the sample into a column.

The goal of GC is to separate and detect components of a mixture as efficiently as possible and it is thus desirable to have a measure of the efficiency of a given chromatographic column. One common way to express column efficiency is by calculating the height of theoretical plate (H) which is the length of the column divided by the number of theoretical plates.

$$H = \frac{L}{N}$$

Where H is the height of theoretical plate, cm; L is column length, cm; N is the number of theoretical plates of a column with respect to a particular compound. N can be calculated using the following equation:

$$N = 16\left(\frac{t_R}{W}\right)^2 = 5.54\left(\frac{t_R}{W_{1/2}}\right)^2$$

Where W and $W_{1/2}$ are the peak width and the peak width measured at half of the peak height measured in the same unit as t_R respectively, cm.

It is well established that the varying efficiency of a gas chromatographic column can be rationalized from the standpoint of kinetic theory of gases and the peak broadening phenomenon is the result of various diffusion and mass transfer processes between different phases. The Van Deemeter equation is usually adopted to describe the results of these processes

$$H = A + \frac{B}{u} + Cu$$

Where H is the height of theoretical plate, cm; u is linear velocity of the carrier gas, $cm \cdot s^{-1}$; A, B and C are eddy diffusion coefficient, cm; longitudinal diffusion coefficient, $cm^2 \cdot s^{-1}$; and mass transfer resistance coefficient, s.

It can be seen that if u is too small, the diffusion of component molecules in the mobile phase intensifies. When u is too large, the mass transfer resistance increases. In both cases, column efficiency decreases. Obviously, there's a conflict over the choice of velocity. However, the equation predicated an optimum flow rate at which the efficiency of the column is at its maximum, and is a useful guide to finding experimentally the best operating condition in using a gas chromatographic column. The flow rate at this time is called the optimal flow rate (u_{opt}), and the corresponding H value is called the minimum height of theoretical plate (H_{min}).

实验 4.5　气相色谱法中流动相速度对柱效的影响

一、实验目的

（1）掌握理论塔板数和理论塔板高度的概念及计算方法。

（2）掌握范德米特（van Deemeter）方程的含义，理解色谱柱柱效与载气流速之间的关系。

二、实验原理

气相色谱法（gas chromatography，GC）是分离、鉴别和定量分析混合物中各种组分的有力工具。它是利用载气将气化的样品带入色谱柱进行分析的方法。

气相色谱法的目标是尽可能地将混合物中的组分分离，因此需要一个衡量色谱柱分离效能的指标。其中之一是计算理论塔板高度（H），其与色谱柱长的关系为

$$H = \frac{L}{N}$$

式中，H 为理论塔板高度，cm；L 为柱长，cm；N 为某指定化合物的理论塔板数。N 又可以按下式计算：

$$N = 16\left(\frac{t_{\mathrm{R}}}{W}\right)^2 = 5.54\left(\frac{t_{\mathrm{R}}}{W_{1/2}}\right)^2$$

式中，W 和 $W_{1/2}$ 为测定 t_{R} 的同时，得到的峰宽和半峰宽，cm。

气相色谱柱的柱效也可以用动力学的观点解释，峰展宽现象是各种扩散和两相间的传质阻抗过程的结果。范德米特方程用于描述这些过程的结果：

$$H = A + \frac{B}{u} + Cu$$

式中，H 为理论塔板高度，cm；u 为载气流速，$\mathrm{cm \cdot s^{-1}}$；A，B，C 分别为涡流扩散系数，cm；纵向扩散系数，$\mathrm{cm^2 \cdot s^{-1}}$；传质阻抗系数，s 。可见，$u$ 过小，组分分子在流动相中的扩散加剧；u 过大，组分在两相中的传质阻力增加。两种情况下均会导致柱效下降。显然，在 u 的选择上发生了矛盾。但可以找到一个合适的流速，兼顾分子扩散和传质阻力的影响，柱效最高，H 值最小，此时的流速称为最佳流速（u_{opt}），相应的 H 值称为最小理论塔板高度（H_{min}）。

三、仪器和试剂

1. 仪器

岛津 GC-14A 气相色谱仪；5% 邻苯二甲酸二壬酯（2 m × 3 mm I.D.）；热导检测器（TCD）；微量注射器（1 μL）。

2. 试剂

正己烷（分析纯）。

Instruments and Chemical Reagents

1. Instruments

Shimadzu GC-14A gas chromatographic system; 5% dinonyl phthalate chromatographic column (2 m × 3 mm I.D.); thermal conductivity detector (TCD); micro-syringe (1 μL).

2. Chemical reagents

n-Hexane (A.R).

Procedure

1. Chromatographic conditions

Chromatographic column: 5% dinonyl phthalate, 2 m × 3 mm I.D.; column temperature: 80 ℃; injection temperature: 85 ℃ ; detector temperature: 80 ℃ ; the current of TCD is 120 mA; carrier gas: H_2.

2. Effect of carrier gas velocity on column efficiency

Turn on the gas chromatograph system as instructed. Adjust the velocity of carrier gas to 90.0 $mL \cdot min^{-1}$. Inject 1.0 μL of *n*-hexane into the injector port, and press the **Start** button on the GC simultaneously. Record the chromatogram until the analyte is eluted. Press the **Stop** button on the computer. Re-adjust the flow rate and wait for it to stabilize. Record the chromatogram for flow rates of 70 $mL \cdot min^{-1}$, 50 $mL \cdot min^{-1}$, 30 $mL \cdot min^{-1}$, 10 $mL \cdot min^{-1}$, 5 $mL \cdot min^{-1}$. Record the t_R and $W_{1/2}$ values.

Data Analysis

(1) Calculate the number of theoretical plates (N) and the height of theoretical plate (H) at each of the flow rate. Plot the H-u curve.

(2) Calculate u_{opt} and the corresponding H_{min}.

Experiment Guidance

1. Preview instruction

(1) Review the basic knowledge of gas chromatography.

(2) Grasp the meaning of the parameters in Van Deemeter equation and their effects on column efficiency.

(3) Understand the detection principle and operation cautions of TCD.

2. Notes

(1) Before the experiment, the carrier gas must be introduced into the GC system and then the power supply turned on. Otherwise, the tungsten wire in the cells may be burned. At the end of the experiment, the temperature should be cooled to below 30℃ , the power supply should be turned off, and then the carrier gas should be turned off.

(2) When using a microsyringe, bubbles must be removed. The needle core should be slowly lifted when the liquid is pumped. If there are bubbles, the needle tip of the syringe can be raised to make the bubbles float up and push out. The injection volume must be accurate and reproducible. Insert and remove the microsyringe at the same rate each time.

3. Discussion

(1) Explain the terms A, B and C in Van Deemter equation and their effects on column efficiency.

(2) What is the most commonly used carrier gas for GC-TCD? And why?

(3) What are the advantages and limitation of the TCD?

(4) For a gas chromatography system with a given column, what are the main factors that affect the operating conditions of separation besides the mobile phase velocity, and what are the results?

四、实验步骤

1. 色谱条件

色谱柱：5% 邻苯二甲酸二壬酯，2 m × 3 mm I.D.；柱温：80 ℃；气化室温度：85 ℃；检测器温度：80 ℃；热导池电流为 120 mA；载气：H_2。

2. 载气流速对柱效的影响

按说明打开气相色谱仪。调整载气流速至 90.0 mL·min^{-1}，吸取 1.0 μL 正己烷注入进样口，同时按下 GC 上的启动按钮。记录色谱图，直至出峰。按计算机上的停止按钮。重新调整流速并等待其稳定。记录流速分别为 70 mL·min^{-1}、50 mL·min^{-1}、30 mL·min^{-1}、10 mL·min^{-1} 和 5 mL·min^{-1} 的色谱图。记录 t_R 和 $W_{1/2}$。

五、数据处理

（1）计算每个流速下色谱柱的 N，计算 H，并绘制 H-u 曲线。

（2）计算最佳线速度（u_{opt}）和最小理论塔板高度（H_{min}）。

六、实验指导

1. 预习要求

（1）复习气相色谱法的基础知识。

（2）掌握范德米特方程中各项含义以及对柱效的影响。

（3）了解热导检测器的工作原理及操作注意事项。

2. 注意事项

（1）实验前，必须先通入载气，再开电源。否则，热导池中的钨丝可能会被烧毁。实验结束时，应先降温至 30 ℃以下，关电源，再关载气。

（2）用微量注射器进样时，必须排除气泡。抽液时应缓慢上提针芯，若有气泡，可将注射器针尖向上，使气泡上浮后推出。注入样品体积必须准确、重现。每次插入和拔出注射器的速度应保持一致。

3. 讨论

（1）请解释范德米特方程中，A，B 和 C 的含义及其对柱效有何影响。

（2）热导检测器常用的载气是什么？为什么？

（3）热导检测器的优缺点是什么？

（4）对于给定色谱柱的气相色谱系统，影响分离的操作条件除了流动相速度外，还有哪些主要因素，影响的结果是什么？

Experiment 4.6 Determination of Alcohol in Tincture by Gas Chromatography

Purpose

(1) To grasp quantitative method of internal standard comparison.

(2) To grasp the gas chromatographic method for determination of alcohol in tincture.

(3) To know the operations for gas chromatographic system.

Principle

Internal standard comparison is generally used for quantitative analysis in gas chromatography because calibration factors of many organic compounds are unknown. First, standard solution of known concentration of analyte is prepared, into which internal standard compound is added. Then sample solution is prepared, which contains internal standard compound of same concentration. After injection these solutions are separated by gas chromatographic system. The concentration of analyte in sample solution can be calculated according to the following formula:

$$c_{\text{sample}}=\frac{(A_i/A_s)_{\text{sample}}}{(A_i/A_s)_{\text{standard}}}\times c_{\text{standard}}$$

Where c_{sample} and c_{standard} are the volume fractions of the components to be measured in the sample solution and the standard solution respectively; $(A_i/A_s)_{\text{sample}}$ and $(A_i/A_s)_{\text{standard}}$ are the peak area ratio of the measured component to the internal standard in sample solution and standard solution respectively.

Tincture is a clear liquid preparation made from the extraction or dissolution of raw drugs with ethanol of specified concentration, which is for oral or external use. It can also be made by diluting liquid extract. Tinctures should be tested for alcohol content unless otherwise specified. The alcohol content in the tincture sample was quantitatively analyzed by internal standard comparison method.

Instruments and Chemicals Reagents

1. Instruments

Agilent 6820 gas chromatographic system; 10% PEG-20M, 102 white supporter, column (2 m × 3 mm I.D.); microsyringe (10 μL); suction pipet (5 mL,10 mL); volumetric flask (100 mL); aurilave.

2. Chemical reagents

Absolute alcohol (A.R.); anhydrous propyl alcohol (internal standard); Tincture sample; double-distilled water.

Procedure

1. Preparation of solutions

(1) Standard solution: Transfer 5.00 mL of absolute alcohol and 5.00 mL of propanol into a

实验 4.6 气相色谱法测定酊剂中乙醇的含量

一、实验目的

（1）掌握内标对比法的定量方法。

（2）掌握酊剂中乙醇含量的气相色谱测定方法。

（3）了解气相色谱仪的使用方法。

二、实验原理

许多有机化合物的校正因子未知，此时可采用内标对比法进行定量。该法是在不知校正因子时内标法的一种应用。先配制已知浓度的标准溶液，将一定量的内标物加入其中，再按相同比例将内标物加入未知浓度的样品中。分别进样，由下式可求出样品中待测组分的含量：

$$c_{样品}=\frac{(A_i/A_s)_{样品}}{(A_i/A_s)_{标准}}\times c_{标准}$$

式中，$c_{样品}$，$c_{标准}$分别为待测组分在样品溶液和标准溶液中的体积分数；$(A_i/A_s)_{样品}$，$(A_i/A_s)_{标准}$分别为样品溶液和标准溶液中待测组分和内标物的峰面积比值。

酊剂系指将原料药物用规定浓度的乙醇提取或溶解而制成的澄清液体制剂，也可用流浸膏稀释制成。供口服或外用。除另有规定外，酊剂应进行乙醇量检查。本实验采用内标对比法对酊剂样品中乙醇量进行定量分析。

三、仪器和试剂

1. 仪器

安捷伦 6820 型气相色谱仪；色谱柱：10% PEG-20M，102 白色担体（2 m × 3 mm I.D.）；微量注射器（10 μL）；移液管（5 mL、10 mL）；容量瓶（100 mL）；洗耳球。

2. 试剂

无水乙醇（A.R.）；丙醇（对照品，内标物）；酊剂样品；二次蒸馏水。

四、实验步骤

1. 溶液配制

（1）标准溶液配制 准确吸取无水乙醇 5.00 mL 及丙醇 5.00 mL，置于 100 mL 容量瓶中，加水稀释至刻度，摇匀。

（2）样品溶液配制 准确吸取酊剂样品 10.00 mL 及丙醇 5.00 mL，置于 100 mL 容量瓶中，加水稀释至刻度，摇匀。

2. 色谱条件

色谱柱：10% PEG-20M，102 白色担体（2 m × 3 mm I.D.）；柱温：80℃；气化室温度：150 ℃；检测器：氢火焰离子化检测器（FID）；检测器温度：200 ℃；N_2（载气）：0.1 MPa；H_2：0.3 MPa；空气：0.4 MPa。

100 mL volumetric flask, dilute to the mark with distilled water and mix well.

(2) Sample solution: Transfer 10.00 mL tincture sample and 5.00 mL propanol exactly into a 100 mL volumetric flask, dilute to the mark with distilled water and mix well.

2. Chromatographic conditions

Column:10% PEG-20M, 102 white supporter, 2 m × 3 mm I.D.; column temperature: 80 ℃; injection temperature: 150℃ ; detector: FID; detector temperature: 200 ℃; N_2 (carrier gas): 0.1 MPa, H_2: 0.3 MPa, Air: 0.4 MPa.

3. Injection

Inject 1.0 μL of standard solution and sample solution under the above conditions, respectively.

Data Analysis

Fill in the blanks in the following table and calculate the concentration of ethanol in sample according to the following formula:

		Retention time/min	Peak area	A_i/A_s	Average
Standard solution 1	Ethanol				
	Propanol				
Standard solution 2	Ethanol				
	Propanol				
Sample solution 1	Ethanol				
	Propanol				
Sample solution 2	Ethanol				
	Propanol				

$$c_{\text{sample}}=\frac{(A_i/A_s)_{\text{sample}}}{(A_i/A_s)_{\text{standard}}}\times 5.00\% \times 10$$

Where $(A_i/A_s)_{\text{sample}}$ and $(A_i/A_s)_{\text{standard}}$ are the peak area ratio of the measured component to the internal standard in sample solution and standard solution respectively. The value of 10 is the dilution ratio and 5.00 % is the concentration of c_{standard}.

Experiment Guidance

1. Preview instruction

(1) Review the basic knowledge of gas chromatography.

(2) Master solution preparation and calculation method of internal standard comparison.

(3) Learn about tinctures.

2. Notes

(1) Use glass volumetric apparatus correctly and prepare standard solution and Sample solution accurately.

3. 进样

在选定的实验条件下，将标准溶液与样品溶液分别进样 1.0 μL。

五、数据处理

将色谱图上有关数据填入下表，按下式计算样品中乙醇的含量。

<table>
<tr><th></th><th></th><th>保留时间/min</th><th>峰面积</th><th>A_i/A_s</th><th>平均值</th></tr>
<tr><td rowspan="2">标准溶液 1</td><td>乙醇</td><td></td><td></td><td rowspan="2"></td><td rowspan="4"></td></tr>
<tr><td>正丙醇</td><td></td><td></td></tr>
<tr><td rowspan="2">标准溶液 2</td><td>乙醇</td><td></td><td></td><td rowspan="2"></td></tr>
<tr><td>正丙醇</td><td></td><td></td></tr>
<tr><td rowspan="2">样品溶液 1</td><td>乙醇</td><td></td><td></td><td rowspan="2"></td><td rowspan="4"></td></tr>
<tr><td>正丙醇</td><td></td><td></td></tr>
<tr><td rowspan="2">样品溶液 2</td><td>乙醇</td><td></td><td></td><td rowspan="2"></td></tr>
<tr><td>正丙醇</td><td></td><td></td></tr>
</table>

$$c_{样品}=\frac{(A_i/A_s)_{样品}}{(A_i/A_s)_{标准}}\times 5.00\%\times 10$$

式中，$(A_i/A_s)_{样品}$，$(A_i/A_s)_{标准}$分别为样品溶液和标准溶液中待测组分和内标物的峰面积比值，10 为稀释倍数，5.00% 为 $c_{标准}$的值。

六、实验指导

1. 预习要求

（1）复习气相色谱法的基础知识。

（2）掌握内标对比法的溶液配制及计算方法。

（3）了解酊剂的有关知识。

2. 注意事项

（1）正确使用容量仪器，准确配制标准溶液和样品溶液。

（2）使用 1 μL 微量注射器，切记不要把针芯拉出针筒外。

（3）吸取样品溶液的注射器，实验后需用乙醇溶剂反复清洗 10 多次，以免针孔堵塞。

（4）内标法只要求被测组分与内标物产生信号即可定量，很适合于中药及复方制剂中有效成分的含量测定。内标物应符合下列要求：

① 样品中不存在的纯物质。

② 稳定的纯品，与样品物理化学性质相近，但不发生化学反应。

③ 与样品组分的色谱峰分离完全，并尽量靠近。

④ 内标物的量应尽量接近被测组分。

（5）氢火焰离子化检测器（FID）主要用于含碳有机化合物的检测，但对非烃类、惰性气体或火焰中难电离或不电离的物质，信号较低或无信号。水是不敏感物质，故本实验中组分的流出顺

(2) Don't pull the valve out of tube when microsyringe (1 μL) is used.

(3) Rinse the microsyringe over ten times with ethanol to prevent filling after experiment.

(4) The internal standard method only requires that the measured components and internal standard substance produce signals and can be quantified, which is suitable for the content determination of active components in Traditional Chinese medicine (TCM) and compound preparations. Requirements of internal standard substance:

A. The sample does not contain the known substance;

B. It is a stable pure product, whose physical and chemical properties similar to the measured component, but no chemical reaction between them;

C. The peak position should be located in the vicinity of the measured component, but are separated completely;

D. The amount should be as close as possible to the measured component.

(5) Hydrogen flame ionization detector (FID) is mainly used for the detection of carbon containing organic compound, but for non-hydrocarbon, inert gas or flame difficult to ionize or non-ionize material, low signal or no signal. Water is an insensitive substance, so in this experiment, the outflow order of components is ethanol and propanol, but there is no water peak.

3. Discussion

(1) What kind of detector are thermal conductivity detector (TCD) and hydrogen flame ionization detector (FID)? What are the characteristics of each?

(2) What is the ratio of H_2, N_2 and Air flow when FID used?

(3) When can internal standard comparison be used? Is the injection volume required to be accurate when using above-mentioned method?

(4) If the carrier gas flow rate changes slightly during the experiment, how does it affect the results?

序是乙醇、丙醇，而无水峰。

3. 讨论

（1）热导检测器和氢火焰离子化检测器各属何种类型检测器？它们各有什么特点？

（2）使用 FID 时，一般 H_2、N_2、Air 三者流量之比是多少？

（3）什么情况下可采用内标对比法？内标对比法定量时，进样量是否要十分准确？

（4）若实验中载气流速稍有变化，对结果有何影响？

Experiment 4.7 Determination of Residual Solvent by Temperature Programmed Capillary Gas Chromatography

Purpose

(1) To master the method of determination of residual solvent in drugs.
(2) To know the application of capillary gas chromatography in the analysis of complex samples.
(3) To know the characteristics of temperature programmed capillary gas chromatography.
(4) To be familiar with quantification by internal standard comparison.

Principle

Residual solvents in pharmaceutical products refer to the organic volatile compounds used in the production of bulk drug, excipients and preparations, but cannot be completely removed during the process. In the process of bulk drug synthesis, the selection of appropriate solvent can increase the yield or determine the properties of the drug, such as crystal type, purity, dissolution rate, etc. Therefore, organic solvent is an essential and very critical substance in drug synthesis reaction. When the level of residual solvent in drugs is higher than the safe value, it will cause harm to human body or the environment. Hence, the control of residual solvent has been paid more and more attention. There are about 70 kinds of residual solvents in drugs. The International Council for Harmonization of Technical Requirements for Pharmaceuticals for Human Use (ICH) has developed guidelines for residual solvents, which are divided into four categories according to the degree of harm to humans and the environment. The pharmacopoeia of various countries, such as USP, BP, EP, JP, ChP has strict standards for the control of residual solvents. Early analytical methods include dry weight loss and spectrophotometry, now commonly use the gas chromatography (GC) system, especially with capillary column and hydrogen flame ionization detector (FID).

In the process of synthesizing Chlorlbenzylidine, methanol, ethanol, acetone, nitromethane, and any other organic solvents used can be determined by temperature programmed capillary GC. Quartz capillary column using PEG-20M as the stationary phase is applied for analysis and four kinds of residual organic solvents can be determined directly by internal standard comparison (*n*-propanol as the internal standard).

Instruments and Chemical Reagents

1. Instruments

Shimadzu GC-2014A; Rtx -Wax capillary column (30 m × 0.53 mm, 0.25 μm); micro-syringe (10 μL);pipettes (1 mL); volumetric flasks (10 mL, 100 mL) ; rubber suction bulb.

2. Chemical reagents

Methanol (A.R.); absolute alcohol (A.R.); acetone (A.R.); nitromethane (A.R.); *n*-propanol (A. R., internal standard substance); chlorlbenzylidine crude drug; double-distilled water.

Procedure

1. Chromatographic conditions

Column: Rtx -Wax capillary column (30 m × 0.53 mm, 0.25 μm); temperature programming:

实验 4.7　程序升温毛细管气相色谱法测定药物中残留溶剂含量

一、实验目的

（1）掌握药物中残留溶剂含量的测定方法。

（2）了解毛细管色谱法在较复杂样品分析中的应用。

（3）了解程序升温气相色谱法的操作特点。

（4）进一步熟悉内标对比法（已知浓度样品对照法）定量。

二、实验原理

药品中的残留溶剂是指在原料药、辅料以及制剂生产中使用的，但在工艺过程中未能完全去除的有机挥发性化合物。在原料药合成工艺中，选择适当的溶剂可提高产量或决定药物的性质，如晶型、纯度、溶解速率等。因此有机溶剂在药物合成反应中是必不可少和非常关键的物质。当药品所含的残留溶剂水平高于安全值时，就会对人体或环境产生危害，因此对残留溶剂的控制已越来越受到人们的关注。药品中残留溶剂的种类有 70 余种，按照对人体和环境的危害程度分为四类，人用药品技术要求国际协调理事会（International council for Harmonization of Technical Requirements for Pharmaceuticals for Human Use，ICH）据此制定了残留溶剂指导原则。各国药典如美国药典、英国药典、欧洲药典、日本药典、中国药典中对残留溶剂控制都有严格的标准。早期的分析方法有干燥失重和分光光度法，现在常用气相色谱法，尤其是采用毛细管柱、氢火焰离子化检测器（FID）的气相色谱分离技术更为常见。

氯苄律定在合成过程中使用了甲醇、乙醇、丙酮、硝基甲烷等有机溶剂，采用毛细管色谱技术并结合程序升温操作，利用PEG-20M交联石英毛细管柱，用内标对比法定量（正丙醇作内标），可直接对此四种残留有机溶剂进行测定。

三、仪器和试剂

1. 仪器

岛津 GC-2014A 型气相色谱仪；Rtx -Wax 毛细管柱（30 m × 0.53 mm，0.25 μm）；微量注射器（10 μL）；移液管（1 mL）；容量瓶（10 mL，100 mL）；洗耳球。

2. 试剂

甲醇（分析纯）；无水乙醇（分析纯）；丙酮（分析纯）；硝基甲烷（分析纯）；正丙醇（分析纯，内标）；氯苄律定原料药；二次蒸馏水。

四、实验步骤

1. 色谱条件

色谱柱：Rtx -Wax 毛细管柱，30 m × 0.53 mm，0.25 μm；程序升温：初始 40 ℃，保持 3 min；以 20 $℃\cdot min^{-1}$ 升温；升到 150 ℃，保持 2 min；气化室温度：200 ℃；检测器：FID；检测器温度：250 ℃；载气：N_2，75 kPa；H_2：50 kPa；空气：50 kPa；分流比：10 ∶ 1；尾吹气：10 $mL\cdot min^{-1}$。

initial 40 ℃, keep for 3 min; heating at 20 ℃·min^{-1}; increase to 150 ℃, maintained for 2 min; temperature of injector: 200 ℃ ; detector: FID; detector temperature: 250 ℃ ; carrier gas: N_2, 75 kPa; H_2: 50 kPa; air: 50 kPa; split ratio: 10 : 1; add flow: 10 mL·min^{-1}.

2. Preparation of solutions

(1) Internal standard and reference stock solution: Accurately pipet proper amount of *n*-propanol, acetone, methanol, ethanol and nitromethane, and add into 100 mL volumetric flask, dilute distilled water to scale, shake well. Dilute the above-mentioned solution and obtain a standard stock solution for each substance.

(2) Mixed standard solution: Transfer stock solution and internal standard (*n*-propanol) 1.00 mL accurately into a 10 mL volumetric flask, add distilled water to the mark, mix well. In this solvent, the concentration of acetone, methanol, ethanol, nitro-methane is 0.109 9 mg·mL^{-1}, 0.065 92 mg·mL^{-1}, 0.109 6 mg·mL^{-1}, 0.055 16 mg·mL^{-1} respectively.

(3) Sample solution: Weigh accurately about 0.200 2 g sample in a 10 mL volumetric flask. Add internal standard 1.00 mL. Add distilled water to the mark, mix well. Tthe concentration of sample is 20.02 mg·mL^{-1}.

3. Injection

Under the above chromatographic condition, inject 1.0 μL of mixed standard solution and sample solution, respectively.

Data Analysis

The content of organic residual solvent in the crude drug can be calculated, respectively, as follows:

$$w_{\text{sample}}=\frac{(A_i/A_s)_{\text{sample}}}{(A_i/A_s)_{\text{standard}}}\times\frac{c_{\text{standard}}}{20.02}\times 100\%$$

Where A_i and A_s are the peak areas of the determined compound and internal standard respectively, while *c* is the concentration of the determined compound, mg·mL^{-1}; 20.02 mg·mL^{-1} is the concentration of sample.

Experiment Guidance

1. Preview instruction

(1) Review internal standard comparison in gas chromatography.

(2) Understand the definition and effect of gradient temperature, splitting and makeup gas.

(3) Understand the classification and characteristics of capillary gas chromatographic column.

2. Notes

(1) When instruments are cooled to original situation and keep steady, inject another sample.

(2) There are many gas chromatography detectors, but only a few are suitable for capillary columns. This is because the detector matched with capillary column must have high sensitivity, fast response and small dead volume. The most commonly used detectors are hydrogen flame ionization detector (FID), flame photometric detector (FPD) and nitrogen phosphorus detector (NPD) are also available.

3. Discussion

(1) What is temperature programming? When is it used?

(2) What are the four categories of residual solvents in drugs according to literatures? Please list which category the solvents measured in this experiment belong to.

(3) What is the split ratio? How do we measure it?

2. 溶液配制

（1）内标和标准物质储备液：准确吸取正丙醇和丙酮、甲醇、乙醇和硝基甲烷适量，置于 100 mL 容量瓶中，蒸馏水稀释至刻度，摇匀。稀释上述溶液，得各物质标准储备液。

（2）混合标准溶液：准确吸取标准储备液和内标溶液各 1.00 mL，置于 10 mL 容量瓶中，蒸馏水稀释至刻度，摇匀。使此溶液中丙酮、甲醇、乙醇和硝基甲烷的浓度分别为 0.109 9 $mg \cdot mL^{-1}$，0.065 92 $mg \cdot mL^{-1}$，0.109 6 $mg \cdot mL^{-1}$，0.055 16 $mg \cdot mL^{-1}$。

（3）样品溶液：取样品约 0.200 2 g，精密称定，置于 10 mL 容量瓶中，准确加入内标溶液 1.00 mL，用水稀释至刻度，摇匀。样品的浓度为 20.02 $mg \cdot mL^{-1}$。

3. 进样

在上述色谱条件下，标准溶液与样品溶液分别进样 1.0 μL。

五、数据处理

根据标准溶液及样品溶液中各待测成分与内标峰面积之比，用下式计算样品中各残留溶剂的含量。

$$w_{样品} = \frac{(A_i/A_s)_{样品}}{(A_i/A_s)_{标准品}} \times \frac{c_{标准}}{20.02} \times 100\%$$

式中，A_i 为待测组分峰面积，A_s 为内标峰面积，c 为待测组分的质量浓度，$mg \cdot mL^{-1}$；20.02 $mg \cdot mL^{-1}$ 为样品溶液质量浓度。

六、实验指导

1. 预习要求

（1）复习气相色谱法的内标对比法定量方法。

（2）理解程序升温、分流及尾吹的定义和作用。

（3）了解毛细管气相色谱柱的分类及特点。

2. 注意事项

（1）在一个温度程序执行完成后，须等待色谱仪回到初始状态并稳定后，才能进行下一次进样。

（2）气相色谱检测器很多，但只有几种适用于毛细管柱。这是因为与毛细管柱相匹配的检测器必须具有灵敏度高、响应迅速以及死体积极小的特点。最常用的检测器是氢火焰离子化检测器，火焰光度检测器和氮磷检测器也可使用。

3. 讨论

（1）什么是程序升温？在什么情况下应用程序升温？

（2）查询相关资料，说明药品中残留溶剂分为哪四类，请分别列出本实验中所测溶剂各属哪一类。

（3）何为分流比？如何测算？

Experiment 4.8 Evaluation of the High Performance Liquid Chromatography Performance and Calculation of the Chromatographic Parameters

Purpose

(1) To grasp the parameters for the evaluation of the high performance liquid chromatography's performance and the method for evaluation of those parameters.

(2) To grasp the calculation of the theoretical plate number, height equivalent to a theoretical plate, peak tailing factor and resolution.

(3) To know the general rules for the operation of the high performance liquid chromatography equipment.

Principle

1. HPLC performance

There are general parameters for the evaluation of high performance liquid chromatography (HPLC) performance even for different types of HPLC equipment. These parameters include the flow accuracy, noise, drift, qualitative reproducibility and quantitative reproducibility.

(1) Flow accuracy: it is expressed by relative standard deviation of repeated measurement of flow rate, which reflects the repeatability of instrumental flow rate.

(2) Noise: the fluctuation of the baseline caused by various accidental factors. The magnitude of noise is expressed in baseline bandwidth, usually with the unit of in millivolts or amperes.

(3) Drift: a slow change of the baseline to a certain direction, which is expressed as the change of baseline per unit time.

(4) Qualitative reproducibility: repeatability of retention time of a component under the same experimental condition, which is usually expressed as the relative standard deviation (RSD) of the retention time difference of the separated component (Δt_R). Eligibility criteria is RSD$\leqslant$1%.

(5) Quantitative reproducibility: repeatability of peak area (or peak height) of a component under the same experimental condition, which is usually expressed as the relative standard deviation (RSD) of peak area ratio (or peak height ratio) of the separated component. Eligibility criteria is RSD$\leqslant$2%.

2. Chromatographic parameters

HPLC chromatographic parameters include qualitative parameters, quantitative parameters, column efficiency parameters and separation parameters. In this experiment, we use theoretical plate number, peak asymmetry and resolution to evaluate the column performance.

(1) Theoretical plate number: Theoretical plate number (N) is one of important parameters to evaluate the column performance. It reflects the characteristic of the column, which is commonly used to evaluate the column efficiency. The more the theoretical plate number, the smaller the height equivalent to a theoretical plate, and the higher the column efficiency.

$$N = 5.54\left(\frac{t_R}{W_{1/2}}\right)^2$$

实验 4.8　高效液相色谱仪的性能考察及色谱参数的测定

一、实验目的

（1）掌握高效液相色谱仪性能考察及色谱参数测定的方法。

（2）掌握色谱柱理论塔板数、理论塔板高度、色谱峰拖尾因子和分离度的计算方法。

（3）了解高效液相色谱仪的一般使用方法。

二、实验原理

1. 高效液相色谱仪的性能指标

不同型号的高效液相色谱仪的技术参数均有一定的要求。常见的高效液相色谱仪的性能指标包括流量精度、噪声、漂移、定性重复性及定量重复性。

（1）流量精度：以重复测定流量的相对标准差表示，体现了仪器流量的重复性。

（2）噪声：由于各种偶然因素引起的基线的起伏。噪声的大小用基线带宽表示，通常以毫伏或安培为单位。

（3）漂移：基线向一定方向的缓慢变化，用单位时间内基线水平的变化来表示。

（4）定性重复性：在相同实验条件下，两组分保留时间的重复性。定性重复性通常以多次测定被分离两组分的保留时间之差（Δt_R）的相对标准差 RSD 表示。合格标准是 RSD≤1%。

（5）定量重复性：在相同实验条件下，两组分色谱峰面积（或峰高）的重复性。定量重复性通常以多次测定被分离两组分的峰面积比（峰高比）的相对标准差 RSD 表示。合格标准是 RSD≤2%。

2. 色谱参数

高效液相色谱参数包括定性参数、定量参数、柱效参数和分离参数等。本实验主要评价色谱柱性能的好坏，涉及的主要参数包括理论塔板数、峰对称性及分离度。

（1）理论塔板数　理论塔板数 N 是评价色谱柱性能的重要指标之一，它反映了色谱柱本身的特征，一般用它来衡量柱效。理论塔板数越多，理论塔板高度越小，柱效越高。

$$N = 5.54\left(\frac{t_R}{W_{1/2}}\right)^2$$

式中，N 为理论塔板数；t_R 为保留时间，min；$W_{1/2}$ 为半峰宽，cm。

（2）峰对称性　色谱柱的热力学性质和柱内填充的均匀程度，会影响色谱峰的对称性。峰对称性用拖尾因子 f_s 表示。

$$f_s = \frac{W_{0.05h}}{2A}$$

式中，$W_{0.05h}$ 为 0.05 倍峰高处的峰宽，cm；色谱峰顶点至基线的垂线将色谱峰分开的两部分 A 和 B，A 为前半峰的长度。

where N is theoretical plate number; t_R is retention time, min; $W_{1/2}$ is peak width at the half peak height, cm.

(2) Peak asymmetry: Peak asymmetry is affected by the thermodynamic characteristics and packing uniformity of the column. Peak asymmetry is expressed by peak tailing factor, f_s.

$$f_s = \frac{W_{0.05h}}{2A}$$

where $W_{0.05h}$ is peak width at the one twentieth of peak height, cm; part A (A) and part B are two parts where the peak is divided by the vertical line from the peak to the baseline, cm.

(3) Resolution: Resolution is used to evaluate the separation efficiency of the neighboring peaks of two components, which is expressed as R.

$$R = \frac{2(t_{R2} - t_{R1})}{W_1 + W_2}$$

where t_{R2} and t_{R1} are retention time of the two adjacent peaks (peak of component 2 appears late), min; W_1 and W_2 are peak width of component 1 and component 2, cm.

Instruments and Chemical Reagents

1. Instruments

HPLC system (Shimadzu LC-10A); UV detector; C_{18} reversed-phase column (150 mm × 4.6 mm, 5.0 μm); microsyringe (100 μL); volumetric flask (10 mL).

2. Chemical reagents

Benzene (A.R.); toluene (A.R.); methanol (HPLC grade); double-distilled water.

Procedure

1. Preparation of solution

Prepare a mixture of benzene and toluene in methanol (1 : 1 000, *V/V*), which is used as sample solution.

2. Instrument status check

Check whether the mobile phase is sufficient, observe the flow path of the mobile phase, and confirm that the waste liquid outlet has been connected.

3. Measurement of the flow accuracy

Measure the actual flow rate when the indicating flow rate is 1.0 $mL \cdot min^{-1}$, 2.0 $mL \cdot min^{-1}$ and 3.0 $mL \cdot min^{-1}$. Use a 10 mL volumetric flask to collect the efflux, accurately record the time required for the outflow of 10 mL, and calculate the flow rate in the unit of $mL \cdot min^{-1}$. Repeat the above determination 5 times.

4. Chromatographic conditions

Mobile phase: methanol-water (95 : 5, *V/V*);

Stationary phase: C_{18} reversed-phase column (150 mm × 4.6 mm, 5.0 μm);

Detection wavelength: 254 nm;

Flow rate: 1.0 $mL \cdot min^{-1}$.

5. Determination of noise and drift

After the instrument is stable, set the detector sensitivity at a higher level until the noise can be detected, and record the baseline for 1 h. Noise is measured as the maximum width of peak to valley of baseline fluctuation. Drift is measured as the difference between the end position and the starting

（3）分离度 分离度是从色谱峰判断相邻两分离组分在色谱柱中总分离效能的指标，用 R 表示。

$$R=\frac{2(t_{R2}-t_{R1})}{W_1+W_2}$$

式中，t_{R2}、t_{R1} 分别为相邻两组分的保留时间（组分 2 后出峰），min；W_1、W_2 分别为组分 1 和组分 2 的色谱峰的峰宽，cm。

三、仪器和试剂

1. 仪器

高效液相色谱仪（岛津 LC-10A）；紫外检测器；C_{18} 反相键合相色谱柱（150 mm × 4.6 mm，5.0 μm）；微量注射器（100 μL）；容量瓶（10 mL）。

2. 试剂

苯（分析纯）；甲苯（分析纯）；甲醇（色谱纯）；二次蒸馏水。

四、实验步骤

1. 样品溶液的配制

配制苯和甲苯的甲醇溶液（1 ∶ 1 000，体积比）作为样品溶液。

2. 仪器状态检查

检查流动相是否够用，观察流动相流路，确认废液出口已接好。

3. 流量精度的测定

在指示流速分别为 1.0 $mL\cdot min^{-1}$、2.0 $mL\cdot min^{-1}$、3.0 $mL\cdot min^{-1}$ 时，测定实际流速。用 10 mL 容量瓶在流动相出口处接收流出液，准确记录流出 10 mL 所用的时间，并换算成流速（$mL\cdot min^{-1}$），重复测定 5 次，并记录。

4. 色谱条件的设定

流动相：甲醇-水（95 ∶ 5，体积比）；

固定相：C_{18} 反相键合相色谱柱（150 mm × 4.6 mm，5.0 μm）；

检测波长：254 nm；

流速：1.0 $mL\cdot min^{-1}$。

5. 噪声和漂移的测定

待仪器稳定后，将检测器灵敏度放在较高档至能测出噪声，记录基线 1 h。测定基线波动的峰对谷的最大宽度为噪声。基线带中心的结尾位置与起始位置之差为漂移。

6. 进样

待仪器基线稳定后，进样 20 μL 样品溶液，记录色谱图。

五、数据处理

（1）计算 3 种不同指示流量下的实际流量，评价色谱仪的流量精度。

（2）根据基线结果，计算色谱仪的噪声和漂移。

（3）根据苯和甲苯混合物的色谱峰，分别计算两种被分离组分的理论塔板数 N。

position of the baseline band center.

6. Sample injection

When the baseline is stable, inject 20 μL of the sample solution under the above chromatographic condition, and record the chromatogram.

Data Analysis

(1) Calculate the actual flow rates at three different indicating flow rates, and evaluate the flow accuracy of the HPLC instrument.

(2) Calculate the noise and drift according to the baseline result.

(3) According to the chromatographic peak of benzene and toluene, calculate the theoretical plate numbers of benzene and toluene, respectively.

(4) According to the chromatographic peak of benzene and toluene, calculate the peak tailing factors of benzene and toluene, respectively.

(5) Calculate the resolution of benzene and toluene.

Experiment Guidance

1. Preview instruction

(1) Review the related content of high performance liquid chromatography.

(2) Be familiar with the instrumentation of HPLC and parameters for evaluation of column performance.

(3) Understand the requirements and preparation methods of HPLC mobile phase.

2. Notes

(1) Solvents used in HPLC must be purified. Water must be freshly double-distilled or deionized before used.

(2) Mobile phase must be degassed before used. The commonly used degassing methods include vacuum pump decompression degassing, heating reflux degassing, ultrasonic degassing, and Helium-blowing degassing.

(3) Before sampling, wash the microsyringe several times with methanol or acetone, and then rinse it several times with sample solution. Suck excessive sample, put the microsyringe needle upward to expel bubbles, and adjust the sample volume to the required amount. After injection, rinse the microsyringe several times with methanol or acetone.

(4) Rinse the column with methanol for 20-30 min to protect the column after experiment. If the mobile phase contains salt or buffer, firstly rinse the column with water, and then with methanol to protect the column.

(5) When calculating the chromatographic parameters, the unit of t_R and $W_{1/2}$ should be identical.

3. Discussion

(1) Why to measure the parameters to evaluate the HPLC performance?

(2) Why must the mobile phase be degassed before use?

(3) According to the principle of reversed-phase chromatography, explain the efflux order of benzene and toluene.

(4) In reversed-phase chromatography, what is the proper pH range of the mobile phase?

（4）根据苯和甲苯混合物的色谱峰，分别计算两种被分离组分的拖尾因子 f_s。

（5）计算苯和甲苯的分离度 R。

六、实验指导

1. 预习要求

（1）复习高效液相色谱相关内容。

（2）熟悉高效液相色谱仪的组成和评估色谱性能的参数。

（3）了解高效液相色谱流动相的要求及配制方法。

2. 注意事项

（1）高效液相色谱中所用的溶剂均需经过纯化处理。水要用新鲜的二次蒸馏水或经脱离子处理的蒸馏水。

（2）流动相经脱气处理后才能使用。常用的脱气方法有水泵减压抽吸脱气法、加热回流脱气法、超声波脱气法和吹氦脱气法。

（3）取样时，先用甲醇或丙酮清洗微量注射器几次，后用样品溶液清洗几次，然后吸取过量样品，将注射器针尖向上，除去注射器内的气泡并将所取样品调至所需的量。进样后，微量注射器要用甲醇或丙酮洗涤数次。

（4）为了保护色谱柱，实验结束后，反相色谱柱需用甲醇冲洗 20~30 min。若流动相中含盐或缓冲溶液，则先用水冲洗，再用甲醇冲洗。

（5）计算色谱参数时，应注意 t_R 和 $W_{1/2}$ 单位一致。

3. 讨论

（1）为什么要对高效液相色谱仪的性能指标进行检测？

（2）流动相在使用前为什么要脱气？

（3）根据反相色谱机制，说明苯、甲苯在反相色谱中的出峰顺序。

（4）在反相色谱中，流动相的 pH 应控制在什么范围内？

Experiment 4.9 Determination of Salicylic Acid Impurity in Aspirin by High Performance Liquid Chromatography

Purpose

(1) To grasp the assay of salicylic acid impurity in aspirin by high performance liquid chromatography.

(2) To be familiar with manual injection in high performance liquid chromatography.

Principle

Aspirin, also known as acetylsalicylic acid, is a commonly used analgesic. In recent years, aspirin has been found to inhibit platelet aggregation, which has been clinically used to prevent postoperative thrombosis, transient ischemic attack, myocardial infarction and so on. Salicylic acid is the main hydrolysate of aspirin.

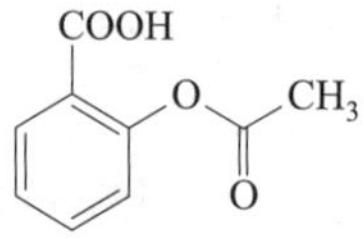

acetylsalicylic acid

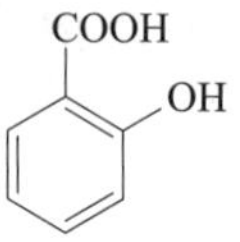

salicylic acid

Chromatography can be used to separate multiple components in the mixture, and provide quantitative basis with the relative standard deviation of 1%-2%. In chromatography, the peak area or peak height is directly proportional to the content of the component, therefore peak area can be used for quantitative analysis. Commonly used quantitative methods include normalization method, external standard method, internal standard method, and standard curve method. In this experiment, a simple and effective high performance liquid chromatography (HPLC) method was designed for the determination of salicylic acid impurities in aspirin raw materials. The external standard method was used to compare the peak area of the standard substance and the sample solution, and the quantitative calculation was carried out with the following formula:

$$\varphi_{sA}\,(\%)=\frac{A_i}{A_s}\times\frac{\varphi_s\times 10}{W_{sample}}\times 100\%$$

where φ_s is the concentration of salicylic acid standard solution, $mg\cdot mL^{-1}$; A_i and A_s are the peak areas of standard solution and sample solution, respectively; W_{sample} is the mass of aspirin raw materials, mg.

Instruments and Chemical Reagents

1. Instruments

HPLC system (Shimadzu LC-10A); UV detector; C_{18} reversed-phase column (150 mm × 4.6 mm , 5.0 μm); analytical balance; microsyringe (100 μL); mortar; funnel; volumetric flask (10 mL).

2. Chemical reagents

Salicylic acid (reference substance); aspirin (raw materials); methanol (HPLC grade). HAc (A.R.);

实验 4.9　高效液相色谱法测定阿司匹林中杂质的含量

一、实验目的

（1）掌握利用外标法测定阿司匹林原料药中水杨酸杂质的方法。

（2）熟悉高效液相色谱仪的手动进样操作。

二、实验原理

阿司匹林，又名乙酰水杨酸，是一种常用的镇痛药。近年来发现阿司匹林对血小板聚集有抑制作用，临床上用于预防术后血栓的形成、短暂脑缺血发作、心肌梗死等。水杨酸是阿司匹林主要的水解产物。

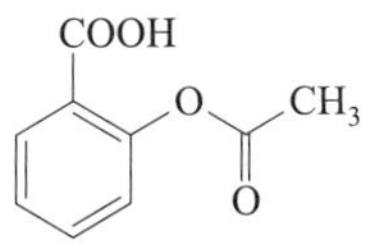

乙酰水杨酸

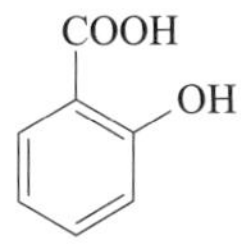

水杨酸

色谱法既能分离多组分混合物，又能提供定量依据，且定量结果的相对标准偏差为 1%~2%。色谱法中，峰高或峰面积与组分的含量成正比，可利用峰面积进行定量。常用的定量方法有归一化法、外标法、内标法、标准曲线法等。本实验设计了一种简单有效的高效液相色谱法，用于测定阿司匹林原料药中水杨酸杂质的含量，并可利用外标法，通过与标准品的峰面积比较，用下式进行定量计算：

$$\varphi_{\text{水杨酸}}\ (\%)=\frac{A_i}{A_\text{s}}\times\frac{\varphi_s\times 10}{W_{\text{样品}}}\times 100\%$$

式中，φ_s 为水杨酸标准溶液浓度，$\text{mg}\cdot\text{mL}^{-1}$；$A_i$ 和 A_s 分别为样品溶液和标准溶液中水杨酸的峰面积；$W_{\text{样品}}$为阿司匹林样品的质量，mg。

三、仪器和试剂

1. 仪器

高效液相色谱仪（岛津 LC-10A）；紫外检测器；ODS 色谱柱（150 mm × 4.6 mm，5.0 μm）；分析天平；微量注射器（100 μL）；研钵；砂芯漏斗；容量瓶（10 mL）。

2. 试剂

水杨酸（对照品）；阿司匹林（原料药）；甲醇（色谱纯）；冰醋酸（分析纯）；二次蒸馏水。

四、实验步骤

1. 溶液的配制

（1）标准溶液：用甲醇配制约含水杨酸 0.02 $\text{mg}\cdot\text{mL}^{-1}$ 的标准溶液，记录标准溶液浓度 C_s。

double-distilled water.

Procedure

1. Preparation of solutions

(1) Standard solution: prepare salicylic acid standard solution by methanol with known concentration about 0.02 mg·mL^{-1} and record the accurate concentration as C_s.

(2) Sample solution: Grind the aspirin raw materials to find powder, accurately weigh about 20 mg to a 10 mL volumetric flask, dilute with methanol to the scale, and mix well for use.

2. Chromatographic conditions

Mobile phase: methanol-water-acetic acid (80 : 20 : 1, *V/V/V*);

Stationary phase: C_{18} reversed-phase column (150 mm × 4.6 mm, 5.0 μm);

Detection wavelength: 302 nm;

Flow rate: 1.0 mL·min^{-1}.

3. Sample injection

Separately inject 20 μL of standard solution and sample solution into the HPLC system, record retention times and peak areas in the chromatograms. Repeat three times.

Data Analysis

(1) According to the retention time of the standard solution, identify the peak of salicylic acid in the sample solution.

(2) Calculate the weight percentage of salicylic acid in the aspirin raw materials.

Experiment Guidance

1. Preview instruction

(1) Review the related content of high performance liquid chromatography.

(2) Be familiar with the operation of HPLC and the external comparison method for quantitative analysis.

(3) Understand the scope and significance of impurity limits in drugs.

2. Notes

(1) Solvents should be filtered and degassed before used.

(2) The accuracy of external standard method is largely dependent on the stability of operation conditions and the reproducibility of injection volumes. Compared with GC, six-port valve was used in HPLC, which greatly improve the accuracy of injection volume.

(3) Rinse the column with methanol after the experiment.

3. Discussion

(1) Why can external method be used for quantitative analysis in HPLC?

(2) What are the advantages and disadvantages of external standard method when compared with the internal standard method?

（2）样品溶液：将阿司匹林原料药研磨成细粉，精密称取约 20 mg 至 10 mL 容量瓶，用甲醇稀释至刻度，混匀待用。

2. 色谱条件的设定

流动相：甲醇–水–冰醋酸（80 ∶ 20 ∶ 1，体积比）；

固定相：C_{18} 反相键合相色谱柱（150 mm × 4.6 mm，5.0 μm）；

检测波长：302 nm；

流速：1.0 $mL \cdot min^{-1}$。

3. 进样测定

分别将 20 μL 的水杨酸标准溶液和阿司匹林样品溶液进样至色谱仪，记录色谱图，重复 3 次。根据色谱图，记录水杨酸峰的保留时间和峰面积。

五、数据处理

（1）根据水杨酸标准溶液的保留时间，确定样品溶液中水杨酸对应的色谱峰。

（2）计算阿司匹林样品中水杨酸的百分含量。

六、实验指导

1. 预习要求

（1）复习高效液相色谱相关内容。

（2）熟悉高效液相色谱仪的进样操作和外标对比法进行定量分析的方法。

（3）了解药品中杂质限量范围及意义。

2. 注意事项

（1）溶剂在使用前必须经过滤和除气泡处理。

（2）外标法的准确性取决于操作条件的稳定性和进样量的重现性。高效液相色谱采用六通阀进样，定量环的设定大大提高了进样的准确性。

（3）实验结束后用甲醇冲洗色谱柱。

3. 讨论

（1）为什么高效液相色谱可以用外标法定量？

（2）和内标法相比，外标法的优缺点各有哪些？

Experiment 4.10 Determination of Caffeine in Food by High Performance Liquid Chromatography

Purpose

1. To grasp the standard curve method for determination of caffeine in food by high performance liquid chromatography.
2. To understand the principle and applications of reversed-phase chromatography.

Principle

Caffeine, with the chemical name of 1, 3, 7-trimethylxanthine and the molecular formula of $C_8H_{10}O_2N_4$, belongs to xanthine derivatives, which is an alkaloid that can be extracted from tea or coffee. It is a kind of central nervous stimulant, which can excite the cerebral cortex and excite people's spirit. Caffeine is clinically used to treat neurasthenia and coma resuscitation, but large dose or long-term use will cause harm to human body. Caffeine in coffee is about 1.2%−1.8%, in tea is about 2.0%−4.7%. One compound aspirin tablet (APC) contains 35 mg of caffeine.

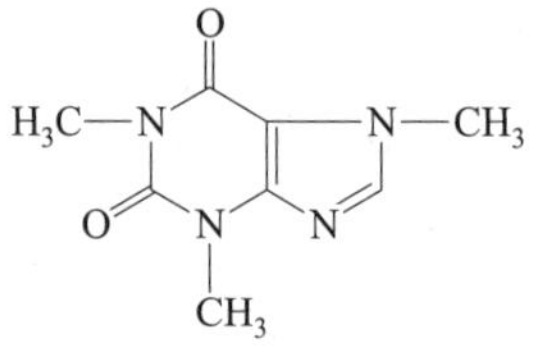

caffeine

In this experiment, reversed-phase high performance liquid chromatography was used to detect caffeine by use of UV detector and to determine the content of caffeine in food or drugs by standard curve method. While direct sample injection is simple, it may reduce the lifetime of the chromatographic column due to the complex nature of the real sample. Therefore, it is necessary to pretreat the sample to eliminate the coexisting interferents, so as to improve the accuracy and protect the column.

Instruments and Chemical Reagents

1. Instruments

HPLC system (Shimadzu LC-10A); C_{18} reversed-phase column (150 mm × 4.6 mm, 5.0 μm); analytical balance; mortar; sonicator; microsyringe (100 μL); volumetric flask (10 mL, 25 mL, and 100 mL); pipette (1 mL and 5 mL); 0.45 μm micropore membrane.

2. Chemical reagents

Caffeine (A.R.); methanol (HPLC grade); beverage of cola or coffee; double-distilled water.

Procedure

1. Preparation of solutions

(1) Caffeine standard series solution: accurately weigh about 25 mg of caffeine standard

实验 4.10 高效液相色谱法测定食品中咖啡因的含量

一、实验目的

1. 掌握利用标准曲线法定量测定食品中咖啡因含量的方法。
2. 理解反相色谱的原理和应用。

二、实验原理

咖啡因又称咖啡碱,化学名为 1,3,7-三甲基黄嘌呤,分子式为 $C_8H_{10}O_2N_4$,属于黄嘌呤衍生物,是可从茶叶或咖啡中提取而得的一种生物碱。它是一种中枢神经兴奋剂,能兴奋大脑皮层,使人精神兴奋,临床上用于治疗神经衰弱和昏迷复苏,但大剂量或长期使用会对人体造成危害。咖啡中咖啡因含量为 1.2%~1.8%,茶叶中咖啡因含量为 2.0%~4.7%,每片复方阿司匹林(APC)药片含咖啡因 35 mg。

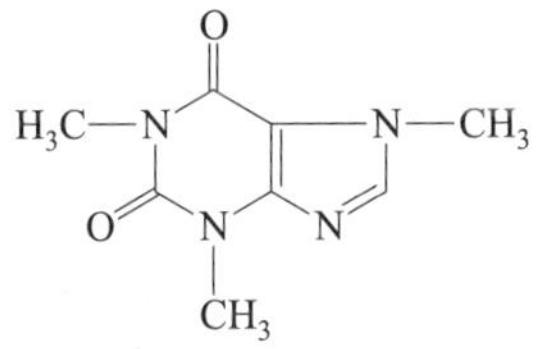

咖啡因

本实验采用反相高效液相色谱法(reversed phase high performance liquid chromatography),用紫外检测器进行检测,以一系列咖啡因标准溶液建立标准曲线,可实现各类食品、药品中咖啡因含量的测定。由于实际样品成分复杂,如果直接进样,虽然操作简单,但会影响色谱柱寿命,因此需对样品进行预处理,消除共存的干扰物,以提高定量的准确度,并可以保护色谱柱。

三、仪器和试剂

1. 仪器

高效液相色谱仪(岛津 LC-10A);ODS 色谱柱(150 mm × 4.6 mm,5.0 μm);分析天平;研钵;超声清洗器;微量注射器(100 μL);容量瓶(10 mL,25 mL,100 mL);移液管(1 mL,5 mL);0.45 μm 微孔滤膜。

2. 试剂

咖啡因(分析纯);甲醇(色谱纯);二次蒸馏水;可乐或咖啡饮料等。

四、实验步骤

1. 溶液的配制

(1)咖啡因标准溶液:取咖啡因对照品约 25 mg,精密称定,置于 100 mL 容量瓶中,加入甲醇至溶解,稀释至刻度,摇匀。分别准确吸取 0.00 mL、1.00 mL、2.00 mL、3.00 mL、4.00 mL 上述

substance, put it into a 100 mL volumetric flask, add methanol to dissolve, dilute to the scale, and mix well. Pipette 0.00 mL, 1.00 mL, 2.00 mL, 3.00 mL, and 4.00 mL of the above solution into 10 mL volumetric flasks, dilute to the scale with methanol, and mix well for use.

(2) Sample solution: pipette 5.00 mL of the Coke into 10 mL volumetric flask, dilute with water to the scale, and mix well. Accurately weigh about 50 mg of grinded tea or coffee solid sample, add appropriate amount of water and put into the sonicator for 60 min. After cooling down to the room temperature, dilute the sample with water to 25 mL, and mix well. The sample solution was filtered with a 0.45 μm filter before use.

2. Chromatographic conditions

Mobile phase: methanol-water (30 : 70, *V/V*);

Stationary phase: C_{18} reversed phase column (150 mm × 4.6 mm, 5.0 μm);

Detection wavelength: 273 nm;

Flow rate: 1.0 $mL \cdot min^{-1}$.

3. Sample injection

When the baseline of the HPLC system is stable, separately inject 20 μL of caffeine standard solution and sample solution into the HPLC system, record retention times and peak areas of caffeine in the chromatograms. Repeat three times.

Data Analysis

(1) According to the chromatograms of caffeine standard series solution, draw the standard curve of peak area of caffeine and its concentration, and fit it linearly.

(2) According to the peak area of caffeine in the sample solution and the above standard curve, calculate the content of caffeine in food (in the unit of $mg \cdot g^{-1}$ or $mg \cdot mL^{-1}$).

Experiment Guidance

1. Preview instruction

(1) Review the related content of high performance liquid chromatography.

(2) Be familiar with the operation of HPLC and the standard curve method for quantitative analysis.

(3) Understand the preparation method of series of standard solutions.

(4) Understand the composition and characteristics of reversed-phase HPLC.

2. Notes

(1) Solvents should be filtered and degassed before used.

(2) When determining caffeine standard series solution, the peak area is determined in the increasing order of concentration.

(3) Rinse the column with methanol after the experiment.

3. Discussion

(1) What should be paid attention to when preparing standard series solution?

(2) Why should the sample solution be filtered during sample pretreatment?

溶液于 10 mL 容量瓶中，稀释至刻度，摇匀，即得。

（2）咖啡因样品溶液：准确吸取市售可乐型饮料 5.00 mL，加水稀释定容至 10 mL，摇匀。取约 50 mg 粉碎均匀的茶叶或咖啡类固体样品，精密称定，置于 25 mL 容量瓶中，加适量水，超声提取 60 min，冷却至室温后，用水定容至 25 mL，摇匀。样品溶液用 0.45 μm 滤膜过滤后待用。

2. 色谱条件的设定

流动相：甲醇–水（30 ∶ 70，体积比）；

固定相：C_{18} 反相键合相色谱柱（150 mm × 4.6 mm，5.0 μm）；

检测波长：273 nm；

流速：1.0 $mL\cdot min^{-1}$。

3. 进样测定

待高效液相色谱仪基线稳定后，分别准确注入 20 μL 咖啡因系列标准溶液和样品溶液，记录色谱图，重复 3 次。根据色谱图，分别记录每次进样的保留时间和峰面积。

五、数据处理

（1）根据咖啡因标准系列溶液的色谱图，绘制咖啡因峰面积与其浓度的标准曲线，并进行线性拟合。

（2）根据样品中咖啡因色谱峰的峰面积和标准曲线，计算食品中咖啡因的含量(依据实际样品，用 $mg\cdot g^{-1}$ 或 $mg\cdot mL^{-1}$ 表示)。

六、实验指导

1. 预习要求

（1）复习高效液相色谱相关内容。

（2）熟悉高效液相色谱仪的使用和标准曲线法进行定量分析的方法。

（3）了解系列标准溶液的配制方法。

（4）了解反相高效液相色谱的组成及特点。

2. 注意事项

（1）溶剂在使用前必须经过滤和除气泡处理。

（2）咖啡因标准系列溶液测定时，按照浓度由低到高的顺序依次测定标准溶液的峰面积。

（3）实验结束后用甲醇冲洗色谱柱。

3. 讨论

（1）标准系列溶液配制时需注意什么？

（2）样品前处理时，为什么要将溶液过滤？

Experiment 4.11 Determination of Nandrolone Phenylpropionate by High Performance Liquid Chromatography

Purpose

(1) To grasp the principle and application of internal standard method for quantitative analysis in chromatography.

(2) To be familiar with the operation of high performance liquid chromatography equipment.

Principle

Internal standard comparison method, as a kind of internal standard method, is one of the quantitative analysis methods in chromatography. After selecting suitable pure substance as internal standard, the reference solution and sample solution containing the same amount of internal standard were prepared, respectively. After analysis by high performance liquid chromatography (HPLC), the peak areas of internal standard (is) and target component (i) were measured. The concentration of components to be measured in the solution could be calculated according to the following formula:

$$w(\%)=\frac{(A_i / A_{\text{is}})_{\text{sample}}}{(A_i / A_{\text{is}})_{\text{reference}}}\times\frac{c_{\text{reference}}}{c_{\text{sample}}}\times 100\%$$

where $w(\%)$ is the weight percentage of the target component; $(A_i / A_{\text{is}})_{\text{sample}}$ is the peak area ratio of target component and internal standard in the sample solution; $(A_i / A_{\text{is}})_{\text{reference}}$ is the peak area ratio of target component and internal standard in the reference solution; $c_{\text{reference}}$ is the concentration of target component in the reference solution, mg·mL^{-1}; c_{sample} is the concentration of sample solution, mg·mL^{-1}.

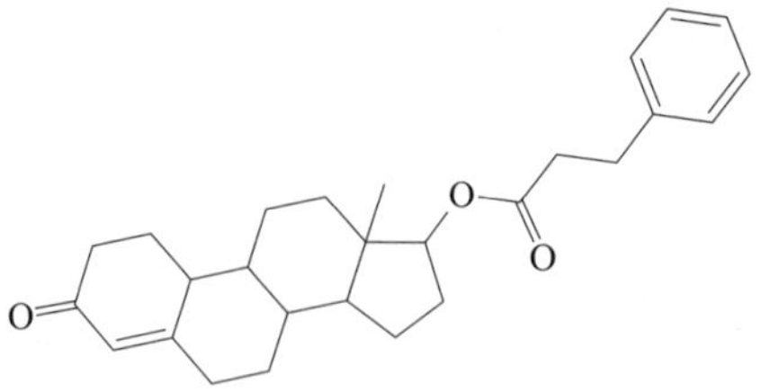

nandrolone phenylpropionate

Instruments and Chemical Reagents

1. Instruments

HPLC system (Shimadzu LC-10A); C_{18} reversed-phase column (150 mm × 4.6 mm, 5.0 μm); microsyringe (100 μL); volumetric flask (5 mL); pipette (1 mL); 0.45 μm micropore membrane.

2. Chemical reagents

Nandrolone Phenylpropionate (NP, raw material); nandrolone phenylpropionate (NP, standard); testosteroni propionas (TP, internal stanard); methanol (HPLC grade); double-distilled water.

实验 4.11　高效液相色谱法测定苯丙酸诺龙的含量

一、实验目的

（1）掌握色谱法中的内标法定量的原理和方法。

（2）进一步熟悉高效液相色谱仪的操作规程。

二、实验原理

内标对比法是内标法的一种，是高效液相色谱中的定量分析方法之一。所谓内标法是指以一定量的纯物质作为内标物，分别配制含有等量内标物的对照品溶液和样品溶液，经高效液相色谱分析后，测得上述两份溶液中内标物（is）和被测组分（i）的峰面积，根据样品和内标物的重量及其相应的峰面积比，求出某组分的含量。当只要测定样品中某几个组分，而样品中所测组分不能全部出峰时，可用内标法测量。对于某组分（i）其含量计算公式为

$$w(\%)=\frac{(A_i / A_{\text{is}})_{样品}}{(A_i / A_{\text{is}})_{对照}}\times\frac{c_{对照}}{c_{样品}}\times 100\%$$

式中，w（%）为待测组分的百分含量；$(A_i / A_{\text{is}})_{样品}$ 为样品溶液中待测组分和内标物峰面积之比；$(A_i / A_{\text{is}})_{对照}$ 为对照品溶液中待测组分和内标物峰面积之比；$c_{对照}$为对照品溶液中待测组分的质量浓度，$\text{mg}\cdot\text{mL}^{-1}$；$c_{样品}$为样品溶液的质量浓度，$\text{mg}\cdot\text{mL}^{-1}$。

本实验测定的苯丙酸诺龙的结构如下所示。

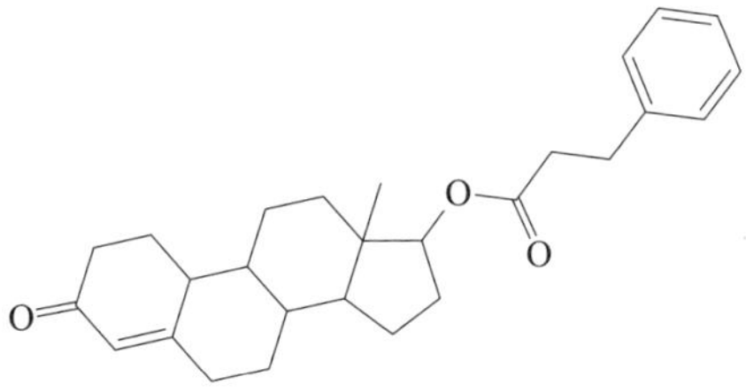

苯丙酸诺龙

三、仪器和试剂

1. 仪器

高效液相色谱仪（岛津 LC-10A）；ODS 色谱柱（150 mm × 4.6 mm，5.0 μm）；微量注射器（100 μL）；容量瓶（5 mL）；移液管（1 mL）；0.45 μm 微孔滤膜。

2. 试剂

苯丙酸诺龙原料药；苯丙酸诺龙标准品；丙酸睾丸素（标准品、内标物）；甲醇（色谱纯）；二次蒸馏水。

Procedure

1. Preparation of the solutions

(1) Stock solution: accurately weigh NP standard, TP and NP sample, respectively. Dilute the above three chemicals to prepare stock solutions.

(2) Reference solution: pipette 1.00 mL of TP stock solution and 1.00 mL NP standard stock solution into a 5 mL of volumetric flask, dilute to the scale with methanol, and mix well for use.

(3) Sample solution: pipette 1.00 mL of TP stock solution and 1.00 mL NP sample stock solution into a 5 mL of volumetric flask, dilute to the scale with methanol, and mix well for use.

2. Chromatographic conditions

Mobile phase: methanol-water (95 : 5, *V/V*);

Stationary phase: C_{18} reversed phase column (150 mm × 4.6 mm, 5.0 μm);

Detection wavelength: 241 nm;

Flow rate: 1.0 $mL \cdot min^{-1}$.

3. Suitabilitiy of chromatographic system

Prepare the mixture of NP standard and TP and inject into the HPLC system with the above chromatographic conditions. The theoretical plate number of NP should be larger than 600, and the resolution of NP and TP should be larger than 1.5.

4. Sample injection

When the baseline of the HPLC system is stable, separately inject 20 μL of reference solution and sample solution into the HPLC system, record retention times and peak areas in the chromatograms. Repeat three times.

Data Analysis

According to the above mentioned formula, calculate the percentage concentration of NP.

Experiment Guidance

1. Preview instruction

(1) Review the related content of high performance liquid chromatography.

(2) Be familiar with standard curve method and internal standard comparison method of internal standard method.

(3) Be familiar with solution preparation process of internal standard comparison method.

(4) Understand the principles of selecting appropriate internal standards.

2. Notes

(1) Solvents should be filtered and degassed before use.

(2) The resolution of NP and TP can be achieved by choosing column with proper length, adjusting the flow rate and optimizing the ratio of methanol and water.

(3) Rinse the column with methanol after the experiment.

3. Discussion

(1) What are the requirements for an ideal internal standard?

(2) What are the advantages of the internal standard method compared with the external standard method?

四、实验步骤

1. 溶液的配制

（1）储备液的配制：分别精密称取苯丙酸诺龙标准品、丙酸睾丸素标准品及苯丙酸诺龙原料药，用甲醇稀释成三个相应浓度储备液。

（2）对照品溶液的配制：精密量取丙酸睾丸素储备液 1.00 mL 和苯丙酸诺龙标准品储备液 1.00 mL，移入同一 5 mL 容量瓶中，用甲醇稀释至刻度，摇匀。

（3）样品溶液的配制：精密量取丙酸睾丸素储备液 1.00 mL 和苯丙酸诺龙标原料药储备液 1.00 mL，移入同一 5 mL 容量瓶中，用甲醇稀释至刻度，摇匀。

2. 色谱条件的设定

流动相：甲醇–水（95 ∶ 5，体积比）；

固定相：C_{18} 反相键合相色谱柱（150 mm × 4.6 mm，5.0 μm）；

检测波长：241 nm；

流速：1.0 mL·min^{-1}。

3. 色谱系统适应性考察

配制苯丙酸诺龙和丙酸睾丸素标准混合溶液，在上述色谱条件下进样，塔板数按苯丙酸诺龙峰计算应不低于 600，苯丙酸诺龙和内标物的分离度应大于 1.5。

4. 样品的测定

待高效液相色谱仪基线稳定后，分别准确注入 20 μL 对照品溶液和样品溶液，记录色谱图，重复 3 次。根据色谱图，分别记录每次进样的保留时间和峰面积。

五、数据处理

按内标对比法公式计算苯丙酸诺龙的百分含量。

六、实验指导

1. 预习要求

（1）复习高效液相色谱相关内容。

（2）熟悉内标法中的标准曲线法及对比法。

（3）熟悉内标对比法的溶液配制过程。

（4）了解选择合适内标物的原则。

2. 注意事项

（1）溶剂在使用前必须经过滤和除气泡处理。

（2）实验中可通过选择合适长度的色谱柱，调整流速或流动相中甲醇和水的比例，使苯丙酸诺龙与内标物的分离度达到定量分析的要求。

（3）实验结束后用甲醇冲洗色谱柱。

3. 讨论

（1）如何选择内标物？

（2）与外标法相比，内标法有哪些优点？

Experiment 4.12 Determination of Sulfamethoxazole and Trimethoprim in Compound Sulfamethoxazole Tablet by Capillary Electrophoresis

Purpose

(1) To understand the separation mechanism of capillary electrophoresis and its applications in the analysis of complex systems.

(2) To be familiar with the structure of capillary electrophoresis instrument.

Principle

Capillary electrophoresis (CE) is a kind of high resolution liquid phase separation technology, which uses capillary tube with inner diameter of 20-100 μm as separation channel and high voltage direct current electric field as driving force, according to the differences of migration velocity and distribution behavior of components in samples. CE has the advantages of high speed, high resolution, high efficiency, less samples required, low cost and wide application range. It has been rapidly developed in the fields of molecular biology analysis (DNA, PCR product analysis and human genome determination, peptide and protein analysis), chiral separation, drug analysis, clinical detection, environmental monitoring, ion analysis, single cell and single molecule monitoring, etc.

The CE separation modes include: capillary zone electrophoresis (CZE), micellar electrokinetic capillary chromatography (MECC), capillary isoelectric focusing (CIEF), capillary isoelectrophoresis. (CITP), affinity capillary electrophoresis (ACE), nonaqueous capillary electrophoresis (NACE) and so on. In the detection mode of CE, there are many detectors with high sensitivity, such as ultraviolet detector (UVD), laserinduced fluorescence detector (LIFD), diode-array detector (DAD) and electrochemical detector (ECD).

Compound sulfamethoxazole tablet is one of the most commonly used antibacterial agent among sulfonamides. It contains sulfamethoxazole (SMZ) and trimethoprim (TMP). In this experiment, sulfamethoxazole and trimethoprim in compound sulfamethoxazole tablets were separated by capillary electrophoresis, and their contents were determined by internal standard comparison method (internal standard is caffeine), respectively. The calculation formula is as follows:

$$c_{\text{sample}}=\frac{(A_i/A_s)_{\text{sample}}}{(A_i/A_s)_{\text{standard}}}\times c_{\text{standard}}$$

Where c is the concentration of the component to be measured, mg·mL^{-1}; A_i and A_s are the peak areas of the component to be measured and the internal standard, respectively.

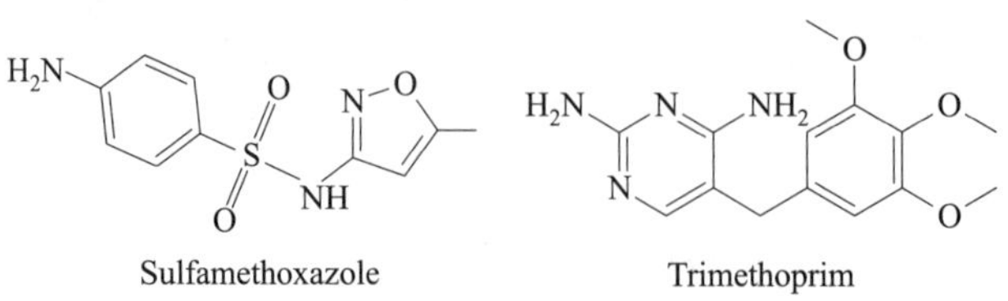

Sulfamethoxazole Trimethoprim

实验 4.12 毛细管电泳法测定复方新诺明片中的磺胺甲噁唑和甲氧苄氨嘧啶

一、实验目的

（1）了解毛细管电泳法的分离机理及其在复杂体系分析中的应用。

（2）熟悉毛细管电泳仪的结构。

二、实验原理

毛细管电泳（capillary electrophoresis，CE）是一类以内径为 20~100 μm 的毛细管为分离通道、以高压直流电场为驱动力，根据样品中各组分之间迁移速率和分配行为上的差异而实现分离的一类分离度极高的液相分离技术。CE 具有高速、高分辨、高效率、所需样品少、成本低及应用范围广等优点，在分子生物学分析（DNA、PCR 产物分析及人类基因组测定、肽和蛋白分析）、手性分离、药物分析、临床检测、环境监测、离子分析和单细胞、单分子监测等领域得到了迅速发展。

CE 分离模式有毛细管区带电泳（capillary zone electrophoresis，CZE）、胶束电动毛细管色谱（micellar electrokinetic capillary chromatography，MECC）、毛细管凝胶电泳（capillary gel electrophoresis，CGE）、毛细管等电聚焦（capillary isoelectric focusing，CIEF）、毛细管等速电泳（capillary isotachophoresis，CITP）、亲和毛细管电泳（affinity capillary electrophoresis，ACE）、非水毛细管电泳（nonaqueous capillary electrophoresis，NACE）等。在 CE 的检测模式上，已有多种灵敏度很高的检测器与其匹配，如紫外检测器（UVD）、激光诱导荧光检测器（LIFD）、二极管阵列检测器（DAD）及电化学检测器（ECD）。

复方新诺明片（Compound Sulfamethoxazole Tablet）为磺胺类药物中抗菌最强而且较常用的复方制剂，内含抑菌剂磺胺甲噁唑（SMZ）和抗菌增效剂甲氧苄氨嘧啶（TMP）。本实验通过毛细管电泳法分离复方新诺明片中的磺胺甲噁唑和甲氧苄氨嘧啶，并通过内标对比法（内标为咖啡因）分别测定其含量。计算公式如下：

$$c_{i\,样品}=\frac{(A_i/A_\mathrm{s})_{样品}}{(A_i/A_\mathrm{s})_{标准}}\times c_{i\,标准}$$

式中，c_i% 为待测组分的浓度，$\mathrm{mg\cdot mL^{-1}}$；A_i 和 A_s 分别为待测组分和内标物的峰面积。

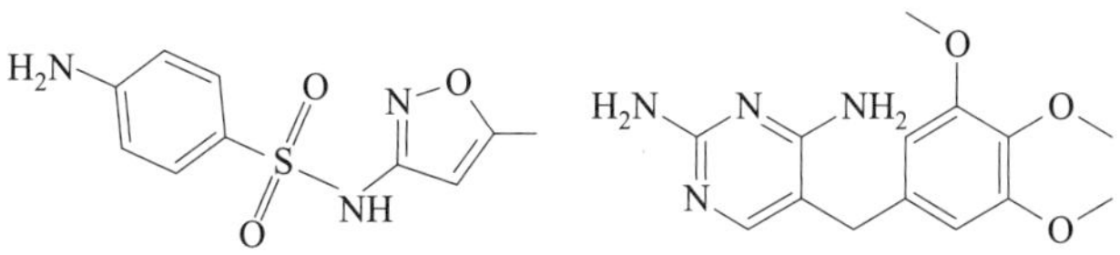

磺胺甲噁唑　　　　甲氧苄氨嘧啶

Instruments and Chemical Reagents

1. Instruments

Agilent CE-3D capillary electrophoresis instrument; analytical balance; ultrasonic apparatus; pipette (5 mL); mortar; uncoated elastic quartz capillary (50 cm × 50 μm I.D.); volumetric flask (100 mL).

2. Chemical reagents

Sulfamethoxazole reference substance; trimethoprim reference substance; caffeine reference substance (internal standard); compound sulfamethoxazole tablets (commercially available); borax (A.R.); phosphoric acid (A.R.) ; sodium hydroxide (A.R.); 95% ethanol; ultrapure water.

Procedure

1. Preparation of solutions

(1) Preparation of internal standard solution

Dissolve 40 mg of caffeine, accurately weighed, into a 100 mL volumetric flask, add appropriate amount of water, dissolve it by ultrasonic wave, dilute it to the volume with water, mix well.

(2) Preparation of reference solutions

Dissolve 40 mg of SMZ and 16 mg of TMP, accurately weighed, into a 100 mL volumetric flask, add 5 mL of 95% ethanol and 2 mL of 0.1 mol · L^{-1} sodium hydroxide solution, dissolve them by ultrasonic wave for 5 min, and then dilute them to the volume with water, mix well. Transfer accurately 3.0 mL of the above solution into a 10 mL volumetric flask, add 2.0 mL of the internal standard solution precisely, dilute with water to the volume, and mix well.

(3) Preparation of sample solution

Take 10 tablets of this product, accurately weighed and grind them, accurately weighed and take an appropriate amount of fine powder (about equivalent to SMZ 40 mg and TMP 16 mg), put them into a 100 mL volumetric flask, add 5 mL of 95% ethanol and 2 mL of 0.1 mol · L^{-1} sodium hydroxide solution. Dissolve them by ultrasound for 5 min, dilute them with water to the volume, mix well. Filter the solution and the filtrate is as the stock solution. Transfer accurately 3.0 mL of the above solution into a 10 mL volumetric flask, add 2.0 mL of the internal standard solution precisely, dilute with water to the volume, and mix well.

2. Conditions of capillary electrophoresis

Uncoated elastic quartz capillary (50 cm × 50 μm I.D., effective length 41.5 cm); detection wavelength 214 nm; pressure injection 30 mbar × 10 s; operating voltage 20 kV; temperature 30 ℃ ; Operating buffer 20 mmol · L^{-1}; borax solution (pH 6.0 adjusted by phosphoric acid). Before each electrophoresis run, the capillary tubes were washed with 0.1 mol · L^{-1} sodium hydroxide solution, water and running buffer for 3 min. All solutions were filtered by microporous membrane with pore size of 0.45 μm before use.

3. Injection

The control solution and the test solution were injected respectively under the selected experimental conditions.

三、仪器与试剂

1. 仪器

Agilent CE-3D 毛细管电泳仪；分析天平；超声仪；移液管（5 mL）；研钵；未涂层弹性石英毛细管（50 cm × 50 μm I.D.）；容量瓶（100 mL，10 mL）。

2. 试剂

磺胺甲噁唑对照品；甲氧苄氨嘧啶对照品；咖啡因对照品（内标）；复方新诺明片（市售）；硼砂（分析纯）；磷酸（分析纯）；氢氧化钠（分析纯）；95% 乙醇；超纯水。

四、实验步骤

1. 溶液的配制

（1）内标溶液的配制　取咖啡因 40 mg，精密称定，置于 100 mL 容量瓶中，加适量水，超声使之溶解，用水稀释至刻度，摇匀，即得。

（2）对照溶液的配制　取对照品 SMZ 40 mg和 TMP 16 mg，精密称定，置于同一 100 mL 容量瓶中，加 95% 乙醇 5 mL，0.1 mol·L^{-1} 氢氧化钠溶液 2 mL，超声 5 min 使之溶解，用水稀释至刻度，摇匀。精密量取上述溶液 3.0 mL，置于 10 mL 容量瓶中，精密加入内标溶液 2.0 mL，用水稀释至刻度，摇匀，即得。

（3）供试溶液的配制　取本品 10 片，精密称定，研细，精密称取细粉适量（约相当于 SMZ 40 mg 和 TMP 16 mg），置于 100 mL 容量瓶中，加 95% 乙醇 5 mL，0.1 mol·L^{-1} 氢氧化钠溶液 2 mL，超声 5 min 使之溶解，用水稀释至刻度，摇匀。精密量取此上述溶液 3.0 mL，置于 10 mL 容量瓶中，精密加入内标溶液 2.0 mL，用水稀释至刻度，摇匀，即得。

2. 毛细管电泳条件

未涂层弹性石英毛细管（50 cm × 50 μm I.D.，有效长度 41.5 cm）；检测波长 214 nm；压力进样 30 mbar × 10 s；运行电压 20 kV；温度 30 ℃；运行缓冲液为 20 mmol·L^{-1}；硼砂溶液（磷酸调 pH=6.0）。每次电泳运行前用 0.1 mol·L^{-1} 氢氧化钠溶液、水及运行缓冲液各冲洗毛细管 3 min。所有溶液使用前经过孔径为 0.45 μm 微孔滤膜过滤。

3. 进样

在选定的实验条件下，将对照溶液和供试溶液分别进样。

五、数据处理

根据电泳谱图中的相关数据，计算样品中 SMZ 和 TMP 的含量。

六、实验指导

1. 预习要求

（1）了解毛细管电泳法的分离机理。

（2）了解毛细管电泳仪的结构。

（3）复习内标对比法在药物定量分析中的应用。

Data Analysis

The contents of SMZ and TMP in the sample were calculated according to the relevant data in the electrophoretic spectrum.

Experiment Guidance

1. Preview instruction

(1) Grasp the separation mechanism of capillary electrophoresis.

(2) Understand the structure of capillary electrophoresis instrument.

(3) Review the application of internal standard comparison method in drug quantitative analysis.

2. Notes

(1) The results showed that the solubility of SMZ and TMP in water was poor. The two components in compound sulfamethoxazole tablets could be extracted completely with 95% ethanol and 0.1 mol · L^{-1} sodium hydroxide solution and ultrasonic wave for 5 min, and the above solvents did not interfere with the determination of the two components and internal standard under the selected electrophoresis conditions.

(2) In order to prevent the capillary from being blocked by fine particles, all solutions are filtered by microporous membrane with pore size of 0.45 μm before use.

3. Discussion

Why is the content of each component determined by internal standard comparison method in this experiment?

2. 注意事项

（1）SMZ 和 TMP 在水中的溶解度较差，用一定量 95% 乙醇和 0.1 mol·L^{-1} 氢氧化钠溶液，超声 5 min，即能够将复方新诺明片中两组分提取完全，且上述溶剂在所选电泳条件下不干扰两组分及内标的测定。

（2）为防止细颗粒物堵塞毛细管，所有溶液使用前经过孔径为 0.45 μm 微孔滤膜过滤。

3. 讨论

本实验中为何采用内标对比法测定各组分的含量？

Experiment 4.13 Separation of Chiral Drug Enantiomer by Capillary Zone Electrophoresis

Purpose

(1) To be familiar with the principle and operation of capillary zone electrophoresis.
(2) To know the application of capillary zone electrophoresis in chiral separation.

Principle

Capillary electrophoresis (CE) is a kind of chromatographic method which uses high-voltage electric field as driving force, capillary as separation channel, and electrolyte as electrophoresis medium. Separation by CE is achieved according to the difference of mobility and distribution behavior of sample components in electrolyte. In capillary zone electrophoresis (CZE), the migration velocity of particles in capillary is equal to the vector sum of electrophoretic migration and electroosmotic flow (EOF). The movement direction of positive ion is the same as that of electroosmotic flow, so it flows out first and is in the front part of electrophoresis zone. The electrophoretic migration velocity of neutral particles is zero, so the migration velocity is equivalent to that of electroosmotic flow, and it is in the middle part of electrophoresis zone. The movement direction of negative ion is opposite to that of electroosmotic flow, so it is in the later part of electrophoresis zone. In this way, particles with different charges could be separated in the mixed components.

CE has the advantages of high separation efficiency, high sensitivity, rapid analysis and less sample consumption. It has shown great potential in the field of bioanalysis, especially in chiral separation. The separation of enantiomers requires the addition of chiral selectors, such as cyclodextrins, crown ethers, bile salts and chiral selective metal complexes.

Ofloxacin, a chiral drug, is a commonly used broad-spectrum antibiotics, which has good killing effect on gram-positive cocci and most of Enterobacteriaceae bacteria. Levofloxacin is the *S*-enantiomer of ofloxacin, which has a more extensive antibacterial effect, not only against gram-positive and gram-negative cocci, but also against chlamydia and mycoplasma.

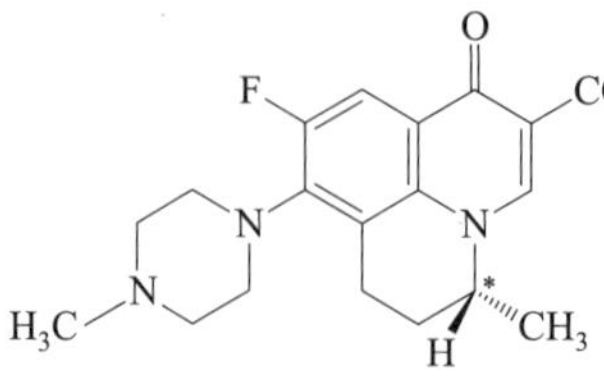

Ofloxacin

In this experiment, a method for the separation of levofloxacin by CZE was developed by use of dimethyl-β-cyclodextrin (DM-β-CD) as chiral selector.

实验 4.13　毛细管区带电泳法分离手性药物对映异构体

一、实验目的

（1）熟悉毛细管区带电泳的基本原理和仪器的操作方法。

（2）了解毛细管电泳法在拆分对映异构体中的应用。

二、实验原理

毛细管电泳（capillary electrophoresis，CE）是以高压电场为驱动力，以毛细管为分离通道，以电解质为电泳介质，根据样品组分在电解质中的淌度和分配行为的差异而实现分离的一种色谱方法。在毛细管区带电泳（capillary zone electrophoresis，CZE）中，粒子在毛细管内的迁移速度等于电泳迁移和电渗流（electroosmotic flow，EOF）两种速度的矢量和。正离子的运动方向和电渗流相同，故最先流出，处于电泳区带较前部分；中性粒子的电泳迁移速度为零，故其迁移速度相当于电渗流速度，处于电泳区带中间部分；负离子的运动方向和电渗流方向相反，故其在电泳区带较后部分，从而实现混合组分的分离。

毛细管电泳法具有高分离效率、高灵敏度、快速、样品消耗量少等优点，在生物医药样品的分析特别是手性分离方面显示出了巨大的优势。对映异构体的分离需要加入手性选择剂，常用的有环糊精、冠醚、胆汁酸盐、手性选择性金属配合物等。

氧氟沙星是一种常用的广谱抗菌药，为手性药物，对革兰氏阳性球菌和多数肠杆菌科细菌具有良好的杀灭作用。左氧氟沙星是氧氟沙星的左旋异构体，具有更广泛的抗菌作用，不仅对革兰氏阳性、革兰氏阴性球菌具有较强的抗菌作用，对衣原体、支原体亦有较强作用。

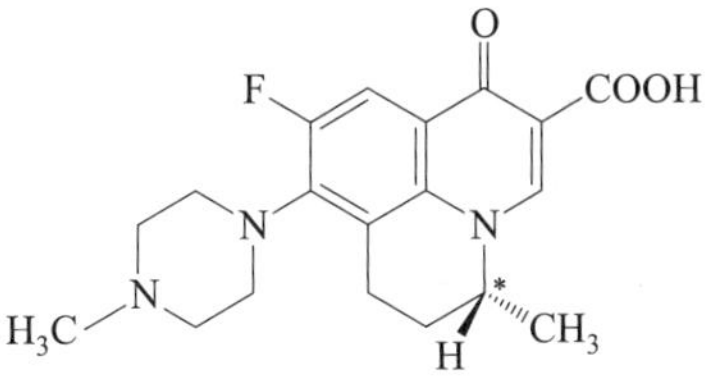

氧氟沙星

本实验采用二甲基-β-环糊精（DM-β-CD）为手性选择剂，设计了一种利用毛细管区带电泳法分离左氧氟沙星的方法。

三、仪器和试剂

1. 仪器

Agilent ^{3D} CE G1600AX 毛细管电泳仪；pH 计；分析天平；超声波清洗机；熔融石英毛细管（50 cm × 50 μm I.D.，有效长度 41.5 cm）；0.45 μm 微孔滤膜。

2. 试剂

左氧氟沙星（对照品）；氧氟沙星（对照品）；二甲基-β-环糊精（DM-β-CD）；磷酸二氢钾（分

Instruments and Chemical Reagents

1. Instruments

Agilent ^{3D} CE G1600AX Capillary electrophoresis; pH meter; analytical balance; sonicator; fused quartz capillary (50 cm $\times$ 50 μm I.D. ,effective length 41.5 cm); 0.45 μm micropore membrane.

2. Chemical reagents

Ofloxacin (reference substance); levofloxacin (reference substance); DM-β-CD (A. R.); KH_2PO_4(A.R.), H_3PO_4 (A. R.); double-distilled water; NaOH solution (0.1 mol·L^{-1}).

Procedure

1. Preparation of solutions

(1) Background electrolyte solution: weigh appropriate amount of KH_2PO_4 and DM-β-CD to prepare 0.07 mol·L^{-1} KH_2PO_4 solution containing 0.04 mol·L^{-1} DM-β-CD. The pH of the solution was adjusted to 2.5 with H_3PO_4. The electrolyte is filtered with 0.45 μm micropore membrane and degassed in the sonicator before used.

(2) Sample solution: accurately weigh appropriate amount of ofloxacin and levofloxacin, and then dissolve in water to prepare the sample solutions with the concentration of 1.4 mg·mL^{-1}, respectively. Sample solutions are filtered with 0.45 μm micropore membrane and degassed in the sonicator before used.

2. Electrophoresis conditions

Concentration of DM-β-CD: 0.04 mol·L^{-1};

Electrolyte buffer: 0.07 mol·L^{-1} KH_2PO_4 solution (pH=2.5);

Applied voltage: 20 kV;

Detection wavelength: 280 nm;

Capillary temperature: 25 ℃ .

3. Injection

(1) Open the CE apparatus, pre-warm it until stable signal is observed.

(2) Before analysis, capillary is sequentially washed with 0.1 mol·L^{-1} NaOH solution, double-distilled water, and electrolyte buffer solution for 5 min, and finally balanced in the buffer solution for 10 min under the applied voltage of 20 kV.

(3) After the baseline is stable, turn off the high-voltage power supply, and inject the sample by pressure injection with certain time. Record the electrophoretogram of ofloxacin and levofloxacin, respectively.

Data Analysis

(1) Record the electrophoretogram of ofloxacin and levofloxacin.

(2) Calculate the proportion of *S*-enantiomer and *R*-enantiomer in ofloxacin and levofloxacin by normalization method.

Experiment Guidance

1. Preview instruction

(1) Be familiar with separation principle of CZE and various factors affecting separation.

析纯)；磷酸(分析纯)；二次蒸馏水；0.1 mol·L^{-1} 氢氧化钠溶液。

四、实验步骤

1. 溶液的配制

（1）电解质溶液：称取适量磷酸二氢钾配制成浓度为 0.07 mol·L^{-1} 的溶液，用磷酸调节 pH 至 2.5，并加入适量 DM-β-CD，使其浓度为 0.04 mol·L^{-1}。配好的电解质溶液经 0.45 μm 微孔滤膜过滤，超声脱气后备用。

（2）样品溶液：分别精确称取氧氟沙星和左氧氟沙星适量，用二次蒸馏水溶解，配制成 1.4 mg·mL^{-1} 的溶液。样品溶液经 0.45 μm 微孔滤膜过滤，超声脱气后备用。

2. 电泳条件的设定

DM-β-CD 浓度：0.04 mol·L^{-1}；

电泳缓冲液：0.07 mol·L^{-1} 磷酸二氢钾溶液（pH=2.5）；

分离电压：20 kV；

检测波长：280 nm；

柱温：25 ℃。

3. 进样分析

（1）打开毛细管电泳仪，预热至检测器输出信号稳定。

（2）每次分析前，毛细管依次用氢氧化钠溶液（0.1 mol·L^{-1}）和二次蒸馏水各冲洗 5 min，再用电解质溶液冲洗 5 min，并将毛细管的两端分别插入位于电极处的缓冲溶液瓶中，将直流电压调至 20 kV，平衡 10 min。

（3）待记录仪基线稳定后，关闭高压电源，用压力进样方式进样，并设定进样时间，待样品峰出现后记录其迁移时间，并记录图谱。

五、数据处理

（1）记录氧氟沙星和左氧氟沙星的手性分离电泳图谱。

（2）利用面积归一化法分别计算氧氟沙星和左氧氟沙星样品中左旋体和右旋体的比例。

六、实验指导

1. 预习要求

（1）熟悉毛细管区带电泳的分离原理及影响分离的各种因素。

（2）熟悉 CE 的一般操作过程和实验注意事项。

（3）了解手性药物的对映异构体的基础知识及药理学差异。

（4）了解毛细管电泳手性拆分药物对映异构体的原理。

2. 注意事项

（1）电解质溶液浓度、pH、柱温和电压等均是影响毛细管电泳分离效果的主要因素，因此需优化上述条件，改善分离度。

（2）DM-β-CD 的浓度会显著影响对映体的分离，需仔细调节。

（3）实验结束后，需用二次蒸馏水清洗毛细管，以免残留的缓冲溶液堵塞毛细管。

(2) Be familiar with CE general operation process and experimental precautions.

(3) Understand the basic knowledge and pharmacological differences of enantiomers of chiral drugs.

(4) Understand the principle of chiral separation of drug enantiomers by CE.

2. Notes

(1) Some important factors, such as concentration of electrolyte solution, pH, column temperature and applied voltage, can affect the separation of CE, so it is necessary to optimize the above conditions to improve the resolution.

(2) The concentration of DM-β-CD can significantly affect the separation of enantiomers, which should be carefully adjusted.

(3) After the experiment, the capillary tube should be cleaned with double-distilled water to prevent the residual buffer solution from blocking the capillary.

3. Discussion

(1) Why the column efficiency of CZE is more efficient than it of HPLC?

(2) What are the factors for the band broadening in CE?

(3) What kind of drug is suitable for CZE?

3. 讨论

（1）毛细管区带电泳比高效液相色谱柱效高的原因是什么？

（2）在毛细管电泳中，影响谱带展宽的因素有哪些？

（3）毛细管区带电泳适用于哪类药物的分析？

Chapter 5 Chromatography-Mass Spectrometry

Experiment 5.1 Performance Verification of Gas Chromatography-Mass Spectrometer

Purpose

(1) To understand the significance of performance verification of gas chromatography-mass spectrometer.

(2) To master the basic process of performance verification of gas chromatography-mass spectrometer.

Principle

In recent years, mass spectrometry technology has made rapid development, and has been widely and deeply applied in food detection, environmental monitoring, drug research, forensic toxicology, life science as well as clinical examination. Compared with the traditional analytical methods, chromatography-mass spectrometry can detect a wide range of compounds (polar and nonpolar), and simultaneously detect multiple target compounds by obtaining rich structural information of compounds. It has powerful qualitative and quantitative functions, and has the advantages of short analysis time, high sensitivity, strong specificity and high accuracy.

Before using chromatography-mass spectrometry technology to carry out analytical experiments and research, the equipment that affects the detection results should be maintained and calibrated regularly, and the performance parameters such as the stability and reliability of the detection system should be verified, so as to ensure that the performance of the detection system can continuously meet the requirements of accurate determination after maintenance.

Gas chromatography-mass spectrometry (GC-MS) is the first developed chromatography-mass spectrometry technology GC is suitable for the separation and analysis of compounds which are easy to gasify and have good thermal stability at operating temperature, as well as the mobile phase used in gas chromatography is gas (such as N_2, He, H_2, etc.), which is easy to match the requirements of mass spectrometry detector for sample ionization and high vacuum detection. In addition, 70 eV electron ionization (EI) source is usually used to ionize the samples when GC-MS is combined, which can obtain abundant information of ion fragments of compounds. Searching the spectral library of these fragment ions is conducive to the rapid structural identification and analysis of compounds.

In order to ensure the accuracy and sensitivity of analysis and determination, GC-EI-MS instrument needs performance verification after installation or maintenance, which mainly includes mass spectrum tuning and GC-MS instrument performance parameter calibration. In this experiment, Shimadzu GCMS-

第五章　色谱–质谱联用法

实验 5.1　气相色谱–质谱仪器性能验证

一、实验目的

（1）了解气相色谱–质谱仪器性能验证的意义。

（2）掌握气相色谱–质谱仪器性能验证的基本流程。

二、实验原理

近年来，质谱法取得了快速的发展，在食品检测、环境监测、药物研究、法医毒理、生命科学和临床检验中得到了广泛和深入的应用。与传统分析手段相比，色谱–质谱联用法可分析检测的化合物范围广（极性和非极性），且可以同时检测多种目标化合物，获取丰富的化合物结构信息，定性和定量功能强大，具有分析时间短、灵敏度高、特异性强、准确度高等优点。

在使用色谱–质谱法开展分析实验和研究前，实验室应对影响检测结果的设备进行维护及校准，并验证检测系统的稳定性和可靠性等性能参数，以确保仪器维护保养后其检测系统性能持续满足准确测定的要求。

气相色谱–质谱（GC–MS）联用法是最早发展起来的色谱–质谱联用技术。气相色谱适用于分离分析操作温度下易气化、热稳定性好的化合物，且气相色谱所用流动相为气体（如 N_2、He、H_2 等），易与质谱检测器对于样品离子化和检测时高真空的要求相匹配。此外，GC–MS 联用时一般采用 70 eV 的电子轰击源（electron ionization，EI）对样品电离，可得到丰富的化合物离子碎片信息，对这些碎片离子进行谱库检索，利于化合物的快速结构鉴定和分析。

为了保证分析测定的准确度和灵敏度，GC–EI–MS 仪器在安装或者维护后，都需要进行性能验证，主要包含质谱的调谐（tuning）和 GC–MS 仪器性能参数校准两部分。本文以岛津（Shimadzu）GCMS–QP 2010 Ultra 气相色谱–质谱联用仪为例，其质谱调谐所涉及的灵敏度调整、质量分辨率调整、质量数校正和相对强度校正等操作均可由工作站软件完成。调谐所用标样为全氟三丁胺［$(CF_3—CF_2—CF_2—CF_2)_3—N$，$C_{12}NF_{27}$，PFTBA］，可提供 *m/z* 69、*m/z* 131、*m/z* 219、*m/z* 414、*m/z* 502 和 *m/z* 614 等主要碎片离子，对质谱进行调谐校正。质谱的调谐通过后，将调谐结果与 JJF1164—2018《气相色谱–质谱联用仪校准规范》及设备制造商对该仪器的性能要求相比较，包括质谱的质量范围、质量分辨率、质量准确性。最后，再利用标准物质（八氟萘）对 GC–MS 的性能参数（如信噪比、峰面积与保留时间重复性等）进行校准与验证。

QP 2010 Ultra gas chromatography-mass spectrometer of Shimadzu company in Japan is taken as an example. The sensitivity adjustment, mass resolution adjustment, mass number correction and relative intensity correction involved in mass spectrum tuning can be completed by its workstation software. The standard sample used for tuning is perfluorotributylamine [(CF_3—CF_2—CF_2—CF_2)$_3$—N, $C_{12}NF_{27}$, PFTBA], which can provide major fragment ions with *m/z* 69, *m/z* 131, *m/z* 219, *m/z* 414, *m/z* 502 and *m/z* 614 to tune the mass spectrum. After the mass spectrum tuning is passed, the tuning results are compared with the performance requirements of "Calibration specification for gas chromatography-mass spectrometer" (JJF1164—2018) and the equipment manufacturer for the instrument, including the mass range, mass resolution, mass accuracy and other results of the mass spectrum. Finally, the standard material (octafluoronaphthalene) is used to calibrate and verify the performance parameters of GC-MS, such as signal-to-noise ratio, peak area and repeatability of retention time.

Instruments and Chemical Reagents

1. Instruments

Shimadzu GCMS-QP 2010 Ultra gas chromatography-mass spectrometer; capillary gas chromatography column DB-5MS (30 m × 0.25 mm, 0.25 μm); micro-syringe (10 μL); pipette (100 μL); volumetric flask (10 mL).

2. Chemical reagents

Perfluorotributylamine (PFTBA, A.R.); octafluoronaphthalene(A.R.); isooctane (HPLC grade); helium (purity≥99.9%).

Procedure

1. Mass spectrum tuning

Perfluorotributylamine (PFTBA) was used as the tuning sample, and the injection pump was used to inject the sample directly. The mass range, mass resolution, sensitivity, mass number and relative intensity of the instrument were adjusted and corrected until the tuning passed.

(1) Parameter setting: The mass spectrum electron bombardment energy was set at 70 eV, the mass to charge ratio (mass-to-charge ratio, *m/z*) was set at 10–700, and the ion source temperature was set at 200 ℃. For the automatic tuning parameter setting of conventional analysis, the FWHM (full width at half maximum) of peak profile can be set as 0.6 for the adjustment of quality resolution, and the target quality can be set as *m/z* 264 for the adjustment of sensitivity; for the high quality number analysis, in order to obtain stable quantitative results, the quality resolution of automatic tuning parameter is set as 0.7–0.8 (FWHM), and the sensitivity adjustment is still set as *m/z* 264.

(2) Tuning method and result check: After the instrument is stable, the automatic tuning command or manual tuning can be executed through the instrument workstation software. After tuning, name and save the tuning file, and check the tuning results, as shown in Figure 5–1.

If the tuning is failed, it is necessary to check whether the vacuum degree, system tightness, filament, ion source, PFTBA margin, capillary column interface, etc. are normal. After eliminating the problem, the automatic tuning can be carried out again.

2. Calibration and verification of GC-MS instrument performance parameters

(1) Quality range calibration: After the instrument was tuned, the mass spectrum peaks of greater than *m/z* 600 (or equal to *m/z* 600) were observed (*m/z* 614 and *m/z* 615 in PFTBA). According to "Calibration specification for gas chromatography-mass spectrometer" (JJF1164—2018), it is required

三、仪器与试剂

1. 仪器

岛津 GCMS-QP 2010 Ultra 气相色谱-质谱联用仪；DB-5MS 毛细管气相色谱柱（30 m × 0.25 mm，0.25 μm）；微量注射器（10 μL）；移液管或移液器（100 μL）；容量瓶（10 mL）。

2. 试剂

全氟三丁胺（PFTBA）（分析纯）；八氟萘（分析纯）；异辛烷（色谱纯）；高纯氦气。

四、实验步骤

1. 质谱的调谐

利用全氟三丁胺（PFTBA）为调谐样品，注射泵直接进样，对仪器的质量范围、质量分辨率、灵敏度、质量数和相对强度进行调整与校正，直到调谐通过。

（1）参数设定　将质谱电子轰击能量设为 70 eV，离子扫描范围设为质荷比（mass-to-charge ratio，*m/z*）10~700，离子源温度设为 200 ℃。对于常规分析的自动调谐参数设定，质量分辨率的调整可设定峰轮廓的半高宽（FWHM）为 0.6，灵敏度的调整可设定目标质量为 *m/z* 264；对于高质量数分析，为了得到稳定的定量结果，将自动调谐参数中质量分辨率设为 0.7~0.8（FWHM），灵敏度调节仍设为 *m/z* 264。

（2）调谐方法和结果的检查　在仪器稳定后，通过仪器工作站软件执行自动调谐命令或者手动方式进行调谐。调谐完成后，将调谐文件命名并保存，并对调谐结果进行检查，见图 5-1。

如果调谐无法通过，需检查真空度、系统密闭性、灯丝、离子源、PFTBA 余量、毛细管柱接口等是否正常，排除问题后，再进行自动调谐。

2. GC-MS 仪器性能参数校准与验证

（1）质量范围校准　仪器调谐通过后，观察调谐结果中是否出现大于 *m/z* 600（含 *m/z* 600）的质谱峰（PFTBA 中符合条件的为 *m/z* 614 和 *m/z* 615）。根据 JJF1164—2018《气相色谱-质谱联用仪校准规范》，要求能检出 *m/z* 600 以上（含 *m/z* 600）的质谱峰。

（2）质量分辨率（mass resolution）校准　质量分辨率是质谱仪分辨两个相邻质谱峰的质量差的能力，常用某离子峰峰高 50% 处的峰宽度（简称半高宽）来表示，记为 FWHM 或 $W_{1/2}$，单位为 u（原子质量单位，atomic mass unit，amu 或 u）。

仪器调谐通过后，记录 PFTBA 中主要碎片离子 *m/z* 69、*m/z* 219 和 *m/z* 502 峰的 $W_{1/2}$。根据 JJF1164—2018《气相色谱-质谱联用仪校准规范》，$W_{1/2}$<1 u 为合格。

（3）质量准确性（mass accuracy）校准　质量准确性是指质谱仪对离子质量的测定值与理论值之间的偏差。

仪器调谐通过后，记录 PFTBA 碎片离子 *m/z* 69、*m/z* 131、*m/z* 219、*m/z* 414、*m/z* 502 和 *m/z* 614 的实测质量数，有效数字保留到小数点后 2 位，计算实测值与标准值之差。根据设备制造商对 GCMS-QP 2010 Ultra 的性能要求，差值在 ± 0.1 u 以内为合格。

（4）信噪比（signal-to-noise ratio）校准　质谱中的基线噪声（baseline noise）是指其基线峰底与峰谷之间的宽度。被测样品信号强度 S 与基线噪声强度 N 的比值，即为信噪比。

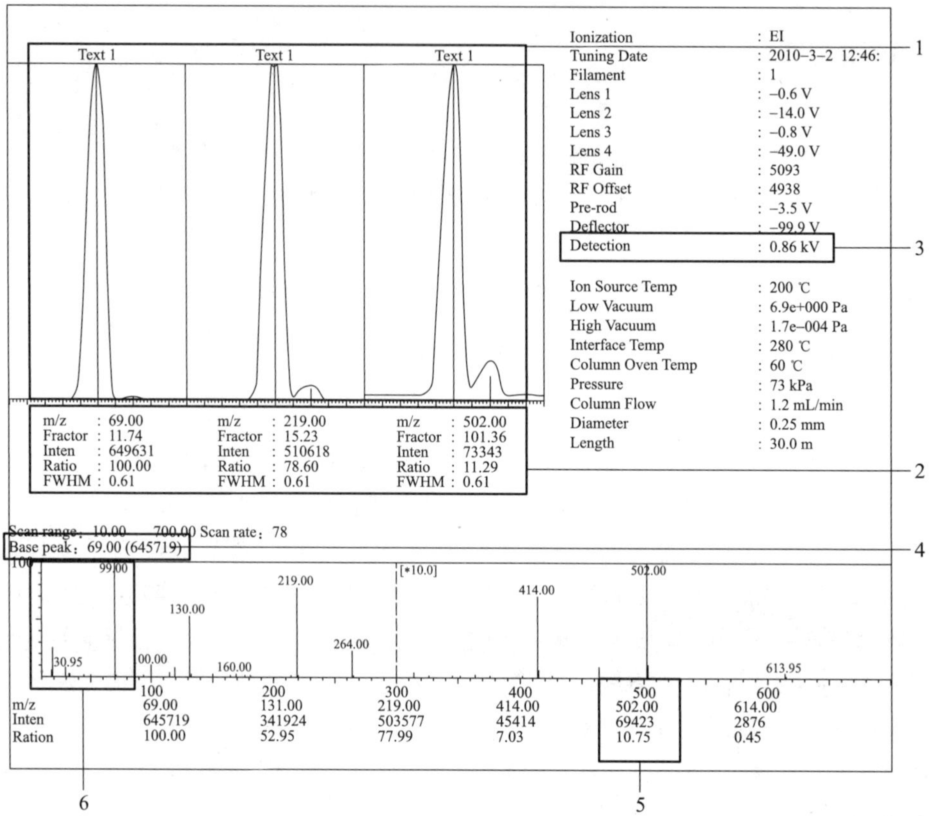

Figure 5–1 Tuning method and result check

Box 1: check whether the peak shape has obvious bifurcation and whether the peak shape is symmetrical;

Box 2: check if FWHM is within 0.6 ± 0.1;

Box 3: check whether the detector voltage exceeds 1.5 kV;

Box 4: check whether the base peak value is 18 or 69;

Box 5: check whether the relative strength ratio of *m/z* 502 is greater than 2%;

Box 6: check whether the peak intensity of *m/z* 69 is at least twice that of *m/z* 28.

to be able to detect mass spectrum peaks with *m/z* 600 or above (including *m/z* 600).

(2) Mass resolution calibration:Mass resolution is the ability of mass spectrometer to distinguish the mass difference between two adjacent mass peaks. It is usually expressed by the peak width at 50% of the height of an ion peak (abbreviated as FWHM or $W_{1/2}$), and the unit is u (atomic mass unit, amu or U).

After tuning, $W_{1/2}$ of *m/z* 69, *m/z* 219 and *m/z* 502 were recorded. According to "Calibration specification for gas chromatography-mass spectrometer" (JJF1164—2018), $W_{1/2} < 1$ u is qualified.

(3) Mass accuracy calibration:Mass accuracy refers to the deviation between the mass measured by mass spectrometer and the theoretical value.

After the instrument is tuned, record the measured mass of pftba fragment ions *m/z* 69, *m/z* 131, *m/z* 219, *m/z* 414, *m/z* 502 and *m/z* 614, and keep the effective value to 2 decimal places. Calculate the difference between the measured value and the standard value. According to the performance requirements of GCMS-QP 2010 Ultra from the equipment manufacturer, the difference is within ± 0.1 u.

(4) Signal to noise ratio calibration: Baseline noise in mass spectrometry refers to the width

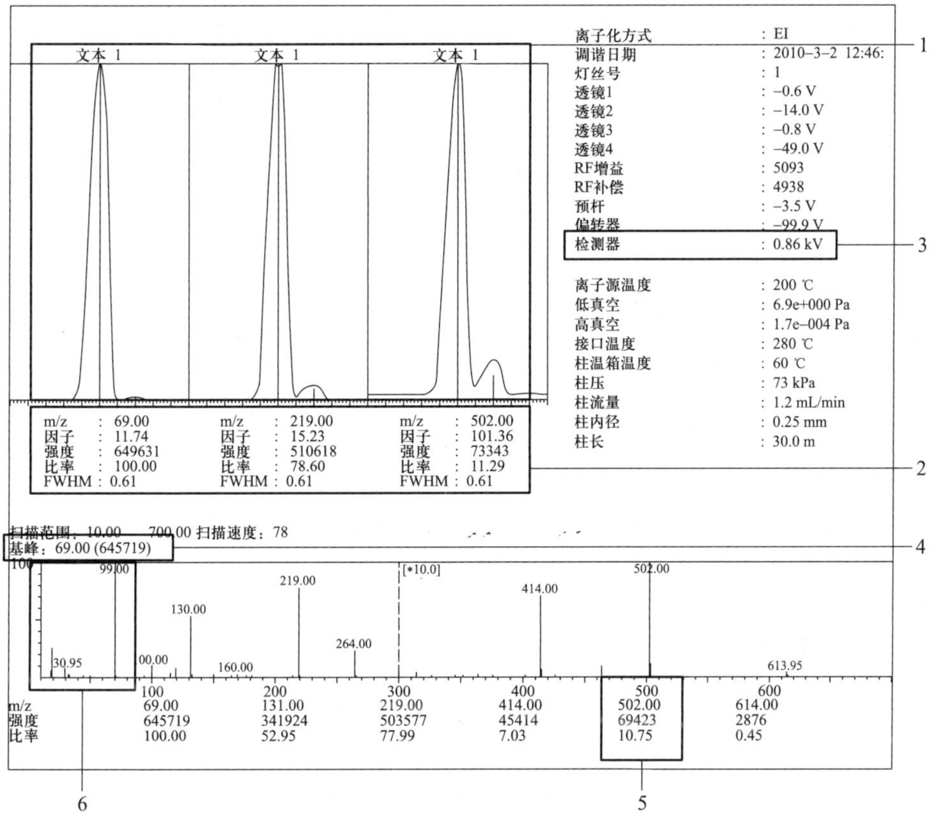

图 5–1　调谐方法和结果检查

框 1 处：检查峰形是否有明显的分叉，峰形是否对称；

框 2 处：检查半高宽（FWHM）值是否在 0.6 ± 0.1 范围内；

框 3 处：检查检测器电压是否超过 1.5 kV；

框 4 处：检查基峰值是否为 18 或 69；

框 5 处：检查 *m/z* 502 的相对强度比例是否大于 2%；

框 6 处：检查 *m/z* 69 的峰强度是否至少是 *m/z* 28 峰强度的两倍。

仪器调谐通过后，将气相色谱进样口温度设为 250 ℃，传输线温度设为 270 ℃，载气流速设为 1.0 mL·min^{-1}，不分流进样，进样量 1.0 μL，升温程序为起始温度 60 ℃，保留 0 min，然后以 10 ℃·min^{-1} 速率升温至 220 ℃，保留 2 min；质谱离子扫描范围设为 *m/z* 50~300，其他参数以调谐时确定的值作为校准参数。

注入 1 μL 八氟萘–异辛烷标准液（100 pg·μL^{-1}），连续 6 次。采集完成后从总离子流图中提取特征离子 *m/z* 272 的质量色谱图，读取特征离子峰高（H_{272}）和基线噪声（H_n，在特征离子峰后 0.5~1.0 min 范围内选取其峰谷值），按照公式 $S/N=H_{272}/H_n$ 计算其信噪比。以 6 次进样结果的算式平均值作为信噪比测试结果。根据 JJF1164—2018《气相色谱–质谱联用仪校准规范》的性能标准，要求 $S/N \geqslant 10$。

（5）峰面积与保留时间重复性校准　用信噪比校准实验结果，从采集完成后的总离子流图中提取相应特征离子 *m/z* 272 的质量色谱图，按照质量色谱峰进行积分，记录峰面积，计算 *m/z* 272 离子峰面积的相对标准偏差（RSD，或变异系数 CV），根据 JJF1164—2018《气相色谱–质谱联用

between the baseline peak bottom and peak valley. The signal-to-noise ratio is the ratio of the signal strength S of the sample to the baseline noise strength N.

After tuning the instrument, set the temperature of gas chromatography injection port as 250 ℃, the temperature of transmission line as 270 ℃, the flow rate of carrier gas as 1.0 $mL \cdot min^{-1}$, the injection volume as 1.0 μL, the initial temperature as 60 ℃ for 0 min, and then raise the temperature to 220 ℃ at the rate of 10 ℃/min for 2 min; set the ion scanning range of mass spectrometry as *m/z* 50–300. For other parameters, the values determined during tuning are used as calibration parameters.

Octafluoronaphthalene isooctane standard solution of 1 μL (100 pg /μL) was injected for 6 times. After collection, extract the mass chromatogram of characteristic ion *m/z* 272 from the total ion flow diagram, read the peak height of characteristic ion (H_{272}) and baseline noise (H_n), select the peak valley value within the range of 0.5–1.0 min after the characteristic ion peak, and calculate the signal-to-noise ratio according to the formula $S/N = H_{272}/H_n$ noise. The average value of six injection results is taken as the signal-to-noise ratio test result. According to the performance standard of "Calibration specification for gas chromatography-mass spectrometer" (JJF1164—2018), $S/N \geqslant 10$ is required.

(5) Repeatability calibration of peak area and retention time: The mass chromatogram of the corresponding characteristic ion *m/z* 272 was extracted from the total ion flow diagram after the collection. The mass chromatogram was integrated according to the mass chromatogram peak, the peak area was recorded, and the *m/z* 272 was calculated The relative standard deviation (RSD, or CV) of ion peak area is required to be less than or equal to 10% ($n = 6$) according to the performance standard of "Calibration specification for gas chromatography mass spectrometer" (JJF1164—2018). The CV of *m/z* 272 ion retention time (RT) was calculated. According to the performance requirements of GCMS-QP 2010 Ultra by the equipment manufacturer, CV≤1.0% was qualified.

Experiment Guidance

1. Preview instruction

(1) Review the basic principle and instrument composition of gas chromatography and mass spectrometry, respectively.

(2) Understand the experimental contents of gas chromatography-mass spectrometer performance verification.

2. Notes

(1) The performance verification of GC-MS instrument is related to the requirements and executive standards of each laboratory analysis and determination. If there is any conflict between the standards, the standards with updated or higher requirements should be referred to for implementation.

(2) After tuning calibration and performance verification, the accuracy and reliability of the test results should be ensured in many ways. If the quality control samples in the laboratory and the quality evaluation between laboratories are used to compare the test results, the working performance of the instrument can be ensured, and the accurate and reliable test results can be provided.

(3) The calibration interval of GC-MS is determined by many factors, such as the use of the instrument, the user, the quality of the instrument itself. Generally, it does not exceed 2 years. If the important parts are replaced, repaired, reinstalled or the performance of the instrument is in doubt, it should be calibrated at any time.

3. Discussion

What are the contents of GC-MS tuning and instrument performance parameter calibration, respectively?

仪校准规范》的性能标准，要求 CV≤10%（n=6）。计算 m/z 272 离子保留时间（retention time，RT）的 CV，根据设备制造商对 GCMS-QP 2010 Ultra 的性能要求，CV≤1.0% 为合格。

五、实验指导

1. 预习要求

（1）复习气相色谱和质谱的基本原理和仪器构成。

（2）了解气相色谱-质谱仪器性能验证的实验内容。

2. 注意事项

（1）GC-MS 仪器的性能验证与各实验室分析测定的要求和执行标准相关，如果各标准有冲突，应参照具有更新或者更高要求的标准实施。

（2）仪器经过调谐校正和性能验证后，还应继续从多途径来保证检测结果的准确性和可靠性。如采用实验室内质控样品、实验室间质评等比对检测结果，确保仪器的工作性能良好，可以提供准确和可靠的检测结果。

（3）GC-MS 的校准时间间隔长短是由仪器的使用情况、使用者、仪器本身质量等诸多因素决定的，一般不超过 2 年。如果更换重要部件、维修、重新安装或者对仪器性能有怀疑时，应随时校准。

3. 讨论

GC-MS 的调谐和仪器性能参数校准分别包含哪些内容？

Experiment 5.2 Performance Verification of High Performance Liquid Chromatography-Mass Spectrometer

Purpose

(1) To understand the significance of performance verification of high performance liquid chromatography-mass spectrometer.

(2) To master the process of performance verification of high performance liquid chromatography-mass spectrometer.

Principle

High performance liquid chromatography-mass spectrometry (HPLC-MS,or LC-MS) combines the high separation ability of chromatography for complex samples with the advantages of MS, such as high selectivity, high sensitivity and providing relative molecular weight and structure information, which reflects the mutual advantages of chromatography and mass spectrometry supplement. HPLC-MS overcomes the shortcomings of gas chromatography-mass spectrometry (GC-MS) in the analysis of highly polar, nonvolatile and thermally unstable compounds. Its application range is not limited by the boiling point and molecular weight of samples. It has been widely used in many fields such as drug research, food safety, molecular biology and environmental analysis.

In LC-MS, in order to meet the requirements of mass spectrometry detection, a special interface is needed to remove the solvent from the effluent of the liquid chromatography column and ionize the separated sample. At present, almost all LC-MS uses atmospheric pressure ionization (API) as the interface and ion source of LC-MS, and the electrospray ion source (electrospray ionization, ESI) is the most widely used.

Similar to the requirements of GC-MS detection instrument, before using LC-MS technology to carry out analysis experiment and research, the laboratory should maintain and calibrate the LC-MS equipment that affects the detection results, and verify the performance parameters such as the stability and reliability of the detection system, so as to ensure that the performance of the detection system can continuously meet the requirements of accurate measurement after the maintenance of the instrument.

According to the performance requirements of the equipment manufacturer for the instrument and JJF 1317—2011"Calibration specification for liquid chromatography-mass spectrometer", the performance verification of Shimadzu UFLCXR/LCMS-2020 LC-MS instrument mainly includes tuning of mass spectrum and calibration of LC-ESI-MS instrument performance parameters. The mixture of polyethylene glycol (PEG 200/600/1000) and raffinose is used as the tuning solution to tune the mass spectrometer. After the mass spectrometer is tuned, the performance parameters (sensitivity, mass resolution, mass number accuracy, peak area and repeatability of retention time, etc.) of LC-MS are calibrated and verified by standard materials (such as reserpine).

Instruments and Chemical Reagents

1. Instruments

Shimadzu UFLCXR/LCMS-2020 HPLC-MS; HPLC column C_{18} (100 mm × 21 mm, 1.8 μm);

实验 5.2　高效液相色谱-质谱仪器性能验证

一、实验目的

（1）了解高效液相色谱-质谱仪器性能验证的意义。

（2）掌握高效液相色谱-质谱仪器性能验证的流程。

二、实验原理

高效液相色谱-质谱联用法（HPLC-MS，简称液相色谱-质谱法，LC-MS）以液相色谱作为分离系统，质谱为检测系统，将色谱对复杂样品的高分离能力，与MS具有高选择性、高灵敏度及能够提供相对分子质量与结构信息的优点结合起来，体现了色谱和质谱技术优势的互补。HPLC-MS克服了气相色谱-质谱（GC-MS）不能分析强极性、难挥发、热不稳定性化合物的缺点，应用范围不受样品沸点和相对分子质量的限制，分析范围广，在药物研究、食品安全、分子生物学研究和环境分析等许多领域得到了广泛应用。

LC-MS中，为了满足质谱检测的要求，需采用特殊接口，以去除液相色谱柱后流出物中的溶剂，并使得分离出的样品离子化。目前几乎所有的LC-MS都使用大气压电离源（atmospheric pressure ionization，API）作为LC-MS的接口和离子源，其中电喷雾离子源（electrospray ionization，ESI）应用最为广泛。

与GC-MS检测仪器要求类似，在使用LC-MS技术开展分析实验和研究前，实验室应对影响检测结果的LC-MS设备进行维护及校准，并验证检测系统的稳定性和可靠性等性能参数，以确保仪器维护保养后其检测系统性能持续满足准确测定的要求。

根据设备制造商对仪器的性能要求和JJF 1317—2011《液相色谱-质谱联用仪校准规范》，岛津UFLCXR/LCMS-2020液相色谱-质谱联用仪器的性能验证主要包含质谱的调谐（tuning）和LC-ESI-MS仪器性能参数校准两部分。采用聚乙二醇（PEG 200/600/1000）与棉籽糖（raffinose）的混合物作为调谐液，对质谱仪进行调谐。质谱的调谐通过后，利用标准物质（如利血平）对LC-MS的性能参数（灵敏度、质量分辨率、质量数准确度、峰面积和保留时间的重复性等）进行校准与验证。

三、仪器与试剂

1. 仪器

岛津UFLCXR/LCMS-2020液相色谱-质谱联用仪；高效液相色谱柱C_{18}（100 mm × 2.1 mm，1.8 μm）；移液管（100 μL）；容量瓶（10 mL）。

2. 试剂

甲醇（色谱纯），乙腈（色谱纯），醋酸铵（分析纯），甲酸（分析纯），氨水（分析纯），PEG标准样品（包括PEG 200、PEG 600和PEG 1000），棉籽糖（对照品），利血平（对照品），去离子水。

pipette (100 μL); volumetric flask (10 mL).

2. Chemical reagents

Methanol (HPLC grade); acetonitrile (HPLC grade); ammonium acetate (A.R.); formic acid (A.R.); ammonia (A.R.); PEG standard samples (including PEG 200, PEG 600 and PEG 1000); raffinose (standard); reserpine (standard) ; deionized water.

Procedure

1. Instrument operating conditions

HPLC mobile phase 1 (ESI + mode): methanol-water-formic acid (80:20:0.1, *V/V*); mobile phase 2 (ESI mode): methanol-water-formic acid-ammonia (80:20:0.1:0.2, *V/V*); the flow rate was 0.2–0.4 $mL \cdot min^{-1}$ (no split flow).

Tuning solution solvent (about 1 L): Take 500 mL of methanol, 500 mL of deionized water, 1 mL of acetonitrile and 14.5 mg of ammonium acetate, respectively, dissolve and mix them thoroughly.

PEG stock solution: Take 15 μL of PEG 200, 20 μL of PEG 600 and 150 μL of PEG 1000 standard samples, respectively, add 100 mL of tuning solution solvent, mix well.

Mixed tuning standard solution (PEG mix + raffinose): Take 1 mL PEG stock solution, dilute it with tuning solvent at the ratio of 1/100, and add raffinose at the concentration of 50 $mg \cdot L^{-1}$.

Reserpine standard solution 1 (for direct injection by syringe pump): 1.00 $ng \cdot \mu L^{-1}$ (isopropanol: water = 1/1, *V/V*); reserpine standard solution 2 (for injection by HPLC column): 100 $pg \cdot \mu L^{-1}$ (mobile phase of HPLC).

2. Mass spectrum tuning

The sensitivity, resolution, mass number and relative intensity of the instrument are adjusted and corrected by injecting mixed tuning standard solution directly into the workstation software. There are two tuning modes: automatic tuning and manual tuning.

(1) Mass spectrum parameter setting: The FWHM of the peak profile is usually set to 0.6 to adjust the quality resolution of the instrument. Other parameters adopt the default values of automatic tuning of the instrument (for example, the atomization gas flow rate of the ion source is 1.5 $L \cdot min^{-1}$, the drying gas flow rate is 5.0 $L \cdot min^{-1}$, the capillary voltage is 4.5 kV, etc.).

(2) Inspection of tuning results: Click the "auto tuning start" button to start tuning. After tuning, name and save the tuning file, and check the tuning results (Figure 5–2).

If the tuning cannot pass, it is necessary to check whether the instrument parameter setting and tuning liquid flow path are normal; after the problem is solved, the automatic tuning can be carried out.

3. Calibration and verification of LC-MS instrument performance parameters

(1) Quality accuracy calibration: After tuning the instrument, set the scanning range to *m/z* 604–614, ESI positive ion mode, inject reserpine standard solution 1 (about 10 ng) directly by injection pump, observe the mass spectrum, record the measured mass number of reserpine characteristic fragment ion *m/z* 609, keep the significant number to 2 decimal places, and calculate the measured value and theoretical value (*m/z* 609). According to "Calibration specification for liquid chromatography-mass spectrometer" (JJF1317—2011), it is qualified if the difference does not exceed ± 0.5 u.

(2) Quality resolution calibration: After the instrument was tuned, the scanning range of MS was set to *m/z* 606–612, ESI positive ion mode, reserpine standard solution 1 (about 5 ng) was injected by injection pump directly, the mass spectrum was observed, and FWHM (or $W_{1/2}$) of *m/z* 609 mass spectrum peak of reserpine characteristic fragment ion was recorded. According to "Calibration specification for liquid

四、实验步骤

1. 仪器操作条件

液相色谱流动相 1（ESI+模式使用）：甲醇–水–甲酸（80：20：0.1，体积比）；流动相 2（ESI–模式使用）：甲醇–水–甲酸–氨水（80：20：0.1：0.2，体积比）；流速均为 0.2~0.4 mL·min^{-1}（不分流）。

调谐液溶剂（约按 1 L 配制）：分别取甲醇 500 mL，去离子水 500 mL，乙腈 1 mL，醋酸铵 14.5 mg，充分溶解混合，即得。

PEG 储备液：分别取 15 μL PEG 200、20 μL PEG 600 和 150 μL PEG 1000 三种标样，加调谐液溶剂 100 mL，混匀，即得。

混合调谐标准液（PEG Mix + raffinose）：取 1 mL PEG 储备液，用调谐液溶剂以 1/100 比例稀释后，按 50 mg·L^{-1} 的浓度加入棉籽糖，即得。

利血平标准溶液 1（通过注射泵直接进样用）：1.00 ng·μL^{-1}（溶剂为异丙醇：水=1/1，体积比）；利血平标准溶液 2（通过液相色谱柱进样用）：100 pg·μL^{-1}（溶剂为液相色谱流动相）。

2. 质谱的调谐

通过工作站软件，利用注射泵直接进样方式注入混合调谐标准液（PEG Mix+raffinose），对仪器的灵敏度、分辨率、质量数和相对强度进行调整与校正。有自动调谐和手动调谐两种调谐模式可供选择。

（1）质谱参数设定　通常设定峰轮廓的半高宽（FWHM）为 0.6 来调整仪器的质量分辨率。其他参数采用仪器自动调谐的默认值（如离子源雾化气流速为 1.5 L·min^{-1}，干燥气流速为 5.0 L·min^{-1}，毛细管电压为 4.5 kV 等）。

（2）调谐结果的检查　点击“自动调谐开始”按钮，仪器开始调谐。调谐完成后，将调谐文件命名并保存，并对调谐结果进行检查，见图 5–2。

如果调谐无法通过，需检查仪器参数设置和调谐液流路等是否正常；排除问题后，再进行自动调谐。

3. LC–MS 仪器性能参数校准与验证

（1）质量准确性校准　仪器调谐通过后，将扫描范围设为 m/z 604~614，ESI 正离子模式，利用注射泵直接进样方式注入利血平标准溶液 1（约 10 ng），观察质谱图，记录利血平特征碎片离子 m/z 609 的实测质量数，有效数字保留到小数点后 2 位，计算其实测值与理论值（m/z 609.28）之差 ΔM。根据 JJF1317—2011《液相色谱–质谱联用仪校准规范》，差值不超过 ± 0.5 u 为合格。

（2）质量分辨率校准　仪器调谐通过后，将质谱扫描范围设为 m/z 606~612，ESI 正离子模式，利用注射泵直接进样方式注入利血平标准溶液 1（约 5 ng），观察质谱图，记录利血平特征碎片离子 m/z 609 质谱峰的半高宽 FWHM（或 $W_{1/2}$），根据 JJF1317—2011《液相色谱–质谱联用仪校准规范》，$W_{1/2}$<1 u 为合格。

（3）信噪比校准　仪器调谐通过后，将质谱扫描范围设为 m/z 606~612，分别采用 ESI+和 ESI–离子模式，利用注射泵直接进样方式注入利血平标准溶液 1，对质谱仪的各项参数（即毛细管电压值、锥孔电压值、碰撞能量、雾化气温度和气流大小等）进行优化，使利血平质谱峰在

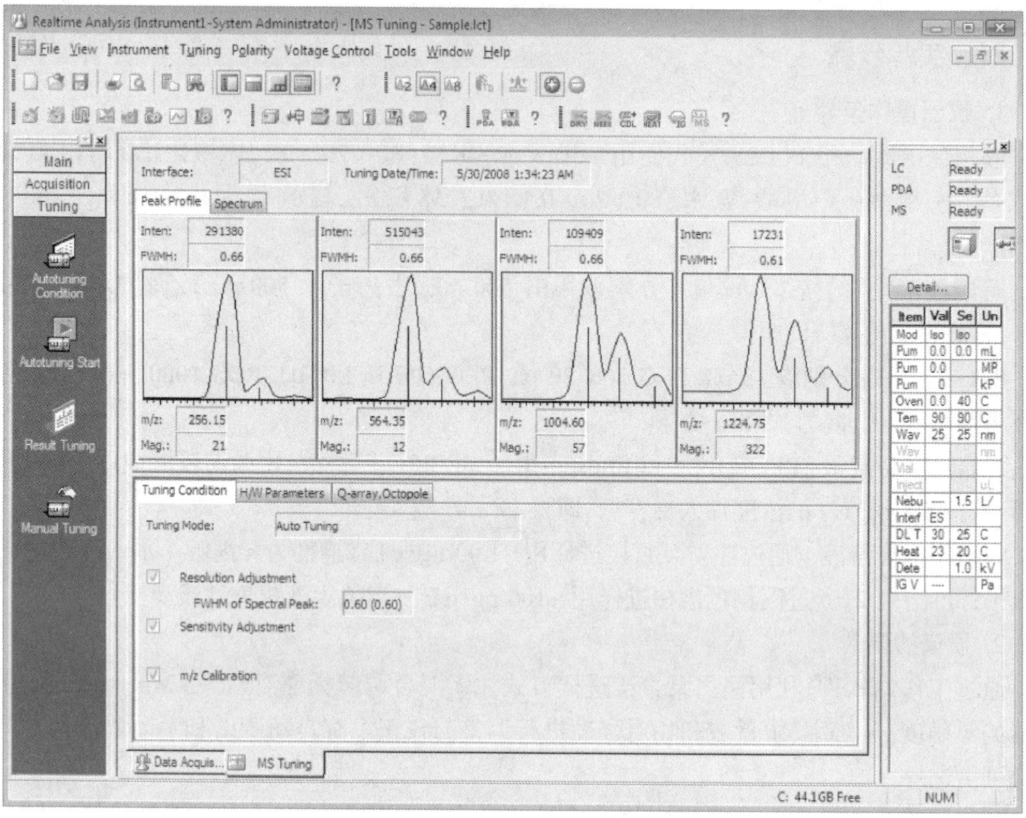

Figure 5–2 Inspection of tuning results

chromatography-mass spectrometer" (JJF1317—2011), it is qualified when $W_{1/2}$ is less than1 u.

(3) SNR calibration: After the instrument was tuned, the mass spectrum scanning range was set to *m/z* 606–612, and reserpine standard solution 1 was injected by injection pump in ESI + and ESI-ion mode respectively. The parameters of the mass spectrometer, such as capillary voltage, cone hole voltage, collision energy, atomization gas temperature and gas flow size, were optimized to make the mass spectrum peak of reserpine at *m/z* 609 has the highest response.

The threshold value of MS data was set to 0, and the characteristic fragment ion was set to *m/z* 609. Using mobile phase 1 and mobile phase 2, 5 μL of reserpine standard solution 2 (100 $pg\cdot\mu L^{-1}$) was injected into the column in ESI + and ESI-mode, respectively. Observe the chromatogram, record the peak height HS and the baseline noise HN (the difference between the peak and valley values of the baseline output signal within 1–3 min after the chromatographic peak), calculate the signal-to-noise ratio according to the formula $S/N = H_s/H_n$, and continuously measure for 6 times, and take the average value of the 6 results as the signal-to-noise ratio measurement result. According to"Calibration specification for liquid chromatography-mass spectrometer" (JJF1317—2011), $S/N \geqslant 10:1$ is required.

(4) Repeatability calibration of peak area and retention time: After instrument tuning and signal-to-noise ratio calibration, the threshold value of mass spectrum data was set to 0, the characteristic fragment ion was set to *m/z* 609, the mobile phase 1 was used, and 5 μL reserpine standard solution 2 (100 $pg\cdot\mu L^{-1}$) was injected into the chromatographic column in ESI + mode. Observe the chromatogram, record the peak area and retention time of the chromatographic peak, continuously

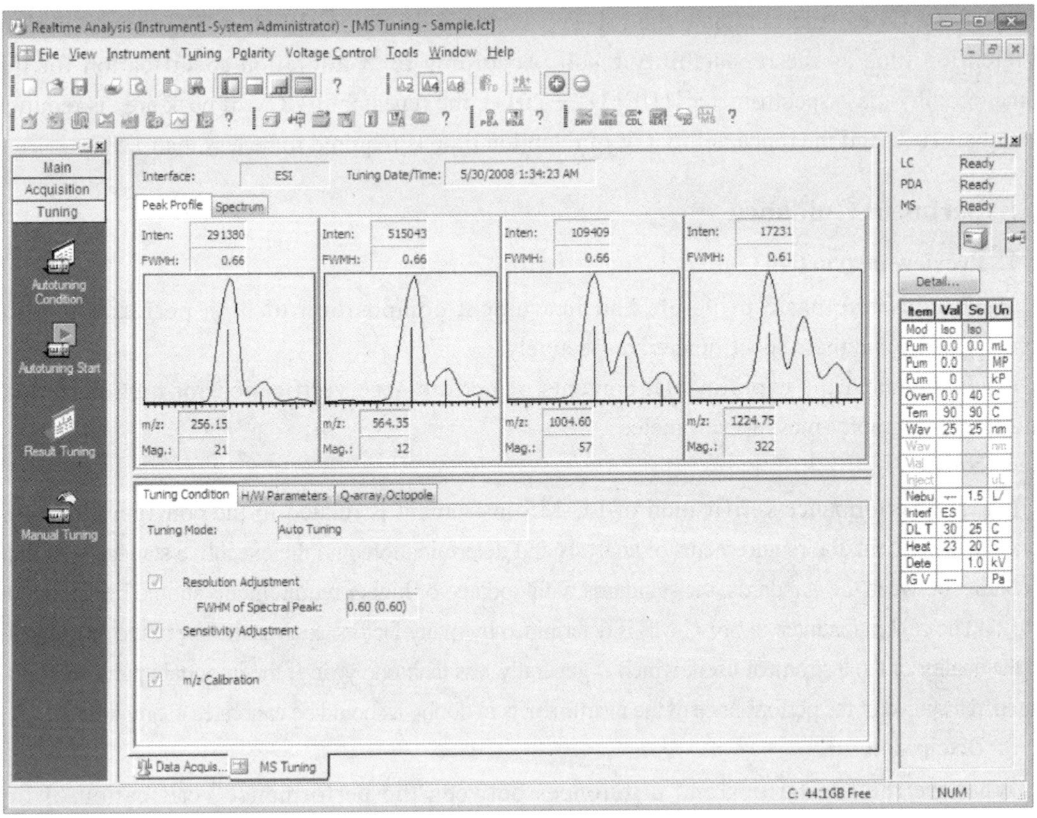

图 5-2 调谐结果的检查

m/z 609 的响应最高。

将质谱采集数据的阈值设为 0，设置特征碎片离子为 *m/z* 609。分别采用流动相 1 和流动相 2，在 ESI+和 ESI-模式下，经色谱柱注入 5 μL 利血平标准溶液 2（100 pg·μL^{-1}）。观察色谱图，记录其色谱峰峰高 H_s 和基线噪声 H_n（色谱峰后 1~3 min 内基线输出信号的峰谷值之差），根据公式 $S/N=H_s/H_n$ 计算信噪比，连续测量 6 次，以 6 次结果的平均值作为信噪比测量结果。根据 JJF1317—2011《液相色谱-质谱联用仪校准规范》，要求 $S/N \geq 10:1$。

（4）峰面积与保留时间重复性校准　仪器调谐通过、信噪比校准后，将质谱采集数据的阈值设为 0，设置特征碎片离子为 *m/z* 609，采用流动相 1，在 ESI+模式下，经色谱柱注入 5 μL 利血平标准溶液 2（100 pg·μL^{-1}）。观察色谱图，记录其色谱峰的峰面积和保留时间，连续测量 6 次，计算其峰面积和保留时间的相对标准偏差（RSD，或 CV），作为重复性结果。根据 JJF1317—2011《液相色谱-质谱联用仪校准规范》，要求峰面积的重复性 CV≤10%，保留时间的重复性 CV≤1.5%。

五、实验指导

1. 预习要求

（1）复习高效液相色谱和质谱的基本原理和仪器构成。

（2）了解高效液相色谱-质谱仪器性能验证的实验内容。

measure for 6 times, and calculate the relative standard deviation (RSD, or CV) of the peak area and retention time as the repeatability result. According to "Calibration specification for liquid chromatography-mass spectrometer" (JJF1317—2011), the repeatability CV of peak area is required to be less than 10%, and the repeatability CV of retention time is required to be less than 1.5%.

Experiment Guidance

1. Preview instruction

(1) Review the basic principle and instrument composition of high performance liquid chromatography and mass spectrometer, respectively.

(2) Understand the experimental contents of performance verification for high performance liquid chromatography-mass spectrometer.

2. Notes

(1) The performance verification of LC-MS instrument is related to the configuration of each laboratory instrument, the requirements of analysis and determination, and the executive standards. If there is any conflict between the standards, the standards with updated or higher requirements should be referred to.

(2) The calibration interval of LC-MS is determined by many factors, such as the use of the instrument, the user, the quality of the instrument itself, which is generally less than one year. If the important parts are replaced, repaired, reinstalled or the performance of the instrument is in doubt, it should be calibrated at any time.

3. Discussion

What are the similarities and differences between the performance verification of liquid chromatography-mass spectrometer and gas chromatography-mass spectrometer?

2. 注意事项

（1）LC-MS 仪器的性能验证与各实验室仪器的配置、分析测定的要求和执行标准相关，如果各标准有冲突，应参照具有更新或者更高要求的标准来实施或者执行。

（2）LC-MS 的校准时间间隔长短是由仪器的使用情况、使用者、仪器本身质量等诸多因素决定的，一般不超过 1 年。如果更换重要部件、维修、重新安装或者对仪器性能有怀疑时，应随时校准。

3. 讨论

液相色谱-质谱联用仪器的性能验证与气相色谱-质谱联用仪器的性能验证的异同点是什么？

Experiment 5.3 Determination of Eugenol in *Caryophylli Flos* by Gas Chromatography-Mass Spectrometry

Purpose

(1) To grasp the basic principle of gas chromatography-mass spectrometry and the components of the instrument.

(2) To be familiar with the experimental process of gas chromatography-mass spectrometry and the analysis method of experimental results.

(3) To be familiar with qualitative and quantitative analysis methods of gas chromatography-mass spectrometry.

Principle

Gas chromatography (GC) is widely used in the determination of volatile and thermostable compounds in petrochemical, environmental monitoring, food analysis, medicine and health and other fields. In the range of application, gas chromatography has the advantages of high separation efficiency, fast analysis speed, less sample consumption and high detection sensitivity. The components of gas chromatograph include carrier gas system, sample injection system, chromatographic column and column temperature oven, detection system and data processing system. The commonly used detectors in GC include hydrogen flame ionization detector and thermal conductivity detector, but these detectors usually cannot give the structural information of the components to be determined.

The mass spectrometer can obtain the structural information of compounds by measuring molecular ions, fragment ions or other characteristic ions. The gas chromatograph and the mass spectrometer are connected through a transmission line (or interface), as shown in Figure 5-3 (a), which constitutes a gas chromatography-mass spectrometer. After gas chromatography separation, the mixture becomes the chromatographic peak of a single component, and then it is introduced into the mass spectrometer through the transmission line for analysis, so as to obtain the mass spectrum of a single component in the mixture [Figure 5-3 (b)]. Gas chromatography-mass spectrometry (GC-MS) can be used to identify compounds

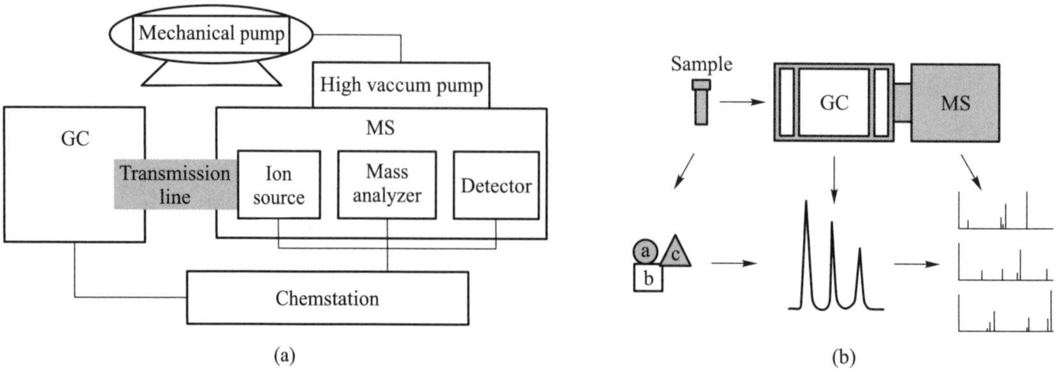

Figure 5-3 Components of GC-MS instrument (a) process of sample analysis (b)

实验 5.3　气相色谱-质谱联用法测定丁香中的丁香酚

一、实验目的

（1）掌握气相色谱-质谱法的基本原理和仪器的组成。

（2）熟悉气相色谱-质谱法的实验过程、实验结果的分析方法。

（3）熟悉气相色谱-质谱法的定性及定量分析方法。

二、实验原理

气相色谱法（gas chromatography，GC）常用于测定易挥发且热稳定的化合物，广泛应用于石油化学、环境监测、食品分析、医药卫生等领域。在应用范围内，气相色谱法具有分离效率高、分析速度快、样品用量少、检测灵敏度高等优点。气相色谱仪的组成部分包括载气系统、进样系统、色谱柱和柱温箱、检测系统和数据处理系统，其中检测系统常用的检测器包括氢火焰离子化检测器和热导检测器等，但这些检测器通常不能给出待测组分的结构信息。

质谱仪可以通过测定化合物的分子离子、碎片离子或其他特征离子获得其结构信息。将气相色谱仪和质谱仪通过传输线（或接口）连接，如图 5-3（a）所示，即组成了气质联用仪。混合物经过气相色谱分离后成为单个组分的色谱峰，然后依次经过传输线导入到质谱仪中进行分析，从而获得混合物中单个组分的质谱信息［图 5-3（b）］。气相色谱-质谱联用法（gas chromatography-mass spectrometry，GC-MS）可以同时用保留时间和质谱图（SCAN 扫描模式）对化合物进行定性鉴别，也可以用质谱检测得到的总离子流色谱图（total ion chromatogram，TIC）或选择离子监测（selected ion monitoring，SIM）进行定量分析。

丁香为桃金娘科植物丁香 *Eugenia caryophyllata* Thunb. 的干燥花蕾（图 5-4），具有温中降逆、散寒止痛、温肾助阳的作用。丁香的主要成分为挥发油，挥发油中含有丁香油酚（Eugenol，$C_{10}H_{12}O_2$，结构见图 5-4，在挥发油中含量为 72%~90%）、乙酰丁香油酚、*β*-石竹烯（*β*-Caryophyllene），以及甲基正戊基酮、水杨酸甲酯、葎草烯（Humuleno）、苯甲醛、苄醇、间甲氧基苯甲醛、乙酸苄酯、胡椒酚（Chavicol）、*α*-衣兰烯（*α*-Ylangene）等成分。《中国药典》（2020 年版）一部丁香项下规定

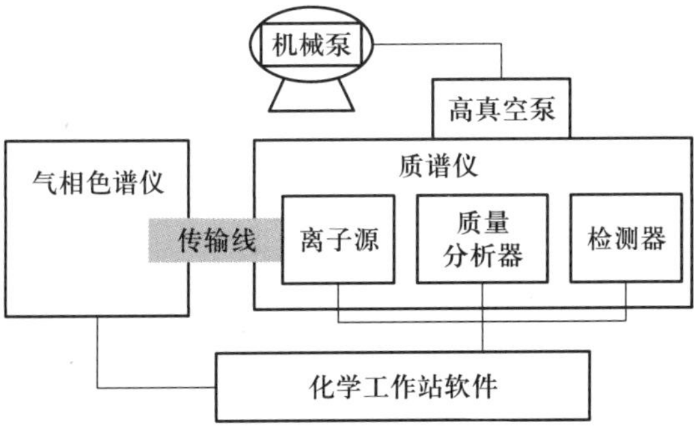

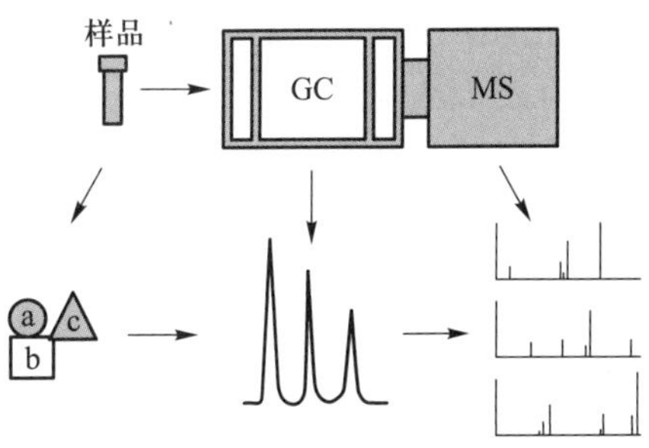

图 5-3　GC-MS 联用仪组成部分示意图（a）和分析流程图（b）

qualitatively by retention time and mass spectrum (SCAN mode), and also can be used for quantitative analysis by total ion chromatogram (TIC) or selective ion monitoring (SIM).

Caryophylli flos is the dried flower bud of *Eugenia caryophyllata Thunb.* (see Figure 5–4). It has the functions of warming the middle and reducing adverse reactions, dispersing cold and relieving pain, warming the kidney and helping Yang. The main component of caryophylli flos is volatile oil, which contains eugenol ($C_{10}H_{12}O_2$, see Figure 5–4 for structure, 72%–90% in the oil), acetyl-eugenol, β-caryophyllene, methyl n-pentyl ketone, methyl salicylate, humuleno, benzaldehyde, benzyl alcohol, m-methoxy-benzaldehyde, benzyl acetate, chavicol, α-ylangene, etc. The content of eugenol in *caryophylli flos* should not be less than 11.0% according to the ChP (2020 Editon, Volume Ⅰ).

(a) (b) (c)

Figure 5–4 Plant of *Eugenia caryophyllata Thunb.* (a), *Caryophylli flos* (b) and structure of eugenol (c)

In this experiment, the content of eugenol in *Caryophylli Flos* is determined by GC-MS with external standard method:

$$w_{\text{Eugenol}}(\%)=\frac{\dfrac{A_i}{A_s}\times c_s\times 20\times 500}{W}\times 100\%$$

Where A_i is the chromatographic peak area of eugenol in the sample solution; A_s is the chromatographic peak area of the standard solution; c_s is the concentration of the reference solution, $mg\cdot mL^{-1}$; W is the sampling mass, g; 20 and 500 are dilution multiples.

Instruments and Chemical Reagents

1. Instruments

Shimadzu GCMS-QP 2010Ultra GC-MS system; DB-5MS chromatographic column (30 m × 0.25 mm, 0.25 μm); Ultrasonic cleaner; volumetric flask(50 mL, 100 mL); analytical balance.

2. Chemical reagents

Eugenol (standard); *Caryophylli Flos* (herb); methanol (A.R.).

Procedure

1. Preparation of standard solutions

Weighing accurately about 5 mg eugenol reference substance into a 100 mL volumetric flask, add methanol to make a 0.05 $mg\cdot mL^{-1}$ solution as the reference substance solution for qualitative

(a)　　(b)　　(c)

图 5–4　丁香原植物（a）、丁香药材（b）和丁香酚（c）的结构

丁香药材中含丁香酚不得少于 11.0%。

本实验采用 GC–MS 联用技术，外标法测定丁香药材中丁香酚的含量，计算公式如下：

$$w_{丁香酚}(\%)=\frac{\frac{A_i}{A_s}\times c_s\times 20\times 500}{W}\times 100\%$$

式中，A_i 为样品中丁香酚的色谱峰面积；A_s 为对照品色谱峰面积；c_s 为对照品溶液的质量浓度，$mg\cdot mL^{-1}$；W 为取样量，g；20 和 500 为稀释倍数。

三、仪器和试剂

1. 仪器

岛津 GCMS–QP2010Ultra 气质联用仪；DB–5MS 色谱柱（30 m × 0.25 mm，0.25 μm）；超声波清洗机；容量瓶（50 mL，100 mL）；分析天平。

2. 试剂

丁香酚对照品；丁香药材；甲醇（分析纯）。

四、实验步骤

1. 对照品溶液的制备

取丁香酚对照品 5 mg，精密称定，置于 100 mL 容量瓶中，加甲醇制成 0.05 $mg\cdot mL^{-1}$ 溶液，作为定性分析溶液。再取上述部分溶液，稀释成 0.005 $mg\cdot mL^{-1}$ 溶液，作为定量分析的对照品溶液。

2. 供试品溶液的制备

取本品粉末（过二号筛）约 0.3 g，精密称定，置于具塞锥形瓶中，精密加入甲醇 20 mL，称定质量，超声处理 15 min，放置至室温，再称定质量，用甲醇补足减失的质量，摇匀，滤过，取续滤液，作为供试品贮备液。

取供试品贮备液 0.1 mL 到 50 mL 容量瓶中，加甲醇稀释至刻度，作为供试品溶液。

3. 实验条件

GC 条件：色谱柱为 DB–5MS（30 m × 0.25 mm，0.25 μm），载气为 He，纯度>99.999%；色谱柱温度：初温 80 ℃，以 20 $℃\cdot min^{-1}$ 升至 230 ℃保持 4.0 min；进样口温度 230 ℃；进样方式：分

analysis. The above solution was then diluted into 0.005 $mg \cdot mL^{-1}$ solution as a quantitative analysis solution.

2. Preparation of test solutions

Take about 0.3 g of the powder of *Caryophylli Flos* (passing through No.2 sieve) and weigh it accurately, put into a triangle flask with stopper. Transfer 20 mL of methanol into the flask and weigh it. After ultrasonic treatment for 15 minutes, place it at room temperature and weigh it again, use methanol to make up the lost weight. Shake well and filter. Take the filtrate as the stock test solution. Take this stock solution 0.1 mL to 50 mL volumetric bottles, diluted to scale with methanol, and used as the analysis solution.

3. Experiment conditions

GC condition: the chromatographic column was DB-5MS (30 m × 0.25 mm, 0.25 μm), carrier gas: He (purity>99.999%); column temperature: the initial temperature was 80 ℃, rising to 230 ℃ by the rate of 20 $℃ \cdot min^{-1}$, and maintain for 4 min; injector temperature 230 ℃; injection method: split; Split ratio: 20:1; column flow rate: 1 $mL \cdot min^{-1}$; injection volume: 1 μL.

MS condition: ionization mode: electron ion source (EI);ionization energy:70 eV; voltage of electron multiplier: 1.2 kV; qualitative analysis: SCAN, range 65–200 *m/z*; quantitative analysis: SIM, quantitative ion *m/z* 164; ion source temperature: 230 ℃; GC-MS interface temperature: 280 ℃; solvent delay time: 3.0 min.

4. Determination method

(1) Inject 1 μL of the qualitative analysis solution (0.05 $mg \cdot mL^{-1}$) into GC-MS, record the chromatogram and mass spectrometry, for standard spectral library search.

(2) Inject 1 μL of standard solution (0.005 $mg \cdot mL^{-1}$) and sample solution into GC-MS for three times, respectively, record the chromatogram and response value of *m/z* 164 ion. The content of eugenol in the sample was calculated according to the content calculation formula.

Data Analysis

Record the peak area of eugenol in the reference solution and sample solution, fill in the table below, and calculate the content of eugenol in *Caryophylli Flos* with the average value of peak area.

No. of injection	Peaks	Peak area	Average of peak area	*w*/%
Standard solution	Eugenol			
	Eugenol			
	Eugenol			
Sample solution	Eugenol			
	Eugenol			
	Eugenol			

流进样；分流比：20∶1；柱流量：1 mL·min^{-1}；进样体积：1 μL。

MS 条件：电离方式为电子轰击离子源（EI）；电离能量为 70 eV；电子倍增器电压为 1.2 kV；定性分析：SCAN 扫描模式，质量扫描范围为 65~200 *m/z*；定量分析：SIM 扫描模式，定量离子 *m/z* 为 164；离子源温度：230 ℃；GC-MS 接口温度：280 ℃；溶剂延迟时间：3.0 min。

4. 测定方法

（1）取定性分析样品溶液 1 μL，进样至 GC-MS，记录色谱图和质谱图，用于标准谱库检索。

（2）分别取定量分析的对照品和供试品溶液各 1 μL，进样至 GC-MS，记录色谱图，测定目标 *m/z* 为 164 的离子的响应值。对照品和供试品溶液各进样三次。按含量计算公式计算丁香中丁香酚的含量。

五、数据处理

记录对照品溶液和样品溶液中丁香酚的峰面积，填入下表，用峰面积平均值计算丁香酚在药材中的含量。

进样次数	色谱峰	峰面积	峰面积平均值	含量/%
对照品溶液	丁香酚			
	丁香酚			
	丁香酚			
样品溶液	丁香酚			
	丁香酚			
	丁香酚			

六、实验指导

1. 预习要求

（1）复习 GC-MS 的基本原理及分析方法。

（2）熟悉 GC-MS 的仪器构成及操作。

（3）了解 GC-MS 的优缺点及其在药物分析中的应用。

2. 注意事项

（1）样品分析前应确认 GC-MS 系统的真空度是否达到分析要求。

（2）在 GC-MS 中，MS 检测器采集数据有两种模式：SCAN（全扫描）和 SIM（选择离子监测），其中 SCAN 连续扫描采集选定质荷比范围内所有离子的信号，可以获得化合物的质谱图，通过自动检索能够得到化合物的结构，常用于定性分析，峰形及灵敏度稍差；而 SIM 只监测采集某几个所选的特征离子的信号，灵敏度高，峰形好，主要用于定量分析。

（3）丁香药材需粉碎后提取，否则提取不完全；丁香酚易挥发，粉碎后不能放置过久测定。

Experiment Guidance

1. Preview instruction

(1) Review the basic principle and analysis method of GC-MS.

(2) Be familiar with GC-MS instrument structure and operation.

(3) Know the advantage and disadvantage of GC-MS and its application in drug analysis.

2. Notes

(1) Before analysis, it should be confirmed whether the vacuum degree of GC-MS system meets the analysis requirements.

(2) In GC-MS, MS detector data collection has two modes: SCAN (full scan) and SIM (selected ion monitoring). SCAN mode can scan all ions in the selected mass-to-charge ratio continuously to obtain mass spectrum and get compounds′ structure by automatical searching, which is often used in qualitative analysis. In this mode, peak shape and sensitivity is a bit poor; SIM only monitors and collects signals of a few selected characteristic ions, with high sensitivity and good peak shape, which is mainly used for quantitative analysis.

(3) *Caryophylli Flos* should be extracted after crushing, otherwise the extraction is incomplete. Eugenol is easy to volatilize, so it can′t be stored for a long time after crushing.

3. Discussion

(1) In gas chromatography, what are the advantages of using mass spectrometry compared with other detectors?

(2) What requirements are needed for the interface of GC-MS?

(3) Which ion sources are commonly used in GC-MS?

(4) Why helium is often used as carrier gas in GC-MS?

3. 讨论

（1）气相色谱使用质谱检测与其他检测器相比有哪些优势？

（2）GC-MS 联用仪对接口有什么要求？

（3）GC-MS 联用仪常用的离子源有哪些？

（4）GC-MS 分析时常用氦气作为载气的原因是什么？

Experiment 5.4 Determination of *p*-Phenylenediamine in Hair Dyes by Gas Chromatography-Mass Spectrometry

Purpose

(1) To be familiar with the basic principle and operation of gas chromatography-mass spectrometry method for quantitative analysis.

(2) To understand the principle of selective ion mode mass spectrometry.

(3) To understand the treatment of hair dyes.

Principle

Oxidized dyes are widely used as raw materials for hair dyes. Phenylenediamine (*o*-phenylenediamine, *p*-phenylenediamine and *m*-phenylenediamine) is a common oxidant dye in organic hair dyes. In the process of hair dyeing, phenylenediamine is oxidized to dye intermediate under the action of oxidant, and the intermediate reacts with coupling agent of hydroquinone to produce color. But *o*-phenylenediamine, *m*-phenylenediamine and *p*-phenylenediamine are toxic chemicals, which can be absorbed through the skin, cause skin rash and liver damage. In 2019, the newly implemented "Hygienic standard for cosmetics" listed *p*-phenylenediamine in oxidized hair dyes as restricted substances, and stipulated that the maximum allowable concentration of *p*-phenylenediamine in cosmetics was 6%, while *o*-phenylenediamine and *m*-phenylenediamine were listed as prohibited substances. Although it has been reported that many analytical methods can be used to detect phenylenediamine compounds, gas chromatography-mass spectrometry (GC-MS) has the advantages of high qualitative accuracy and high detection sensitivity. In this experiment, the selective ion monitoring (SIM) mode of GC-MS was used to determine the content of *p*-phenylenediamine in hair dyes, and the standard curve was used to determine its content.

Instruments and Chemical Reagents

1. Instruments

Shimadzu GCMS-QP2010Ultra GC-MS system; DB-5MS chromatographic column (30 m × 0.25 mm, 0.25 μm); analytical balance; centrifuge tube (10 mL); centrifuge; volumetric flask(10 mL, 25 mL).

2. Chemical reagents

p-phenylenediamine (analytical purity, ⩾99%); ethyl acetate (A.R.); sodium chloride (A.R.); 1% sodium sulfite solution.

Procedure

1. Preparation of reference solutions

Take an appropriate amount of *p*-phenylenediamine reference substance, accurately weigh it, add ethyl acetate to make a solution containing 1 mg per 1 mL, which is used as the reference stock solution. Take 0.1 mL, 0.5 mL, 1.0 mL, 1.5 mL and 2.0 mL of stock solution respectively, put them into a 10 mL volumetric flask, add ethyl acetate to the marked line, shake well, and used as a series of standard solutions.

2. Preparation of test solutions

(1) Powder sample:Accurately weigh a proper amount of powder sample (containing about 25 mg

实验 5.4 气相色谱-质谱联用法检测染发剂中的对苯二胺类物质

一、实验目的

（1）熟悉气相色谱-质谱联用法进行含量测定的基本原理和操作。

（2）了解选择离子模式质谱分析原理。

（3）了解染发剂样品的处理方法。

二、实验原理

氧化型染料是目前广泛应用的染发剂原料。苯二胺（邻苯二胺、对苯二胺和间苯二胺）是有机染发剂中常用氧化剂染料。在染发过程中，苯二胺在氧化剂的作用下，被氧化为染料中间体，该中间体又在苯二酚类偶合剂的作用下发生耦合反应后产生颜色而染发。但邻苯二胺、间苯二胺、对苯二胺 3 种同分异构体均是有毒化学物质，可经皮肤被吸收，引起皮疹和使肝脏受损害。《化妆品卫生规范》（2019 年版）将氧化型染发剂中对苯二胺列为限用物质，规定其在化妆品中最大允许浓度为 6%，而将邻苯二胺和间苯二胺列为禁用物质。虽然文献报道多种分析方法均可用于检测苯二胺类化合物，但使用气相色谱-质谱法（gas chromatography-mass spectrometry，GC-MS）测定氧化型染发剂中的苯二胺，具有定性准确和检测灵敏度高等优点。本实验采用 GC-MS 中的选择离子监测（selective ion monitoring，SIM）模式检测染发剂中的对苯二胺，利用标准曲线法测定其含量。

三、仪器和试剂

1. 仪器

岛津 GCMS-QP2010Ultra 气质联用仪；DB-5MS 色谱柱（30 m × 0.25 mm，0.25 μm）；分析天平；离心管（10 mL）；离心机；容量瓶（10 mL，25 mL）。

2. 试剂

对苯二胺（分析纯，≥99%）；乙酸乙酯（分析纯）；氯化钠（分析纯）；1% 亚硫酸钠溶液。

四、实验步骤

1. 对照品溶液的制备

取对苯二胺对照品适量，精密称定，加乙酸乙酯制成每 1 mL 含 1 mg 的溶液，作为对照品储备液。分别移取对照品储备液 0.1 mL、0.5 mL、1.0 mL、1.5 mL、2.0 mL 置于 10 mL 容量瓶中，用乙酸乙酯定容至刻度，摇匀，制成系列标准溶液。

2. 供试品溶液的制备

（1）粉剂样品　精密称取粉剂样品适量（含对苯二胺约 25 mg），置于 25 mL 容量瓶中，用乙酸乙酯稀释至刻度，避光静置约 4 h，取出过滤，精密移取续滤液 1 mL，置于 10 mL 容量瓶中，用乙酸乙酯稀释至刻度，摇匀，作为粉剂样品溶液。

（2）水剂样品　精密称取水剂样品适量（含对苯二胺约 25 mg），置于 10 mL 离心管中，

of *p*-phenylenediamine), put it into a 25 mL volumetric flask, dilute it to the scale with ethyl acetate, keep it still for about 4 h in dark, take it out for filtration, transfer 1 mL of filtrate to 10 mL volumetric flask, dilute to the scale with ethyl acetate, mix well, used as the powder sample solution.

(2) Water sample:Accurately weigh an appropriate amount of water sample (containing about 25 mg of *p*-phenylenediamine), place it in a 10 mL centrifuge tube, add 2 mL of 1% sodium sulfite solution, 0.2 g sodium chloride and 5 mL of ethyl acetate, cover the plug tightly, vibrate for 30 seconds, place it in a centrifuge (2 000 $r \cdot min^{-1}$) for 10 minutes, stand for several minutes, separate the supernatant, extract the lower aqueous solution twice with 5 mL of ethyl acetate, separate the upper solution and combine the extract of ethyl acetate into a 25 mL volumetric flask, add ethyl acetate to the marked line, shake well, used as the water sample solution.

3. Experimental conditions

Chromatographic conditions: the column was DB-5MS (30 m × 0.25 mm, 0.25 μm), the carrier gas was He (purity >99.999%), the flow rate was 1.2 $mL \cdot min^{-1}$. Temperature programming: 90 ℃ maintained for 1 min, increased to 180 ℃ at the rate of 15 $℃ \cdot min^{-1}$, maintained for 1 min, and then increased to 270 ℃ at the rate of 30 $℃ \cdot min^{-1}$, maintained for 1 min. The injector was set at 250 ℃, the injection volume was 1 μL, and the split ratio was 20 : 1.

MS conditions: the transfer line temperature was 200 ℃, and the solvent delay time was 2.5 min; The ionization mode is EI ion source, and its temperature was set at 200 ℃; The ionization energy is 70 eV; The acquisition mode is SIM; The monitoring ion scanning range is *m/z* 40–350, the detection ions were *m/z* 108, 91, 80 and 54 and the quantitative ions were *m/z* 108.

4. Determination method

1 μL of each standard solution and 1 μL of sample solution are injected into the GC-MS system, and analyzed respectively. Record the peak area of each component in standard and sample solutions.

Data Analysis

The working curve was drawn based on the peak area of series standard solution with concentration of *p*-phenylenediamine, and the concentration of *p*-phenylenediamine in the sample to be determined was calculated according to the working curve.

Experiment Guidance

1. Preview instruction

(1) Review the basic principle and analysis method of GC-MS.

(2) Be familiar with the basic principle and operation of external standard method.

(3) Understand the application of GC-MS method in the quality control of daily life products.

2. Notes

(1) Phenylenediamine compounds are easy to oxidize, so sodium sulfite solution should be added in the treatment process and it should be operated under dark conditions.

(2) Adding sodium chloride to the water sample can prevent emulsification.

(3) During the operation, the volatilization of ethyl acetate should be avoided as far as possible. And the whole process should be carried out in the fume hood.

3. Discussion

(1) What types of products can be detected by GC-MS in daily life?

(2) What is the definition of solvent delay? What is its role in the whole process?

加 1% 亚硫酸钠溶液 2 mL、0.2 g 氯化钠和 5 mL 乙酸乙酯，盖紧塞子，振荡 30 s，放置离心机（2 000 $r \cdot min^{-1}$）中分离 10 min，静置片刻，分出上层溶液，下层水溶液再用 5 mL 乙酸乙酯萃取 2 次，分出上层溶液，合并萃取液，并用乙酸乙酯定容至 25 mL 容量瓶中，摇匀，精密移取该溶液 1 mL，置于 10 mL 容量瓶中，用乙酸乙酯稀释至刻度，摇匀，作为水剂样品溶液。

3. 实验条件

色谱条件：色谱柱为 DB-5MS（30 m × 0.25 mm，0.25 μm），载气为 He，纯度>99.999%；流速 1.2 $mL \cdot min^{-1}$；程序升温：初始温度为 90 ℃，保持 1 min，15 $℃ \cdot min^{-1}$ 升至 180 ℃，保持 1 min，再以 30 $℃ \cdot min^{-1}$ 升至 270 ℃，保持 1 min。进样口温度为 250 ℃，进样量 1 μL；进样方式：分流进样；分流比：20 ∶ 1。

质谱条件：接口温度为 200 ℃，溶剂延迟时间为 2.5 min；电离方式为 EI 离子源，温度为 200 ℃，电离能量为 70 eV；采集方式为 SIM；选择监测离子扫描范围 40~350 *m/z*，检测离子为 *m/z* 108、91、80 和 54，定量离子 *m/z* 为 108。

4. 测定方法

分别精密吸取系列标准溶液与样品溶液各 1 μL，注入 GC-MS，测定峰面积。

五、数据处理

以标准溶液峰面积-对苯二胺浓度绘制工作曲线，根据工作曲线方程计算待测样品中对苯二胺的含量。

六、实验指导

1. 预习要求

（1）复习 GC-MS 的基本原理及分析方法。

（2）熟悉 GC-MS 中外标法定量检测的基本原理和操作方法。

（3）了解 GC-MS 法在日常生活品质量监测中的应用。

2. 注意事项

（1）苯二胺类化合物容易氧化，因此处理过程中加入亚硫酸钠溶液，且应在避光条件下操作。

（2）水剂样品中加入氯化钠可防止乳化。

（3）操作过程中应尽量防止乙酸乙酯挥发造成测定误差，且全程应在通风橱中进行。

3. 讨论

（1）日常生活中哪些产品可采用 GC-MS 法进行质量检测？

（2）何谓溶剂延迟？其作用是什么？

Experiment 5.5 Determination of Paracetamol by Liquid Chromatography-Mass Spectrometry

Purpose

(1) To understand the component of liquid chromatography-mass spectrometer.

(2) To master the basic principle and method of liquid chromatography-mass spectrometry detection.

(3) To understand the application of liquid chromatography-mass spectrometry in drug analysis.

Principle

Liquid chromatography-mass spectrometry (LC-MS) is mainly composed of high performance liquid chromatography and mass spectrometry It is a combination of high separation characteristics of HPLC and high sensitivity detection characteristics of MS. LC-MS is mainly used in drug analysis: drug structure information acquisition, molecular weight determination; drug quality control (impurities, isomers, degradation products research); drug in vivo process analysis, drug metabolites research, blood drug concentration detection, etc.

HPLC instrument consists of infusion pump, injection system, chromatographic column, detector and chemical workstation. The main function of the chemical workstation is responsible for the operation of the whole instrument system and data processing. The detector is usually equipped with UV diode array detector and mass spectrometer detector.

The mass spectrometer is mainly composed of injection system, ion source, mass analyzer, detector, data acquisition and analysis.

The sample enters the ion source through the injection system, ionizes into various ion fragments with different mass to charge ratios (m/z) due to different structures, and then the ion fragments with sample information are accelerated into the mass analyzer. Under the action of magnetic field, the radius of ion motion is proportional to the square root of its mass to charge ratio, so that the ions with different mass to charge ratios are separated in the magnetic field, and the ions are separated According to the mass charge ratio, the samples arrive at the detector in turn. After recording, the mass spectrum of the sample is obtained.

At present, the commonly used ionization methods include electrospray ionization (ESI) and atmospheric pressure chemical ionization (APCI). The principle of electrospray ionization is that the components to be measured (chromatographic effluent) enter the ion source through a terminal high voltage capillary, and the tiny droplets produced by nitrogen atomization are removed by solvent under the action of heating and nitrogen flow, forming a single charge or more single charged gaseous ions (such as M^+, $[M+Na]^+$, $[M+H]^+$, $[M+K]^+$, $[M+NH_4]^+$, etc.) These ions are then transferred from atmospheric pressure to the high vacuum of the mass spectrometer through the step-by-step decompression region, and detected by the mass analyzer. According to different mass charge ratios, the mass spectrum chromatogram is output after data processing.

The common scanning methods in mass spectrometry include full scan, selective ion monitor (SIM) and

实验 5.5　液相色谱-质谱法测定对乙酰氨基酚的含量

一、实验目的

（1）了解液相色谱-质谱仪器的结构。

（2）掌握液相色谱-质谱法检测的基本原理和方法。

（3）了解液相色谱-质谱法在药物分析中的应用。

二、实验原理

液相色谱-质谱法（liquid chromatography-mass spectrometry，LC-MS）主要由高效液相色谱仪和质谱仪所组成，是一种结合 HPLC 的高分离特性和 MS 的高灵敏度检测特性的联用技术，其在药物分析中主要用于药物结构信息的获取、相对分子质量的确定、药物质量控制（杂质、异构体、降解物研究等）以及药物体内过程分析、药物代谢产物研究、血药浓度的检测等。

高效液相色谱仪由输液泵、进样系统、色谱柱、检测器、化学工作站等组成。化学工作站的主要功能是负责整个仪器系统的运行和数据的处理。检测器通常配备紫外二极管阵列检测器和质谱检测器。

质谱仪主要由进样系统、离子源、质量分析器、检测器和数据采集及分析五大部分组成。

样品通过进样系统进入离子源，由于结构不同而电离为各种不同质荷比（m/z）的离子碎片，而后带有样品信息的离子碎片被加速进入质量分析器，在磁场作用下，离子的运动半径与其质荷比的平方根成正比，因而使不同质荷比的离子在磁场中被分离，并按质荷比大小依次抵达检测器，经记录即得样品的质谱。

目前常用的离子化方式有电喷雾离子化（electrospray ionization，ESI）和大气压化学离子化（atmospheric pressure chemical ionization，APCI）。电喷雾离子化的原理是：待测组分（色谱流出物）通过一终端加有高电压的毛细管进入离子源，氮气雾化，产生的微小液滴，在加热和氮气流作用下去除溶剂，形成单电荷或多单电荷的气态离子（如 M^+、$[M+Na]^+$、$[M+H]^+$、$[M+K]^+$、$[M+NH_4]^+$等）。这些离子再经过逐步减压区域，从大气压状态传送到质谱仪的高真空中，由质量分析器检测，按不同的质荷比，经过数据处理，输出质谱-色谱图。

质谱中常见的扫描方式包括全扫描（full scan）、选择离子监测（SIM）和选择反应监测（SRM）。全扫描是质量分析器在给定的时间内无间断地从第一个质荷比扫描到最后一个质荷比。全扫描实验用于测定或确认未知化合物的身份，或鉴定未知混合物中的每一个组分。SIM 和 SRM 是对某一个或某一组特定离子进行检测的技术，主要被用于痕量分析以及在数量众多的样品中快速筛选目标化合物。

本实验分别对对乙酰氨基酚对照品和对乙酰氨基酚样品进行选择离子监测，通过测定对乙酰氨基酚对照品的准分子离子峰$[M+H]^+$（m/z 152）的强度，采用外标法测定对乙酰氨基酚样品的含量，其计算公式如下：

selective reaction monitor (SRM). Full scan means that the mass analyzer scans continuously from the first mass charge ratio to the last mass charge ratio in a given time. Full scan experiments are used to determine or confirm the identity of unknown compounds, or to identify each component in an unknown mixture. SIM and SRM are the technology to detect a specific ion or group of ions, and are mainly used for trace analysis as well as rapid screening of target compounds in a large number of samples.

In this experiment, selective ion monitoring was carried out for paracetamol reference substance and paracetamol sample respectively. Through the strength of quasi-molecular ion peak $[M+H]^+$ (*m/z* 152) of paracetamol reference substance, the percentage content of paracetamol sample was determined by external standard method. The calculation formula is as follows:

$$w_{\text{paracetamol}}(\%)=\frac{A_{\text{sample}}}{A_{\text{standard}}}\times\frac{m_{\text{standard}}}{m_{\text{sample}}}\times 100\%$$

Where m is the sample weight of paracetamol reference substance and sample respectively, mg; and A is the peak area of reference substance and sample corresponding to the selective ion monitoring (SIM) result of $[M+H]^+$ (*m/z* 152) in LC-MS mass spectra, respectively.

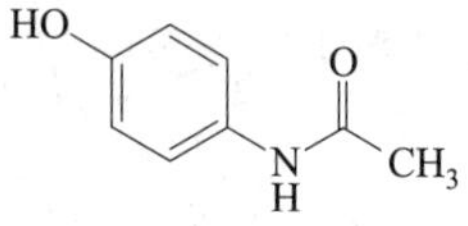

paracetamol

Instruments and Chemical Reagents

1. Instruments

Shimadzu LCMS-2020 system; ODS chromatographic column (150 mm × 2.1 mm, 5 μm); analytical balance; volumetric flask (10 mL, 50 mL, and 100 mL); pipette (1 mL, 5 mL); mortar.

2. Chemical reagents

Paracetamol reference substance; paracetamol tablets; methanol (HPLC grade); ultrapure water.

Procedure

1. Solution preparation

(1) Preparation of reference solution

Accurately weigh about 10 mg of paracetamol reference substance into a 10 mL volumetric flask, add methanol to dissolve and then dilute to volume, mix well. Transfer 0.2 mL of the above solution into a 10 mL flask, add mobile phase to dilute it to volume, mix well.

(2) Preparation of test solution

Accurately weigh about 10 mg of paracetamol sample in a 10 mL volumetric flask, add methanol to dissolve and dilute to volume, mix well. Transfer 0.2 mL of the above solution into a 10 mL flask accurately, dilute with mobile phase to volume, mix well.

$$w_{对乙酰氨基酚}(\%)=\frac{A_{样品}}{A_{对照}}\times\frac{m_{对照}}{m_{样品}}\times 100\%$$

式中，$m_{对照}$和$m_{样品}$分别为对乙酰氨基酚对照品和样品的称样量，mg；$A_{对照}$和$A_{样品}$分别为LC–MS质谱图中[M+H]$^+$（*m/z* 152）的选择离子监测（SIM）结果所对应的对照品和样品的峰面积。

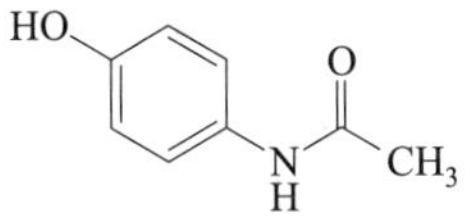

对乙酰氨基酚

三、仪器与试剂

1. 仪器

岛津LCMS–2020液质联用系统；ODS色谱柱（150 mm ×2.1 mm，5 μm）；分析天平；容量瓶（10 mL，50 mL，100 mL）；移液管（1 mL，5 mL）；研钵。

2. 试剂

对乙酰氨基酚对照品；对乙酰氨基酚片剂；甲醇（色谱纯）；超纯水。

四、实验步骤

1. 溶液的配制

（1）对照品溶液的配制　取对乙酰氨基酚对照品约10 mg，精密称定，置于10 mL容量瓶中，加甲醇溶解并稀释至刻度线，混合均匀。精密量取上述溶液0.2 mL置于10 mL容量瓶中，加流动相稀释至刻度，摇匀，即得。

（2）供试品溶液的配制　取对乙酰氨基酚样品约10 mg，精密称定，置于10 mL容量瓶中，加甲醇溶解并稀释至刻度线，混合均匀。精密量取上述滤液0.2 mL置于10 mL容量瓶中，加流动相稀释至刻度，摇匀，即得。

2. 色谱条件和质谱条件

（1）色谱条件　色谱柱：ODS柱（150 mm×2.1 mm，5 μm）；流动相：甲醇–水（25∶75，体积比）；流速：0.3 mL·min^{-1}；进样量：5 μL；检测波长：244 nm。

（2）质谱条件　电喷雾离子源（ESI）；扫描模式：正、负离子模式；扫描范围：50~400 amu；脱溶剂温度：250 ℃；雾化气流速：1.5 L·min^{-1}；干燥气流速：5.0 L·min^{-1}；干燥气温度：250 ℃；离子喷射电压：1 100 V。

3. 实验结果

对乙酰氨基酚对照品紫外吸收光谱图，HPLC–UV色谱图，正、负离子总离子流图，正、负离子质谱图分别见图5–5~图5–9。

2. Chromatographic and mass spectrometric conditions

(1) Chromatographic conditions

Chromatographic column: ODS (150 mm × 2.1 mm, 5 μm); mobile phase: methanol-water (25:75, *V/V*); flow rate: 0.3 mL·min^{-1}; injection volume: 5 μL; detection wavelength: 244 nm.

(2) Mass spectrometry conditions

Electrospray ion source (ESI); scanning mode: positive and negative ion mode; scanning range: 50~400 amu; desolvent temperature: 250 ℃; atomization gas flow rate: 1.5 L·min^{-1}; drying gas flow rate: 5.0 L·min^{-1}; drying gas temperature: 250 ℃; ion jet voltage: 1 100 V.

(3) Results

UV absorption spectrum, HPLC-UV chromatogram, total ion chromatogram, and positive and negative ion mass spectra of paracetamol reference substance are shown in Figure 5–5 to Figure 5–9, respectively.

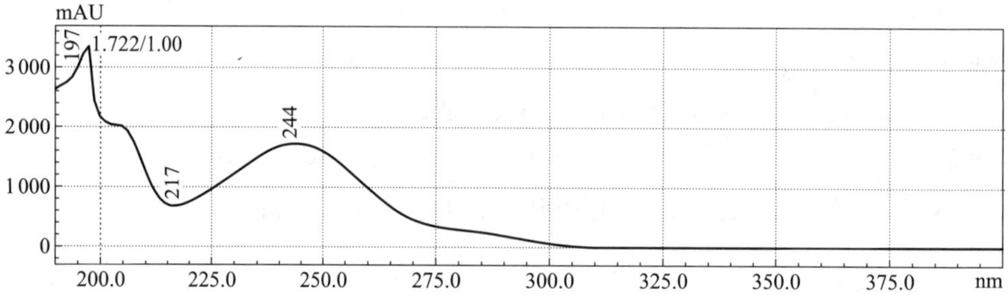

Figure 5–5 UV absorption spectrum of paracetamol reference substance

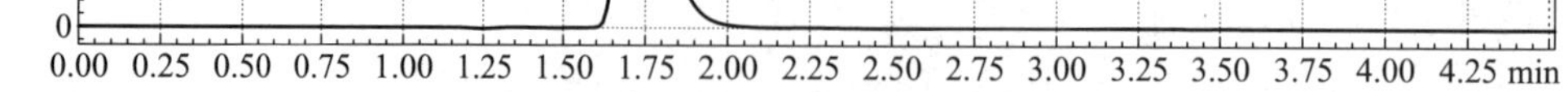

Figure 5–6 HPLC-UV chromatogram of paracetamol reference substance

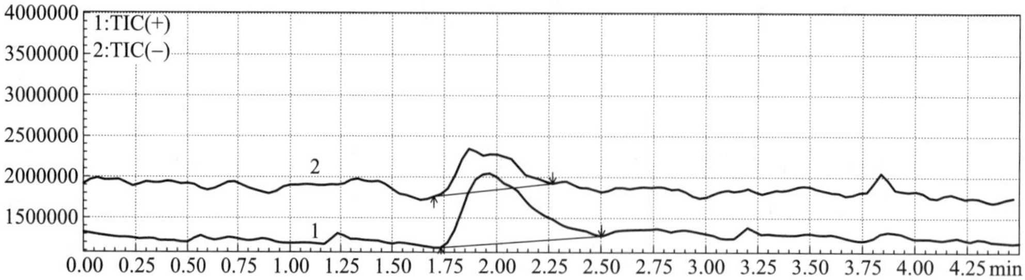

Figure 5–7 Total ion chromatogram (TIC) of paracetamol

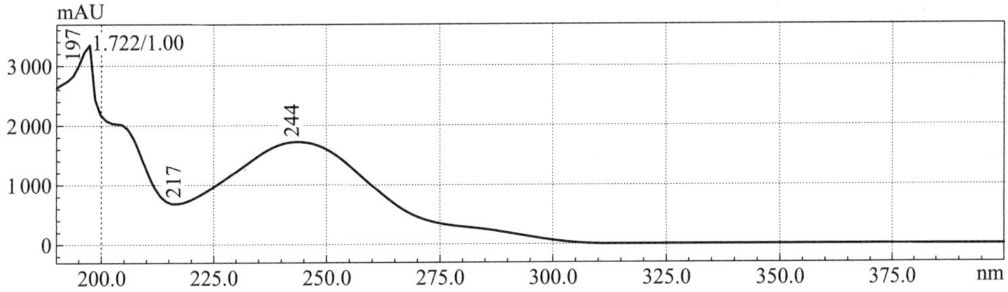

图 5–5　对乙酰氨基酚对照品紫外吸收光谱图

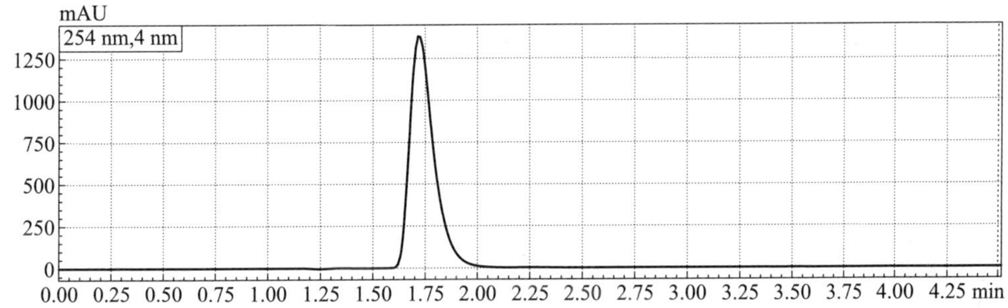

图 5–6　对乙酰氨基酚对照品 HPLC–UV 色谱图

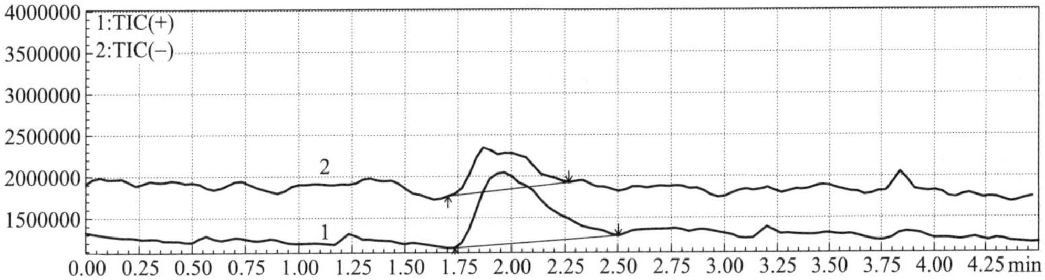

图 5–7　对乙酰氨基酚正、负离子总离子流图

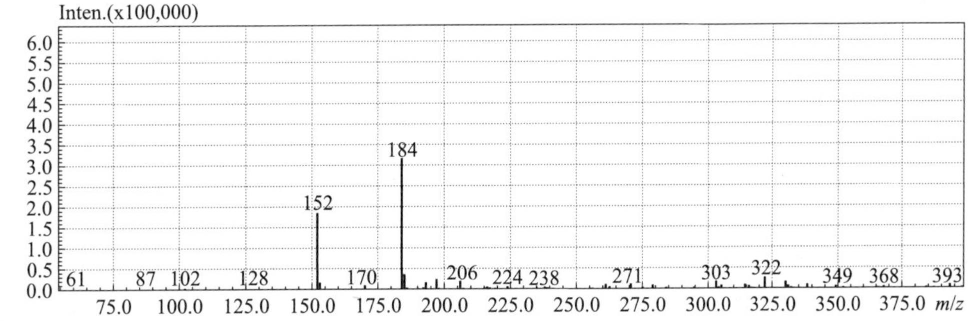

图 5–8　对乙酰氨基酚正离子质谱图

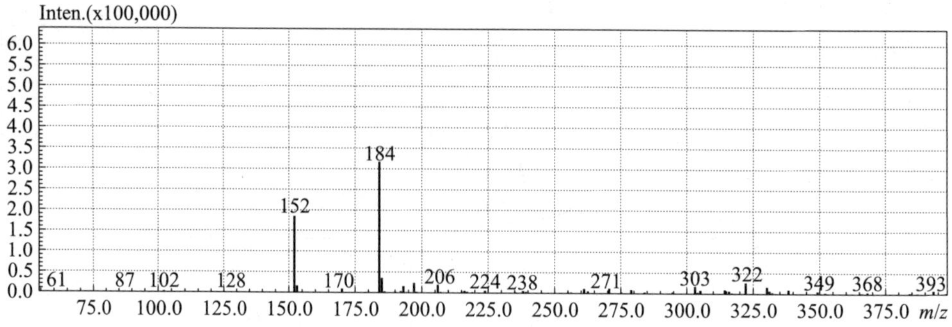

Figure 5–8 Positive ion mass spectrum of paracetamol

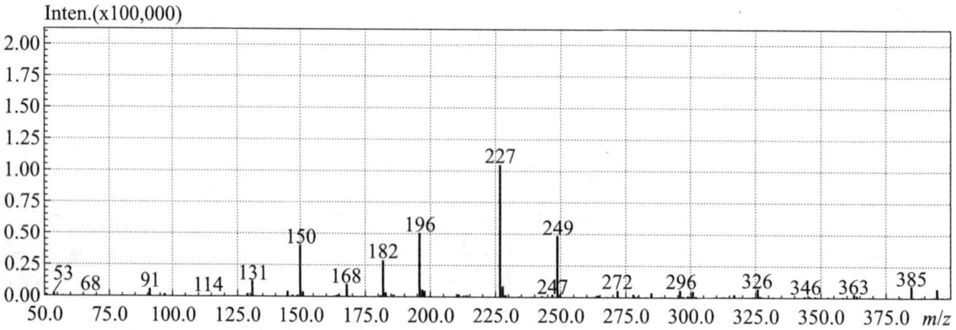

Figure 5–9 Negative ion mass spectrum of paracetamol

Data analysis

The percentage content of paracetamol sample is determined by external standard method.

Experiment Guidance

1. Preview instruction

(1) Understand the structure of LC-MS instrument.

(2) Understand the basic principle and method of LC-MS quantitative determination in drug analysis.

2. Notes

(1) The mobile phase solvent must use high-purity reagents, and the mobile phase must not contain nonvolatile substances.

(2) The sample solution must be purified.

3. Discussion

(1) MS is used to detect the charged ions. How to improve the sensitivity and selectivity of the determination?

(2) The suitable flow rate of LC-MS is 0.3 $mL \cdot min^{-1}$, and that of conventional analytical column is 1.0 $mL \cdot min^{-1}$. Can the later be used for LC-MS analysis, and what method can be adopted to achieve it?

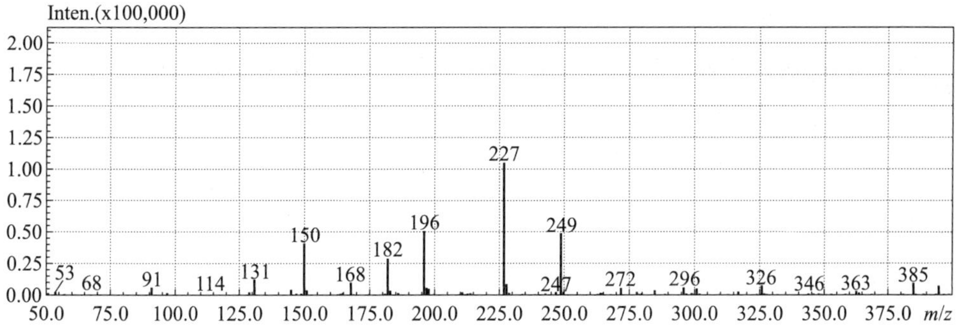

图 5-9 对乙酰氨基酚负离子质谱

五、数据处理

采用外标法测定对乙酰氨基酚样品的含量。

六、实验指导

1. 预习要求

（1）了解 LC-MS 仪器的结构。

（2）了解 LC-MS 在药物分析中定量测定的基本原理和方法。

2. 注意事项

（1）流动相溶剂必须采用高纯试剂，流动相中不得含有不挥发的物质。

（2）样品溶液必须经过纯化处理。

3. 讨论

（1）MS 检测的是带电离子，怎样提高测定的灵敏度和选择性？

（2）LC-MS 适宜的流速为 0.3 $mL \cdot min^{-1}$，常规分析柱通常的流速为 1 $mL \cdot min^{-1}$，后者能否用于 LC-MS 分析？可采取什么方法得到实现？

Experiment 5.6 Determination of Sulfonamides by Liquid Chromatography-Mass Spectrometry

Purpose

(1) To grasp the principle and application of liquid chromatography-mass spectrometry.

(2) To be familiar with basic operation of qualitative and quantitative analysis using liquid chromatography-mass spectrometry.

Principle

Mass spectrometry (MS) is an analytical method to determine the mass to charge ratio (*m/z*) of the sample ions. Samples are firstly ionized by an ion source. Because of the different moving behaviors of different ions in the electric field or magnetic field, the sample ions can be separated according to the *m/z*. The qualitative and quantitative results can be obtained by analyzing the mass spectrum.

The mass spectrometer consists of ion source, mass analyzer, detector, and vacuum system. Ion source is used to ionize the sample, and then the sample ions can be separated in the mass analyzer according to different *m/z*. The detector can obtain the signal and then the spectrum can be obtained. As organic, inorganic, and isotopic samples have different forms and properties, the ion source, mass analyzer and detector are different.

Mass spectrometer is a good qualitative analysis instrument, but it can't help to separate the mixture. The hyphenation of chromatography and mass spectrometry provide a good approach to separate and identify target analyte at the same time. As early as the 1960s, the research of gas chromatography-mass spectrometry (GC-MS) technology was started. At the end of 1970s, the development of GC-MS has reached a very high level, and liquid chromatography-mass spectrometry (LC-MS) has been studied. In the late 1980s, with the emergence of atmospheric pressure ionization technology, the development of liquid chromatography-mass spectrometry (LC-MS) reached a new stage.

In this experiment, three sulfonamides were identified and determined by LC-MS.

Instruments and Chemical Reagents

1. Instruments

Shimadzu LCMS-2020 system; ODS chromatographic column (150 mm × 2.1 mm, 5 μm); sonicator; analytical balance; microsyringe (10 μL); volumetric flask (10 mL, 25 mL, and 100 mL); 0.45 μm micropore membrane.

2. Chemical reagents

Methanol (HPLC grade); ammonium acetate (HPLC grade); sulfadiazine (A. R.); sulfamethazine (A. R.); sulfamethoxazole (A. R.); double-distilled water.

实验 5.6 液相色谱–质谱联用法测定磺胺类抗生素

一、实验目的

（1）掌握液相色谱–质谱联用法的基本工作原理和应用。

（2）熟悉利用液相色谱–质谱联用法进行定性、定量分析的基本操作。

二、实验原理

质谱分析法（mass spectrometry，MS）是通过对被测样品离子的质荷比的测定来进行分析的一种方法。被分析的样品首先通过离子源进行离子化，由于不同离子在电场或磁场的运动行为不同，可将离子按质荷比（*m/z*）分开而得到质谱。通过样品的质谱和相关信息，可以得到样品的定性定量结果。

质谱仪的基本组成包括离子源、质量分析器、检测器和真空系统。质谱仪首先必须有电离装置把样品电离为离子，再通过质量分析器把不同质荷比的离子分开，经检测器检测之后可以得到样品的质谱图。由于有机样品、无机样品和同位素样品等具有不同形态、性质和不同的分析要求，所用的电离装置、质量分析装置和检测装置有所不同。

质谱仪是一种很好的定性分析仪器，但其对混合物的分离无能为力。色谱–质谱联用法则能发挥各自专长，使分离和鉴定同时进行。早在 20 世纪 60 年代就开始了 GC–MS（gas chromatography-mass spectrometry）的研究，并出现了早期的气相色谱–质谱联用仪。20 世纪 70 年代末，这种联用仪器已经达到很高的水平，同时开始研究液相色谱–质谱联用法（liquid chromatography-mass spectrometry，LC–MS）。到了 20 世纪 80 年代后期，随着大气压电离技术的出现，液相色谱–质谱联用仪的发展到达新的阶段。

本实验利用 LC–MS 鉴别和测定 3 种磺胺类抗生素。

三、仪器和试剂

1. 仪器

岛津 LCMS–2020 液相色谱–质谱联用仪；ODS 色谱柱（150 mm × 2.1 mm，5 μm）；超声波清洗器；分析天平；微量注射器（10 μL）；容量瓶（10 mL，25 mL，100 mL）；0.45 μm 微孔滤膜。

2. 试剂

甲醇（色谱纯）；乙酸铵（色谱纯）；磺胺嘧啶（分析纯）；磺胺二甲嘧啶（分析纯）；磺胺甲噁唑（分析纯）；二次蒸馏水。

四、实验步骤

1. 溶液的配制

（1）新鲜配制 0.01 $mol \cdot L^{-1}$ 乙酸铵（含 0.1% 甲酸）溶液。

（2）按甲醇∶0.01 $mol \cdot L^{-1}$ 乙酸铵=20∶80（体积比）配制流动相，超声脱气 10 min。经 0.45 μm 微孔滤膜过滤后使用。

Procedure

1. Preparation of solutions

(1) Prepare 0.01 mol·L^{-1} ammonium acetate solution containing 0.1% formic acid.

(2) Prepare mobile phase with methanol: 10 mM ammonium acetate = 20:80 (*V/V*). The mobile phase was degassed by ultrasonic for 10 min and filtered by 0.45 μm micropore membrane.

(3) Prepare the reference solution of sulfadiazine, sulfamethazine, and sulfamethoxazole mixture with mobile phase as solvent. The concentration of each component was 200 ng·mL^{-1}. Solution was filtered by 0.45 μm micropore membrane.

2. Instrument setups

Turn on the liquid chromatography, install the chromatographic column, set the flow rate at 0.5 mL·min^{-1}, set the ion source parameters and ion pair 250.9/155.9, 254.0/92.1, 279.0/155.9, and observe whether the column pressure is normal.

3. Injection

After the baseline is stable, inject 5 μL of reference solution and sample solution, respectively, and record the chromatogram.

Data Analysis

(1) According to the retention time and the characteristic parent ion/daughter ion, identify the chromatographic peaks.

(2) Calculate the content of the three sulfonamides by using external standard method, according to peak area and the known concentration of the reference solution.

Experiment Guidance

1. Preview instruction

(1) Review the principle and instrument structure of liquid chromatography-mass spectrometry.

(2) Understand the methods of qualitative and quantitative analysis by liquid chromatography-mass spectrometry.

(3) Understand the basic operation and experimental precautions of liquid chromatography-mass spectrometry system.

2. Notes

(1) The sample and solvent should be filtered by 0.45 μm micropore membrane before use.

(2) The vacuum level of mass spectrometer should be more than 10^{-6} psi.①

3. Discussion

(1) What are the characteristics of HPLC-MS compared with HPLC-UV?

(2) Discuss on the research progress and application of HPLC-MS.

---

① 1 psi=6.895 kPa。

（3）以流动相为溶剂，配制磺胺嘧啶、磺胺二甲嘧啶和磺胺甲噁唑的对照品混合溶液，每种组分的浓度均为 200 ng·mL^{-1}。经 0.45 μm 微孔滤膜过滤后待用。

2. 仪器参数的设定

开启液相色谱仪，安装色谱柱，设置流速为 0.5 mL·min^{-1}，离子源参数、离子对 250.9/155.9；254.0/92.1；279.0/155.9 等参数，观察柱压是否正常。

3. 样品的测定

待基线稳定后，分别将 5 μL 对照品溶液和供试品溶液进样，记录色谱图。

五、数据处理

（1）根据保留时间及各待测物的特征母离子/子离子对色谱峰，定性分析色谱图中的色谱峰。

（2）采用外标一点法根据已知浓度的对照品溶液各待测物的峰面积，计算样品溶液中相应组分的含量。

六、实验指导

1. 预习要求

（1）复习液相色谱–质谱联用法工作原理及仪器构造。

（2）了解液相色谱–质谱联用法进行定性定量分析方法。

（3）了解液相色谱–质谱联用系统的基本操作及实验注意事项。

2. 注意事项

（1）样品和溶剂须经 0.45 μm 的微孔滤膜过滤后方可使用。

（2）质谱的真空度一般要大于 10^{-6} psi① 方可正常工作。

3. 思考题

（1）HPLC–MS 与 HPLC–UV 相比有何特点？

（2）结合自己的兴趣，谈谈 HPLC–MS 的研究进展及应用。

① 1 psi=6.895 kPa。

Experiment 5.7 Determination of Isosorbide-5-Mononitrate in Human Plasma by Ultra-high Performance Liquid Chromatography-Mass Spectrometry

Purpose

(1) To be familiar with the principle of ultra-performance liquid chromatography-mass spectrometry.

(2) To understand the method and procedure for the determination of isosorbide-5-mononitrate in human plasma by ultra-performance liquid chromatography-mass spectrometry.

Principle

High performance liquid chromatography-mass spectrometry (HPLC-MS) takes full advantage of the separation capacity of HPLC and the high sensitivity and specificity of MS, and establishes a powerful means of substance identification and determination through appropriate interface connection. At present, HPLC-MS has become one of the most important instrumental analytical methods in modern pharmaceutical research fields, including pharmacokinetics, identification of drug trace impurities, analysis of drug degradation products, and screening of natural products. Ultra-high performance liquid chromatography (UPLC) is based on the theory and principle of HPLC. Using small stationary phase (particle size less than 2 μm) and very low system volume, it improves the resolution, analysis speed, sensitivity and peak capacity of liquid chromatography. Ultra-performance liquid chromatography-mass spectrometry (UPLC-MS) further combines the high efficiency of LC with the high sensitivity of MS to improve the separation efficiency and shorten the analysis time, which is a development and progress of HPLC-MS technology.

Isosorbide 5-mononitrate (5-ISMN) is the main active metabolite of isosorbide dinitrate (ISDN) in vivo, and its main pharmacological activity is to relax smooth muscle. Compared with ISDN, 5-ISMN has the characteristics of rapid absorption, no first pass effect and high bioavailability, which has become a new generation of nitrate drugs.

The content of 5-ISMN in human plasma was determined by UPLC-MS with acetaminophen as internal standard. The structural of 5-ISMN is as follows:

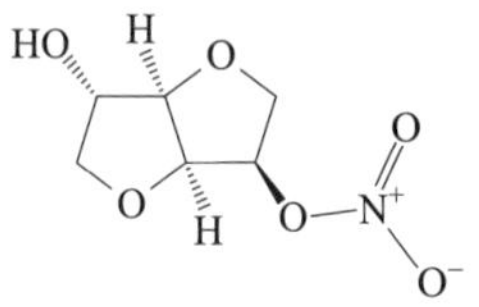

5-ISMN

Instruments and Chemical Reagents

1. Instruments

WATERS UPLC-TOF-MS system, equipped with automatic sampler, column temperature box, four-element solvent pump, ESI ion source and WATERS QUANLYNX data processing system; ACQUITY UPLC Hss T3 Column (50 mm × 2. 1 mm, 1.8 μm); MILLI-Q-Reference pure water

实验 5.7　超高效液相色谱–质谱联用法测定人血浆中单硝酸异山梨酯

一、实验目的

（1）熟悉超高效液相色谱–质谱仪的基本原理。

（2）了解超高效液相色谱–质谱联用法测定人血浆中单硝酸异山梨酯的方法和步骤。

二、实验原理

高效液相色谱–质谱联用法（high performance liquid chromatography-mass spectrometry，HPLC–MS）是充分利用高效液相色谱的分离能力与质谱的高灵敏度和专属性，通过适当的接口连接，构建的一种强大的物质鉴定和测定的手段。目前，HPLC–MS 已成为包括药物代谢动力学研究、药物微量杂质鉴定和药物降解产物的分析、天然产物筛选等在内的现代药学研究领域中十分重要的仪器分析方法之一。超高效液相色谱法（ultra-high performance liquid chromatography，UPLC）借助于 HPLC 的理论和原理，利用小颗粒固定相(粒径小于 2 μm)、非常低的系统体积、快速检测手段等技术，使分离度、分析速度、检测灵敏度、色谱峰容量大大提高，从而全面提升了液相色谱的分离分析效能。超高效液相色谱–质谱联用法（ultra-high performance liquid chromatography-mass spectrometry，UPLC–MS）进一步将液相色谱的高效分离能力与质谱的高灵敏度结合，提高了分离效率，缩短了分析时间，是 HPLC–MS 技术的发展和进步。

5–单硝酸异山梨酯（isosorbide 5–mononitrate，5–ISMN）是抗心肌缺血药硝酸异山梨酯（isosorbide dinitrate，ISDN）的体内主要活性代谢产物，其主要药理活性是松弛平滑肌。与 ISDN 相比，5–ISMN 具有吸收迅速、无首过效应、生物利用度高等特点，已成为新一代硝酸酯类药。

本实验利用 UPLC–MS 联用仪，以对乙酰氨基酚为内标物，测定人血浆中 5–ISMN 的含量。5–ISMN 的结构式如下：

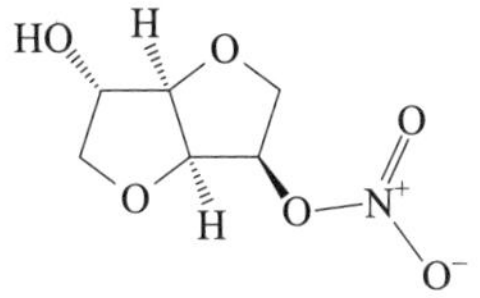

5–ISMN

三、仪器和试剂

1. 仪器

WATERS 超高效液相色谱–飞行时间质谱联用系统，配有自动进样器、柱温箱、四元溶剂泵、ESI 离子源及 WATERS QUANLYNX 数据处理系统；ACQUITYUPLC Hss T3 色谱柱（50 mm × 2.1 mm，1.8 μm）；MILLI–Q–Reference 纯水机；ASONE TM–2F 微型旋涡混合仪。

machine; ASONE TM-2F micro vortex mixer.

2. Chemical reagents

Isosorbide 5-mononitrate (reference substance); acetaminophen (reference substance); acetonitrile, formic acid (HPLC grade); ethyl acetate (A.R.); dichloromethane(A.R.); blank human plasma; ultrapure water.

Procedure

1. Preparation of solutions

(1) 5-ISMN reference solution: 10 mg of 5-ISMN, dried to constant weight, was weighed and placed in a 50 mL flask, dissolved and diluted with acetonitrile to prepare 200 $\mu g \cdot mL^{-1}$ stock solution, then diluted with acetonitrile to obtain 0.20 $\mu g \cdot mL^{-1}$, 0.25 $\mu g \cdot mL^{-1}$, 0.50 $\mu g \cdot mL^{-1}$, 1.00 $\mu g \cdot mL^{-1}$, 1.25 $\mu g \cdot mL^{-1}$, 2.50 $\mu g \cdot mL^{-1}$, 5.00 $\mu g \cdot mL^{-1}$, 8.00 $\mu g \cdot mL^{-1}$, 10.00 $\mu g \cdot mL^{-1}$ standard solutions. Use the solutions as soon as possible after preparation.

(2) Internal standard solution: 10 mg of paracetamol reference was weighed and placed in a 50 mL measuring bottle, dissolved and diluted with acetonitrile-water (20 : 80, *V/V*) to obtain a stock solution with a concentration of 200 $\mu g \cdot mL^{-1}$, and then diluted to a concentration of 1 $\mu g \cdot mL^{-1}$ as the internal standard solution.

(3) Plasma sample treatment: 200 μL blank human plasma was pipetted, 20 μL internal standard solution (1 $\mu g \cdot mL^{-1}$) was added, and the solution was vortexed for 1 min. Add ethyl acetate and dichloromethane (80 : 20, *V/V*) 3 000 μL, vortex for 1 min, centrifuge for 5 min at 4 000 $r \cdot min^{-1}$, extract the upper organic phase at 2 550 μL, dry with N_2 at 40 ℃, and remix with 200 μL mobile phase. Centrifugation at 12 000 $r \cdot min^{-1}$ for 5 min, supernatant was taken and injected for analysis.

(4) Standard curve solution: 20 μL of 5-ISMN reference solution with different concentrations were taken and placed in 10 mL centrifuge tubes. After drying with N_2, 200 μL of blank plasma was added to prepare the corresponding 5-ISMN plasma concentrations of 0.02 $\mu g \cdot mL^{-1}$, 0.05 $\mu g \cdot mL^{-1}$, 0.10 $\mu g \cdot mL^{-1}$, 0.25 $\mu g \cdot mL^{-1}$, 0.50 $\mu g \cdot mL^{-1}$, 1.00 $\mu g \cdot mL^{-1}$samples according to the plasma sample treatment procure.

2. Instrument operating conditions

(1) The chromatographic conditions:

Column: ACQUITY UPLC Hss T3 (50 mm × 2. 1 mm, 1.8 μm); mobile phase: 0. 1 % aqueous formic acid (A)-acetonitrile(B) with gradient elution (Table 5–1); flow rate: 0.5 $mL \cdot min^{-1}$; column temperature: 30 ℃; injection volume: 10 μL; analysis time: 3.0 min.

Table 5–1 Gradient elution procure

Time	Mobile phase composition	
	A	B
0.0 min	90%	10%
2.0 min	10%	90%
2.5 min	10%	90%
3.0 min	90%	10%

(2) MS conditions:

Ion source: ESI source; Capillary voltage: 500 V; Capillary temperature; 350 ℃; Dry gas flow

2. 试剂

单硝酸异山梨酯（对照品）；对乙酰氨基酚（对照品）；乙腈、甲酸（色谱纯）；乙酸乙酯（分析纯）；二氯甲烷（分析纯）；空白人血浆；超纯水。

四、实验步骤

1. 溶液的配制

（1）5–ISMN 对照品溶液：称取干燥至恒重的 5–ISMN 对照品 10 mg，置于 50 mL 容量瓶中，用乙腈溶解并稀释，配制成 200 μg·mL^{-1} 的储备液，再用乙腈稀释成 0.20 μg·mL^{-1}，0.25 μg·mL^{-1}，0.50 μg·mL^{-1}，1.00 μg·mL^{-1}，1.25 μg·mL^{-1}，2.50 μg·mL^{-1}，5.00 μg·mL^{-1}，8.00 μg·mL^{-1}，10.00 μg·mL^{-1} 的系列对照品溶液。现用现配。

（2）内标溶液：称取对乙酰氨基酚对照品 10 mg，置于 50 mL 容量瓶中，用乙腈–水（20∶80，体积比）溶解并稀释，得到浓度为 200 μg·mL^{-1} 的对乙酰氨基酚储备液，并稀释成浓度为 1 μg·mL^{-1} 溶液作为内标溶液。

（3）血浆样品处理：移取空白人血浆 200 μL，加入内标溶液（1 μg·mL^{-1}）20 μL，涡旋 1 min。加入乙酸乙酯–二氯甲烷（80∶20，体积比）3 000 μL，涡旋 1 min，4 000 r·min^{-1} 离心 5 min，提取上层有机相 2 550 μL，40 ℃下 N_2 吹干，用流动相 200 μL 复溶，12 000 r·min^{-1} 离心 5 min，取上清液进样分析。

（4）标准曲线溶液：分别取不同浓度的 5–ISMN 对照品溶液各 20 μL，置于 10 mL 离心管中，氮气吹干后加入空白血浆 200 μL，配制成相当于 5–ISMN 血浆浓度为 0.02 μg·mL^{-1}，0.05 μg·mL^{-1}，0.10 μg·mL^{-1}，0.25 μg·mL^{-1}，0.50 μg·mL^{-1}，1.00 μg·mL^{-1} 的样品，按血浆样品处理方法处理。

2. 仪器操作条件

（1）色谱条件：色谱柱：ACQUITY UPLC Hss T3（50 mm × 2.1 mm，1.8 μm）；流动相：0.1% 甲酸水溶液（A）—乙腈（B），梯度洗脱，洗脱程序见表 5–1；流速：0.5 mL·min^{-1}；柱温：30 ℃：进样量：10 μL；分析时间：3.0 min。

表 5–1　色谱洗脱条件

时间	流动相比例	
	A	B
0.0 min	90%	10%
2.0 min	10%	90%
2.5 min	10%	90%
3.0 min	90%	10%

（2）质谱条件：离子源：ESI 源；毛细管电压：500 V；毛细管温度；350 ℃；干燥气流速：600 mL·h^{-1}；辅助气流速：10 mL·h^{-1}；负离子 V 模式检测；扫描范围：*m/z* 100~1 000。5–ISMN 与对乙酰氨基酚在 ESI 离子化方式下，主要生成［M+HCOO］$^{-}$和［M+H］$^{-}$分子离子峰，分别为 *m/z* 236.04

rate: 600 mL·h^{-1}; Auxiliary gas flow rate: 10 mL·h^{-1}; Negative ion V mode detection: scanning range: *m/z* 100~1 000. The molecular ion peaks of $[M+ HCOO]^-$ and $[M+H]^-$, *m/z* 236.04 and *m/z* 150.05, were generated by the ESI ionization of 5-ISMN and acetaminophen.

3. Sample analysis

Standard solutions are injected to obtain the standard curve. The plasma sample is reinjected (treated as plasma sample procure) and the chromatogram is recorded. The t_R of 5-ISMN and acetaminophen are 0.85 min and 0.66 min, respectively.

Data Analysis

The 5-ISMN concentration is the abscissa, and the ratio of the 5-ISMN peak area to the internal standard peak area is the ordinate. The weighted least square method is used to perform linear regression operation, and the linear equation and quantification are obtained.

Experiment Guidance

1. Preview instruction

(1) Understand the chemical properties of 5-ISMN and the basic principles of qualitative and quantitative LC-MS.

(2) Understand the similarities and differences between UPLC-MS and HPLC-MS and their operation methods.

(3) Understand the treatment methods and precautions of 5-ISMN plasma samples.

(4) Understand the method validation of component measurement in plasma samples.

2. Notes

(1) 5-ISMN is a small molecular compound of adipose group with double ring, which has a rigid molecular structure, and is unstable both in light and heat. It is easy to fragment in the process of ionization and dehydrogenation to form negative ions. In this experiment, 5-ISMN is mainly combined with formic acid molecules in mobile phase to form $[M + HCOO]^-$ after fragmentation in the ion source, which has a stable signal. It has good retention and peak shape.

(2) Due to the large number of components in the biological sample, the concentration of the substances to be measured is relatively low and the fluctuation range is large, so the biological sample must be properly pretreated, otherwise other components in the sample may cause interference, and will cause great pollution to the chromatographic column and instrument.

(3) Matrix effect (ME) caused by the sample matrix and interferences from metabolites have direct or indirect impact on responses. The endogenous substance in biological fluid interferes with the determination of the sample for ion suppression or enhancement of compounds analyzed by LC-MS. This effect may reduce or increase the intensity of amalyte ions and affect the accuracy of the assay. There are two methods for quantitative assessment of the ME, absolute versus relative ME.

3. Discussion

(1) Compare the similarities and differences between electrospray ionization and atmospheric pressure chemical ionization.

(2) What are the commonly used biological sample pretreatment methods?

和 m/z 150.05。

3. 进样分析

先进标准溶液，得标准曲线；再进样待测血浆样品(按血浆样品处理方法处理)，记录色谱图。5-ISMN 和内标对乙酰氨基酚的保留时间分别为 0.85 min 和 0.66 min。

五、数据处理

以待测物 5-ISMN 浓度为横坐标，5-ISMN 色谱峰面积与内标色谱峰面积的比值为纵坐标，用加权最小二乘法进行线性回归运算，求得线性方程和定量。

六、实验指导

1. 预习要求

(1) 了解 5-ISMN 的化学性质和 LC-MS 的定性、定量的基本原理。

(2) 了解 UPLC-MS 与 HPLC-MS 的异同点及其操作方法。

(3) 了解 5-ISMN 血浆样品的处理方法和注意事项。

(4) 了解血浆样品中组分含量测量的方法学研究内容。

2. 注意事项

(1) 5-ISMN 是带有双环的脂肪族小分子化合物，具有刚性分子结构，且光、热均不稳定，离子化过程中容易碎裂，并脱氢形成负离子。本实验中 5-ISMN 在离子源中碎裂后主要与流动相中甲酸分子结合形成 $[M+HCOO]^-$ 分子离子峰，该峰信号稳定，有较好的保留和峰形。

(2) 由于生物样品中的成分较多，待测物浓度相对较低且波动范围较大，因此必须对生物样品进行适当的预处理，否则样品中的其他成分可能产生干扰，且会对色谱柱和仪器产生较大的污染。

(3) 基质效应(matrix effect, ME)是由于样品中存在干扰物质，对响应造成直接或间接的影响。LC-MS 分析时，内源性物质使待测物的离子化效率降低或增强，影响定量分析结果准确率。ME 的评价方法分为绝对 ME 评价和相对 ME 评价。

3. 讨论

(1) 试比较电喷雾离子化和大气压化学离子化两种离子化方式的异同点。

(2) 常用的生物样品预处理方法有哪些？

Chapter 6 Designing Experiment

6.1 Overview

The selection of qualitative and quantitative analysis methods is a very important part of instrumental analysis experiment. In the actual production practice and scientific research work, the exclusive, sensitive and reproducible analysis methods shall be selected according to the analysis object (inorganic and organic), the content of the analyte (major, micro or trace components), as well as the matrix contained in the analyte (blood, tissue, soil, water, Chinese herbal medicine extract, and pharmaceutical excipients), etc.

When we need to conduct qualitative and quantitative analysis on a sample, sometimes we can find the mature analysis methods directly from relevant references or standards and regulations at all levels. However, some analytical tasks are difficult to find a completely matched analytical method for reference, which requires the analyst to modify or optimize the reference method appropriately according to the specific conditions of the sample to be analyzed (such as compound properties, content, and matrix that may interfere with the determination, etc.) and establish a new and applicable analytical method. If the composition of the analyte to be analyzed is very complex (such as Chinese herbal medicine, compound preparation, and multiple drug residues, etc.), it is also necessary to complete the verification of extraction and content determination methodology before formulating the corresponding analysis method or determination standard.

In addition, it is worth mentioning that instrumental analysis is a subject of multi-disciplinary technology integration and keeping pace with the times. The analysis method of samples is not unique and invariable. When designing and selecting the analytical methods for a certain type of sample, we should discuss and compare the characteristics of different methods from as many angles as possible, as well as select the most appropriate method for methodological research and practice according to the conditions of our own laboratory.

第六章　设计类实验

6.1　概述

定性、定量分析方法的选择是仪器分析实验中非常重要的组成部分。在实际生产实践和科学研究工作中，要根据分析对象(无机物、有机物)、待分析物的含量(常量、微量或者痕量组分)、待分析物所包含的基质(血液、组织、土壤、水分、中药材提取物、药品辅料)等，综合考虑，选择专属、灵敏、重现性好的分析方法。

当需要对某个样品进行定性、定量分析时，有时可以直接从有关的参考资料或者各级标准、法规中查到成熟的分析方法。但是有些分析任务难以找到完全匹配的分析方法来参考，这就要求分析工者能够根据待分析样品的具体情况(如化合物性质、含量、可能干扰测定的基质等)，对参考方法进行适当的修改或者优化，建立新的适用的分析方法。如果待分析物的组成非常复杂(如中草药、复方制剂、药物多残留等)，还需要经过完备的提取和含量测定方法学验证，才能制定出相应的分析方法或者测定标准。

另外，仪器分析是一个多学科技术融合、与时俱进的学科，样品的分析方法并不是唯一的、一成不变的。在设计、选取某类样品的分析方法时，应尽可能多角度地讨论、比较不同方法的特点，并根据自己实验室的条件，选择最合适的方法进行方法学研究和实践。

6.2 General Steps of Designing for the Analysis Scheme

When formulating the experimental scheme and process, the following aspects can be comprehensively considered:

(1) Select the appropriate analysis method according to the properties and content of the analyte and its matrix.

If the purity and content of the substance to be measured are relatively high, the content determination methods of titration analysis and chromatographic analysis are preferred. For the content determination of some items, there are also relevant methods and instruments that can be selected directly. For example, the Karl Fischer moisture meter can be used for the determination of moisture in active pharmaceutical ingredients (API).

If the content of the substance to be measured is less than 1%, the instrument analysis method with high sensitivity is generally selected, such as spectrophotometry, electrochemistry or chromatography.

If the substance to be tested is a mixture, it shall be separated first and then analyzed as well as determined separately. At this time, the analysis method of chromatography-spectrum or chromatography-mass spectrometry is preferred.

If the matrix of the sample is complex and will interfere with the determination of the components to be tested, it shall be extracted first, and the extraction effect shall be investigated methodologically, and then the analysis and determination shall be considered.

(2) Pre-test shall be carried out, and the accuracy and reliability of the method shall be ensured through standard addition, recovery, reproducibility, durability and other experiments.

(3) The existing experimental conditions of the laboratory, such as instruments, equipment, samples and reagents, shall be used as much as possible, and the consumption of samples and reagents shall be estimated according to the experimental purpose and scheme, so as to save reagents and samples as much as possible. Evaluate the safety of the selected reagent, list the experimental precautions, and clarify the treatment methods of reagent and experimental waste.

(4) Design the experimental scheme and list the detailed experimental steps, mainly including:

① Experimental purpose;

② The nature of the analyte to be analyzed;

③ Experimental principle and calculation formula of experimental results;

④ Required instruments and reagents;

⑤ Experimental steps;

⑥ Original data record form;

⑦ Experimental precautions;

⑧ References.

(5) After the experiment, a complete experimental report shall be written. In addition to the contents of the above experimental design scheme, it shall also state:

① Experimental data analysis and results;

② The evaluation and discussion of the experimental scheme designed by ourselves. If there is any modification or revision, it shall be indicated in the discussion, or the experimental scheme shall be redesigned.

6.2　分析方案设计的一般步骤

拟定实验方案和过程时，可以从以下几方面综合考虑：

（1）根据待分析物及其基质的性质和含量，选择合适的分析方法。

如果待测物纯度和含量都比较高，优选滴定分析和色谱分析的含量测定方法。有些项目的含量测定，也有相关方法和仪器可以直接参考选用，比如原料药中水分的测定，就可以利用卡尔·费歇尔水分测定仪进行测定。

如果待测物含量在 1% 以下，一般选择灵敏度较高的仪器分析方法，如分光光度法、电化学法或者色谱分析法。

如果待测物是混合物，应先分离，再分别分析测定，此时优先选用色谱-光谱或者色谱-质谱联用的分析方法。

如果样品所处的基质比较复杂，会干扰待测组分的测定，应先进行提取，并对提取效果进行方法学考察，再考虑分析测定。

（2）应进行预实验，并且通过标准添加、回收率、重现性、耐用性等实验，来确保方法的准确性和可靠性。

（3）应尽可能利用实验室现有的实验条件，如仪器、设备、样品、试剂，并按照实验目的和方案，预估试样和试剂的使用量，尽可能节约试剂和样品。对所选用试剂的安全性进行评估，列出实验注意事项，并阐明试剂、实验废弃物处理方法。

（4）应撰写设计实验方案，列出详细的实验步骤，主要包含：

① 实验目的；

② 待分析物的性质；

③ 实验原理及实验结果的计算公式；

④ 所需仪器和试剂；

⑤ 实验步骤；

⑥ 原始数据记录表格；

⑦ 实验注意事项；

⑧ 参考资料。

（5）实验结束后，应撰写完整的实验报告，除上述实验设计方案的内容外，还应写明：

① 实验数据分析与结果；

② 对自己设计的实验方案的评价和讨论。如有修改或者订正，应在讨论中注明，或者重新拟定设计实验方案。

6.3 Analysis of Scheme Design Cases

In order to consolidate students' basic knowledge and operation skills of instrumental analysis, improve students' ability to analyze and solve problems in instrumental analysis experiments, and give full play to students' subjective initiative and teamwork spirit, this chapter provides some cases and experimental topics of comprehensive design experiments for teachers and students to choose.

6.3　分析方案设计案例

为了巩固学生所学仪器分析的基础知识和操作技能，提高学生分析、解决仪器分析实验中的问题，发挥学生的主观能动性和团队合作精神，本章提供了一些综合设计实验的案例和实验题目，供教师和学生选择。

6.4 Typical Example of Designing Experiment

Identification, Structure Analysis and Determination of Paracetanol Experimental Scheme Design and Validation

Purpose

(1) To investigate students' ability of review and organize literature by mastering the structure and properties of paracetamol, understand the main basis and requirements of identification, structure confirmation and content determination of paracetamol based on the literatures.

(2) To investigate the students' ability to comprehensively use the knowledge and skills they have learned by designing reasonable and feasible methods for the identification, structure confirmation and content determination of paracetamol.

(3) To investigate students' ability of comprehensive analysis of standard spectra by learning the general method of structure confirmation of organic drugs.

(4) To investigate the students' ability of correctly operating various instruments, solving problems and analyzing problems in the process of experiment.

(5) To investigate the students' abilities to comprehensively use the data analysis knowledge, correctly analyze and reasonably evaluate the obtained experimental data.

Principle

1. Identification of paracetamol

Paracetamol can be identified by chemical reaction and infrared spectroscopy based on its chemical structure and it can also be identified according to the consistency of the retention time of sample compared with the retention time of reference substance in HPLC chromatogram. The specific process is brief.

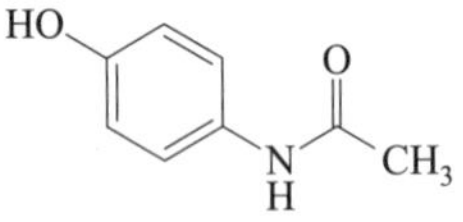

Paracetamol

2. Structure confirmation of paracetamol

The structure of acetaminophen can be confirmed by spectra of UV, IR, ^{1}H-NMR, ESI-MS and EI-MS, respectively.

3. Determination of paracetamol

The content of paracetamol was determined by UV spectrophotometry and HPLC, respectively. The external standard method was used for quantitative analysis.

(1) UV: $$w_{\text{paracetanol}}(\%)=\frac{A_{\text{sample}}}{A_{\text{standard}}}\times\frac{m_{\text{standard}}}{m_{\text{sample}}}\times 100\%$$

Where *m* is the weight of paracetanol sample and standard, respectively, mg; *A* is the UV absorbance of standard and sample, respectively.

6.4　设计类实验示例

对乙酰氨基酚的鉴别、结构确证及含量测定实验方案的设计及验证

一、实验目的

（1）通过文献查阅，掌握对乙酰氨基酚的结构及性质，了解对乙酰氨基酚鉴别、结构确证及含量测定的主要依据与要求，考查学生查阅文献、整理文献的能力。

（2）设计出合理可行的对乙酰氨基酚鉴别、结构确证及含量测定方法，考查学生综合运用所学知识和技能的能力。

（3）学习有机药物结构确证的一般方法，考查学生对标准谱图进行综合解析的能力。

（4）考查学生在实验过程中正确操作各种仪器，解决问题，分析问题的能力。

（5）考查学生综合运用所学数据分析知识，对获得的实验数据进行正确分析和合理评价的能力。

二、实验原理

1. 对乙酰氨基酚的鉴别

可根据对乙酰氨基酚的化学结构，分别采用化学反应和红外光谱法进行鉴别；也可根据HPLC色谱图，与对照品对比保留时间的一致性进行鉴别。具体过程略。

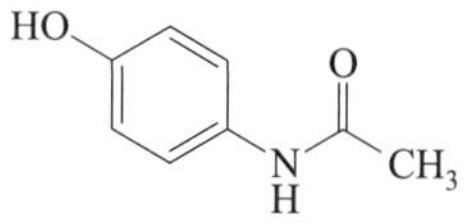

对乙酰氨基酚

2. 对乙酰氨基酚的结构确证

根据对乙酰氨基酚相关谱图（UV、IR、^{1}H-NMR、ESI-MS 和 EI-MS），对其进行结构确证。

3. 对乙酰氨基酚的含量测定

分别采用紫外分光光度法和高效液相色谱法测定对乙酰氨基酚的含量，均采用外标法进行定量分析。

（1）UV：$w_{对乙酰氨基酚}(\%)=\dfrac{A_{样品}}{A_{对照}}\times\dfrac{m_{对照}}{m_{样品}}\times 100\%$

式中，m 分别为对照品和样品的称样量，mg；A 分别为对照品和样品的吸光度。

（2）HPLC：$w_{对乙酰氨基酚}(\%)=\dfrac{A_{样品}}{A_{对照}}\times\dfrac{m_{对照}}{m_{样品}}\times 100\%$

式中，m 分别为对照品和样品的称样量，mg；A 分别为 HPLC 色谱图中对照品和样品的峰面积。

(2) HPLC: $w_{\text{paracetanol}}(\%)=\frac{A_{\text{sample}}}{A_{\text{standard}}}\times\frac{m_{\text{standard}}}{m_{\text{sample}}}\times 100\%$

Where m is the weight of paracetanol sample and standard, respectively, mg; A is the peak area of standard and sample in HPLC chromatogram, respectively.

Instruments and Chemical Reagents

1. Instruments

UV-752 spectrophotometer; Shimadzu UV-2100 spectrophotometer; Shimadzu FTIR-8400S; Shimadzu HPLC-10A; HPLC20A-MS; Thermo Picospin 80 NMR spectrometer; BS-25 electronic balance.

ODS column (150 mm × 4.6 mm, 5 μm); quartz cell; 100 μL micro-syringe; 0.45 μm filter membrane; agate mortar; volumetric flasks (10, 100 and 250 mL).

2. Chemical reagents

Paracetanol reference substance (99.9%); paracetanol bulk drug; 0.4% NaOH solution; methanol (HPLC grade); secondary distilled water; KBr (spectrum grade).

Procedure

1. Contents assay by UV spectroscopy

(1) Selection of wavelength for determination:Accurately weigh about 40 mg of paracetanol reference substance, dissolve in 50 mL of 0.4% NaOH solution and 50 mL of water sequentially into a 250 mL volumetric flask, and then dilute with waster to volume, mix well. Transfer accurately 5 mL of the above solution into a 50 mL flask, add 10 mL of 0.4% NaOH solution and dilute with water to volume, mix well.

Measure the absorbance of the diluted solution in the wavelength range of 200–400 nm. The λ_{max} can be obtained based on the absorbance graph.

(2) Preparation of sample solution: Accurately weigh about 40 mg paracetanol bulk drug, dissolve in 50 mL of 0.4% NaOH solution and 50 mL of water sequentially into a 250 mL volumetric flask, and then dilute with waster to volume, mix well. Transfer accurately 5 mL of the above solution into a 50 mL flask, add 10 mL of 0.4% NaOH solution and dilute with water to volume, mix well.

(3) Determination: The cells were calibrated under the selected wavelength. Measure the absorbance of the reference solution and the sample solution, respectively. The contents of paracetanol bulk drug can be obtained by external standard method.

2. Contents assay by HPLC

(1) Chromatographic conditions: Stationary phase: ODS column (150 mm × 4.6 mm, 5 μm); mobile phase: methanol-water (40 : 60, *V/V*); flow rate: 0.8 mL·min^{-1}; UV wavelength: 257 nm; injection volume: 20 μL

(2) Preparation of reference solution: Accurately weigh about 100 mg of paracetanol reference substance, dissolve in mobile phase into a 100 mL volumetric flask and dilute to volume, mix well. Transfer accurately 1 mL of the above solution into a 10 mL flask and dilute with mobile phase to volume, mix well.

(3) Preparation of sample solution: Accurately weigh about 100 mg of paracetanol bulk drug, dissolve in mobile phase into a 100 mL volumetric flask and dilute to volume, mix well. Transfer accurately 1 mL of the above solution into a 10 mL flask and dilute with mobile phase to volume, mix well.

(4) Determination: Inject 20 μL of paracetanol reference solution and sample solution into the HPLC system and record the chromatograms, respectively. The contents of paracetanol bulk drug can

三、仪器和试剂

1. 仪器

紫外分光光度计（UV-752 型分光光度计）；岛津 UV-2100 紫外分光光度计；FTIR-8400S 红外分光光度计；HPLC-10A 高效液相色谱仪；HPLC20A-MS 高效液相色谱-质谱联用仪；Thermo Picospin 80 核磁共振波谱仪；BS-25 电子天平。

ODS 色谱柱（150 × 4.6 mm，5 μm）；石英比色皿；100 μL 微量注射器；0.45 μm 微孔滤膜；玛瑙研钵；容量瓶（10 mL、100 mL、250 mL）。

2. 试剂

对乙酰氨基酚对照品（99.9%）；对乙酰氨基酚原料；0.4% NaOH 水溶液；甲醇（色谱纯）；二次蒸馏水；KBr（光谱纯）。

四、实验步骤

1. 含量测定（紫外分光光度法）

（1）测定波长的选择　取对乙酰氨基酚对照品约 40 mg，精密称定，置于 250 mL 容量瓶中，加 0.4% NaOH 溶液 50 mL，加水 50 mL，溶解后，用水稀释至刻度，摇匀。精密量取该溶液 5.00 mL 至 50 mL 容量瓶中，加 0.4% NaOH 溶液 10 mL，加水至刻度，摇匀，即得对照品溶液。

取该溶液，用紫外光谱扫描仪在 200~400 nm 波长范围内扫描对乙酰氨基酚紫外吸收曲线，选择 λ_{max} 为测定波长。

（2）供试品溶液的配制　取对乙酰氨基酚原料药约 40 mg，精密称定，置于 250 mL 容量瓶中，加 0.4 % NaOH 溶液 50 mL，加水 50 mL，溶解后，用水稀释至刻度，摇匀。精密量取该溶液 5.00 mL，置于 50 mL 容量瓶中，加 0.4% NaOH 溶液 10 mL，加水至刻度，摇匀，即得供试品溶液。

（3）对乙酰氨基酚含量测定　取石英比色皿一对，在（1）中测定的 λ_{max} 处进行比色皿配对，分别测定（1）和（2）中制备的对乙酰氨基酚对照品溶液和对乙酰氨基酚供试品溶液的吸光度，按外标法计算对乙酰氨基酚的百分含量。

2. 含量测定（高效液相色谱法）

（1）色谱条件　固定相：ODS 色谱柱（150 × 4.6 mm，5 μm）；流动相：甲醇-水（40 : 60，*V/V*）；流速：0.8 $mL \cdot min^{-1}$；测定波长：257 nm；进样量：20 μL。

（2）对照品溶液的配制　取对乙酰氨基酚对照品约 100 mg，精密称定，置于 100 mL 容量瓶中，加流动相适量，溶解后，用流动相稀释定容至刻度、摇匀。精密量取该溶液 1.00 mL 至 10 mL 容量瓶中，加流动相稀释至刻度，摇匀，即得。

（3）供试品溶液的配制　取对乙酰氨基酚原料药约 100 mg，精密称定，置 100 mL 容量瓶中，加流动相适量，溶解后，用流动相稀释定容至刻度、摇匀。精密量取该溶液 1.00 mL 至 10 mL 容量瓶中，加流动相稀释至刻度，摇匀，即得。

（4）对乙酰氨基酚的含量测定　分别精密量取（2）和（3）中制备的对乙酰氨基酚对照品溶液和对乙酰氨基酚供试品溶液各 20 μL，注入高效液相色谱仪，记录色谱图。按外标法计算对乙酰氨基酚的含量。

be obtained by external standard method.

3. Plotting of the IR spectrum of paracetanol

Weigh about 2 mg of paracetanol, mix it with 200 mg of KBr (spectrum grade) in an agate mortar and triturate the mixture under the infrared lamp. Preparation of IR sample is according to the standard procedure. Recommended press is 1 ton lasting for 3–5 min. Then put the transparent slice of KBr with sample into the detection window and plot the IR spectrum.

According to the IR spectrum of sample, figure out the vibration style causing characteristic absorption and deduce what functional groups the compound may be composed of.

4. Structure confirmation of paracetamol

The chemical structure of paracetamol will be confirmed according to the correlation spectra (UV, IR, ^{1}H-NMR, ESI-MS and EI-MS, see Figure 6–1 to Figure 6–5).

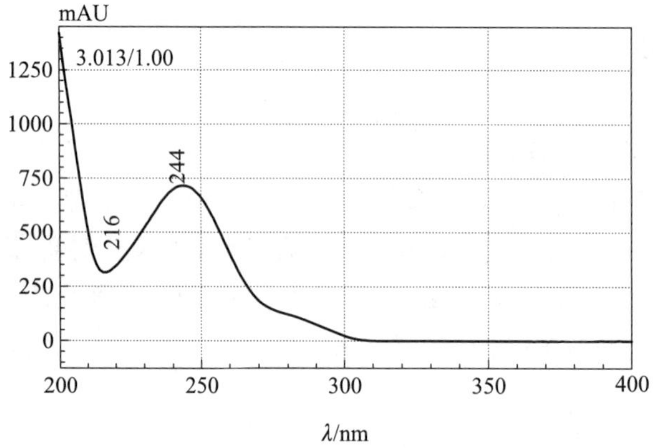

Figure 6–1 UV absorption spectrum of paracetamol

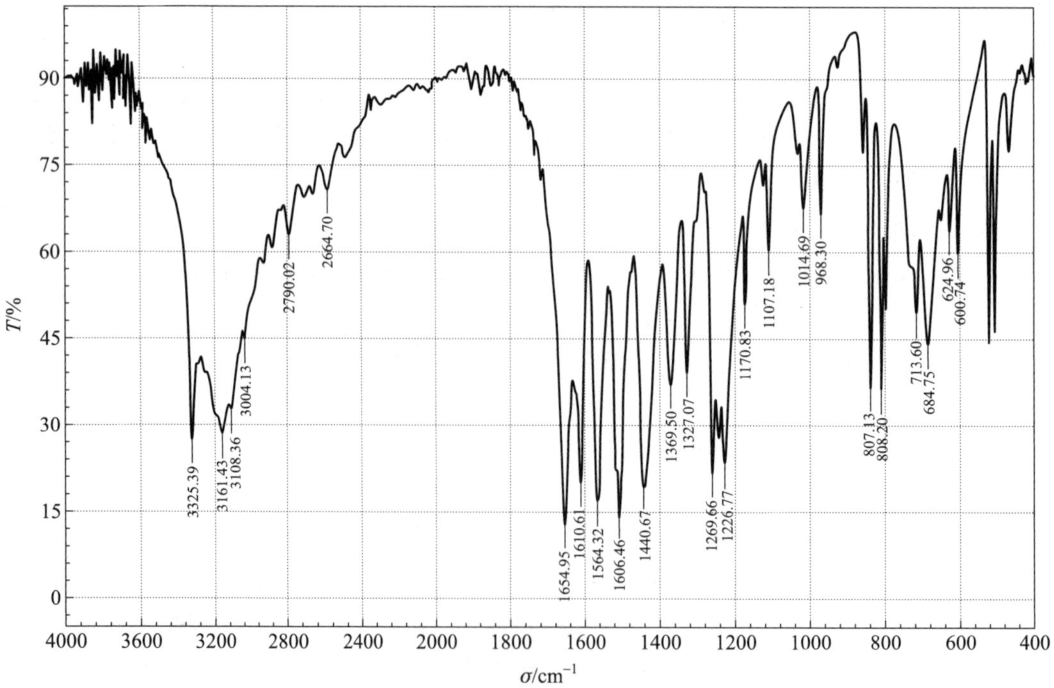

Figure 6–2 FTIR absorption spectrum of paracetamol

3. 对乙酰氨基酚红外光谱的绘制

取对乙酰氨基酚约 2 mg,置玛瑙研钵中,加入干燥的光谱纯 KBr 约 200 mg 作为分散剂,充分研磨混匀,挑取混匀的粉末适量置红外压片模具中,按红外压片的要求(规范压片参考压力为 1 ton①,参考时间为 3~5 min)。压制的片子应呈透明状,且无明显的颗粒状样品。将压好的片装入片架,放入红外分光光度计中进行红外光谱的扫描测定。本品测定以空气的红外谱图为空白。将空白校正的对乙酰氨基酚谱图进行处理,记录主要吸收峰用于结构确证。

4. 对乙酰氨基酚结构确证

根据对乙酰氨基酚相关谱图(UV、IR、^{1}H-NMR、ESI-MS、EI-MS,见图 6-1~ 图 6-5),对其结构进行确证。

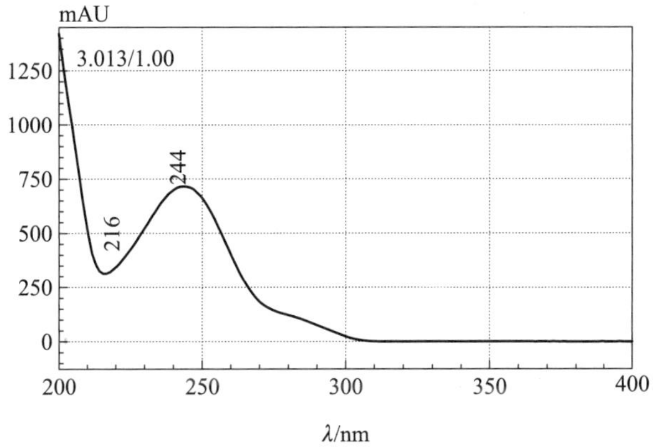

图 6-1　对乙酰氨基酚的紫外光谱图

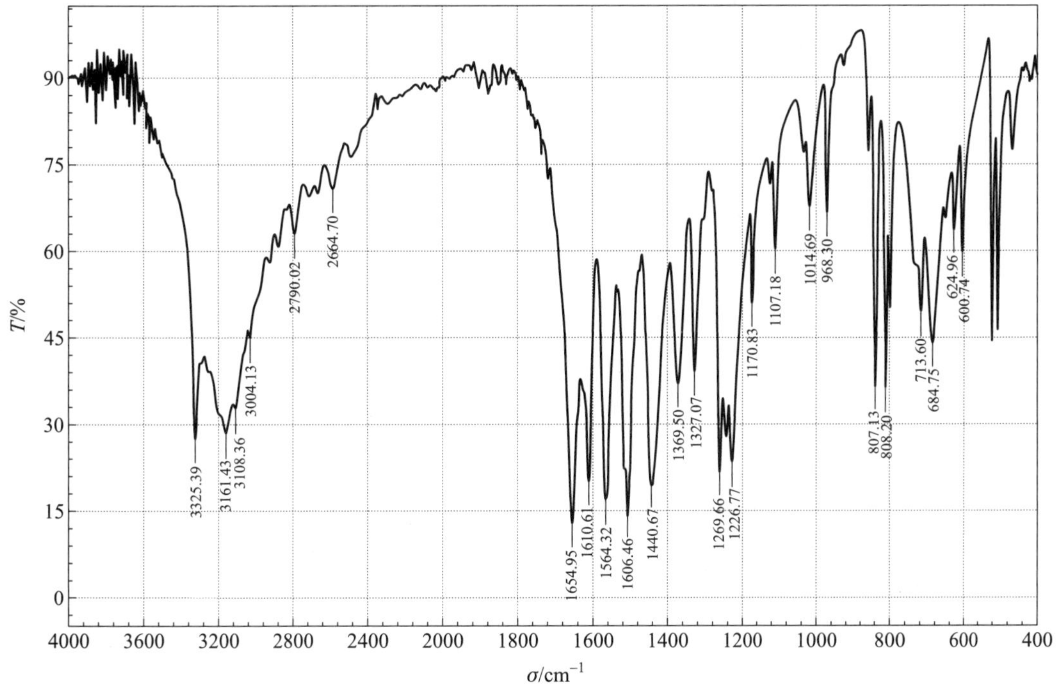

图 6-2　对乙酰氨基酚的红外光谱图

① ton(吨)为质量单位,1 ton 产生的压力为 9.8 kN。

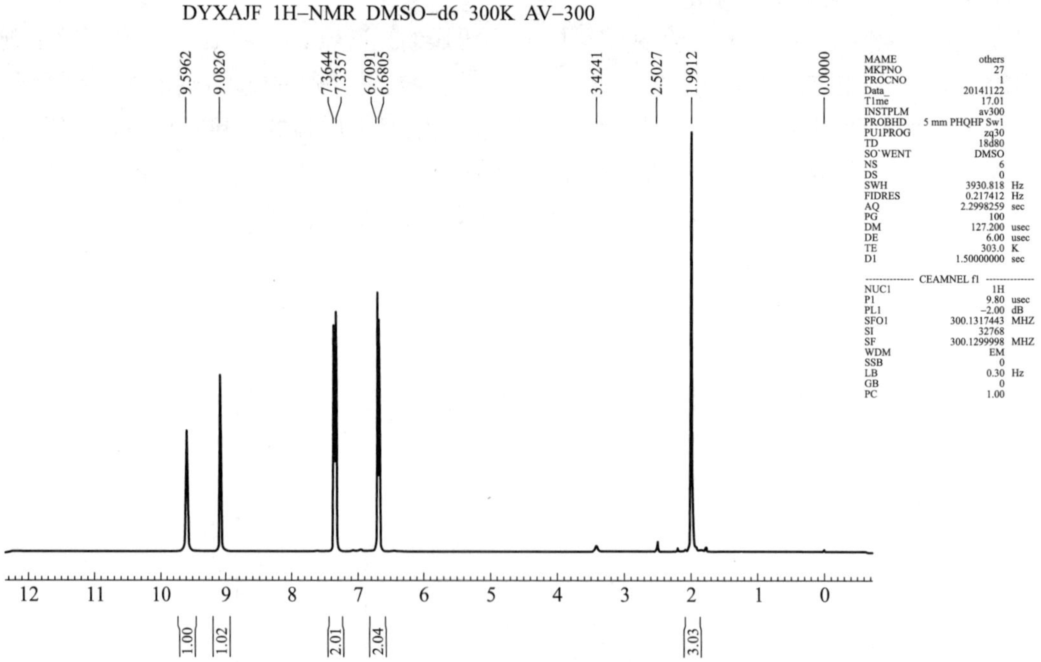

Figure 6–3 ^{1}H-NMR spectrum of paracetamol

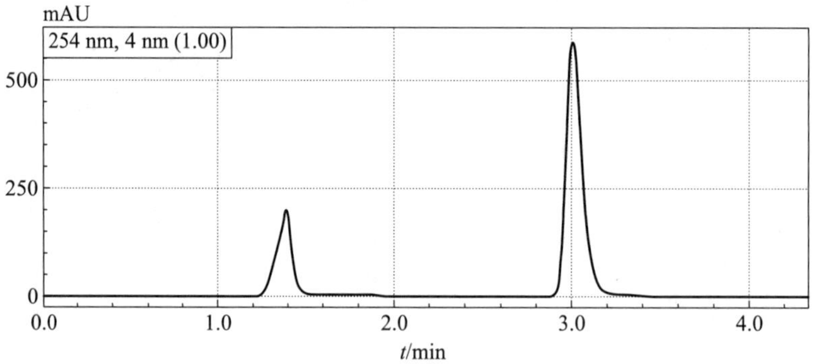

(a)

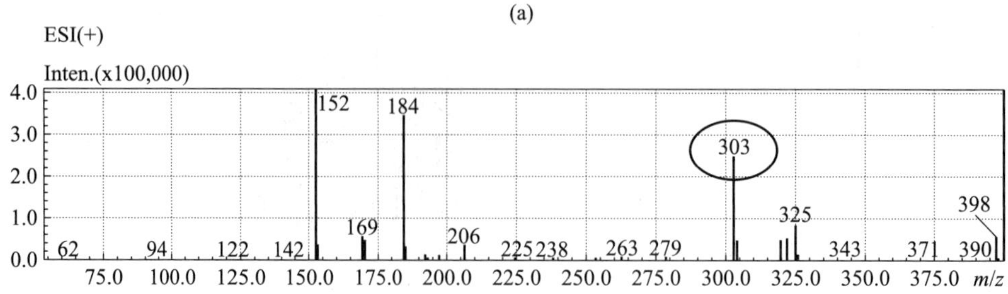

m/z 152, $[M+H]^+$

m/z 184, $[M+CH_3OH+H]^+$

m/z 303, $[2M+H]^+$

(b)

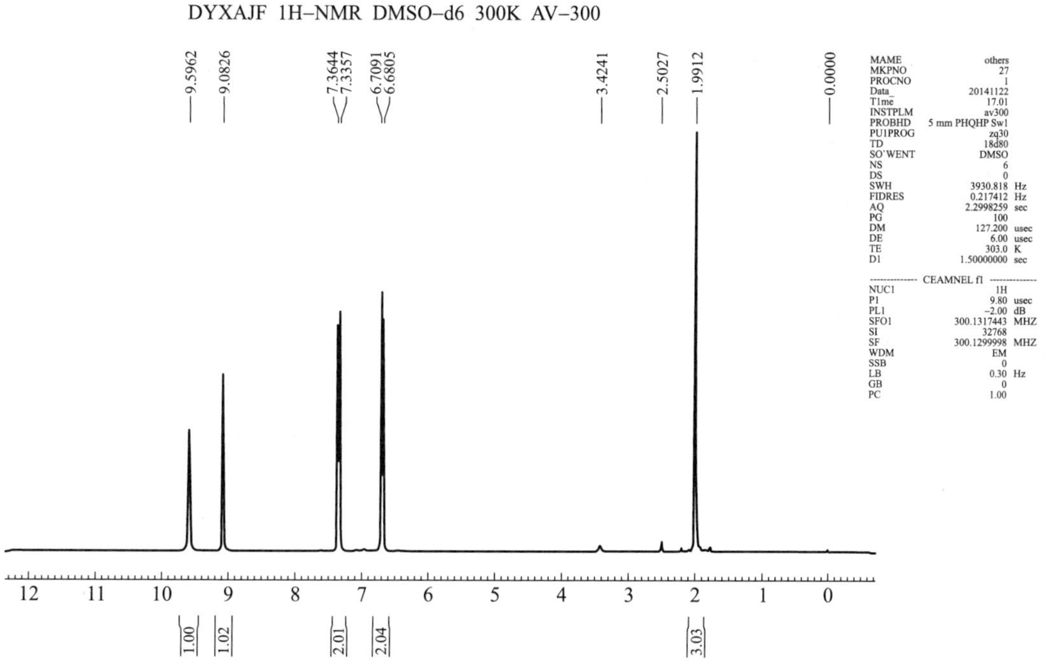

图 6–3　对乙酰氨基酚的核磁共振氢谱图

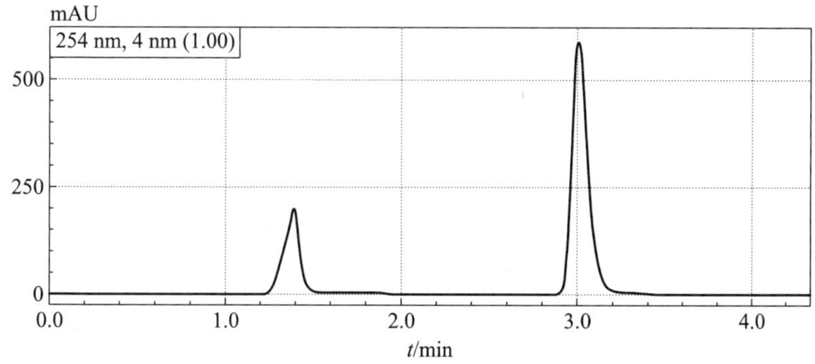

(a)

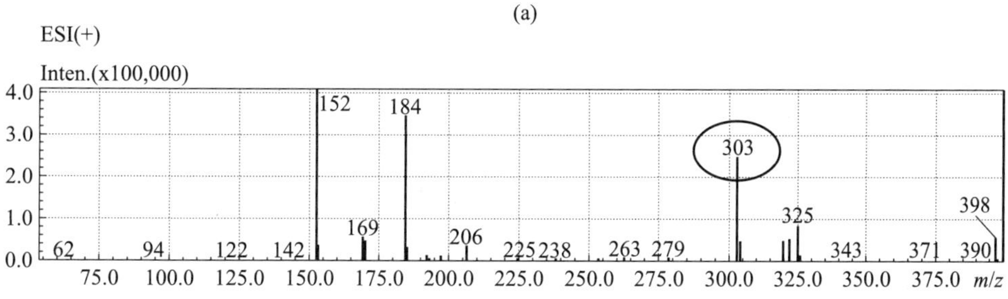

m/z 152, $[M+H]^+$

m/z 184, $[M+CH_3OH+H]^+$

m/z 303, $[2M+H]^+$

(b)

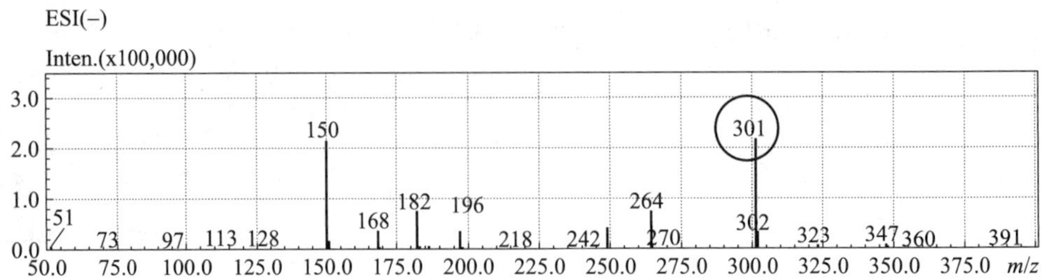

m/z 150, $[M-H]^-$

m/z 182, $[M-H+CH_3OH]^-$

m/z 301, $[2M-H]^-$

(c)

Figure 6–4 Total ion flow (a) and positive and negative ion (b, c) mass spectra of paracetamol (ESI-MS)

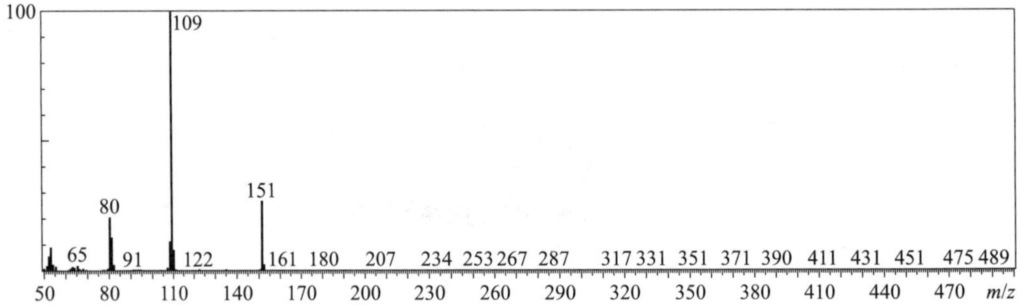

Figure 6–5 Mass spectrum of paracetamol (EI-MS)

Experiment Guidance

1. Preview instruction

(1) Understand the structure and properties of acetaminophen.

(2) Master the main basis and requirements for the identification, structure confirmation and content determination of acetaminophen.

(3) Review the application methods of common instruments, such as infrared spectrophotometer, ultraviolet spectrophotometer and high performance liquid chromatograph.

2. Notes

Paracetanol is soluble easily in hot water or ethanol. Therefore, in UV method, 0.4% of NaOH solution was added to the sample solution to promote dissolution since paracetanol is more stable in weak basic solution, which is used in Chinese pharmacopoeia. While in HPLC assay, the method to promote dissolution of paracetanol was conducted by heating or ultrasonic instead of by using 0.4% of NaOH solution.

3. Discussion

(1) In this experiment, different solvents are used for the determination of acetaminophen by UV spectrophotometry and HPLC.Why?

(2) When the structure of acetaminophen is confirmed according to the relevant spectra (UV, IR, ^{1}H-NMR, ESI-MS and EI-MS), what are the chemical structure confirmation principles of each spectrum and the structural information provided?

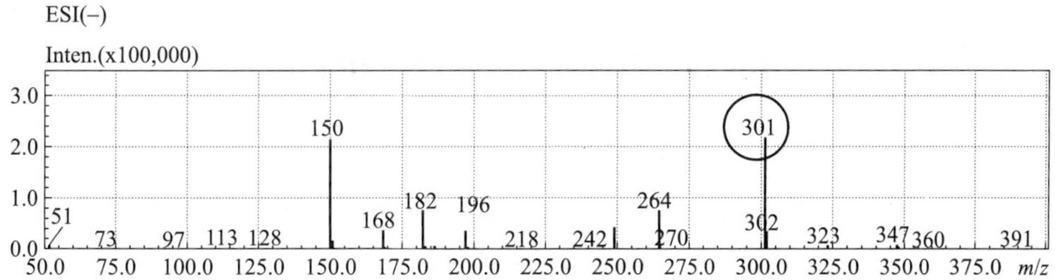

m/z 150, $[M-H]^-$

m/z 182, $[M-H+CH_3OH]^-$

m/z 301, $[2M-H]^-$

(c)

图 6–4　对乙酰氨基酚的总离子流图（a），正负离子（b，c）质谱图（ESI-MS）

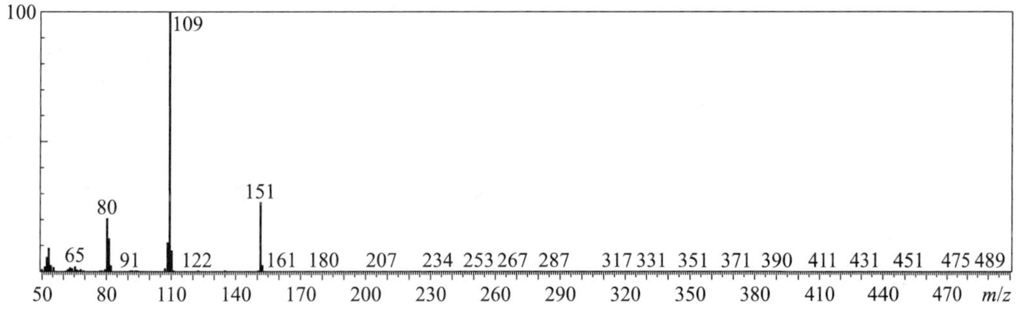

图 6–5　对乙酰氨基酚的质谱图（EI-MS）

五、实验指导

1. 预习要求

（1）了解对乙酰氨基酚的结构及性质。

（2）掌握对乙酰氨基酚鉴别、结构确证及含量测定的主要依据与要求。

（3）复习常用的红外分光光度计、紫外分光光度计和高效液相色谱仪等仪器的使用方法。

2. 注意事项

对乙酰氨基酚在热水或乙醇中易溶，在水中微溶。紫外测定方法在供试品溶液与对照品溶液中加入的 0.4% NaOH 溶液是为了促进溶解，在弱碱性溶液中，对乙酰氨基酚性质稳定，该法也是《中国药典》采用的方法。高效液相色谱测定法中不能使用氢氧化钠溶液作为溶剂，为促进对照品及样品溶解，采用超声溶解的方法。

3. 讨论

（1）本实验中分别采用紫外分光光度法和高效液相色谱法进行对乙酰氨基酚含量测定时，使用的溶剂不同，其原因是什么？

（2）根据对乙酰氨基酚的相关谱图（UV、IR、^{1}H-NMR、ESI-MS 和 EI-MS）对其进行结构确证时，各类谱图的化学结构确证原理和提供的结构信息有哪些？

6.5 Reference Topics of Designing Experiment

I Separation and Determination of Preservatives Sodium Benzoate and Potassium Sorbate in Oral Syrup Preparation

1. Research background

Oral liquid preparations mostly use water as the solvent. Affected by many factors, they are easy to be polluted by microorganisms, especially syrup and traditional Chinese medicine preparations, which contain nutrients and are more likely to breed microorganisms.

Preservatives are chemicals that can prevent or inhibit the growth and development of pathogenic microorganisms. They are widely used in all kinds of oral and external liquid preparations and semi-solid preparations to ensure the biological stability of drugs. They are one of the important components of preparation prescriptions. There are many kinds of preservatives. Acidic preservatives commonly used in oral liquid preparations, such as benzoic acid and sodium salt, sorbic acid and potassium salt, can affect or block the metabolic process by combining with the enzyme system of pathogenic microorganisms.

Due to the toxicity of preservatives, for example, benzoic acid has certain toxicity to the liver and certain irritation to the stomach, skin, eyes and mucous membrane. The adverse reactions of sorbic acid are mainly reported as irritant and contact dermatitis. Who now stipulates that the total allowable daily intake of these substances is 5 $mg \cdot kg^{-1}$ body weight and 25 $mg \cdot kg^{-1}$ body weight based on benzoic acid and sorbic acid, respectively.

Therefore, preservatives are one of the key components in the prescription of oral liquid preparations. Whether they are used correctly and reasonably is directly related to the quality and safety of drugs.

This experiment is to separate and determine the content of sodium benzoate and potassium sorbate in oral syrup preparation.

2. Tips for experimental design methods

Before designing the experimental scheme, we should clarify the experimental purpose and analysis object, understand the physical and chemical properties of the analyte and the matrix that may interfere with the determination, then select the analysis method according to the properties of the target compound, and finally determine the experimental scheme in combination with the laboratory conditions.

The objects to be analyzed in this experiment are sodium benzoate and potassium sorbate, which are organic compounds with π-π conjugated structure and have strong UV absorption in the near UV region. Therefore, the detection methods with UV absorption characteristics are considered first. The possible applicable methods include UV visible spectrophotometry, high performance liquid

6.5 设计类实验参考选题

I 口服糖浆制剂中防腐剂苯甲酸钠和山梨酸钾的分离和测定

1. 研究背景

口服液体制剂多以水为溶媒,受诸多因素的影响,易为微生物所污染,尤其是糖浆类和中药类制剂,内含营养物质,更易滋生微生物。

防腐剂是指能防止或抑制病原性微生物生长发育的化学药品,广泛应用于各类口服、外用液体制剂和半固体制剂中,以保证药品的生物学稳定性,是制剂处方的重要组成之一。防腐剂种类很多,口服液体制剂中常用酸性防腐剂,如苯甲酸及钠盐、山梨酸及钾盐等,可通过与病原微生物酶系统结合,影响或阻断其新陈代谢过程。

由于防腐剂本身存在着毒性,如苯甲酸对肝有一定毒性,对胃、皮肤、眼和黏膜均有一定刺激性,山梨酸不良反应报道主要也是刺激性和接触性皮炎。世界卫生组织(WHO)规定该类物质日允许总摄入量以苯甲酸和山梨酸计分别为每千克体重 5 mg 和 25 mg。

因此,防腐剂作为口服液体制剂处方中的关键组成部分之一,其正确合理使用与否,直接关系到药品的质量和安全。

本实验拟对口服糖浆制剂中的苯甲酸钠和山梨酸钾两种防腐剂进行分离和含量测定。

2. 实验设计方法提示

在具体设计实验方案前,应明确实验目的和分析对象,了解待分析物的理化性质和可能干扰测定的基质,然后根据目标化合物性质选择分析方法,最后结合实验室条件,确定实验方案。

本实验待分析的对象是苯甲酸钠和山梨酸钾,均为具有 π-π 共轭结构的有机化合物,在近紫外光区有较强的紫外吸收,因此首先考虑具有紫外吸收特性的检测方法,可能适用的方法有紫外-可见分光光度法、高效液相色谱法(紫外检测)、薄层色谱法、纸色谱法等。

苯甲酸钠和山梨酸钾在水溶剂中处于解离状态,可利用其具有带电基团的特点,选择离子色谱法或者毛细管电泳法进行分离测定。

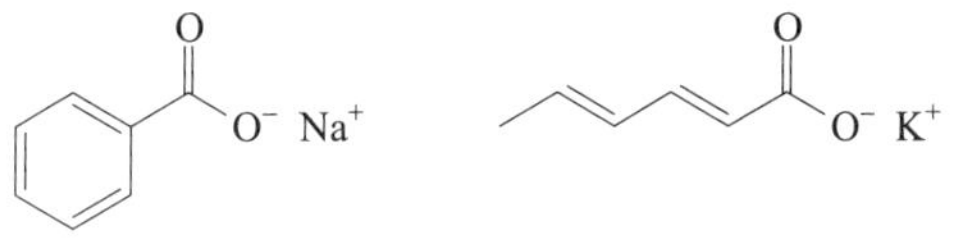

苯甲酸钠　　　　山梨酸钾

chromatography (UV detection), thin layer chromatography, paper chromatography, etc.

Sodium benzoate and potassium sorbate are in dissociation state in aqueous solvent, so they can be separated and determined by ion chromatography or capillary electrophoresis.

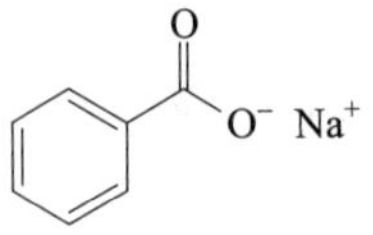

Sodium benzoate

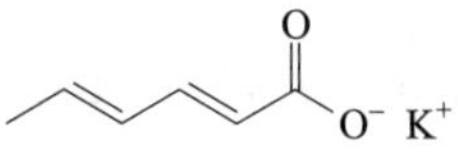

Potassium sorbate

The matrix of the compound to be analyzed is liquid syrup preparation, which may contain pharmaceutical components, sugar, aromatics, colorants, etc. the influence of these components on the determination of the target compound should be considered when designing the experiment. The target compound can be separated and purified by sample pretreatment technology (such as solid phase extraction) before determination, or more sensitive and exclusive determination methods (such as gas chromatography derivatization, high performance liquid chromatography-mass spectrometry, and fluorescence analysis) can be selected.

待分析化合物所处的基质为液体糖浆类制剂，其中可能含有药物成分、糖分、芳香剂、着色剂等，设计实验时要考虑这些成分对目标化合物测定的影响。可通过样品前处理技术（如固相萃取）分离纯化目标化合物后再进行测定，或者选择更加灵敏、专属的测定方法（如气相色谱衍生化、高效液相色谱-质谱联用、荧光分析法等）。

II Analysis and Determination of Amino Acid Mixture

1. Research background

Amino acids are compounds formed after the hydrogen atom on the carbon atom of carboxylic acid is replaced by amino group. It contains two functional groups: basic amino group and acidic carboxyl group. The chemical formula is $RCHNH_2COOH$.

Amino acids are the basic substances that constitute the protein required for animal nutrition. They can play the following roles in human body through metabolism: ① synthesis of tissue protein; ② Turn into ammonia containing substances such as acid, hormone, antibody and creatine; ③ Into carbohydrates and fats; ④ It is oxidized to carbon dioxide, water and urea to produce energy.

Similar to hydroxy acids, amino acids can be divided into amino acids according to their different positions on the carbon chain α-, β-, γ-, ω-amino acids, but the amino acids obtained after protein hydrolysis are α-amino acids. There are only 22 kinds of amino acids, including glycine, alanine, valine, leucine, isoleucine, methionine (methionine), proline, tryptophan, serine, tyrosine, cysteine, phenylalanine, asparagine, glutamine, threonine, aspartic acid, glutamate, lysine, arginine, histidine selenium cysteine and pyrrole lysine (found only in a few bacteria).

2. Tips for experimental design methods

Amino acids contain both acidic and basic groups, which are amphoteric compounds. Due to the different relative molecular weight and isoelectric point of various amino acids, in the buffer solution of the same pH, different amino acids not only have different charge conditions, but also have different swimming directions and rate in the electric field. Therefore, based on this difference, the mixture of amino acids can be separated by electrophoresis.

Amino acids basically exist in the form of facultative ions or dipole ions in aqueous solution or crystal. Therefore, anion exchange chromatographic column and conductivity detector can also be used to separate and analyze mixed amino acids.

All kinds of common amino acids have light absorption in the far ultraviolet region (< 200 nm) and no light absorption in the visible region (360–760 nm); In the ultraviolet region (near ultraviolet region) (220–300 nm), only phenylalanine, tyrosine and tryptophan have light absorption ability, because their R groups contain benzene ring conjugated double bond system. Phenylalanine λ_{max} = 259 nm, tyrosine λ_{max} = 278 nm, tryptophan λ_{max} = 259 nm, proteins generally contain these three amino acid residues. Therefore, the UV absorption characteristics at 280 nm wavelength can be used to quantitatively detect the content of proteins.

High performance liquid chromatography is the preferred method for on-line simultaneous analysis of amino acid mixtures. However, due to the lack of chromogenic groups and weak UV absorption of most amino acids, it is necessary to carry out pre column derivatization of amino acids, that is, using phenyl isothiocyanate (PITC) as derivatization reagent, the HPLC-UV analysis of mixed amino acids can be realized at 254 nm.

Ⅱ 氨基酸混合物的分析测定

1. 研究背景

氨基酸是羧酸碳原子上的氢原子被氨基取代后形成的化合物，含有碱性氨基和酸性羧基两种官能团，化学式是 $RCHNH_2COOH$。

氨基酸是构成动物营养所需蛋白质的基本物质，在人体内通过代谢可以发挥下列作用：①合成组织蛋白质；②变成酸、激素、抗体、肌酸等含氨物质；③转变为糖类和脂肪；④氧化成二氧化碳和水及尿素，产生能量。

与羟基酸类似，氨基酸可按照氨基连在碳链上的不同位置而分为 α-，β-，γ-，ω-氨基酸，但经蛋白质水解后得到的氨基酸都是 α-氨基酸，而且仅有 22 种，包括甘氨酸、丙氨酸、缬氨酸、亮氨酸、异亮氨酸、甲硫氨酸（蛋氨酸）、脯氨酸、色氨酸、丝氨酸、酪氨酸、半胱氨酸、苯丙氨酸、天冬酰胺、谷氨酰胺、苏氨酸、天冬氨酸、谷氨酸、赖氨酸、精氨酸、组氨酸、硒半胱氨酸和吡咯赖氨酸（仅在少数细菌中发现）。

2. 实验设计方法提示

氨基酸中同时含有酸性基团和碱性基团，是两性化合物。由于各种氨基酸的相对分子质量和等电点不同，在相同 pH 的缓冲溶液中，不同的氨基酸不仅所带电荷状况有差异，而且在电场中的泳动方向和速率也不同。因此，可基于这种差异，采用电泳技术分离氨基酸的混合物。

氨基酸在水溶液或结晶内基本上均以兼性离子或偶极离子的形式存在，因此也可以利用阴离子交换色谱柱和电导检测器，实现混合氨基酸的分离分析。

各种常见的氨基酸在远紫外区（<200 nm）均有光吸收，在可见光区域（360~760 nm）均无光吸收；在紫外区（近紫外区）（220~300 nm）只有苯丙氨酸、酪氨酸、色氨酸三种氨基酸有光吸收能力，因为它们的 R 基含有苯环共轭双键系统。其中苯丙氨酸 λ_{max} = 259 nm、酪氨酸 λ_{max} = 278 nm、色氨酸 λ_{max} = 259 nm，蛋白质一般都含有这三种氨酸残基，因此，可以利用 280 nm 波长处的紫外吸收特性定量检测蛋白质的含量。

高效液相色谱法是氨基酸混合物在线同时分析的优选方法，但是由于大部分氨基酸缺少生色基团，紫外吸收弱，因此需对氨基酸进行柱前衍生，即以异硫氰酸苯酯（PITC）作为衍生试剂，可在 254 nm 实现混合氨基酸的 HPLC-UV 分析。

也可以通过在背景电解质中添加强紫外吸收试剂，采用毛细管电泳-间接紫外吸收法测定无紫外吸收的混合氨基酸的含量。

氨基酸自动分析仪是利用样品各种氨基酸组分的结构不同、酸碱性、极性及分子大小不同，在阳离子交换柱上将它们分离，采用不同 pH 离子浓度的缓冲液将各氨基酸组分依次洗脱

The content of mixed amino acids without UV absorption can also be determined by capillary electrophoresis indirect UV absorption method by adding strong UV absorption reagent to the background electrolyte.

The automatic amino acid analyzer separates various amino acid components in the sample according to their different structure, acidity, alkalinity, polarity and molecular size on the cation exchange column by eluting each amino acid component in turn using buffer solution with different pH value and ion concentration. And then each amino acid component is mixed one by one with the ninhydrin reagent in another way, followed by flowing into the spiral reaction tube for the color reaction to form the blue purple products with λ_{max} = 570 nm and the yellow products (hydroxyproline and ninhydrin) with λ_{max} = 440 nm. The amino acid components can be qualitatively and quantitatively analyzed by comparing with standard amino acids according to the Lambert-Beer law.

下来，再逐个与另一流路的茚三酮试剂混合，然后共同流至螺旋反应管中进行显色反应，形成 λ_{max} = 570 nm 的蓝紫色产物和 λ_{max} = 440 nm 的黄色产物（羟脯氨酸与茚三酮），根据朗伯-比尔定律，可通过与标准氨基酸比较，实现定性和定量分析。

Ⅲ Determination of Multivitamins in Compound Vitamin B Tablet

1. Research background

Compound vitamin B tablets are vitamin over-the-counter drugs. They are composed of vitamin B_1, vitamin B_2, nicotinamide, vitamin B_6 and calcium *d*-pantothenate. They are compound preparations and are suitable for the prevention and treatment of malnutrition, anorexia, beriberi, pellagra, etc. caused by the lack of B vitamins. Among them, vitamin B_1 is an important component of coenzymes required for glucose metabolism; Vitamin B_2 is an important coenzyme component for tissue respiration; Vitamin B_6 is the accessory group of many enzymes and participates in the metabolism of amino acids and fats; Nicotinamide is a component of coenzyme Ⅰ and Ⅱ, which is necessary for lipid metabolism and oxidation of tissue respiration; Calcium pantothenate is a component of coenzyme A and participates in the metabolism of sugar, fat and protein. Compound vitamin B tablets are only included in Volume Ⅰ of chemical drugs and preparations (WS1-73 (B)-89) of drug standards of the Ministry of Health of the People's Republic of China. There is no such variety abroad, so the United States Pharmacopoeia (USP), British Pharmacopoeia (BP), European Pharmacopoeia (EP) and Japanese Pharmacopoeia (JP) are not included.

2. Tips for experimental design methods

According to their different chemical structures and properties, the drug standards of the Ministry of Health of the People's Republic of China (Volume Ⅰ of chemicals and preparations, WS1-73 (B)-89) respectively adopt three methods to determine the contents of three vitamins (vitamin B_1 by gravimetric analysis, vitamin B_2 by ultraviolet spectrophotometry and nicotinamide by acid-base titration). The operation is cumbersome and time-consuming, and the contents of vitamin B_6 and calcium pantothenate are not determined, so "one test and multiple evaluation" cannot be realized.

For the simultaneous determination of multicomponent compounds in complex system, chromatographic analysis method is preferred. High performance liquid chromatography can be considered to realize the separation and quantitative determination of five components at the same time. In addition, capillary electrophoresis and LC-MS can also be used for qualitative and quantitative analysis.

Spectroscopy can also be used for the analysis of complex components. For example, the simultaneous determination of multiple vitamins in vitamin B tablets can be realized by computational spectrophotometry, colorimetry and quantitative nuclear magnetic resonance spectroscopy.

Ⅲ　复合维生素 B 片中多种维生素的含量测定

1. 研究背景

复合维生素 B 片是维生素类非处方药，由维生素 B_1、维生素 B_2、烟酰胺、维生素 B_6 及右旋泛酸钙组成，属于复方制剂，适用于预防和治疗 B 族维生素缺乏所致的营养不良、厌食、脚气病、糙皮病等。其中，维生素 B_1 是糖代谢所需辅酶的重要组成成分；维生素 B_2 为组织呼吸所需的重要辅酶组成成分；维生素 B_6 为多种酶的辅基，参与氨基酸及脂肪的代谢；烟酰胺为辅酶Ⅰ及Ⅱ的组分，是脂质代谢、组织呼吸的氧化作用所必需的成分；泛酸钙为辅酶 A 的组分，参与糖、脂肪、蛋白质的代谢。复合维生素 B 片只收载于《中华人民共和国卫生部药品标准》化学药品与制剂第一册[WS1-73(B)-89]。国外无该品种，因此美国药典(USP)、英国药典(BP)、欧洲药典(EP)及日本药典(JP)均没有收载。

2. 实验设计方法提示

根据其不同的化学结构和性质，《中华人民共和国卫生部药品标准》[化学药品与制剂第一册，WS1-73(B)-89]中分别采用三种方法测定其中三种维生素的含量(采用重量分析法测定维生素 B_1，紫外分光光度法测定维生素 B_2，酸碱滴定法测定烟酰胺的含量)，操作烦琐费时，且并未对维生素 B_6 和泛酸钙的含量进行测定，不能实现“一测多评”。

对于复杂体系中多组分化合物的同时测定，首选色谱分析方法。可以考虑采用高效液相色谱法，同时实现五种成分的分离和定量测定。另外，也可以采用毛细管电泳法、LC-MS 联用法等进行定性、定量分析。

光谱法也可以用于复杂组分的分析，比如通过采用计算分光光度法、比色法及定量核磁共振波谱法，实现维生素 B 片中多种维生素的同时测定。

Ⅳ Separation and Determination of Tea Polyphenols in Tea

1. Research background

Tea polyphenols (TP), also known as tea tannin, is a kind of polyhydroxy compounds and the general name of phenolic compounds in tea. Tea polyphenols are not only the main bioactive components in tea, but also an important source of bitterness, astringency and color in tea. It is also one of the important indexes to evaluate the quality of tea. When determining the content of tea polyphenols in tea, a variety of analytical methods can be used to separate and detect according to the structure and properties of tea polyphenols, so as to evaluate the quality and classification of tea.

According to the main chemical components, tea polyphenols are divided into four categories: catechins, flavonoids, anthocyanins and phenolic acids. The content of catechins is the highest, accounting for about 70% of tea polyphenols. Catechins are mainly epicatechin (EC), epicatechin gallate (ECG), epicatechin (EGC) and epicatechin gallate (EGCG).

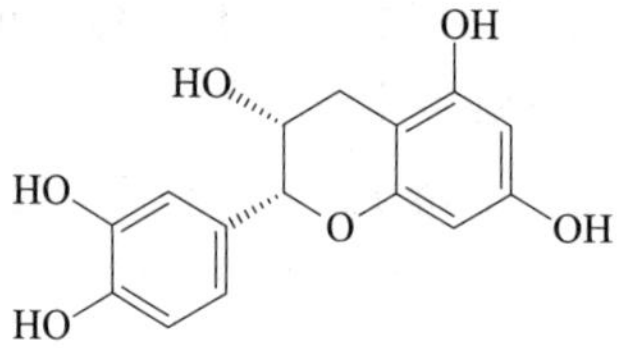

EC

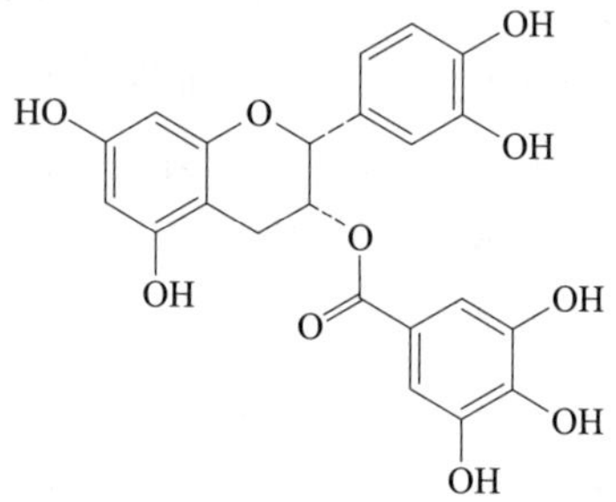

ECG

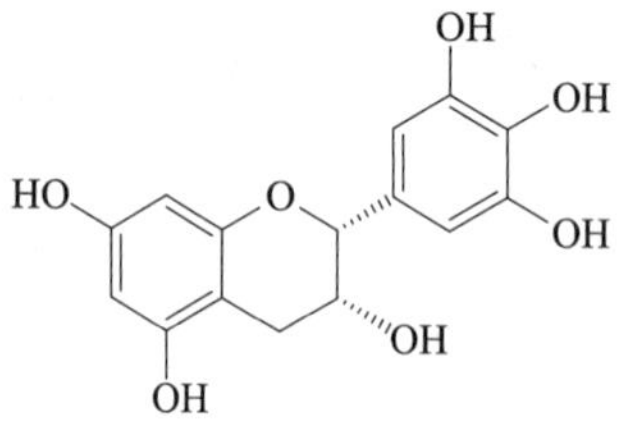

EGC

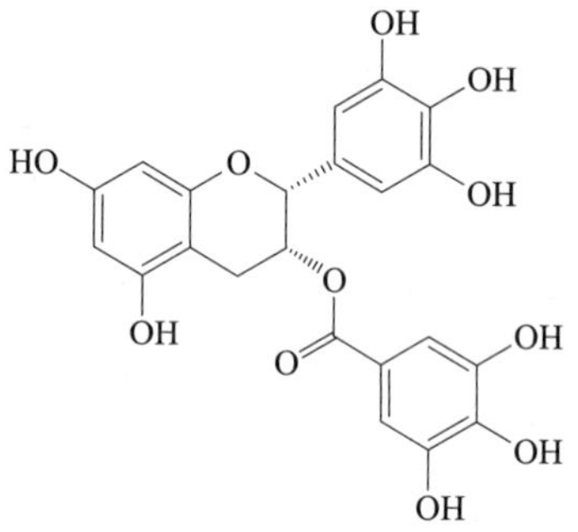

EGCG

2. Tips for experimental design methods

Spectrophotometry is a common method to determine the content of polyphenols by using the absorbance of the measured substance at a specific wavelength and then detecting and analyzing according to the linear relationship between the absorbance and the concentration of the measured substance. It mainly includes ultraviolet spectrophotometry (UV), ferrous tartrate colorimetry and folinol colorimetry. Polyphenols form green black compounds with iron ions and have strong absorption in the ultraviolet-visable region. Based on this characteristic, polyphenols can be detected by UV–Vis spectrophotometry. However,

Ⅳ　茶叶中茶多酚类物质的分离测定

1. 研究背景

茶多酚（Tea Polyphenols，TP）又名茶鞣质，是一类多羟基类化合物，是茶中酚类化合物的总称。茶多酚不仅是茶叶中的主要生物活性成分，而且是茶中苦味、涩味和色泽的重要来源，也是评价茶叶品质的重要指标之一。在测定茶叶中的茶多酚含量时，可根据茶多酚的结构和性质，采用多种分析方法分离和检测，从而评价茶叶品质和分级。

茶多酚按主要化学成分分为儿茶素类、黄酮类、花青素类、酚酸类四大类物质，其中以儿茶素含量最高，约占茶多酚的 70%。儿茶素主要为表儿茶素（EC）、表儿茶素没食子酸酯（ECG），表没食子儿茶素（EGC）和表没食子儿茶素没食子酸酯（EGCG）4 种物质。

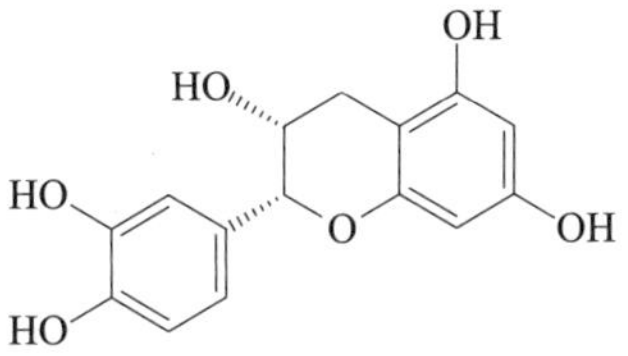

EC

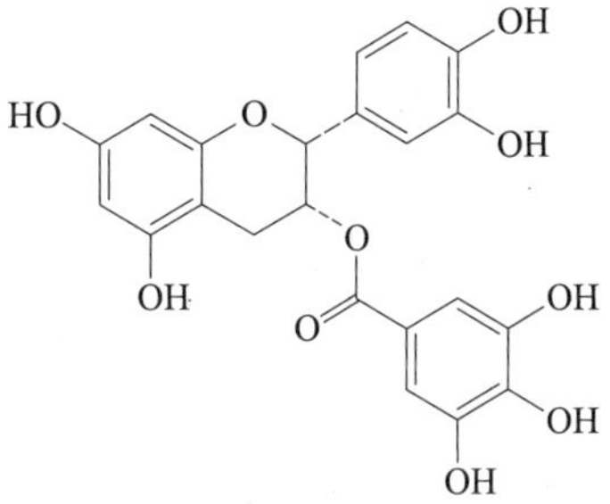

ECG

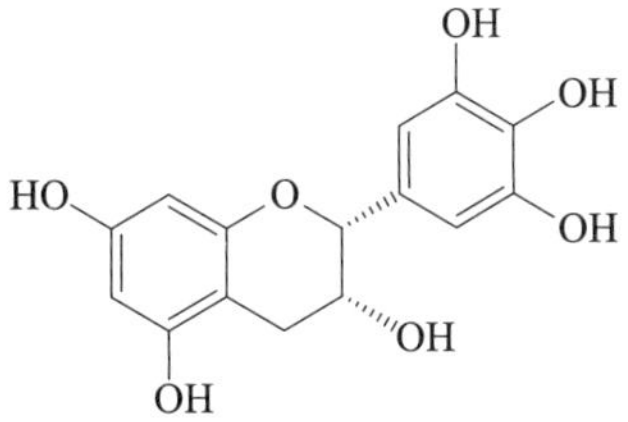

EGC

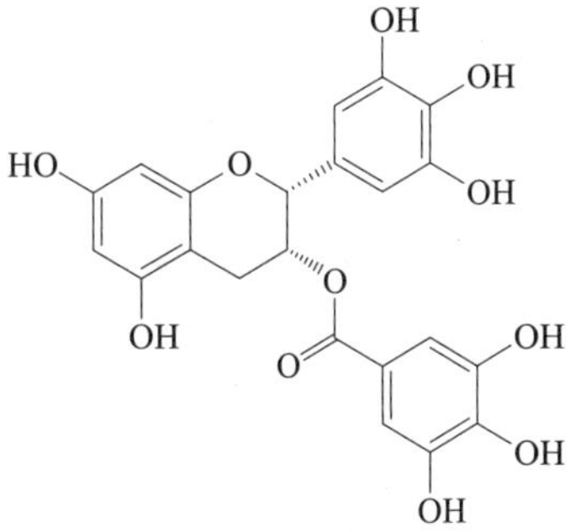

EGCG

2. 实验设计方法提示

分光光度法（spectrophotometry）是利用被测物质在特定波长下的吸光度，再根据吸光度与被测物质浓度之间的线性关系进行检测分析的方法，是测定多酚类物质含量的常用方法，主要包括紫外–可见分光光度法（UV 法）、酒石酸亚铁比色法和福林酚比色法。多酚类物质可与铁离子生成绿黑色化合物，有较强烈的紫外 – 可见吸收，利用这一特性，能用紫外 – 可见分光光度法快速检测多酚类物质的含量，但要注意茶叶提取物中的咖啡因等物质也具有类似的吸收，可能导致测量结果有较大偏差；酒石酸亚铁比色法的原理是在一定的 pH 条件下，茶叶中多酚类物质与 Fe^{2+}形成蓝紫色配位化合物，在可见光区有特定的波长吸收，该法快捷、简便，是行业内茶多酚测定被广泛采用的检测方法；福林酚比色法是国家标准中各种茶叶中茶多酚含量的检测方

it should be noted that caffeine and other substances in tea extract also have similar absorption, which may lead to large deviation in the measurement results; The principle of ferrous tartrate colorimetry is that under certain pH conditions, polyphenols in tea form blue purple coordination compounds with Fe^{2+}, and have specific wavelength absorption in the visible region. This method is fast and simple. It is a widely used detection method of tea polyphenols in the industry; Folin phenol colorimetry is a method for detecting the content of tea polyphenols in various tea leaves in the national standard. It uses Folin phenol reagent to oxidize hydroxyl groups in tea polyphenols to form blue substances with specific absorption wavelength. The content of tea polyphenols determined by this method is relatively more accurate, but it takes a long time, and Folin phenol reagent is relatively expensive.

Three dimensional fluorescence spectroscopy (3D-EEM) and near infrared spectroscopy (NIR) are analytical methods that have developed rapidly in recent decades. They are relatively simple, rapid, sensitive and accurate. They can be used as alternative methods for the analysis and detection of tea polyphenols.

Chromatographic analysis has high accuracy and sensitivity, and can accurately determine multiple components at the same time. It is usually used to separate and determine complex substrates, such as qualitative and quantitative analysis of various tea polyphenol monomers in tea soup, mainly including column chromatography, high performance liquid chromatography, high performance thin layer chromatography, liquid chromatography-mass spectrometry, etc. In addition, liquid chromatography-mass spectrometry can also realize the separation and identification of trace or trace components.

Electrochemical analysis (EA) is a qualitative and quantitative method based on the electrochemical properties and change law of tea polyphenols in tea through the relationship between electrochemical parameters (such as potential, conductivity and current) and the concentration of tested substances. It has good repeatability, accuracy and short time. It can be used for the rapid detection of tea polyphenols.

Capillary electrophoresis (CE) uses the migration speeds of different particles to reach the detector at different speeds for detection, and produces an electrophoresis map distributed according to time. CE has the advantages of high efficiency, rapidity and simplicity, but it also has some disadvantages, such as narrow linear range, poor reproducibility, low analysis accuracy and large error.

In the actual analysis of tea polyphenols in tea, appropriate analysis methods should be selected according to the composition, content and laboratory instruments and equipment of the compounds to be tested.

法，它是利用福林酚试剂氧化茶多酚中的羟基，形成特定吸收波长的蓝色物质，该方法测定的茶多酚含量相对更准确，但耗时长，且福林酚试剂相对昂贵。

三维荧光光谱法（three-dimensional fluorescence spectrometry，3D-EEM）和近红外光谱法（near infrared spectrometry，NIR）是近几十年来发展较迅速的分析方法，操作相对简便、快速、灵敏度高、测定结果相对准确，可作为茶多酚分析检测时的替代方法。

色谱分析法精确度和灵敏性较高，可同时准确测定多组分，通常用于分离和测定复杂基质，如茶汤中各类茶多酚单体的定性、定量分析，主要有柱色谱法、高效液相色谱法、高效薄层色谱法、液相色谱-质谱联用法等。此外，液相色谱-质谱联用方法还可以实现微量或者痕量组分的分离和鉴定。

电化学分析法（electrochemical analysis，EA）是基于茶叶中茶多酚的电化学性质及其变化规律，通过电化学参数（如电位、电导、电流）与被测物质浓度间的关系进行定性定量的方法，重复性和准确性好、时间短，可用于茶多酚的快速检测。

毛细管电泳法（capillary electrophoresis，CE）是利用不同粒子的迁移速度，最终以不同的速度到达检测器进行检测，产生按时间分布的电泳图谱。CE 具有高效、快速、简便等优点，但是也存在线性范围窄、重现性差、分析精度不高、误差大等缺点。

实际进行茶叶中茶多酚类化合物的分析时，应根据待测化合物的组成、含量和实验室仪器设备，选择合适的分析方法。

V Determination of Trace Elements Copper, Iron and Zinc in Human Hair

1. Research background

Copper, iron and zinc are essential trace elements for human body, which play a very important role in human growth and development, intelligence and personality. The selection of samples for trace element analysis is very important. Human hair is an important part of human metabolic system. It is easy to collect and has a certain accumulation effect (it can reflect the status of trace elements in the body for weeks or even months). Therefore, the long-term metabolism and nutritional status of trace elements in the body can be evaluated by measuring the content of trace elements in hair.

2. Tips for experimental design methods

For the determination of trace elements copper, iron and zinc in human hair, atomic absorption spectrophotometry (AAS), inductively coupled plasma spectrometry (ICP-AES), X-ray fluorescence spectrometry and polarography can be selected according to the characteristics of inorganic metal elements. During determination, different sample pretreatment methods need to be selected according to the analysis methods used.

V　人发中微量元素铜、铁、锌的测定

1. 研究背景

铜、铁、锌等是人体必需的微量元素，对人体的生长发育和智力、性格等起着非常重要的作用。微量元素分析中样品的选择至关重要。人体的头发是人新陈代谢系统的重要组成部分，它易于采集，而且具有一定的积累作用(可以反映机体几个星期甚至几个月体内微量元素的状况)。因此，利用测定头发中微量元素的含量，可以评价体内微量元素长期的代谢和营养状况。

2. 实验设计方法提示

人发中微量元素铜、铁、锌的测定，可以根据待测物为无机金属元素的特性，选择原子吸收分光光度法(AAS)、电感耦合等离子体光谱法(ICP-AES)、X射线荧光光谱法和极谱法等。测定时，需要根据使用的分析方法，选择不同的样品前处理方法。

Ⅵ Determination of Saponins in *Panax Notoginseng*

1. Research background

Panax notoginseng (Burk.) F.H.Chen is a perennial herb of Araliaceae ginseng in Acanthopanax family. It has the functions of hemostasis, promoting blood circulation and tonifying blood. The main component of Panax notoginseng is saponin, which plays a certain role in anti-shock, anti-aging, anti-cell proliferation, anti-arrhythmia and anti-tumor. Different Panax notoginseng medicinal materials contain different saponins and contents due to the influence of medicinal material sources, processing technology and other factors. Therefore, the qualitative and quantitative analysis of saponins in Panax notoginseng is of great significance to control the quality of Panax notoginseng and the modernization of traditional Chinese medicine.

2. Tips for experimental design methods

HPLC and HPLC-MS are the first choices for the analysis of saponins in Panax notoginseng. They have obvious advantages in accuracy, specificity, sensitivity and operation feasibility.

Capillary electrophoresis is suitable for the separation of compounds with high polarity, high separation efficiency and low analysis cost. It can also be used for the separation and analysis of saponins.

Thin layer chromatography is simple, rapid and intuitive. It also has a certain application in the separation and identification of complex components of traditional Chinese medicine.

Near infrared spectroscopy is also used for the analysis and quality control of complex components of traditional Chinese medicine in recent years because of its advantages of no loss of samples, no pollution and fast analysis speed. However, in practical application, it is necessary to establish a mathematical model to ensure the high accuracy of the reference method, so as to ensure the scientific and effective results of quantitative analysis.

Ⅵ　中药材三七中皂苷类成分的测定

1. 研究背景

三七是五加科（Araliaceae）人参属多年生草本植物三七［Panax notoginseng（Burk.）F.H.Chen］的干燥根及根茎，具有止血、活血、补血等作用。三七的主要成分为皂苷，在抗休克、抗衰老、抗细胞增殖、抗心律失常及抗肿瘤等方面发挥一定的功效。因药材来源及炮制工艺等因素的影响，不同三七药材中含有的皂苷类成分、含量均不同。因此，对三七药材中的皂苷类成分进行定性、定量分析，对控制药材质量和中药现代化具有重要的意义。

2. 实验设计方法提示

HPLC 法及 HPLC-MS 联用法是三七中皂苷类成分分析的首选方法，在准确性、专属性、灵敏度、操作可行性等方面均具有明显优势。

毛细管电泳法适宜分离极性较大化合物，分离效率高、分析成本低，也可用于皂苷类成分的分离分析。

薄层色谱法操作简单、快速、直观，在中药复杂组分的分离鉴别方面也具有一定的应用。

近红外光谱法由于其具有不损失样品、无污染、分析速度快等优点，近年来也被用于中药复杂组分的分析和质量控制。但是实际应用时，需要建立数学模型，保证参比方法具有较高的准确性，才能确保定量分析的结果科学、有效。

参考文献

Reference

附　　录

Appendix

附录一　0–95 ℃时标准缓冲溶液的 pH

附录二　部分元素的光谱线

附录三　主要基团的红外特征吸收

附录四　一些质子类型的 ^1H 化学位移范围

附录五　气相色谱常用固定液

附录六　气相色谱常用载体

附录七　一些气体和蒸气的导热系数

附录八　气相色谱中相对重量校正因子（f）

附录九　反相液相色谱常用固定相

附录十　液相色谱常用流动相的性质

附录十一　$m/z \leqslant 105$ 的常见碎片离子及其中性分子